Greene County Tennessee

Death Record
Abstracts

Volume 1: 1908-1918

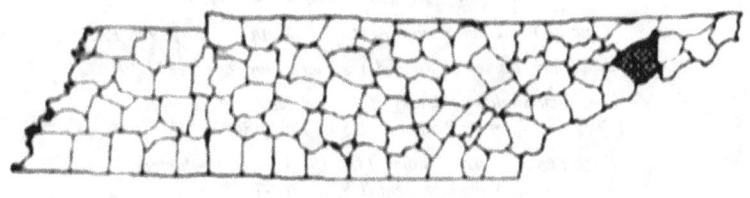

Eddie M. Nikazy

HERITAGE BOOKS
2007

HERITAGE BOOKS
AN IMPRINT OF HERITAGE BOOKS, INC.

Books, CDs, and more—Worldwide

For our listing of thousands of titles see our website
at
www.HeritageBooks.com

Published 2007 by
HERITAGE BOOKS, INC.
Publishing Division
65 East Main Street
Westminster, Maryland 21157-5026

Copyright © 1997 Eddie M. Nikazy

Other books by the author:

Abstracts of Death Records for Johnson County, Tennessee, 1908 to 1941
Carter County, Tennessee Deaths, 1926-1934
Carter County, Tennessee Record Abstracts, Death Records, 1908-1925
Carter County, Tennessee Record Abstracts, Marriages, 1871-1920
Forgotten Soldiers: History of the 2nd Tennessee Volunteer Infantry Regiment (USA), 1861-1865
Forgotten Soldiers: History of the 4th Tennessee Volunteer Infantry Regiment (USA), 1863-1865
Sullivan County, Tennessee Death Records, 1908-1918, Volume 1
Sullivan County, Tennessee Death Records, 1919-1925, Volume 2
Unicoi County, Tennessee Death Record Abstracts, 1908-1936
Washington County, Tennessee Death Record Abstracts, 1908-1916

All rights reserved. No part of this book may be reproduced or transmitted in any form or by any means, electronic or mechanical, including photocopying, recording or by any information storage and retrieval system without written permission from the author, except for the inclusion of brief quotations in a review.

International Standard Book Number: 978-0-7884-0660-4

TABLE OF CONTENTS

Preface:..v.

Death Record Abstracts:..1.

Name Index:...295.

PREFACE

Formed from Washington County, North Carolina, in 1783, Greene County played a prominent role in the settlement of the frontier. As early as 1772 Jacob Brown and several families from neighboring North Carolina settled on the banks of the Nolachuckey River in present day Greene County. A little over a decade later, the county would serve as the site for the capitol of the short lived State of Franklin. Greene County is named in honor of General Nathaniel Greene, a Revolutionary War hero.

This volume contains Tennessee death record abstract for Greene County for the years 1908 through 1918. Death records were first filed for rural Tennessee counties beginning in 1908. Records, for the years 1908 through 1912 did not record the names of parents and in 1913 deaths were not recorded. Beginning in 1914, the State imposed more stringent recording requirements and the records included parents names, the name of the informant, and place of burial. The index contains 8,049 names. Records contained herein were compiled from microfilm of the original records.

The majority of names contained in this volume were direct descendants of early settlers of Greene County. As the records show, many migrated to Greene County from neighboring, Cocke, Hawkins, Hamblen, Sullivan, Washington, Carter and Johnson Counties. In addition, many records show North Carolina as the place of birth or place of birth of the parents.

Important facts about this volume:

1.) Name spelling variations have been preserved. The compiler made no effort to confirm or verify spelling.
2.) Record numbers shown in the compilation correspond with those on file in the Tennessee State Library and Archives.
3.) The place of birth is stated when the place of birth of the deceased or parents is recorded other than Greene County.
4.) An entry following the informant's name indicates the recorded place of residence.
5.) The cause of death is quoted as it appears in the official record.

1

LAFOLLETTE, Joseph; age: 66; death cause: "paralysis"; died: 10 Nov. 1909; record # 30351.

KING, Infant; female; stillborn; died: 4 Oct. 1911; record # 30352.

GURGER, Infant; male; black; age: 3 days; death cause: not stated; died: 15 May 1912; record # 30353.

REYNOLDS, Alfred; age: 75 years, 3 months; married; born: near Ottway; death cause: "lung trouble"; died: 22 Aug. 1911; record # 30354.

MIDDLETON, Mariah Jane; age: 72; married; born: Bethesda; death cause: "general breakdown"; died: 5 Jul. 1911; record # 30355.

SELF, W.R.; age: 57; married; born: Pilot Noble; death cause: "stomach trouble"; died at Watertown on 7 Apr. 1912; record # 30356.

WHINREY, B.F.; age: 78; married; born: Rheatown; death cause: "lagrippe and rheumatism"; died: 22 Feb. 1912, record # 30357.

GRAHAM, Infant; male; age not stated; died: 30 Jan. 1912; record # 30358.

MCNEESE, Mrs. Rolina; age: 59; widow; death cause: "consumption"; died: 3 Jan. 1912; record # 30359.

MARSHALL, L.B.; age: 55; married; death cause: "paralysis"; died near Mt. Zion on 9 May 1912; record # 30360.

REED, Infant; male; age: 3 months; death cause: "spinal trouble"; died 15 Jan. 1912; record # 30361.

BAILES, Mary E.: age: 11 months; death cause: "infantile paralysis"; died: 18 Jul. 1911; record # 30362.

GRAY, Andrew P.; age: 7; death cause: "flux"; died: 11 Sep.1911; record # 30363.

MOORE, Mrs. Sarah; age: 62; married; death cause: "female trouble"; died at Afton on 13 Nov. 1911; record # 30364.

COLLINS, L.R.; age: 68; married; born: Greene County; death cause: "consumption of bowels"; died: 2 Aug. 1911; record # 30365.

MOORE, Infant; male; age: not stated; died: 16 Jan. 1912; record # 30366.

MOPPIN, Lydia; age: 58; single; born: Sinking Creek; death cause: "paralysis"; died: 13 Mar.1912, record # 30367.

RUPE, Littie; age: 42, married; born: Virginia; death cause: "consumption"; died: 5 Oct. 1911; record # 30368.

FRY, Dovie; age: 33; married; born at Marvin; died: 10 Aug. 1911; record # 30376.

FRY, Infant; female; age: 1 day; death cause: "unknown"; died at Marvin on 10 Aug. 1912; record # 30377.

BARB, Clifford; age: 5; death cause: "accidental gunshot"; died at Marvin on 25 Jan. 1912; record # 30378.

BURRIS, Anna; age: 65; married; death cause: "neuralgia"; died: 18 Nov. 1911; record # 30379.

ILLEGIBLE, Infant; female; death cause: "stillborn"; died: 2 Feb. 1912, record # 30380.

CRAFT, William Jackson; age: 8 months; death cause: "meningitis"; died at Mt. Carmel on 4 Apr. 1912; record # 30381.

LIPTRAP, Tomas; age: 50; married; death cause: "dysentery"; died at Chuckey on 10 May 1911; record # 30382.

PICKERING, Puris; age: 82; married; death cause: "old age"; died at Chuckey on 22 May 1911; record # 30383.

ST HILAS, Joseph; age: 60; married; born: Canada; death cause: "Brights disease"; died at Chuckey on (day not stated) Mar.1911; record # 30384.

LAYUCK, Eugene; age: 13; born: Scranton, PA; death cause: "typhoid"; died at Frogmore on 1 Oct. 1910, record # 30385.

REMAINE, J.E.; age: 79; married; born: Scott County, VA; death cause: "Brights disease"; died at Frogmore on 31 Oct. 1911; record # 30386.

CASSADY, George; age: 76; married; "old soldier"; death cause: "kidney trouble"; died: 16 Apr. 1911; record # 30387.

MCCRAY, Edith; age: 10; death cause: "inflammation of bowels"; died: 28 Nov. 1910; record # 30388.

COLLET, Melvina; age: 65; married; death cause: "pneumonia fever"; died at Limestone, TN on 15 Feb. 1911; record # 30389.

JOHNSON, Addie; age: 52 years and 3 days; married; born: Scott County, VA; death cause: "pneumonia fever"; died: 1 Mar.1911; record # 30390.

CAMPBELL, R.E.; age: 72; married; born: Morristown; death cause: "kidney trouble"; died: 14 Nov. 1910; record # 30391.

BASKET, Infant; female, age: 11 days; death cause; not stated; died 9 Dec. 1910; record # 30392.

ROBERTS, Vernie; age: 26; single; school teacher; death cause: "measles"; died: 29 Apr. 1911; record # 30393.
DICKSON, Gladis; age: 6 weeks; death cause: "hives"; died 11 Mar.1911; record # 30394.
HAYS, Infant; female; died at birth on 21 Feb. 1911; record # 30395.
HAYS, William Alexander; age: 77; married; death cause: "(illegible) poison"; died: 19 Feb. 1911; record # 30396.
PATTERSON, Y.M.; age: 42; married; death cause: "consumption"; died 12 Nov. 1911; record # 30397.
CRAWFORD, Jessie L.; age: 2; death cause: "pneumonia"; died: 10 may 1911; record # 30398.
HAYS, Joseph H.; age: 61; married: death cause: "consumption"; died: 22 Feb. 1911; record # 30399.
HUNT, Susiana; age: 81; married; death cause: "old age"; died 24 Feb. 1911; record # 30400.
HAYS, Lexie Glenda; age: 3 months; death cause: "tuberculosis"; died: 15 Feb. 1911; record # 30401.
BENNET, Zack; black; age: 60; single; born in South Carolina; death cause: "kidney trouble"; died: 14 Aug. 1910; record # 30402.
JEFFERS, Ruphus; age: 30; married; death cause: "dropsy"; died (day not stated) May 1911; record # 30403.
THURNBURG, Ernest: age: 14 months; death cause: "dyre (illegible)"; died 23 Jun. 1911, record # 30404.
THURNBURG, Blanch; age: 1 year and 9 months; death cause: "cholera"; died: 13 Jan. 1911; record # 30405.
DYKES, Clarence; age: 7; death cause: "lung trouble"; died: 3 May 1911; record # 30406.
BRANDON, Etta; age: 30; single; death cause: "heart trouble"; died: 30 Apr. 1911; record # 30407.
CRAWFORD, Zella; age: 3; death cause: "spasms"; died: 10 May 1911; record # 30408.
CRAWFORD, Etta; age: 50; married; born: Sullivan County, TN; death cause: "dropsy"; died: 24 Jul. 1911, record # 30409.
MORELOCK, Ana; age: 83; married; born: Beech Creek, Hawkins County, TN; death cause: "consumption"; died: 25 Oct. 1911; record # 30410.

P..(illegible): female; age: 75; married; died: 20 Jan. 1912; record # 30411.
STARNES, Anay; age: 60; married; death cause: "heart failure"; died: 8 Aug. 1910; record # 30412.
JONES, Infant; male; age: 3 months; death cause: not stated; died: 27 Nov. 1911; record # 30413.
JUSTICE, Henry; age: 75; married; born: Otway, TN; death cause: "bronchitis"; died: 2 Dec. 1911; record # 30414.
MCANIS, Archibald; age: 67; married; death cause: "dropsy"; died 21 Mar.1912, record # 30414.
GASS, Joe; age: 50; married; death cause: "cancer"; died: 11 Oct. 1911; record # 30416.
JUSTICE, James; age: 80; married; death cause: not stated; died: 2 Feb. 1912, record # 30416.
BROWN, Ross; age: 15; death cause: "tuberculosis"; died: 1 Jun. 1912, record # 30418.
WEEMS, Marion; age: 50; married; born: Missouri; death cause: "pneumonia"; died: 8 Mar.1912, record # 30417.
RAGSDALE, Elizabeth; age: 49; married; death cause: "heart failure"; died: 9 Dec. 1911; record # 30420.
GASS, Conrad; age: 5; death cause: "membranous croup"; died: 9 Dec. 1911; record # 30421.
LUSTER, Lorenda; age: 80; married; born: Greeneville; death cause: not stated; died: 28 Jul. 1911; record # 30422.
REYNOLDS, James; age: 60; married; born: Baileyton, TN; death cause: "pneumonia"; died: 17 Dec. 1911; record # 30423.
REYNOLDS, Catherine; age: 60; married; born: Baileyton, TN; death cause: "pneumonia"; died: 19 Dec. 1911; record # 30424.
MILLIGAN, Dewey; age: 14; death cause: "tuberculosis"; died: 31 Jan. 1911, record # 30425.
WHITE, Matilda; age: 71; married; death cause: "pneumonia"; born: Baileyton, TN; died: 20 Mar.1912; record # 30426.
MALONE, Bewley; age: 16; death cause: "typhoid fever"; died: 21 Oct. 1911; record # 30427.
MALONE, Andy; age: 28; single, death cause: "typhoid fever"; died: 14 Oct. 1911; record # 30428.

JUSTICE, James: age: 74; married; born: Baileyton, TN; death cause: "bronchitis"; died: 1 Feb. 1911; record # 30429.

RAGSDALE, Bessie: age: 18; married; death cause: "measles"; died: 5 Jul. 1911; record # 30430.

JONES, Naoma; age: 1; death cause: "membranous croup"; died: 5 Nov. 1911; record # 30431.

BAILEY, George A.; age: 65; married; death cause: "pneumonia"; died in New Mexico on 22 Feb. 1912; record # 30432.

LAUGHTERS, Lawrence; age: 5; death cause: "membranous croup"; died: 11 Nov. 1911; record # 30433.

LAUGHTERS, Faun: female; age: 3; death cause: "membranous croup"; died: 22 Aug. 1911; record # 30434.

THOMPSON, Infant; female; age: 1 day; death cause: not stated; died: 20 Mar.1911; record # 30435.

UNIDENTIFIED, Infant; male; death cause: not stated; died: 31 Oct. 1911; record # 30436.

UNIDENTIFIED, Infant; male; death cause: not stated; died: 31 Oct. 1911; record # 30437.

PAINTER, Rosa; age: 69; married; death cause: "heart trouble"; died: 6 Jun. 1912; record # 30438.

WHITE, Carl V.; age: 20; married; born: Sullivan County, TN; death cause: "accident in factory"; died at Knoxville on 7 Apr. 1912; record # 30439.

MCMILLAN, Lidia; black; age: 20 years and 5 days; married; school teacher; born: Rogersville, TN; death cause: "child bed fever"; died at Bulls Gap on 12 Mar.1912; record # 30440.

GLASPIE, Allice; black; age: 45; married; death cause: "pneumonia"; died at Bulls Gap on 15 Nov. 1912; record # 30441.

HAUN, Hazel; age: 2 months and 20 days; death cause: "hives"; died at Bulls Gap on 25 Oct. 1911; record # 30442.

LYNCH, W.K.; age: 66; married; born: Hamblen County; death cause: "pneumonia"; died at Mohawk, TN., on 2 Aug. 1911; record # 30443.

MCPERAN, Laura; age: 26; single; death cause: "consumption"; died at Bulls Gap on 7 Oct. 1911; record # 30444.

JANES, Berley; age: 14 months; death cause: "pneumonia fever"; died at Mahawk on 15 Mar.1912; record # 30445.

EXERHART, Bessey; age: 28; married; death cause: "consumption"; died at Mohawk on 7 Oct. 1911; record # 30446.
EXERHART, Stella; age: 17 months; death cause: "pneumonia fever"; died at Mohawk on 21 Jun. 1911; record # 30447.
ILLEGIBLE, Infant; male; death cause: "born dead"; died: 15 Nov. 1911; record # 30448.
GILLESPIE, Alice; black; age: 40; married; death cause: "pneumonia fever"; died at Bulls Gap on 22 Nov. 1912; record # 30449.
REED, Sam; age: 50; married; born: Cocke County; death cause: "consumption"; died at Mohawk on 19 Dec. 1911; record # 30450.
W__(?), Greene; female; age: 3; death cause: "diphtheria"; died 6 Oct. 1910; record # 30451.
W__(?), Sarah F.; age: 11 months; death cause: "inflammation of bowels"; died: 3 Nov. 1910; record # 30452.
MIDDLETON, Rosa: age: 22; married; death cause: "consumption"; died 2 Jul. 1910; record # 30453.
ARMSTRONG, M.B.; age: 81; married; born: Greene County; death cause: "Brights disease"; died: 19 Jun. 1911; record # 30454.
DUNWOODY, John; age: 48; married; death cause: "consumption"; died: 3 May 1911; record # 30455.
MILLER, John N.; age: 67; married; death cause: "general breakdown"; died: 22 Feb. 1911; record # 30456.
WILSON, Jennie; age: 11 weeks; born: Knoxville; death cause: "stomach trouble"; died: 10 Sep.1911; record # 30457.
MCAMIS, John; age: 46; married; death cause: "heart failure"; died: 16 Oct. 1910; record # 30458.
BRITTON, Catherine; age: 88; widow; born: Greene County; death cause: "old age"; died: 18 Jan. 1911; record # 30459.
BRITTON, Margaret; age: 53; single, death cause: "consumption"; died: 15 Nov. 1911; record # 30460.
ROBERTSON, W.W.; age: 58; married; death cause: "blood poison"; died: 20 Feb. 1911; record # 30461.
SQUIBB, C.P.; age: 54; married; born: Washington County; death cause: "heart trouble"; died: 7 Feb. 1911; record # 30462.
RUTHERFORD, Burnas Nadine; age: 4 months and 29 days; death cause: "cholera infantum"; died: 14 Jun. 1909; record # 30463.

WHITE, Mary Suda; age: 10 months and 13 days; death cause: "cholera infantum"; died: 25 Jun. 1909; record # 30464.

WHITE, M. Elizabeth; age: 23; single; death cause: "consumption"; died: 27 Apr. 1909; record # 30465.

LINEBAUGH, Rebecca A.; age: 56; married; death cause: "consumption"; died: 7 Jan. 1909; record # 30466.

HAWKINS, Ema Virginia; age: 24; married; death cause: "consumption"; died: 12 May 1909; record # 30467.

STARNES, Rutha Lucinda; age: 55; married; death cause: "cancer"; died: 8 Jan. 1909; record # 30468.

MORRISON, Robert Earnest; age: 1 year, 11 months and 8 days; death cause: "cholera infantum"; died: 1 Jun. 1909, record # 30469.

GADDIS, Lillie; age: 20; married; death cause: "consumption"; died: 26 May 1909; record # 30470.

WHITE, Burthie; age: 1 year and 7 months; death cause: "cholera infantum"; died: 30 Jun. 1909; record # 30471.

HULSE, Mary; age: 81; widow; death cause: "diarrhea of bowels"; died: 30 May 1909; record # 30472.

ARMITAGE, Mary; age: 38; married; death cause: "smallpox"; died: 26 Mar.1909; record # 30473.

BROWN, John B.; age: 80 years, 8 months and 11 days; married; born: Baileyton, TN; died: 16 Jun. 1909; record # 30474.

LINEBAUGHT, Elizabeth; age: 76; married; born: Baileyton, TN; death cause: "paralysis"; died: 12 Mar.1909; record # 30475.

RAGSDALE, Nan; age: 47; married: death cause: "consumption"; died: 18 Feb. 1909; record # 30476.

MCNEESE, Infant; male; age: 6 weeks; death cause: "flux"; died: 22 Jun. 1909; record # 30477.

WHITE, Laura; age: 60, "to a day"; married; death cause: "consumption"; died: 25 Jun. 1909; record # 30478.

REYNOLDS, Manerve; age: about 90; married; death cause: "old age and heart failure"; died: 28 Feb. 1909; record # 30479.

CASTEEL, Hanah; age: 25; married; death cause: "consumption"; died: 21 Jun. 1909; record # 30480.

HARMON, Joe; age: 45; married; death cause: "hemorrhage of lungs"; died: 26 Nov. 1908; record # 30481.

CASTEEL, William Marton; age: 50; married; death cause: "killed by accident"; died (day not stated) Oct. 1908; record # 30482.

CARTER, Susan; age: 69 years, 8 months; married; death cause: "dropsy"; died: 12 Aug. 1908; record # 30483.

THOMPSON, Mollie; age: 30; death cause: "heart failure"; died: 30 May 1909; record # 30484.

MALONE, Mandy Beatrice; age: 3 years, 3 months; death cause: "convulsion of brain"; died: 7 Oct. 1908; record # 30485.

JUSTICE, Jacob; age: 47; married; death cause: "typhoid fever"; died: 7 Sep.1908; record # 30486.

JUSTICE, Maggie; age: 40; married; death cause: "typhoid fever"; died: 7 Sep.1908; record # 30487.

PRICE, Nettie; black; age: 16; married; death cause: "relapse of typhoid fever"; died: 1 Oct. 1908; record # 30488.

LUMBERTSON, Alice; age: 17; born: Texas; single; death cause: "appendicitis"; died: 13 Sep.1911; record # 30489.

NORTON, Infant; age: 3 days; child of Larson NORTON, death cause: unknown; died: 28 Feb. 1911; record # 30490.

CUTSHALL, Ellen; age: not stated; married; born: North Carolina; died: 17 Jul. 1910; record # 30491.

RAY, Lottie; age: 31 married; born: Madison County, NC; death cause: "dropsy": died; 10 May 1911; record # 30492.

SHAW, Lou; age: 63; born: Virginia; married; death cause: "dysentery"; died: 20 Jun. 1911; record # 30493.

MCCOY, Infant; female; child of Buck MCCOY; death cause: unknown; died: 20 Mar.1911; record # 30494.

BOWMAN, Nela May; age: 1 day; child of Dora BOWMAN; died: 20 Nov. 1910; record # 30495.

COBBLE, Nela May; age: 1 year; death cause: "lung trouble"; died: 2 Aug. 1908; record # 30496.

RADER, J.A.; age: 64; married; death cause: "kidney trouble"; died: 11 Jul. 1908; record # 30497.

CLEMMON, J.L.; age: 66; widower; death cause: "brain disease"; died: 12 Mar.1909; record # 30498.

CLEMMON, Essie; age: 2 months; death cause: "bronchitis"; died: 26 Apr. 1909; record # 30499.

JENKINS, Infant; female; age: 1 day; death cause: not stated; died: 24 Jun. 1909; record # 30500.
BLACK, Ellen; age: not stated; death cause: "female trouble"; date of death not stated; record # 30501.
WILLBORN, Corra; age: 3 years; death cause: "membranous croup"; died (day not stated) Nov. 1908; record # 30502.
COBBLE, Mary Effy; age: 1 year, 10 months; death cause: "membranous croup"; died: 15 Oct. 1908; record # 30503.
RAGAN, Arthur; age: 8; death cause: "membranous croup"; died: 9 Sep.1908; record # 30504.
RAGAN, James; age: 5; death cause: "membranous croup"; died: 22 Oct. 1908; record # 30505.
STAFFORD, Ermel Mary; age: 1 month; death cause: "hives"; died: 4 Oct. 1908; record # 30506.
COBBLE, N.; age: 74; married; death cause: "urina"; died in Madionsville, TN on (day not stated) Apr. 1908; record # 30507.
MCCONNELL, Orpha; age: 14; death cause: "typhoid fever"; died: 12 Jul. 1908; record # 30508.
COBBLE, Washington; age: 82; married; death cause: "old age"; died: (day not stated) Mar.1909; record # 30509.
ILLEGIBLE, Infant; age: 1 month; death cause: "unknown"; died; (day not stated) Feb. 1909; record # 30410.
PETERS, Yauk; age: 50; married; death cause: "pneumonia"; died: 26 Nov. 1910; record # 30511.
REED, Infant; female; age: 7 months (?); death cause: "born dead"; died: 20 Jun. 1911; record 30512.
JUSTIS, Martha; age: 86; widow; born: Greene County; death cause: "dropsy"; died: 15 Apr. 1911; record # 30513.
GRAYHAM, Mary; infant; death cause: "stillborn"; died: 14 Dec. 1910; record # 30514.
BABB, Mollie; age: 50; single; death cause: "stomach trouble"; died: 26 Jun. 1911; record # 30515.
BASKET, John; age: 60; married; death cause: "consumption"; died: 15 Feb. 1911; record # 30516.
WILLIAMS, Laurce; female; age: 50; married; death cause: "consumption"; died: 12 Apr. 1911; record # 30517.

BARRY, George; age: 82; married; born: Greene County; death cause: "peralosis"; died: 10 Feb. 1911; record # 30518.

ROSE, Ninnie; age: 43; married; death cause: "dropsy"; died; 20 Jun. 1911; record # 30519.

SCOTT, Rachle; age: 76; married; born: Carter County; death cause: "flucks"; died: 15 Jun. 1911; record # 30520.

HYDER, William; age: 64; married; born: Carter County; death cause: "pneumonia"; died: 12 Dec. 1910; record # 30521.

REED, Sarah; age: 22; married; death cause: "blood poison"; died: 16 May 1911; record # 30522.

REED, Infant; female; death cause: "born dead"; died: 2 May 1911; record # 30523.

BROWN, Charlie Roscoe; age: 7 months; death cause: (illegible) fever"; died: 29 Jun. 1911; record # 30524.

COLLET, Infant; female; age: 1 day; death cause: "unknown"; died: 2 Apr. 1911; record # 30525.

SHAFER, Ola; age: 55; married; death cause: "consumption"; died: 14 Nov. 1910; record # 30526.

NELSON, Bertha; age: 4; death cause: "measles"; died: 3 May 1911; record # 30527.

MCMACKEN, R.F.; age: 52; married; death cause: "heart failure"; died: 7 Jun. 1911; record # 30528.

REED, Katy; age: 32 (plus); married; death cause: "consumption"; died: 29 Apr. 1911; record # 30529.

SMITH, Bula; age: 3; death cause: "croupe"; died: 10 Feb. 1911; record # 30530.

JACKSON, R.C.; age: 63; married; death cause: "diabetes or Brights disease"; died: 4 Apr. 1911; record # 30531.

YOKELEY, George; age: 55; married; death cause: "heart failure"; died: (day not stated) Feb. 1911; record # 30532.

MORELOCK, Montie; age: 5; death cause: "croupe"; died: 1 Apr. 1911; record # 30533.

DYKES, Mary Walsey; age: 1 year and 2 months; death cause: "choked to death"; died: 6 Aug. 1910; record # 30534.

COMPTON, Nola; age: 4; death cause: "spinal trouble"; died: 29 Jun. 1911; record # 30535.

DOBBINS, Nancy; age: 80; married; death cause: "cancer of stomach"; died: 25 Dec. 1911; record # 30536.
THOMPSON, Hauer; female, age: 75; married; death cause: "paralysis"; died: 8 Nov. 1911; record # 30537.
CONLEY, Nancy; age: 92; married; death cause: "old age and cancer"; died: 10 May 1911; record # 30538.
MIDDLETON, Maggie; age: 38; married; death cause: "consumption"; died: 18 Sep.1911; record # 30539.
HALE, Conway; age: 92; widower; death cause: "old age and pneumonia"; died: 9 Feb. 1909; record # 30540.
SMITH, Infant; male; death cause: "stillborn"; died: 7 Feb. 1909; record # 30541.
STEELE, M.H.; age: 53; married; death cause: "consumption"; died: 15 Jun. 1909; record # 30542.
CAMPBELL, J.A.; age: 28; married; death cause: "typhoid fever"; died: 10 Jun. 1909; record # 30543.
SCRUGGS, Alma; age: 17; single; death cause: "consumption"; died: 10 Aug. 1908; record # 30544.
BIBLE, John T.; age: 9 months; death cause: "meningitis"; died: 28 Sep.1908; record # 30545.
AYERS, J.C.: age: 81; born: Tennessee; married; death cause: "dropsy"; died: 26 Jan. 1909; record # 30546.
HALE, S.P.; age: 50 years, 3 months and 15 days; married; death cause: "pneumonia"; died: 4 Feb. 1909; record # 30547.
UNIDENTIFIED, Infant; male; death cause: "stillborn"; died: 17 Apr. 1909; record # 30548.
UNIDENTIFIED, Infant; male; black; death cause: "stillborn"; died: 4 Apr. 1909; record # 30549.
BRISENDINE, Carlos; age: 19; single; death cause: "typhoid fever"; died: 15 Aug. 1908; record # 30550.
BRISENDINE, Dewey; age: 11; death cause: "typhoid fever"; died: 8 Sep.1908; record # 30551.
COBBLE, Ida; age: 21 years, 11 months and 29 days; married; death cause: "consumption"; died: 28 Oct. 1908; record # 30552.
UNIDENTIFIED, Infant; male; death cause: "stillborn"; died: 28 Oct. 1908; record # 30553.

TAYLOR, Mattie; age: 20 years and 8 months; single; death cause: "pneumonia fever"; died: 7 Aug. 1909; record # 30554.

HULSEY, Infant; male; age: 10 days; death cause: "unknown"; died: 30 Jun. 1911; record # 30555.

EASTERLY, Carl; age: 20; single; death cause: "consumption"; died: 21 Feb. 1910; record # 30556.

UNIDENTIFIED, Infant; female; age: not stated; death cause: not stated; died: 19 Feb. 1910; record # 30557.

GREGG, Elmer Ayers; age: 2; death cause: "pneumonia"; died: 25 Nov. 1909; record # 30558.

AYERS, Samuel D.; age: 85; married; born: Greene County; death cause: "heart failure"; died: 8 Aug. 1909; record # 30559.

AYERS, Lucind; age: 75; married; born: Tennessee; death cause: not stated; died: 10 Dec., 22 Nov. 1909 (record not clear, both dates shown); record # 30560.

PRUIT, Samantha; age: 53; single; death cause: "general break down"; died: 10 Dec. 1909; record # 30561.

RADER, George; age: 68; married; death cause: "abscess of bowels"; died: 11 Mar.1910; record # 30562.

HOLDER, Mollie; age: 38; single; death cause: "by accident"; died: 2 Jun. 1910; record # 30563.

HARRIS, Margarette; age: 75; widow; born: Tennessee; death cause: "dropsy"; died: 15 Nov. 1909; record # 30564.

LANE, J.D.; age: 60; widower; death cause: "cancer"; died: 10 Mar.1910; record # 30565.

LANE, Eliza; age: 55; married; death cause: "cancer"; died: 29 Jul. 1909; record # 30566.

RILEY, Alice; age: 48; married; death cause: "female trouble"; died: 29 May 1910; record # 30567.

MARSHALL, Veral L.; age: 5; death cause: "diphtheria"; died: 12 Nov. 1909; record # 30568.

HARPER, Nancy; age: 70; widow; death cause: "pneumonia"; died: 9 Mar.1910; record # 30569.

HETTIE (?), P.J.; age: 54; married; death cause: "heart trouble"; died: 20 Aug. 1909; record # 30570.

LLOY, Margarette; age: 34; married; death cause: "consumption"; died: 1 Oct. 1909; record # 30571.
LATMONS, Jay; male; age: 4; death cause: "croup"; died: 13 Jan. 1910; record # 30572.
AURINS, Lee; age: 38; married; death cause: not stated; died: 18 Mar.1910; record # 30573.
STEELE, Sallie; age: 18; single; death cause: "consumption"; died: 19 Aug. 1909; record # 30574.
WHITE, Francis; age: 28; married; death cause: "consumption"; died: 20 Jun. 1910; record # 30575.
UNIDENTIFIED, Infant; male; death cause: "still born"; died: 15 Jan. 1910; record # 30576.
UNIDENTIFIED, Infant; female; death cause: "still born"; died: 2 Jan. 1910; record # 30577.
MELTON, Rettie; age: 72; married; death cause: "paralysis"; died: 5 May 1910; record # 30578.
MELTON, William; age: 57; widower; death cause: "paralysis"; died; 16 Jun. 1910; record # 30579.
STROND, Nancy; age: 67; widow; death cause: "paralysis"; died: 27 Feb. 1910; record # 30580.
COLLINS, Chassie Viola; age: 1 month and 2 days; death cause: "fever"; died: 10 Oct. 1908; record # 30581.
CAMPBELL, John; age: 72 years, 1 month and 9 days; widower; born: Jefferson County; death cause: "paralysis"; died: 30 Jul. 1908; record # 30582.
COLLINS, Martha; age: 3 months and 6 days; death cause: "fever"; died: 29 Aug. 1908; record # 30583.
COLLINS, Daniel C.; age: 2 months and 28 days; death cause: "fever"; died: 21 Aug. 1908; record # 30584.
CONDUFF, Susan Ann; age: 63 years, 1 month and 10 days; married; death cause: "heart trouble"; died: 30 Aug. 1908; record # 30585.
CONDUFF, Ida Bell; age: 23; married; death cause: "consumption"; record # 30586.
COLLINS, Madge M.; age: 4 years and 13 days; death cause: "gastritis"; died: 30 Mar.1909; record # 30587.

FRESHONS, Rebecca; age: 83; married; death cause: "neuralgia"; died: 30 Apr. 1909; record # 30588.

FILLERS, Clarence; age: 1 day; death cause: not stated; died: 5 Jan. 1909; record # 30589.

CONNOR, Sarah; age: 79 years, 2 months and 14 days; widow; death cause: "heart trouble"; died: 18 May 1909; record # 30590.

CONNER, Viola; age: 2 weeks; death cause: "hives"; died; 2 May 1909; record # 30591.

MORELOCK, B.W.; age: 59 years, 4 months and 17 days; married; death cause: "heart trouble"; died: 18 Jun. 1909; record # 30592.

RICKER, Terry; age: 2 months and 20 days; death cause: "indigestion"; died: 6 Apr. 1909; record # 30593.

STILLS, Birdie Josephine; age: 1 month and 4 days; death cause: "bole hives"; died: 21 Jun. 1909; record # 30594.

MILLS, Everhart; age: 18 months; death cause: "meningitis"; died: 2 Oct. 1908; record # 30595.

DANIELS, John B.; age: 54; married; death cause: "kidney trouble"; died: 22 Jun. 1908; record # 30596.

LUTTRELL, Dolphes L.; age: 6 weeks; death cause: "stonnic disease"; died: 4 Aug. 1909; record # 30597.

LUTTRELL, Thebia; age: 70 years, 7 months and 7 days; widow; death cause: "ulcer and heart disease"; died: 8 Oct. 1909; record # 30598.

BOWLES, Ira A.; age: 41 years, 6 months and 15 days; married; school teacher; death cause: "consumption"; died: 7 Apr. 1910; record # 30599.

NEAS, Nettie; age: 33 years, 6 months and 21 days; married; death cause: "consumption"; died: 31 Oct. 1909; record # 30600.

UNIDENTIFIED, Infant; male; lived 4 hours; death cause: "premature birth"; died: 22 Jan. 1910; record # 30601.

JACKSON, Beulah V.; age: about 2 years; death cause: "croup"; died: 7 Jan. 1910; record # 30602.

RUPERT, Viola; death cause: "still born"; died: 16 Oct. 1910; record # 30603.

BOWER, Mira; death cause: "still born"; died: 2 Feb. 1910; record # 30604.

SULLIVAN, Alfred; age: about 68; married; born: Buncomb County, NC; death cause: illegible; died: 14 Oct. 1910; record # 30605.

HOLT, James; age: about 68; married; death cause: "paralysis"; died: 22 Mar. 1910; record # 30606.
GABY, Homer Wane; age: 15 days; death cause: "pneumonia"; died: 7 Jan. 1910; record # 30607.
NEAL, Harell (?) F.; female; age: 9 months and 9 days; death cause: "brain fever"; died: 14 Jul. 1909; record # 30608.
WILLIAMS, Thomas R.; age: 11 days; death cause: not stated; died: 21 Feb. 1910; record # 30609.
JUSTIS, Margaret H.; age: 71 years, 1 month and 12 days; married; death cause: "heart failure"; died: 9 Dec. 1909; record # 30610.
KELLER, Mrs. James K.P.; age: 54 years, 10 months and 4 days; married; death cause: "rheumatism and lung trouble"; died: 20 Jun. 1910; record # 30611.
JUSTIS, Margaret Ann; age: 49 years, 1 month and 7 days; single; death cause: "rheumatism"; died: 26 Jun. 1910; record # 30612.
STARNES, Mrs. Jimie; age: 23 years, 9 months and 15 days; married; school teacher; death cause: "inflammation of stomach"; died: 21 Oct. 1909; record # 30613.
NEWBARY, Leahr; age: 69 years, 4 months and 12 days; married; death cause: "lung trouble"; died: 31 Dec. 1909; record # 30614.
COATER, James H.; age: 27 years, 1 month and 1 day; single; school teacher; death cause: "typhoid fever"; died: 7 Aug. 1909; record # 30615.
CARTER, Infant; age: 8 days; death cause: "yellow jaundice"; died: 17 Jun. 1910; record # 30616.
PRESLEY, Ralph; age: 5 days; death cause: "premature birth"; died: 8 Feb. 1910; record # 30617.
NEAL, James R.; age: 43 years, 11 months and 23 days; single; death cause: "consumption"; died: 21 Apr. 1910; record # 30618.
UNIDENTIFIED, Infant; female; death cause: "died at birth"; died: 3 Feb. 1910; record # 30619.
FARRIS, Samuel; age: 18 years, 1 month and 1 day; death cause: "typhoid fever"; died: 26 Dec. 1909; record # 30620.
FARRIS, Robert; age: 16 years, 11 months and 9 days; death cause: "typhoid fever"; died: 3 Apr. 1910; record # 30621.

NEAL, Virna G.; age: 7 months and 13 days; death cause: "bronchial pneumonia"; died: 19 Feb. 1909; record # 30622.

GABY, Inlia; age: 25 years, 6 months and 27 days; single; death cause: "consumption"; died: 3 Jul. 1909; record # 30623.

PRICE, Mollie; age: 51 years, 7 months and 5 days; married; death cause: "ulcer of stomach"; died: 3 Oct. 1909; record # 30624.

KITE, Infant; female; age: 1 day; death cause: "bronchitis"; died: 22 Oct. 1909; record # 30625.

KITE, Infant; male; age: 1 month and 21 days; death cause: "earisiples"; died: 22 Oct. 1909; record # 30626.

FIELDS, Ralph; age: 1 year, 1 month and 21 days; death cause: "bowel trouble"; died: 19 Jul. 1911; record # 30627.

SAYLER, Edith; age: 2 years, 11 months and 18 days; death cause: "diphtheria"; died at J.K.P. SAYLER farm on 21 Oct. 1909; record # 30628.

SAYLER, John; age: 1 year, 1 month and 21 days; death cause: "diphtheria"; died at J.K.P. SAYLER farm on 28 Oct. 1909; record # 30629.

MALLONE, Roy; age: 19; single; death cause: "consumption"; died: 8 Aug. 1909; record # 30630.

GABY, Dorthia Ann; age: 41; married; death cause: "consumption"; died: 29 Dec. 1910; record # 30631.

NEAL, James; age: 44; married; death cause: "consumption"; died: 21 Dec. 1910; record # 30632.

SMITH, Dorthy Estell; age: 9 months and 20 days; death cause: "typhoid fever"; died: 30 Jun. 1910; record # 30633.

SMITH, William Talmage; age: 22; married; born: Morristown; death cause: "capillary bronchitis"; died: 13 Apr. 1911; record # 30634.

SMITH, Mary Catherine; age: 2 years and 6 months; death cause: "capillary bronchitis"; died: 6 Apr. 1911; record # 30635.

CARTER, Hyla; age: 56; married; born: Hawkins County; death cause: "typhoid fever"; died: 12 Nov. 1910; record # 30636.

CARTER, John; age: 60; married; death cause: "heart trouble"; died: 8 Feb. 1911; record # 30637.

CARTER, Robert; age: 16; death cause: "typhoid fever"; died: 18 Nov. 1910; record # 30638.

CARTER, Martha; age: 28; married; death cause: "puerperbl peritonitis"; died: 22 Jan. 1910; record # 30639.

BRITT, Louis; age: 50; married; death cause: "consumption"; died: 25 May 1911; record # 30640.

HARMON, D.M.; age: 64; married; death cause: "tuberculosis of throat"; died: 25 Jul. 1911; record # 30641.

UNIDENTIFIED, Infant; male; age: 3 weeks; death cause: "congenital syphilis"; died: 28 Jan. 1911; record # 30642.

BIBLE, Dessie; age: 9 months; death cause: "consumption"; died: 19 Jan. 1911; record # 30643.

WAITS, Mahala J.; age: 68; married; death cause: "gangrene"; died: 11 Dec. 1910; record # 30644.

KITE, Matilda; age: 55; married; death cause: "consumption"; died: 28 Jan. 1911; record # 30645.

KITE, Lasarath; age: 69; married; born: Hawkins County; death cause: "heart failure"; died: 20 Jun. 1911; record # 30646.

WEEMS, Nancy Ann; age: 72; married; death cause: "consumption"; died: 20 Jun. 1911; record # 30647.

MORRISON, Dellie; age: 6 months; death cause: "hives"; died: 20 Sep.1910; record # 30648.

SPEAR, Elizabeth; age: 76; married; born: Virginia; death cause: "old age"; died: 29 Mar.1912; record # 30649.

MCNEESE, Lacy; age: 24; single; death cause: "typhoid"; died: 30 Aug. 1911; record # 30650.

DEPEW, Eliza; age: 51; married; death cause: "typhoid fever"; died: 3 Sep.1911; record # 30651.

HARTSELL, Mary; age: 84; married; born: Bedford County; death cause: "paralysis"; died: 31 Mar.1911; record # 30652.

REED, James: age: 74; married; death cause: "tuberculosis"; died: 24 Jun. 1912; record # 30653.

MAYERS, Emiline; age: 90; widow; death cause: "abscess"; died: 25 Feb. 1912; record # 30654.

MAHONEY, Anna; age: 32; married; death cause: "spinal meningitis"; died: not stated; death recorded: 18 Jul. 1912; record # 30655.

VEST, Laurence; age: 2; born: North Carolina; death cause: "flux"; died in North Carolina on 9 Sep.1911; record # 30656.

COLLETT, Frank; age: 7; death cause: "pneumonia fever"; died: not stated; death recorded: 18 Jul. 1912; record # 30657.
ANDERSON, M.L.; age: 53; married; death cause: "hemorrhage of brain"; died: 2 Dec. 1912; record # 30658.
BASS, Anna Elizabeth; age: 51; single; death cause: "general affliction"; died: 11 Dec. 1912; record # 30659.
MCCRAY, Jennie; age: 40; married; born: Limestone, TN.; death cause: "consumption"; died: 2 Nov. 1911; record # 30660.
LITTLE, Nat; age: 27; single; born: Washington County; death cause: "consumption"; died: 4 Jun. 1912; record # 30661.
STATEN, Oka R.; male; age: 13; death cause: "heart trouble"; died: 29 Mar.1912; record # 30662.
SHAFER, William; age: 45; married; death cause: "tuberculosis"; died: 17 Oct. 1911; record # 30663.
WINSLOW, Walter S.; age: 5; death cause: "scarlet fever"; died: 4 Feb. 1912; record # 30664.
CAMPBELL, Bettie; age: not stated; married; born: Washington County; death cause: "cancer of stomach"; died: 18 Jul. 1912; record # 30665.
BASKET, Infant; sex: not stated; death cause: "lived just a few minutes"; died: 3 Oct. 1911; record # 30666.
MIDDLETON, Rosa; age: 22; married; death cause: "consumption"; died: 2 Jul. 1911; record # 30667.
BOWMAN, Smith; age: 73; married; born: Greene County; death cause: "old age"; died: 8 Dec. 1911; record # 30668.
DETHRGE, Mable; age: 8 months; death cause: "diarrhea"; died: 20 Mar.1912; record # 30669.
COMPTON, Andrew; age: 20; single; death cause: "consumption"; died: 20 Jun. 1912; record # 30670.
KILDAY, Mourie; male; age: 7 months; death cause: "heart disease"; died: 17 May 1912; record # 30671.
COMPTON, Nellie; age: 3; death cause: "paralysis"; died: 1 Jul. 1911; record # 30672.
DYKES, Essie; age: 22; married; death cause: "child birth"; died: 17 May 1912; record # 30673.
ROBERTS, Sarah M.; age: 61; married; death cause: "tuberculosis"; died: 5 Aug. 1912; record # 30674.

KENNEDY, Lanisa L.; age: 80 years, 5 months and 4 days; widow; born: Limestone, TN.; death cause: "dropsy"; died: 4 Apr. 1909; record # 30675.

COLLETT, William; age: "unknown"; widower; death cause: "heart trouble"; died: 21 Nov. 1908; record # 30676.

DOTY, Alphius; age: 85 years, 1 month and 13 days; widower; death cause: "kidney disease"; died: 17 Apr. 1909; record # 30677.

JAMES, Charles; age: 35; married; death cause: "consumption"; died: 4 Jan. 1909; record # 30678.

KELLEY, George; age: 3 years and 6 months; death cause: "spinal disease"; died: 23 Aug. 1908; record # 30679.

GARDNER, Sarah; age: 27 years, 1 month and 8 days; death cause: "child birth"; died: 28 Aug. 1908; record # 30680.

HOPE, Caroline Matilda; age: 86 years, 2 months and 22 days; death cause: "kidney disease"; died: 15 Mar.1909; record # 30681.

GARDNER, Infant; male; lived 2 hours; death cause: not stated; died: 28 Aug. 1908; record # 30682.

MORRISON, J.Y.; age: 50; born: Hawkins County; married; death cause: "rupture"; died: 28 Dec. 1908; record # 30683.

LOYD, Nancy; age: 17; single; death cause: "female disease"; died: 15 May 1909; record # 30684.

LANE, Milbord; age: 8 months; death cause: "spinal disease"; died: 30 Mar.1909; record # 30685.

DAVIS, Lana; age: 21 years; 2 months and 23 days; married; death cause: "child birth"; died; 13 Oct. 1908; record # 30686.

DAVIS, Infant; female; age: 1 day; death cause: "unknown"; died: 14 Oct. 1908; record # 30687.

CARTER, John P.; age: 71; widower; death cause: "indigestion"; died: 12 Nov. 1911; record # 30688.

KELLER, Major; female; age: 94; widow; born: Virginia; death cause: illegible; died: (day not stated) Feb. 1912; record # 30689.

KELLER, Sindia; age: 69; single; death cause: "pneumonia fever"; died: (day not stated) Mar.1912; record # 30690.

HARTMAN, Lois; age: 3; death cause: "pneumonia"; died: (day not stated) Apr. 1912; record # 30691.

CARTER, Kermit; age: 2; born: New Mexico; death cause: "diphtheria"; died: (day not stated) Oct. 1911; record # 30692.
BURGON, Joe; age: 64; widower; death cause: "heart failure"; died: (day not stated) Jun. 1912; record # 30693.
MYERS, Martha; age: 60; widow; death cause: "pneumonia"; died: (day not stated) Jan. 1912; record # 30694.
MYERS, Bell; age: 25; widow; death cause: "fever"; died: (day not stated) Feb. 1912; record # 30695.
HUNEYCUT; Henry; age: 8; death cause: "fever"; died: (day not stated) Jul. 1911; record # 30696.
HELTON, John; age: 81; widower; born: Greene County; death cause: "senility"; died: 3 May 1912; record # 30697.
UNIDENTIFIED, Infant; male; age: 6 months; death cause: "diphtheria"; date not recorded; record # 30698.
HUMPHREYS, Eliza; age: 63; born: Washington County; married; death cause: "heart failure"; died: 7 Aug. 1911; record # 30699.
ADAMS, Effie J.; age: 38; married; death cause: "pneumonia"; died: 21 Dec. 1911; record # 30700.
THORNBURY, Blanch; age: 17 months; death cause: "cholera infantum"; died: __ Feb. __; death registered: 23 Jul. 1912; record # 30701.
MOORE, Arch; age: 60; married; death cause: "consumption"; died: 22 Feb. 1912; record # 30702.
JEFFERS, Infant; female; death cause: "born dead" on 15 May 1912; record # 30703.
DYKES, James; age: 17; single; death cause: "consumption"; died: 12 May 1912; record # 30704.
HENSLEY, Charley; age: 4; death cause: "burned to death"; died: 20 Dec. 1911; record # 30705.
KILDAY, Mary; age: 7 months; death cause: "heart disease"; died: 17 Mar.1912; record # 30706.
JEFFERS, Essie; age: 22; married; death cause: "child birth"; died: 15 May 1912; record # 30707.
DOTSON, Blanch; age: 20; single; death cause: "spinal meningitis"; died: 22 Jun. 1912; record # 30708.
ADAMS, Melvina; age: 82; born: Washington County; married; death cause: "pneumonia"; died: 13 Dec. 1912; record # 30709.

JOHNSON, Infant; male; death cause: "still born"; died: 10 Mar.1909; record # 30710.
CUTSHALL, Infant; male; death cause: "still born"; died: 3 Jul. 1909; record # 30711.
CUTSHALL, Mary; age: 39; born: North Carolina; married; death cause: "cancer"; died: 20 Dec. 1909; record # 30712.
HARRISON, Rhea Aelene; age: 1 year, 11 months and 13 days; death cause: "diphtheria and kidney trouble"; died: 1 Dec. 1909; record # 30713.
THOMASON, George: age: 50; married; death cause: "consumption"; died: 17 Jul. 1909; record # 30715.
KING, Thomas: age: 76; born: Washington County; single; death cause: "consumption"; died: 17 Jul. 1909; record # 30715.
KNIGHT, Greenville; age: 72; born: North Carolina; married; death cause: "consumption"; died: 22 Mar.1909; record # 30716
SMITH, Frank; age: 19; single; death cause: "by fallen tree"; died: 31 Jul. 1908; record # 30717.
PHILLIPS, Fred; age: 6; death cause: not stated; died: 22 Feb. 1909; record # 30718.
ROSE, Bob; no additional information given; died: 14 May 1908; record # 30719.
PETERS, George: age: 30; single; death cause: "consumption"; died: 1 Apr. 1909; record # 30720.
JOHNSON, Matilda; age: 77; born: Rheatown; single; death cause: "paralysis"; died: 9 Jan. 1909; record # 30721.
UNIDENTIFIED, Infant; male; age: 9 days; death cause: not stated; died: 5 Jun. 1909; record 30722.
GRAY, John; age: 26; single; death cause: "typhoid"; died: 3 Nov. 1908; record # 30723.
LEWIS, James; age: 70; born: Bristol, TN.; widower; death cause: "kidney trouble"; died: 23 Feb. 1909; record # 30724.
PHILLIPS, Carl; age: 10 months; death cause: "cholera and measles"; died: 20 Jun. 1909; record # 30725.
LEWIS, Thomas; age: 20; born: Carter County; single; death cause: "operation"; died: 24 Oct. 1908; record # 30726.

HYDER, James F.; age: 3; death cause: "pneumonia"; died: 8 Dec. 1908; record # 30727.

SWANSON, Aurbrey; age: 11 months; death cause: "flux"; died: 15 Jun. 1909; record # 30728.

WILSON, Margaret; age: 74; married; death cause: "dropsy"; died: 10 Nov. 1908; record # 30729.

BALNS, Hunter; age: 20; single; death cause: "appendicitis"; died: (day not stated) Jun. 1910; record # 30730.

CANNON, William F.M.; age: 66 years, 6 months and 17 days; married; death cause: "cancer"; died: 12 Aug. 1909; record # 30731.

GARDNER, Mary Jane; age: 50 years and 5 months; single; death cause: "consumption"; died: 22 Feb. 1910; record # 30732.

MARSHALL, Ailent; female; age: 6 months; death cause: "unknown"; died: 9 Sep.1910; record # 30733.

BIRD, Hannah Jane; age: 59 years, 1 month and 2 days; married; death cause: "bronchial asthma"; died: 3 Oct. 1909; record # 30734.

KNIPP, Guy; age: 4 years and 26 days; death cause: "diphtheria"; died: 23 Oct. 1909; record # 30735.

KNIPP, Elsie; age: 27 years, 3 months and 1 day; married; death cause: "heart failure"; died: 28 Apr. 1910; record # 30736.

MILLER, Florence; age: 21 years and 3 months; single; death cause: "tuberculosis"; died: (day not stated) Jun. 1910; record # 30737.

DARNELL, John; age: 27 years, 1 month and 5 days; married; death cause: "drowned"; died: 25 May 1910; record # 30738.

MASNEL, Ann; black; age: 75; born: North Carolina; single; death cause: "syphilis"; record # 30739.

CLAYTON, Adeline; black; age: 50; born: Monroe County; married; death cause: "tuberculosis"; died: 8 Apr. 1911; record # 30740.

KENNEDY, Fanney; black; age: 85; single; death cause: "old age"; died 25 Jun. 1911; record # 30741.

LOVE, Elizabeth; black; age: 13 months; death cause: "pneumonia fever"; died: 1 Apr. 1911; record # 30742.

NORTON, Flossie; age: 11; death cause: "diphtheria"; died: 29 Oct. 1909; record # 30743.

DAVENPORT, Ellen; age: 34; born: Washington County; nurse; single; death cause: "typhoid fever"; died: 21 Sep.1909; record # 30744.

GENTRY, James; age: 31; born: Madison County, NC.; married; death cause: "shot"; died: 21 Sep.1909; record # 30745.

RICKER, Dora; age: 48; married; death cause: "pneumonia"; died: 23 May 1910; record # 30747.

BOWMAN, Polly; age: 57; single; death cause: "diarrhea"; died: 8 May 1910; record # 30747.

BOWMAN, Hattie; age: 33; born: Washington County; married; death cause: "stomach trouble"; died: 18 Mar.1910; record # 30748.

FILLERS, Infant; female; death cause: "still born"; died: 3 Apr. 1910; record # 30749.

FANNON, Infant; male; death cause: "still born"; died: 24 Jan. 1910; record # 30750.

REAVES, Infant; male; death cause: "still born"; died: 15 Mar.1910; record # 30751.

FANNING, Oma; age: 35; married; death cause: "consumption"; died: 3 Aug. 1910; record # 30752.

SHELTON, Daphne; age: 5; born: North Carolina; death cause: "fever"; died: 17 Apr. 1910; record # 30753.

RANDOLPH, George; age: 19; born: Yancy County, NC.; single; death cause: "consumption"; died: 6 Jun. 1910; record # 30754.

SEATON, B.T.; age: 69; married; death cause: "diarrhea"; died: 1 May 1910; record # 30755.

CRUM, M.A.; age: 25; married; death cause: "consumption"; died: 6 Mar.1910; record # 30756.

CORBY, James; age: 77; born: Virginia; married; death cause: "pneumonia fever"; died: 17 Oct. 1909; record # 30757.

BROWN, Marian; age: 63; single; death cause: "heart failure"; died: 5 Sep.1909; record # 30758.

BROWLES, E.H.; age: 66; married; death cause: "heart trouble"; died: 3 Dec. 1909; record # 30759.

JONES, Celia V.; age: 2 months; death cause: "unknown"; died: 21 Feb. 1910; record # 30760.

FELLERS, W.A.; age: 44; married; death cause: "dropsy"; died: 24 Apr. 1910; record 30761.

WILLIAMSON, J.W.; age: 73; married; death cause: "dropsy"; died: 7 Feb. 1910; record # 30762.

GREEN, Myrtle; age: 32; married; death cause: "consumption"; died: 29 Jan. 1910; record # 30763.
BROWLES, W.W.; age: 54; married; death cause: "consumption"; died: 31 Aug. 1909; record # 30764.
PAINTER, Osea; male; age: 78; married; merchant; death cause: "paralysis"; died: 27 Aug. 1909; record # 30765.
ROGERS, Hobart; age: 10; death cause: "scarlet fever"; died: 11 Oct. 1909; record # 30766.
ROGERS, Lila; age: 36; married; death cause: "consumption"; died: 3 Jun. 1910; record # 30767.
JENNINGS, J.K.; age: 22; single; death cause: "consumption"; died: 3 Feb. 1910; record # 30768.
DUNBAR, Louise; age: 65; married; death cause: "paralysis"; died: 6 Nov. 1909; record # 30769.
FILLERS, Sarah; age: 41; married; death cause: "dropsy"; died: 10 Jun. 1910; record # 30770.
GRAY, W.A.; age: 76; married; death cause: "consumption"; died: 11 Mar.1910; record # 30771.
GRAY, Crawford; age: 3 days; death cause: "heart trouble"; died: 17 Apr. 1910; record # 30772.
GRAY, Lavada; age: 23; married; death cause: "brain fever"; died: 27 Apr. 1910; record # 30773.
DAVIS, Henry; age: 33; married; death cause: "fever"; died: 27 Jan. 1910; record # 30774.
MATHEWS, Lewis; age: 3; born: Hamblen County; death cause: "scarlet fever"; died; 16 Oct. 1909; record # 30775.
GRAY, G.S.; age: 44; married; death cause: "heart disease"; died: 27 Dec. 1909; record # 30776.
JOHNSON, Lawrence; age: 2; death cause: "pneumonia"; died: 7 Oct. 1909; record # 30777.
MITCHELL, Thomas; age: 14 months; death cause: "flux"; died: 14 Jun. 1910; record # 30778.
RAY, Infant; female; age: 1 month; death cause: "heart disease"; died: 27 Dec. 1909; record # 30779.
MITCHELL, Lucretia; age: 16; married; death cause: "typhoid fever"; died: 2 Aug. 1909; record # 30780.

JOHNSON, W.F.; age: 53; married; death cause: "typhoid fever"; died: 25 Nov. 1909; record # 30781.
WILHOIT, E.M.; age: 76; married; death cause: "unknown"; died: 24 May 1910; record # 30782.
MAUK, Jake; age: 73; born: Washington County; married; death cause: not recorded; died; 24 Dec. 1909; record # 30783.
ROBERTS, Patsy; age: 69; married; death cause: "paralysis"; died: 27 Nov. 1909; record # 30784.
GREGG, Carry; age: 14; death cause: "membranous croup"; died in Cocke County on 1 Oct. 1909; record # 30785.
GREGG, Emory; age: 12; death cause: "membranous croup"; died; 9 Oct. 1909; record # 30786.
GREGG, Jusie; female; age: 10; death cause: "membranous croup"; died: 13 Oct. 1909; record # 30787.
RIVERS, Raymond; age: 2 years and 6 months; death cause: "bold hives"; died: 23 May 1910; record # 30788.
EASTERLY, W. CARL; age: 20; single; death cause: "tuberculosis"; died: 21 Feb. 1910; record # 30789.
GREEN, Kate; age: 72; married; death cause: "paralysis"; died: 16 Dec. 1910; record # 30790.
BOLES, Virginia; age: 29; married; death cause: "tuberculosis"; died: 27 Jul. 1910; record # 30791.
OSBORNE, W.S.; age: 38; married; death cause: "typhoid fever"; died: 11 Dec. 1909; record # 30792.
SHULDS, J.K.P.; age: 62; married; death cause: "Brights disease"; died: 4 Jan. 1910; record # 30793.
CALHUT, Ellen; age: 19; married; death cause: "burned to death"; died: 23 Aug. 1909; record # 30794.
CHANDLEY, William; age: 65; married; death cause: "tuberculosis"; died: 12 May 1910; record # 30794.
GRAYSON, Jane; age: 84; married; death cause: "senile gangrene"; died: 25 Jan. 1910; record # 30796.
SHIELDS, Infant; male; age: 1 day; death cause: "unknown"; died: 28 Dec. 1910; record # 30797.
SOLOMAN, Selma; age: 23; married; death cause: "typhoid fever"; died: 28 Jul. 1909; record # 30798.

GRAY, James; age: 2 months; death cause: "unknown"; died: 13 Apr. 1910; record # 30799.
HUNT, Flora Bertha; age: 27; born: Sullivan County; death cause: "scarlet fever"; died: 12 Aug. 1910; record # 30800.
MURRH, Bruce; age: 19; single; death cause: "typhoid fever"; died: 9 Jun. 1911; record # 30801.
HENRY, Thomas A.; age: 21; single; death cause: "scarffula"; died: 4 Jun. 1911; record # 30802.
MULLENDORE, George; age: 66; married; death cause: "dropsy"; died: 1 Jan. 1911; record # 30803.
SUSONG, Dean Fox; age: 1 year and 4 months; death cause: "stomach disease"; died: 28 Mar.1911; record # 30804.
MILTON, Elizabeth; age: 34; born: Cocke County; married; death cause: "hemorrhage of brain"; died: 16 Feb. 1910; record # 30805.
SEETLES, H.I.; age: 15; death cause: "accidental shot"; died: 9 Jan. 1910; record # 30806.
KESTON, J.V.; age: 15 months; death cause: "lung trouble"; died: 1 Mar.1910; record # 30807.
TATES, Blanch; age: 13 months; death cause: "pneumonia fever"; died: 1 Feb. 1910; record # 30808.
RUSSEL, Mrs. Louisa; age: 79 years and 10 months; widow; death cause: "old age"; died: 10 Jun. 1910; record # 30809.
UNIDENTIFIED, Infant; male; death cause: not stated; died: 24 Jan. 1910; record # 30810.
UNIDENTIFIED, Infant; male; death cause: "unknown"; died: 28 Dec. 1909; record # 30811.
JEFFERS, Robert Taylor; age: 23; single; death cause: "meningitis"; died: 12 Mar.1910; record # 30812.
PEIRCE, Belle D.; age: 2; death cause: "consumption"; died: 1 Mar.1910; record # 30813.
JUSTICE, Hannah J.; age: 54; married; death cause: "heart trouble"; died: 30 Dec. 1909; record # 30814.
MITCHELL, A.J.; age: 67; married; death cause: "abscess"; died: 8 Feb. 1910; record # 30815.
UNIDENTIFIED, Infant; female; age: 9 days; death cause: "unknown"; died: 4 Dec. 1909; record # 30816.

HENSHAW, Nancy; age: 77; married; death cause: "old age"; died: 28 Nov. 1909; record # 30817.
MCLAIN, David; age: 13 months; death cause: "pneumonia"; died: 30 Dec. 1909; record # 30818.
ISLEY, Wilburn; age: 16 months; death cause: "scarlet fever"; died: 20 Sep. 1909; record # 30919.
JUSTICE, T.T.; age: 32; married; death cause: "consumption"; died: 13 Aug. 1909; record # 30820.
BARLOW, Della May; age: 22; married; death cause: "consumption"; died: 26 Mar.1910; record # 30821.
GARBER, Christie A.; age: 64; born: Washington County; death cause: "consumption of bowels"; died: 9 May 1910; record # 30822.
STORY, Carrie; age: 2 months; death cause: "unknown"; died: 2 Feb. 1910; record # 30823.
GRAHAM, Eliza Ann; age: 68; married; death cause: "diarrhea"; died: 20 Aug. 1908; record # 30824.
LONG, A.W.; age: 26; single; death cause: "pneumonia"; died: 25 Nov. 1908; record # 30825.
LONG, John; age: 22; single; death cause: "typhoid fever"; died: 24 Nov. 1908; record # 30826.
UNIDENTIFIED, Infant; male; death cause: "still born"; died: 13 Apr. 1909; record # 30827.
TELOEAT (?), Maty E.; male; age: 12 days; death cause: "unknown"; died: 10 Jan. 1909; record # 30828.
HERTEN, W.J.; age: 73; born: North Carolina; married; death cause: "heart trouble"; died: 15 Nov. 1908; record # 30829.
FORTNER, Mary; age: 22; married; death cause: "lung trouble"; died: 18 Jul. 1908; record # 30830.
HANKINS, John E.; age: 17; single; death cause: "typhoid fever"; died: 6 Dec. 1908; record # 30831.
JESTES, Serel; male; age: 10; death cause: "flux"; died: 31 May 1909; record # 30832.
FLUKS, Margaret; age: 50; married; death cause: "dropsy"; died: 25 Nov. 1908; record # 30833.
HARDEN, Robert R.; age: 21 days; death cause: illegible; died: 30; Jul. 1908; record # 30834.

GASS, M.W.; age: 41; married; death cause: "stomach trouble"; died: 8 Feb. 1909; record # 30835.

GRAHAM, A.T.; age: 52; married; death cause: "lagrip"; died: 15 Jan. 1909; record # 30836.

MYERS, Clara; age: 68; married; death cause: "flux"; died: 28 May 1909; record # 30837.

LANE, Patsy; age: 4; death cause: "pneumonia"; died: 19 Mar.1909; record # 30838.

ANDERSON, Mildred; age: 11 months; death cause: "flux"; died: 26 Jun. 1909; record # 30839.

BRUMLEY, Cathern; age: 45; married; death cause: "heart failure"; died: (day not stated) Mar.1909; record # 30840.

BAILES, Maley; female; age: 12 years and 1 day; death cause: "lung trouble"; died: 8 Mar.1909; record # 30841.

UNIDENTIFIED, Infant; female; age: 10 days; death cause: "bold hives"; died: 17 Feb. 1909; record # 30842.

BARNET, A.J.; age: 83; born: Tennessee; married; death cause: "diabetes"; died: 15 Jun. 1909; record # 30843.

HARTMAN, Elsie Jane; age: 78; married; death cause: "lung trouble"; died: 18 Aug. 1908; record # 30844.

LASEN, Emma; age: 3; death cause: "measles"; died: 16 May 1909; record # 30845.

INSEARE (?), J.H.; age: 54 in May 1909; born: North Carolina; married; death cause: not recorded; died: 14 Jan. 1909; record # 30846.

RITE, Glennss; male; age: 6 weeks; death cause: "bold hives"; died: 16 Sep. 1908; record # 30847.

BANSREL, Infant; age: 4 years and 1 month; death cause: "scarlet fever"; died: 8 Sep. 1908; record # 30848.

JOHNSON, Barbara; age: 78 on the 29th of April; married; death cause: illegible; died; 2 Sep. 1908; record # 30849.

LOWE, Myrtle B.; age: 26; married; death cause: "tuberculosis"; died: 30 Dec. 1911; record # 30850.

LOWE, Henry R.; age: 1; death cause: not stated; died: 8 Mar.1912; record # 30851.

SEAY, Rubin F.; age: 38; married; death cause: "gunshot"; died: 30 Apr. 1912; record # 30852.

KNOTT, Lasey; female; age: 83; single; death cause: "old age"; died: 24 Apr. 1912; record # 30853.
ALLEN, Nancy; age: 91; born: South Carolina; single; death cause: "cancer"; died: 5 Nov. 1911; record # 30854.
BLACK, Thomas; age: 78; born: Indiana; single; death cause: "dropsy"; died: 5 Aug. 1911; record 30855.
COBBLE, John A.; age: 23; married; death cause: "typhoid fever"; died: 2 Jan. 1912; record # 30856.
HARMON, George F.; age: 62; married; death cause: "Brights disease"; died: 28 Jul. 1911; record # 30857.
MCCAMEY, Lydia May Belle; age: 1 year, 1 month and 3 days; death cause: "diphtheria"; died: 12 Apr. 1912; record # 30858.
STILLS, Sista; female; age: 24; married; death cause: "coal"; died: 19 Nov. 1911; record # 30859.
KYKENDALL, Milta; female; age: 85; born: North Carolina; married; death cause: "stomach trouble"; died: 25 Jun. 1912; record # 30860.
JENNINGS, Malinda; age: 72; born: Greene County; married; death cause: not stated; died: 10 Dec. 1912; record # 30861.
RICKER, F.K.; age: 49; married; death cause: "operation"; died: 16 Oct. 1911; record # 30862.
MYERS, Jacob; age: 57; married; death cause: "heart disease"; died: 18 Oct. 1911; record # 30863.
HAWS, Beryl; age: 13 years and 6 months; death cause: "peritonitis"; died: 23 Dec. 1911; record # 30864.
LAMB, Minnie; age: 5 months; death cause: "fever"; died: (day not stated) Jan. 1912; record # 30865.
WADDLE, Arch; age: 4 days; death cause: not stated; died: 7 May 1912; record # 30866.
CONDUFF, Samuel; age: 61; married; death cause: not recorded; died: 31 Oct. 1911; record # 30867.
CUNNINGHAM, Annie; age: 25; born: North Carolina; married; death cause: "consumption"; died: 18 Aug. 1911; record # 30868.
RIKER, Sarah; age: 12; death cause: "coal"; died: 8 Jan. 1912; record # 30869.
LAMB, Alice; age: 5 days; death cause: not stated; died: 17 Dec. 1911; record # 30870.

UNIDENTIFIED, Infant; male; age: 1 day; death cause: not stated; died: 20 Mar.1912; record # 30871.

WARN, Robert; age: 12; days; death cause: "cripple from birth"; died: 12 Feb. 1912; record # 30872.

COLLINS, Lizzie; age: 2; death cause: "croup"; died: 13 Nov. 1911; record # 30873.

LAMB, William; age: 61; married; death cause: not stated; died: 27 Jun. 1912; record # 30874.

BROWN, Liza; age: 43; married; death cause: "scarfulla"; died: 19 Oct. 1911; record # 30875.

PICKERING, Infant; female; age: 3 days; death cause: not stated; died: 13 Feb. 1911; record # 30876.

CARTER, John; age: 46; married; death cause: "abscess on side"; died: 27 May 1911; record # 30877.

CARTRIGHT, Hazel; age: 7; death cause: "diphtheria"; died: 25 Oct. 1911; record # 30878.

MALONE, Mary; age: 81; born: Bluff City, TN.; widow; death cause: "old age"; died: 2 Feb. 1911; record # 30879.

GASS, Infant; male; age: 6 months; death cause: "dropsy"; died: 30 Jun. 1911; record # 30880.

MALONE, Mary Ann; age: 60; widow; death cause: "tuberculosis"; died: 5 Nov. 1911; record # 30881.

CRUMLEY, Abram; age: 77 years and 9 months; born: Baileyton, TN.; married; death cause: "pneumonia and old age"; died: 3 Jan. 1911; record # 30882.

GASS, Hilie; age: 53; married; death cause: "bladder disease"; died: 4 Mar.1911; record # 30883.

COATES, Cloe; age: 2; death cause: "membranous croup"; died: 2 Nov. 1910; record # 30884.

SMITH, Esther; age: 11; death cause: "pneumonia fever"; died: 18 Feb. 1911; record # 30885.

YOAKLEY, George; age: 41; married; Baptist Minister; death cause: "pneumonia fever"; died: 6 Nov. 1910; record # 30886.

KELLER, Jane; age: 60; married; death cause: "tuberculosis of bowels"; died: 26 Nov. 1910; record # 30887.

YOKLEY, Bettie; age: 45; married; death cause: "tuberculosis"; died: 17 May 1911; record # 30888.

LINEBAUGH, John; age: 80 years and 3 months; born: Andersonville, TN.; married; death cause: "old age"; died: 10 Jun. 1911; record # 30889.

COMBS, Robert; age: 3; born: Bluff City, TN.; death cause: "membranous croup"; died: 5 Apr. 1912; record # 30890.

HARMON, Pearl; age: 6; born: Chattanooga, TN.; death cause: "burned"; died: 20 Dec. 1911; record # 30891.

FORTNER, Ruby; age: 5; death cause: "measles and flux"; died: 4 Jul. 1911; record # 30892.

LOVE, Mary; black; age: 40 to 45; married; death cause: not stated; died: 31 Dec. 1911; record # 30893.

MCWAMAR (or McNamar), Jennie V.; age: 1 year and 10 months; death cause: "pneumonia fever"; died: 28 Dec. 1911; record # 30894.

MCDONALD, Herman (?) F.; female; age: 1; death cause: "tuberculosis"; died: 29 Jul. 1911; record # 30895.

COLLINS, A__ (illegible); male; age: 2; death cause: not stated; died: 27 Nov. 1911; record # 30896.

CLOYD, John P.: age: 42; born: Washington County; married; death cause: "pneumonia fever"; died: 25 Mar.1912; record # 30897.

CARMON, Darnell; age: 55; married; death cause: "gall stone"; died: 15 Jan. 1912; record # 30898.

DIXON, Sue; age: 46; married; death cause: "stomach trouble"; died: 2 Oct. 1911; record # 30899.

YOKLEY, Rebecca; age: 81; widow; death cause: "old age"; died: 17 Apr. 1912; record # 30900.

SMITH, Margaret; black; age: 82; born: near Greeneville; death cause: "old age"; died: 20 Dec. 1911; record # 30901.

SHELTON, Peter; black; age: 72; married; death cause: "old age"; died; date not recorded; record # 30902.

UNIDENTIFIED, Infant; female; age: 3; death cause: "brain fever"; died: date not recorded; record # 30903.

ELLIOT, Augusta; female; age: near 4 months; death cause: "brain fever"; died: 18 May 1912; record # 30904.

BROOKS, F.S.; age: 26; married; death cause: "tuberculosis or lung hemorrhage"; died: 3 Dec. 1911; record # 30905.

HEUX, Alice; age: 17; death cause: "unknown"; died: 22 Jul. (year not recorded); record # 30906.

BROOKS, Nellie Clyde; age: 33; married; death cause: "tuberculosis of lungs"; died: 22 Apr. 1911; record # 30907.

ROODA, Edna; age: 2; death cause: "pneumonia and whooping cough"; died: 15 Jan. 1912; record # 30908.

UNIDENTIFIED, Infant; female; age: 1 day; death cause: "unknown"; died: 18 Feb. 1912; record # 30909.

LEMING, Samuel W.; age: 71; married; death cause: "chronic heart failure"; died: 8 Sep. 1911; record # 30910.

DOBSON, Caroline H.; age: 70; married; death cause: "cancer of left breast"; died: 21 Oct. 1911; record # 30911.

GOOD, Elizabeth; age: 82; born: Washington County; widow; death cause: "chronic diarrhea"; died: 27 Sep. 1911; record # 30912.

DOBSON, Thomas: age: 74; married; death cause: "chronic heart failure"; died: 20 Aug. 1911; record # 30913.

FRIDDLE, Infant; male; age: 2 days; unnamed child of James FRIDDLE; death cause: "unknown"; died: 16 May 1912; record # 30914.

MCNEESE, I.P.; male; age: 58; married; death cause: "cancer"; died: 8 Jul. 1910; record # 30915.

MONTGOMERY, Cathern; age: 1 year and 4 months; death cause: "typhoid fever"; died: 24 Jul. 1911; record # 30916.

KIRK, Culman; age: 4; death cause: "brain fever"; died: 29 Jun. 1912; record # 30917.

JOHNSON, Alex; age: not stated; born: Virginia; single; death cause: "tuberculosis; died: (day not stated) Jul. 1911; record # 30918.

THOMPSON, Mattie; age: 1; death cause: "whooping cough"; died: 7 Nov. 1911; record # 30919.

ARNOLD, Selena; black; age: 18; single; death cause: "typhoid"; died: 26 Jun. 1912; record # 30920.

WOODFIN, Matilda; black; age: 61; married; death cause: "hemorrhage of bowels"; died: 22 Sep. 1911; record # 30921.

KAHL, John; age: 29; married; death cause: "tuberculosis"; died: 29 Oct. 1911; record # 30922.

HAYS, Harriett C.; age: 6; death cause: "tubercular meningitis"; died: 31 Dec. 1912; record # 30923.

SCOTT, Hercelese; age: 22; single; death cause: "phalagra"; died: 22; Jun. 1912; record # 30924.

ARWOD, Ed.; age: 34; married; death cause: "tuberculosis"; died: 18 Jun. 1912; record # 30925.

LAWS, Margaret L.; age: 3 months; death cause: "convulsions"; died: 28 Jan. 1912; record # 30926.

LAWS, Charley; age: 2 years and 6 months; death cause: "indigestion"; died: 16 Jun. 1912; record # 30927.

BROBECK, Cecil; age: 6; death cause: "membranous croup"; died: 5 Oct. 1911; record # 30928.

LAWS, Lillie; age: 51; married; death cause: "paralysis or dropsy of heart"; died: 18 Apr. 1912; record # 30929.

BARHAM, Mary A.; age: 45; married; death cause: "nervous prostration"; died: 14 Apr. 1912; record # 30930.

BRIGHT, Infant; male; age: 1 day; death cause: not stated; died: 20 Dec. 1911; record # 30931.

LISTER, Jaunita M.; age: 3; death cause: "whooping cough"; died: 8 Aug. 1911; record # 30932.

UNIDENTIFIED, Infant; male; age: 1 day; death cause: not stated; died: 6 Apr. 1912; record # 30933.

SCOTT, James; age: 26; married; death cause: "pneumonia fever"; died: 11 Feb. 1912; record # 30934.

CHURCH, Edny; age: 31; married; born: Washington County; death cause: not recorded; died in Washington County on 25 Jul. 1911; record # 30935.

MCLAIN, Hobert; age: 4 months; death cause: "thrash"; died: 9 Oct. 1911; record # 30936.

MORRISON, Charles; age: 8; death cause: "fever"; died: 21 Feb. 1912; record # 30937.

BALES, Martha; age: 70; death cause: "lung trouble"; died: 15 Feb. 1912; record # 30938.

STARNES, Wyan (?); age: 22; single; death cause: "dropsy"; died: 4 Apr. 1912; record # 30939.

UANR (?), Carl; age: 14; death cause: "typhoid fever"; died: 19 Jun. 1912; record # 30940.

MORELOCK, Michael; age: 84; married; death cause: "old age"; died: 21 Feb. 1912; record # 30941.

SOUTHERLAND, Martha J.: age: 60 years, 5 months and 2 days; born: Cocke County; widow; death cause: "gastric interitis"; died: 29 Apr. 1912; record # 30942.

LOVE, Odeca A.; age: 28 years and 3 months; single; death cause: "suicide by drinking carbolic acid"; died in Cocke County on 18 Jan. 1912; record # 30943.

PETERS, Earnest G.; age: 1 year, 6 months and 6 days; death cause: "diphtheria"; died: 1 Dec. 1911; record # 30944.

LOVE, Mary; black; age: 44; married; death cause: "enteritis"; died: 31 Dec. 1912; record # 30945.

LOWERY, Elbert; age: 1 month and 5 days; death cause: not stated; died: 25 Oct. 1911; record # 30946.

WHITE, Jacob; age: 68; married; death cause: "abscess of lungs"; died: 17 Jan. 1912; record # 30947.

NEAS, Margaret; age: 79 years and 21 days; married; death cause: "nephritis"; died: 25 Feb. 1912; record # 30948.

RUPERT, David Darius; age: 17 days; death cause: illegible; died: 28 Jan. 1912; record # 30949.

PETERS, Jacob; age: 3 days; death cause: "enteritis"; died: 18 Feb. 1912; record # 30950.

UNIDENTIFIED, Infant; female; age: 16 days; death cause: "bold hives"; died: 2 Jul. (year not stated); record # 30951.

UNIDENTIFIED, Child; male; age: 14; death cause: "typhoid fever"; died: 15 Jun. 1911; record # 30952.

UNIDENTIFIED, Infant; female; age: 2 months; death cause: not stated; died: 1 Jun. 1911; record # 30953.

UNIDENTIFIED, Child; age: 2 years and 6 months; death cause: not stated; died: 23 Aug. 1910; record # 30954.

UNIDENTIFIED, Adult; female; age: 68; married; death cause: "heart trouble"; died in the 18th District on 5 Oct. 1910; record # 30956.

UNIDENTIFIED, Adult; male; age: 74; married; death cause: not stated; died in the 18th District on 25 Sep. 1910; record # 30957.

UNIDENTIFIED, Adult; female; age: 18; married; death cause: "heart failure"; died: 15 Oct. 1910; record 30958.
UNIDENTIFIED, Infant; male; age: 3 weeks; death cause: "born too soon"; died: 8 Mar 1911; record # 30959.
UNIDENTIFIED, Child; female; age: 14; death cause: "fever"; died: 14 Feb. 1911; record # 30960.
UNIDENTIFIED, Adult; female; age: 83; married; death cause: "fever"; died: 13 Jan. 1911; record # 30961.
PITTS, Asabelle; age: 66; married; death cause: "fever"; died; 27 Feb. 1911; record # 30962.
COBBLE, Ricky; age: 13; death cause: "gunshot"; died: 24 Nov. 1910; record # 30963.
BLACK, Polly Ann; age: 16; married; born: Cocke County; death cause: "heart failure"; died: 5 Dec. 1910; record # 30964.
MARISETT, Millie; age: 23; married; death cause: "child birth"; died: 23 Jun. 1911; record # 30965.
KNIPP, Mary; age: 24; married; death cause: "consumption"; died: 23 Oct. 1910; record # 30966.
BIBLE, R.J.; age: 4 months; death cause: "spinal"; died: 23 Oct. 1910; record # 30967.
MCMILLAN, Mary E.; age: 73; single; born: Virginia; death cause: "lagrippe"; died: 25 Feb. 1911; record # 30968.
DOUGHTY, John H.: age: 77; single; born: Loudon County; death cause: "pneumonia"; died: 5 Dec. 1910; record # 30969.
PAXTON, Tiny Vetrice; age: 10 days; death cause: not stated; died: 22 Jun. 1911; record # 30970.
SHEFFEY, John R.; age: 41; married; death cause: "appendicitis"; died: 16 Jan. 1911; record # 30971.
DAVIS, Guy; black; age: 63; married; born: South Carolina; death cause: "dropsy"; died: (day not stated) Oct. 1910; record # 30972.
CASTEEL, T. Henderson; age: 1 day; death cause: "unknown"; died: (day not stated) Oct. 1910; record # 30973.
UNIDENTIFIED, Infant; male; age: 1 day; death cause: "unknown"; died: 31 Aug. 1910; record # 30974.
BOWEN, Marion; age: 3; death cause: "bronchitis"; died: 14 Jul. 1910; record # 30975.

CHRISTIAN, J.H.M.; age: 57; born: Hawkins County; married; death cause: "stomach trouble"; died: 9 Nov. 1910; record # 30976.

WOODS, Nancy; age: 47; born: Hawkins County; married; death cause: "tuberculosis"; died: 13 May 1911; record # 30977.

HILL, William; age: 23; born: Bristol; single, druggist; death cause: "tuberculosis"; died: 15 Dec. 1911; record # 30978.

JOHNSON, David; age: 4 months; death cause: "pneumonia"; died: 1 Nov. 1910; record # 30979.

JAMES, Louise; age: 1 day; death cause: "unknown"; died: 28 Dec. 1910; record # 30980.

DAVIS, Orrin; age: 1; death cause: "unknown"; died: 7 May 1911; record # 30981.

SPEARS, Ruth L.; age; 6; death cause: "measles and croup"; died: 17 Apr. 1911; record # 30982.

SPEARS, Martha; age: 3; death cause: "not certain"; died: 4 May 1911; record # 30983.

ARNOUL, Newton; black; age: 45; married; death cause: "accidental fall from car"; died in Florida on 22 Jan. 1911; record # 30984.

UNIDENTIFIED, Infant; black; male; age: 1 day; death cause: "not known"; died; 15 Feb. 1911; record # 30985.

BIREL (?) (or BIRD), David; age: 66; male; married; death cause: "pneumonia; died: 14 Dec. 1910; record # 30986.

HULL, Mary Ruth; age: 2; death cause: "pneumonia"; died: 9 Jun. 1911; record # 30987.

UNIDENTIFIED, Infants (twins); death cause: not stated; died: 21 May 1912; record # 30988.

GENTRY, George; age: 9 months; death cause: "pneumonia"; died; 19 Dec. 1908; record # 30989.

LOYD, Burlow; age: 22 years, 3 months and 6 days; born: North Carolina; married; death cause: "killed by tree"; died: 10 Aug. 1908; record # 30990.

WEEMS, Mattie; age: 27; single; death cause: "consumption"; died: 29 May 1909; record # 30991.

SHELTON, Infant; male; age: 16 days; death cause: "cholera infantum"; died: 27 Jun. 1909; record # 30992.

SHELTON, Genettie; age: 18 months; death cause: "cholera infantum"; died: 27 Jun. 1909; record # 30993.

JENNINGS, Kennedy H.; age: 7 months and 1 day; death cause: "pneumonia fever"; died: 10 Apr. 1909; record # 30994.

WILHOIT, George Click; age: 1 day; death cause: "unknown"; died: 3 Mar 1909; record # 30995.

MITCHELL, Jesse; age: 1 year and 1 month; death cause: "consumption"; died: 15 Feb. 1909; record # 30996.

GRAY, Troy; age: 3 months and 14 days; death cause: "heart failure"; died: 2 Feb. 1909; record # 30997.

JOHNSON, A.S.; age: 81 years, 3 months and 19 days; born: Limestone, TN.; married; death cause: "unknown"; died: 10 Apr. 1909; record # 30998.

FILLERS, May; age: 7 days; death cause: "unknown"; died: 22 Dec. 1908; record # 30999.

DULANEY, Infant; male; death cause: "still born"; died: 27 Mar 1909; record # 31000.

PRICE, Infant; male; death cause: "still born"; died; 23 Sep. 1908; record # 31001.

BOWMAN, Rachel; age: 56; married; death cause: "consumption"; died; 31 May 1909; record # 31002.

CRUM, Infant; female; death cause: "still born"; died: 1 Sep. 1908; record # 31003.

LAWS, Infant; female; death cause: "still born"; died: 16 Aug. 1908; record # 31004.

FANNING, Sarah; age: 62; married; death cause: "stomach trouble"; died: 11 Jun. 1908, record # 31005.

BOWMAN, Sallie; age: 15; born: Unicoi County; death cause: "dropsy"; died: 25 Aug. 1908; record # 31006.

RICKER, Infant; male; death cause: "still born"; died: 29 Mar 1909; record # 31007.

JONES, Annie; age: 13 months and 9 days; death cause: "pneumonia fever"; died: 28 Nov. 1908; record # 31008.

LAWS, Effie; age: 28; married; death cause: "consumption"; died: 14 Apr. 1909; record # 31009.

WADDLE, Mat; female; age: 52; single death cause: "tumor of stomach"; died: 17 Jan. 1909; record # 31010.

BELT, Belle; age: 40; married; death cause: "consumption"; died: 20 Mar 1909; record # 31011.

BLAKE, Robert; age: 48; married; death cause: "typhoid fever"; died; 20 Jan. 1909; record # 31012.

BROYLES, L.J.; age: 71 years, 3 months and 4 days; married; born at Chuckey; death cause: "dropsy"; died: 18 Nov. 1908; record # 31013.

BROYLES, Martha; age: 82 years, 3 months and 1 day; born at Chuckey; death cause: "heart failure"; died: 7 Jun. 1909; record # 31014.

JANES, G.A.; age: 64; married; death cause: "pneumonia fever"; died: 22 Nov. 1908; record # 31015.

ROGERS, Charlie R.: age: 2 months and 4 days; death cause: "indigestion"; died: 31 May 1909; record # 31016.

KELLER, J.M.; age: 51 years, 10 months and 19 days; married; death cause: "heart failure"; died: 28 May 1909; record # 31017.

NELSON, Joseph M.; age: 64 years, 3 months and 18 days; married; death cause: "diabetes"; died: 13 Jun. 1909; record # 31018.

DAVIS, Isaac; age: 1 month and 5 days; death cause: "hives"; died: 14 Jan. 1909; record # 31019.

MAY (?), Nancy J.; age: 74 years, 9 months and 8 days; married; tailor; death cause: "dropsy"; died at Chuckey on 7 Jan. 1909; record 31020.

WEEMS, Earley; female; age: 7 months and 17 days; death cause: "cholera"; died: 2 Jun. 1909; record # 31021.

BURKHART, Infant; female; died date of birth; death cause: "unknown"; died: 29 Aug. 1908; record # 31022

WILHOIT, William; age: 4 months and 15 days; death cause: "cholera infantum"; died: 23 Jun. 1909; record # 31023.

BROYLES, Lee Roy; died date of birth; death cause: "still born"; died: 30 Apr. 1909; record # 31024.

GRAY, Ida; age: 4 days; death cause: "unknown"; died: 13 Feb. 1909; record # 31025.

GRAY, Moice (?); male; age: 3 days; death cause: "heart failure"; died: 29 Jun. 1909; record # 31026.

ALLRED, Ira Leghetty; male; age: 35 years, 7 months and 9 days; married; death cause: "consumption and dropsy"; died: 2 Mar.1909; record # 31027.

WILLHOIT, Nancy E.; age: 66; married; death cause: "heart failure"; died: 28 Feb. 1909; record # 31028.

PARMAN, Gipsie; age: 5 months; death cause: "fever"; died: 12 Jun. 1909; record # 31029.

WELLS, Jacob P.; age: 94 years, 8 months and 15 days; born: Greene County; married; death cause: "paralysis"; died: 15 Jun. 1909; record # 30130.

CUTSHALL, James Perry; age: 1 month and 1 day; death cause: "whooping cough"; died: 28 Mar.1909; record # 31031.

DIXON, Eller; female; age: 3 years, 11 months and 12 days; death cause: "pneumonia fever"; died: 1 Apr. 1909; record # 31032.

CHANLY, Eulret; male; age: 52 days; death cause: "whooping cough"; died: 24 Feb. 1909; record # 31033.

DIXON, George; age: 42; married; death cause: "consumption"; died: 22 Apr. 1909; record # 31034.

PETERS, Infant; male; age: 21 days; death cause: "whooping cough"; died: 27 Feb. 1909; record # 31035.

HAMILTON, Mary; black; age: 34; married; death cause: "dropsy"; died: 18 May 1909; record # 31036.

LINEBARGER, Alpha I.; female; age: 43; widow; death cause: "tuberculosis"; died: 31 Dec. 1908; record # 31037.

NEASE, Mary Ann; age: not stated; single ("always so"); death cause: "chronic diarrhea"; died: 27 Aug. 1908; record # 31038.

HOUSTON, Penelope; age: about 81; born; Greene County; married; death cause: "chronic bronchitis"; died: 2 Feb. 1909; record # 31039.

GREEG, Joseph; age: 66; born: Cocke County; married; death cause: "dropsy"; died: 7 Apr. 1909; record # 31040.

COX, Walter; age: 4; death cause: illegible; died: 30 Nov. 1911; record # 31041.

BROYLES, W.O.; age: 30; married; death cause: "brain fever"; died: 22 Dec. 1911; record # 31042.

WERNER, N.L.; age: 42; born: Locust Springs, TN.; married; death cause: "heart failure"; died: 11 Apr. 1912; record # 31043.

FORHIE, Martha; age: 59; married; death cause: "consumption"; died: 22 Sep. 1911; record # 31044.

BABB, George; age: 60; single; death cause: "dropsy"; died: 10 Apr. 1912; record # 31045.

HAULSLEY, Serrih; female; age: 72; born: Washington County; married; death cause: "pneumonia fever"; died: 1 Mar.1912; record # 31046.

HAULSLEY, W.H.; age: 63; death cause: "pneumonia fever"; died: 14 Mar.1912; record # 31047.

ELENBURG, Willie; age: 1 year and 11 months; death cause: "pneumonia fever"; died: 1 Nov. 1911; record # 31048.

WILLET, Margaret; age: 60; born: Knox County; married; death cause: "heart failure"; died: 5 Apr. 1912; record # 31049.

SCOT, James; age: 27; married; death cause: "abscess of brain"; died: 11 Feb. 1912; record # 31050.

FERIRIL, Martha; age: 74; married; death cause: "rheumatism"; died: 24 Nov. 1911; record # 31051.

MCSINGER, Mary E.; age: 69; married; death cause: "pneumonia fever"; died: 4 Mar.1912; record # 31052.

MYERS, Mrs. Rosa May; age: 42 years, 11 months and 16 days; married; music teacher; death cause: "indigestion of stomach"; died: 16 May 1912; record # 31053.

HARMON, Delia; age: 41; single; death cause: illegible; died in Knoxville on 9 Nov. 1911; record # 31054.

BRUMLEY, W.P.; age: 75; married; death cause: "pneumonia fever"; died: 8 Nov. 1911; record # 31055.

THOMAS, Jerry; age: about 64; born: Cocke County; married; death cause: "bronchitis"; died: 22 May 1909; record # 31056.

JORDAN, Charlie; black; age: 42; married; death cause: "heart failure"; died: 3 Jul. 1912; record # 31057.

LAMBERTSON, Florence; age: 22; born: Brownwood, Texas; single; death cause: "heart failure"; died: 22 Sep. 1911; record # 31058.

BROBSON, J.M.; age: 64; married; banker; death cause: "apoplexy"; died: 21 Jun. 1912; record # 31059.

KERBOUGH, Dale; age: 3 months; death cause: "whooping cough"; died: 19 Aug. 1911; record # 31060.

SMITH, J.L.; age: 63; married; death cause: "typhoid fever"; died: 5 Dec. 1911; record # 31061.
BRANNON, Cora Mae; age: 5; death cause: "whooping cough"; died: 24 Dec. 1911; record # 31062.
MAXWELL, R.C.; age: 32; born; Wellston, Ohio; married; death cause: "tuberculosis"; died: 10 Nov. 1911; record # 31063.
MCKEE, Sally P.; age: 73; born: Greenville, South Carolina; married; death cause: "lagrippe and weakly decline"; died: 12 Apr. 1912; record # 31064.
PARKER, Lizzie; age: 28; born: Haywood County, NC.; married; death cause: "dropsy, side pleurisy, blood poison"; died: 23 Nov. 1911; record # 31065.
WILSON, Narsessis; female; age: 44; married; death cause: "nervous debility"; died: 30 Apr. 1912; record # 31066.
WILLIAMS, Lena; age: 29; married; death cause; not stated; died: 11 Mar.1912; record # 31067.
BIDDLE, John M.; age: 67; born: Telford Station; married; death cause: "paralysis"; died: 4 Feb. 1912; record # 31068.
DUNCAN, Goober; age: 5 years and 2 days; born: Washington County, VA.; death cause: "indigestion"; died: 19 Oct. 1911; record # 31069.
MOUHEAD, J.A.; age: 59; married; carpenter; death cause: "paralysis"; died: 14 Jun. 1912; record # 31070.
LESTER, G.W.; age: 56; married; death cause: "consumption"; died in Jonesboro on 6 Aug. 1911; record # 31071.
JOHNSON, Alice; black; age: 53; married; death cause: "cancer of womb"; died: 25 Mar.1912; record # 31072.
ALLISON, Jammie; female; age: 28; married; death cause: "tuberculosis"; died: 19 Aug. 1911; record # 31073.
WITT, Alma; age: 5; death cause: "typhoid fever"; died: 21 Dec. 1911; record # 31074.
ROSS, Fred; black; age: 53; widower; death cause: hook worms"; died: 4 Jun. 1912; record # 31075.
GUINN, P.M.; age: 76; married; death cause: "Brights disease"; died: 7 May 1912; record # 31076.
MARSHALL, Clifford; age: 4 months; death cause: "membranous croup"; died: 14 Nov. 1911; record # 31077.

GRAY, A.W.; age: 60; married; death cause: "complication of disease"; died: 6 Jan. 1912; record # 31078.
CLIMER, Ellen; age; 35; married; death cause: "tuberculosis"; died: 21 May 1912; record # 31079.
COBBLE, James; age: 71; married; death cause: "paralysis"; died: 3 Nov. 1011; record # 31080.
KIRK, Luona; age: 1; death cause: "dysentery"; died: 29; Jul. 1911; record # 31081.
STAFFORD, Thomas; age: 44; married; death cause: "paralysis"; died: 16 Jun. 1912; record # 31082.
KIRK, Mollie; age: 46; single; death cause: "appendicitis"; died: 13 Jun. 1912; record # 31083.
SNODDY, Miles; black; age: 60; widower; death cause: "(illegible) complication"; died: (day not stated) Apr. 1912; record # 31084.
RUSSELL, W.M.; black; age: 73; born: Washington County; married; death cause: "apoplexy"; died: 8 Sep. 1910; record # 31085.
BROBECK, Dessie; age: 15 months; death cause: "stomach trouble"; died: 16 Sep. 1910; record # 31086.
STURNS, Iretta; female; age: 5; death cause: not stated; died: 14 Sep. 1910; record # 31087.
WILHOIT, John; age: 35; born: Georgia; married; death cause: "pneumonia fever"; died: 3 Feb. 1911; record # 31088.
OELER, Nannie; age: 17 years and 8 days; single; death cause: "hit by train"; died: 2 Feb. 1911; record # 31089.
MARTIN, Robert; age: 2; death cause: "measles"; died: 10 Mar.1911; record # 31090.
MARTIN, Birdie Kate; age: 5; death cause: "measles and lagrippe"; died: 8 Mar.1911; record # 31091.
WILSON, Sallie; age: 14 years and 3 days; born: Cocke County; death cause: "pneumonia"; died: 9 Jul. 1910; record # 31092.
BURKEY, Hubert; age: 13 months; death cause: "indigestion"; died: 20 Sep. 1910; record # 31093.
PA___ (illegible), Buster; age: 5 months; death cause: "pneumonia"; died: 7 Nov. 1910; record # 31094.
MCCOWN, Bess; age: 19; born: Sweetwater, TN.; married; death cause: "child birth"; died: 21 Jan. 1910; record # 31095.

MCCOWN, Mary; age: 5 months; death cause: "indigestion"; died: 14 May 1911; record # 31096.

HOLT, Sarah; age: 38; married; death cause: "pneumonia"; died: 18 Mar.1911; record # 31097.

PIERCE, Elizabeth; black; age: 74; born: Smith County, VA.; single death cause: "old age"; died: 18 Oct. 1910; record # 31098.

COX, Aleno; age: 3; born: Jefferson County; death cause: "membranous croup"; died: 24 Nov. 1910; record # 31099.

TORBETT, Mattie; age: 40; born: Sullivan County; married; death cause: "tuberculosis"; died: 26 Feb. 1911; record # 31100.

TORBETT, Walter R.; age: 12; born: Piney Flats, Sullivan County; death cause: "spine __"; died: 22 Jan. 1911; record # 31101.

TORBETT, Hugh C.; age: 4 months; death cause: "tuberculosis"; died: 10 Mar.1911; record # 31102.

JONES, Infant; male; age: 5 months; death cause: "diarrhea"; died: 21 Jan. 1911; record # 31103.

THOMAS, Addie; age: 21; single; death cause: "tuberculosis"; died: 18 Feb. 1911; record # 31104.

MALONE, George; age: 18; born: Hawkins County; single; death cause: "tuberculosis"; died: 19 May 1911; record # 31105.

HENDERSON, Malisa; black; age: 16; death cause: "spinal trouble"; died; 16 Dec. 1910; record # 31106.

GENTRY, Ernest Edward; age: 24 days; death cause: "bold hives"; died: 15 Jun. 1911; record # 31107.

LANE, Viola; black; age: 16 years and 8 months; death cause: "tuberculosis"; died: 16 Apr. 1911; record # 31108.

WOODS, Vina; black; age: 18; single; death cause: "tuberculosis"; died; 8 Dec. 1910; record 31109.

JONES, Jennie; age: 12 years and 8 months; death cause: "measles"; died; 19 Apr. 1911; record # 31110.

CHURCH, Nat; age: 3 weeks; death cause: "measles"; died: 21 Jun. 1911; record # 31111.

HOLT, Albert; age: 10; death cause: "blood poison"; died; 14 Sep. 1911; record # 31112.

KIRK, Clara L.; age: 8 hours; death cause: not stated; died: 30 Jan. 1911; record # 31113.

MANUEL, Infant; black; male; age: 5 hours; death cause: not stated; died: 3 Aug. 1910; record # 31114.

ROSS, Nancy A.; age: 78; born: North Carolina; single; death cause: "dropsy"; died: 1 Feb. 1911; record # 31115.

CANNON, Jessie; male; lived a few minutes; death cause: not stated; died: 18 May 1911; record # 31116.

CRADDOCK, John C.; age: 9 months; death cause: "stomach and spine"; died: 30 May 1911; record # 31117.

FORTNER, Ruby; age: 5; death cause: "measles and flux"; died at the Greeneville Orphanage on 4 Jul. 1911; record # 31118.

BIBLE, David; age: 33; married; death cause: "tuberculosis"; died: 13 Feb. 1909; record # 31119.

COBBLE, Ida; age: 37; married; death cause: "fever"; died: 18 Sep. 1909; record # 31120.

BIBLE, Mahalla; age: 75; born: Kentucky; married; death cause: "cancer"; died: 11 May 1910; record # 31121.

KIFER, Infant; sex: not stated; death cause: "born dead"; died: 2 Aug. 1909; record # 31122.

PAXTON, Infant; female; death cause: "born dead"; died: 27 Jan. 1910; record # 31123.

HENRY, B.F.: age: 51; married; death cause: "paralysis"; died: 16 Sep. 1909; record # 31124.

UNIDENTIFIED, Infant; male; death cause: "born dead"; died: 10 Dec. 1910; record # 31125.

TRENT, Mattie; age: 22; born: Hancock County; married; death cause: "fever"; died: 24 Sep. 1909; record # 31126.

SMELLER, James; age: 54; married; death cause: "tuberculosis"; died: 2 Sep.1909; record # 31127.

DILLON, Mary; black; age: 75; married; death cause: "old age"; died: (day not stated) May 1910; record # 31128.

KING, Thomas: age; 72; single; death cause: "consumption"; died: 17 Jul. 1909; record # 31129.

MORELOCK, Alex; age: 63; married; death cause: "consumption"; died: 3 Apr. 1910; record # 31130.

MCAMIS, Nancy; age: 34; married; death cause: "mumps and consumption"; died: 8 Apr. 1911; record # 31131.

MCAMIS, Mrs. Jummie; age: 91; born: Greene County; widow; death cause: "lagrippe"; died: 3 Oct. 1909; record # 31132.
MCNEESE, Infant; male; death cause: "bowles"; died: 11 May 1910; record # 31133.
PHILLIPS, Katherine; age: 63; born: Virginia; married; death cause: "cancer"; died: 4 Feb. 1910; record # 31134.
GRAYHAM, Abraham; age: 74; born: Greene County; merchant; married; death cause: "heart trouble"; died: 25 Apr. 1910; record # 31135.
GRAY, Mary; age: 79; born: Greene County; widow; death cause: "old age"; died: 30 May 1910; record # 31136.
SHEROTT, Mary; age: 72; born: Greene County; married; death cause: "paralysis"; died: 12 Mar. 1910; record # 31137.
BASKET, Dessie; age: 20; single; death cause: "consumption"; died: 10 Feb. 1910; record # 31138.
RANKIN, Eileen; age: 18; single; death cause: "consumption"; died: 15 Nov. 1909; record # 31139.
GAGELY, Mrs. Anna; age: 40; married; death cause: "tuberculosis"; died: 1 Nov. 1909; record # 31140.
JOHNSON, Frank; age: 42; married; death cause: "consumption"; died: 1 Apr. 1910; record # 31141.
BASKET, Kermat; age: 1; death cause: "pneumonia"; died: 25 Apr. 1910; record # 31142.
HUMBARD, Susanne; age: 74; born: Greene County; single; death cause: "old age"; died: 2 May 1910; record # 31143.
BULLINGTON, Edgar; age: 11; death cause: "run over by wagon; died: 17 Mar. 1911; record # 31144.
HARMON, James Edward; age: 5 months and 17 days; death cause: "pneumonia fever"; died: 2 Jun. 1911; record # 31145.
MILTON, Lula Albertie; age: 7 months and 5 days; death cause: "pneumonia"; died: 20 Jun. 1911; record # 31146.
PINKERTON, Cinter C.; male; age: 2 years, 7 months and 10 days; death cause: "tuberculosis"; died: 18 May 1911; record # 31147.
WOODS, Steve; black; age: 63 years and 8 days; married; death cause: "kidney trouble"; died: 23 Mar. 1911; record # 31148.

MELTON, Johnie Livi; age: 1 month and 4 days; death cause: "bold hives"; died: 28 Nov. 1910; record # 31149.

RILEY, Annie; age: about 80; born: Greene County; widow; death cause: "insane"; died: 18 Mar. 1911; record # 31150.

EVERHART, Clayton; age: 1 year, 11 months and 2 days; death cause: "diphtheria"; died: 31 Aug. 1910; record # 31151.

ARNETT, Nannie; age: 1 month and 7 days; death cause: "bold hives"; died: 5 Mar. 1911; record # 31152.

STROUD, Rosco; age: 7 months and 20 days; death cause: "pneumonia fever; died: 22 Sep. 1910; record # 31153.

EVERHART, Stella May; age: 17 months; death cause: "pneumonia fever"; died: 21 Jun. 1911; record # 31154.

S__(illegible), Nancy Jane; age: 43; born: Cocke County; married; death cause: "heart failure"; died: 31 Dec. 1910; record # 31155.

EASTERLY, Frank; age: 8; born: Knoxville; death cause: "appendicitis"; died: (day not stated) Jan. 1910; record # 31156.

BARLOW, James Rose; age: 17 years and 15 days; death cause: "typhoid fever"; died: 3 Dec. 1910; record # 31157.

COBBLE, Kelly Love; age: 5 days; death cause: "bold hives"; died: 21; Nov. 1910; record # 31158.

MARSHALL, Willie Kate; age: 3 days; death cause: "bold hives"; died: 20 Jan. 1911; record # 31159.

REYNOLDS, J.R.; age: 26 years, 4 months and 14 days; born: Washington County, VA.; married; death cause: "paralysis"; died: 28 Jun. 1911; record # 31160.

LINEBARGER, James H.; age: 15 hours; death cause: illegible; died: 20 Oct. 1910; record # 31161.

SMITH, Margaret; age: 70; widow; death cause: "paralysis"; died: 28 Jun. 1911; record # 31162.

HANSEL, W.J.; age: 44 years, 10 months and 4 days; married; death cause: "dropsy"; died: 4 Mar. 1911; record # 31163.

OTTINGER, Mandy; age: 50; single; death cause: illegible; died: 10 Nov. 1910; record # 31164.

SCRUGGS, Emma; age: 48; born: Newport, Cocke County; death cause: "consumption"; died: 9 May 1911; record # 31165.

JOHNSON, Martha; age: 40; married; death cause: "consumption"; died: 17 May 1911; record # 31166.
KIRK, Thomas Edward; age: 3 years and 10 months; death cause: "meningitis"; died: 29 Sep.1910; record # 31167.
EVERETT, Manda; age: 65; widow; death cause: "paralysis"; died: 6 Jan. 1911; record # 31168.
EASTERLY, Kate; age: 86; born: Greene County; single; death cause: illegible; died: 29 Sep. 1910; record # 31169.
LUTTRELL, Robert J.; age: 53; single; death cause: "stomach trouble"; died: 22 Nov. 1910; record # 31170.
DEAN, Davey Andrew; age: 6 months and 13 days; death cause: "bold hives"; died: 31 Oct. 1910; record # 31171.
COUGDAL, John; age: 40 year and 2 months; married; death cause: "pneumonia fever"; died: 13 Apr. 1909; record # 31172.
WAGNER, Paul; age: 15 months; death cause: "flux"; died: 26 Jun. 1909; record # 31173.
ROBINSON, Infants (twins); females; death cause: "still born"; died: 20 Nov. 1908; record # 31174.
COGDAL, Infant; female; death cause: "still born"; died: 2 May 1909; record # 31175.
LAWLESS, Willie; female; age: 3 months; death cause: not stated; died: 28 May 1909; record # 31176.
CLOWERS, Edward; age: 37; married; death cause: "pneumonia"; died: 1 Feb. 1911; record # 31177.
HARRIS, William; age: 50; married; death cause: "pneumonia"; died: 8 Feb. 1911; record # 31178.
CAMPBELL, Harlow; age: 13; death cause: "pneumonia"; died: 7 Feb. 1911; record # 31179.
GREGG, Robert; age: 32; single; death cause: "tuberculosis"; died: 28 Sep.1910; record # 31180.
CAMPBELL, Bessie; age: 17 months; death cause: "membranous croup"; died: 18 Aug. 1910; record # 31181.
SHIELDS, Ivin; age: 20; single; school teacher; death cause: illegible; died: 19 Aug. 1910; record # 31182.
HOGAN, Adolphus; age: 3 months; death cause: "croup"; died: 15 Jan. (year not recorded); record # 31183.

KISK, John Leonard; age: 5 days; death cause: "peritonitis"; died: 27 Oct. 1910; record # 31184.

ROBINSON, William Elmer; age: 2; death cause: "Brights disease"; died: 23 Mar. 1911; record # 31185.

HOOD, Liney; age: 48; married; death cause: "cancer of breast"; died: 21 Mar. 1911; record # 31186.

CHANDLEY, (first name not given); male; age: 70; married; death cause: "tuberculosis"; died: 29 Aug. 1910; record # 31187.

KNIGHT, Infant; male; lived 6 hours; death cause: illegible; died: 29 Jul. 1910; record # 31188.

UNIDENTIFIED, Infant (1 of twins); male; death cause: "not known"; died: 12 Aug. 1910; record # 31189

UNIDENTIFIED, Infant (1 of twins); male; death cause: "not known"; died: 12 Aug. 1910; record # 31190.

BROWN, Jennie; age: 37; single; death cause: "epilepsy"; died: 22 Oct. 1910; record # 31191.

INSCORE, Edna; age: 18 months; death cause: "cholera infantum"; died: date not stated; record # 31192.

WEEMS, Mary; age: 73; married; death cause: "grippe"; died: 18 May 1911; record # 31193.

HARISON, Lucy; black; age: 54; married; death cause: "dropsy"; died: 30 Jan. 1911; record # 31194.

WOODS, Infant; female; child of Charles WOODS; age: 5 months; death cause: "flux"; died: 25 Jun. 1911; record # 30195.

WELLS, Sidney; age: 43; married; death cause: "typhoid fever"; died: 31 May 1911; record # 33196.

SAM, Sophia; age: 65; born: North Carolina; married; death cause: "heart failure"; died: 8 Mar. 1911; record # 31197.

RUSSELL, A.D.; age: 65; married; death cause: "chronic diarrhea"; died: 25 Feb. 1911; record # 31198.

SAULSBURG, William; age: 81; single; death cause: "tuberculosis"; died: 22 Jun. 1911; record # 31199.

SAULSBURG, Louise; age: 1; death cause: "meningitis"; died: 17 May 1911; record # 31200.

GREENWAY, Jesse J.; age: 61; born: Washington County; married; death cause: "Brights disease"; died: 15 May 1911; record # 31201.

HUX, Infant; male; death cause: "still born"; died: 7 Dec. 1910; record # 31202.

UNIDENTIFIED, Infant; black; male; death cause: "still born"; died: 15 Dec. 1910; record # 31203.

LANE, Sophia; age: 67; widow; death cause: "not known"; died: 8 Mar. 1911; record # 31204.

UNIDENTIFIED, Infant; male; death cause: not stated; died: 7 Feb. 1911; record # 31205.

SWIFT, Willie Clyde; age: 15 months; death cause: "cholera infantum"; died: 1 Sep. 1910; record # 31206.

GREGG, Melvina; age: 40; married; death cause: "spinal meningitis"; died: 5 Jun. 1910; record # 30350.

HANKINS, Elijah K.; age: 47; married; death cause: "consumption"; died: 16 Mar.1911; record 31207.

GRAHAM, Bessie; age: 17; single; death cause: "consumption"; died: 7 Feb. 1910; record # 31208.

UNIDENTIFIED, Infant; male; age: 3 days; death cause; "bled to death"; died: 16 May 1911; record # 31209.

SHELTON, Ales (?); female; age: 59; born: Bristol, VA., married; death cause: "pneumonia fever"; died: 12 Jan. 1911; record # 31210.

BROCKELL, Crawford; age: 3 months; death cause: "bold hives"; died: 10 Sep.1910; record # 31211.

HANARD (?), Drelvie; female; age: 3 months; death cause: "pneumonia fever"; died: 28 Oct. 1910; record # 31212.

JENNINGS, Homer; age: not stated; single; death cause: "typhoid fever"; died: 13 Jul. 1911; record # 31213.

JONES, Augusta; age: not stated; death cause: "unknown"; died: 15 Aug. 1911; record # 31214.

BROWN, Willie Y.; age: 24; single; death cause: "tuberculosis"; died at Knoxville on 28 Jun. 1910; record # 31215.

CHATMAN, Lora; age: 24; single; death cause: "typhoid fever"; died: 8 Jul. 1909; record # 31216.

FRAKAR, Sarah; age: 74; married; death cause: "paralysis"; died: 19 Sep.1910; record # 31217.

ELLIS, Susanna; age: 87; born: Rheatown; widow; death cause: "old age"; died: 14 Nov. 1910; record # 31218.

SMITH, Sarah Alice; age: not stated (infant); death cause: not stated; died: 14 Nov. 1910; record # 31219.

FRAKAR, H.D.; age: 85; born: Milburnton; married; death cause: "old age"; died: 27 Feb. 1911; record # 31220.

BR__ (illegible); male; age: 2 years and 6 months; death cause: "flux"; died: 12 Sep.1910; record # 31221.

FREEMAN, Scot; age: 25; married; death cause: "typhoid fever"; died: 20 Aug. 1910; record # 31222.

UNIDENTIFIED, Infant; female; death cause: "still born"; died: 17 Aug. 1910; record # 31223.

UNIDENTIFIED, Infant; male; age: 4 weeks; death cause: "bold hives"; died: 7 Dec. 1910; record # 31224.

MYERS, Martha E.; age: 62; married; death cause: illegible; died: 16 Mar.1911; record # 31225.

CRADDOCK, John Carl; age: 9 months and 3 days; death cause: illegible; died: 30 May 1911; record # 31226.

BANLEY (?), H.V.; age: 80; born: North Carolina; married; death cause: "kidney trouble"; died: 11 Dec. 1910; record # 31227.

ILLEGIBLE, Thelmer; female; age: 1 month and 5 days; death cause: "whooping cough"; died: 10 Jun. 1911; record # 31228.

MEIRIEL, Frank; age: 61; married; death cause: "typhoid fever"; died: 26 Jun. 1911; record # 31229.

UNIDENTIFIED, Infant; male; lived 6 hours; death cause: not stated; died: 26 Feb. 1911; record # 31230.

LANE, Pery; male; age: 20; death cause: illegible; died: 2 Sep.1910; record # 31231.

UNIDENTIFIED, Infant; male; age: 10 days; death cause: not stated; died: 30 May 1911; record # 31232.

MALTSBERGER, Harvy; age: 64 years and 8 months; married; death cause: "dropsy"; died: 6 Aug. 1909; record # 31233.

MCANNIS, Loyd; age: 57; married; death cause: "dropsy"; died: 9 Sep.1909; record # 31234.

WHITE, Archable; age: 70 years, 11 months and 2 days; married; death cause: "tuberculosis"; died: 26 Jan. 1910; record # 31235.

CHATMAN, Sarah; age: not stated; married; death cause: "typhoid fever"; died: 10 Aug. 1909; record # 31236.

MALONE, Truly; age: 3; death cause: "cholera infantum"; died: 2 Jan. 1910; record # 31237.
CASTEEL, Ida; age: 23; married; death cause: "tuberculosis"; died: 9 Sep.1909; record # 31238.
REYNOLDS, Cleo; age: 1 year and 3 months; death cause: "meningitis"; died: (day not stated) May 1910; record # 31239.
CASTEEL, Bonie; female; age: 1 year and 8 months; death cause: "typhoid and meningitis"; died: 14 Aug. 1909; record # 31240.
JUSTICE, Ethel; age: 27; married; death cause: "tuberculosis"; died: 23 Nov. 1911; record # 31241.
COLLINS, J.K.; age: 93 years and 10 months; born: Jockey, Greene County; single; death cause: "old age"; died: 25 Feb. 1909; record # 31242.
GOOD, Mary Hellen; age: about 10 hours; death cause: "premature birth"; died: 25 Jun. 1909; record # 31243.
SALTS, Aleck; age: 70; born: Bowmantown; married; death cause: "abscess"; died: 29 Jun. 1909; record # 31244.
HULSE, Sarah; age: 24; married; death cause: "cancer"; died: 1 Jun. 1909; record # 31245.
SIMONS, Ida; age: 27; rural mail carrier's wife; death cause: not stated; died: 9 May 1909; record # 31246.
FULKERSON, Poff (?); female; age: 87; born: Cedar Creek, TN.; married; death cause: "broken leg"; died: 5 May 1909; record # 31247.
SAYS, Robert; age: 70; married; death cause: "hay fever"; died: 26 Mar.1909; record # 31248.
LOYD, Sinda; age: 69; married; death cause: not stated; died: 27 Jun. 1909; record # 31249.
SMITH, Irene; age: not stated; death cause: illegible; died: 1 Jun. 1909; record # 31250.
PITT, Haysel; female; age: 8 months; death cause: "whooping cough"; died: 5 Feb. 1909; record # 31251.
PITT, Paul; age: 8 months; death cause: "brain fever"; died: 12 Mar.1909; record # 31252.
HENSEL, Georgia; age: 17; single; death cause: "dropsy"; died: 22 Jun. 1909; record # 31253.

CONK, Ronie; male; age: 23; born: Sullivan County; death cause: "gun shot"; died: 3 Oct. 1908; record # 31254.

CARR, Sherman; age: 4; death cause: "whooping cough"; died: 10 Jul. 1909; record # 31255.

LOYD, Julia; age: 20 months; death cause: illegible; died: 7 Nov. 1908; record # 31256.

MCCANISH, James; age: 7 months; death cause: "whooping cough"; died: 6 Sep.1908; record # 31257.

MOORE, Toledo; female; age: 8 months; death cause: "paralysis"; died: 28 Sep.1908; record # 31258.

COLLENS, Johnie; age: 10 months; death cause: "whooping cough"; died: 8 Dec. 1908; record # 31259.

COLLENS, Nancy; age: 10 months; death cause: "whooping cough"; died: 7 Feb. 1909; record # 31260.

SMITH, Evey; female; age: 19; single; death cause: "consumption"; died: 14 May 1909; record # 31261.

BOWSER, C.R.; age: 4 years and 3 months; death cause: "diphtheria and croup"; died: 18 Sep.1908; record # 31252.

DOTY, Ely May; age: 2 years and 5 months; death cause: "whooping cough"; died: 28 Oct. 1909; record # 31263.

DOTY, Roy; age: 7 months; death cause: "whooping cough"; died: 7 Nov. 1908; record # 31264.

ROSE, Mrs. E.M.; age: 31; minister's wife; death cause: "tuberculosis"; died: 11 Feb. 1909; record # 31265.

BOLTON, D.F.; age: 70; born: Virginia; married; death cause: "consumption"; died: 26 Mar.1909; record # 31266.

CARTER, Georgia; age: 15; death cause: "pneumonia fever"; died: 6 Apr. 1909; record # 31267.

ROE, Flora; age: 20 days; infant twin; death cause: "convulsions"; died: 15 Jul. 1908; record # 31268.

ROE, Florence; age: 4 months and 16 days; infant twin; death cause: "whooping cough"; died: 10 Nov. 1908; record # 31269.

MARION, L__ (illegible); female; age: 27; born: Sullivan County; single; death cause: "consumption"; died: 4 Feb. 1909; record # 31270.

CRAMER, Louisa; age: 71; widow of George CRAMER; death cause: "paralysis; died: 17 Aug. 1908; record # 31271.

KENNEDY, Rhoda; black; age: 81; born: near Greeneville; marital status: not stated; death cause: "old age"; died: 6 Apr. 1909; record # 31272.

DOAK, Margaret; age: 72; widow of Mathew DOAK; death cause: "tumor"; died: 12 Jul. 1908; record # 31273.

SPEERS, Martha Louisa; age: 2 months; death cause: "hives"; died: 5 Jul. 1908; record # 31274.

CALHOUN, Effa; age: 5 months; death cause: "consumption"; died: 21 Jul. 1905; record # 31275.

WALLACE, Nona; age: 23; married; death cause: "consumption"; died: 8 Aug. 1908; record # 31276.

FERGUSON, Frank; age: 63; born: Washington County, VA.; married; death cause: "consumption"; died: 23 Jun. 1909; record # 31277.

LAWS, Tilda; age: 65; born: Sullivan County; married; death cause: "nervousness and diarrhea"; died: 26 Jun. 1909; record # 31278.

JOBE, Joseph Russell; age: 1 month; death cause: "unknown"; died: 30 Jun. 1909; record # 31279.

HAMET, Marah; age: 28; born: Wolf Creek, Cocke County; married; death cause: "consumption"; died: 10 Apr. 1908; record # 31280.

RIKER, Infant; lived 1 day; death cause: "unknown"; died: 28 Feb. 1909; record # 31281.

POE, Mary; age: 23; married; death cause: "consumption"; died: 18 Jul. 1908; record # 31282.

HELTON, Dugger; age: 30; married; death cause: "gravel"; died: 8 May 1912; record # 31283.

GILBERT, Sarah; age: 47; born: Madison County, NC.; married; death cause: "female sickness or change of life"; died: 15 Sep.1911; record # 31284.

BOWMAN, Maud; age: 5; death cause: "flux"; died: 18 Apr. 1912; record # 31285.

BOWMAN, Wilson; age: 6 months; death cause: "pneumonia fever"; died: 26 Nov. 1911; record # 31286.

COX, Hareld; age: 1; death cause: "meningitis"; died: 27 Feb. 1912; record # 31287.

LAWS, Infant; female; child of Dora LAWS; death cause: "unknown"; died: 5 Nov. 1911; record # 31288.

BURGNER, Infant; female; child of Ella BURGNER; death cause: "unknown"; died: 12 Feb. 1912; record # 31289.

STREET, Aught; age: 22; born: Mitchell County, NC.; married; death cause: "consumption"; died: 2 Jun. 1912; record # 31290.

BROYLES, Watsell; age: 7 days; death cause: "unknown"; died: 4 Nov. 1911; record # 31291.

DETHERAGE, Birt; age: 34; single; death cause: "consumption"; died: 23 Apr. 1912; record # 31292.

MILLER, Felix; age: 44; married; death cause: "killed with saw log"; died: 9 May 1912; record # 31293.

HAMPTON, B__ (illegible); female; age: 1; death cause: "flux"; died: 2 Jul. 1911; record # 31294.

NELSON, Goolie; age: 4; death cause: "flux"; died: 7 Jul. 1911; record # 31295.

PRATHER, Emmett; lived 1 hour; death cause: "unknown"; died: 12 Oct. 1911; record # 31296.

CUTSHALL, Mirlin; age: 2 months; death cause: "bold hives"; died: 20 Oct. 1911; record # 31297.

ROBERTS, Annie; age: 72; widow; death cause: "cancer"; died: 5 Nov. 1911; record # 31298.

ROBERTS, Infant; lived 3 days; child of Vina ROBERTS; death cause: "unknown"; died: 4 Oct. 1911; record # 31299.

BROYLES, Will F.; age: 66; married; death cause: "typhoid fever"; died: 9 Jun. 1912; record # 31300.

MYSINGER, Martha; age: 30; married; death cause: "consumption"; died: 19 Jun. 1912; record # 31301.

CUTSHALL, F__ (illegible); female; age: 2 months; death cause: "unknown"; died: 27 Dec. 1811; record # 30302.

UNIDENTIFIED, Infant; female; age: 3 weeks; death cause: "unknown"; died: 18 Mar.1912; record # 30303.

HENSLEY, Vena; age: 22; born: Madison County, NC.; single; death cause: "consumption"; died: 7 Jun. 1912; record # 31304.

GENTRY, Bobie; male; age: 22; born: Madison County, NC.; single; death cause: "unknown"; died: 1 Oct. 1911; record # 31305.

MANUL, Fred; black; age: 22 days; death cause: "whooping cough"; died: 7 Jul. 1908; record # 31306.

MCAMIS, Robert; age: 28; married; death cause: "consumption"; died: 26 Jan. 1909; record # 31307.

DAVIS, Sam; black; lived 6 days; death cause: "cold"; died: 1 Apr. 1909; record # 31308.

CARRISON, Howard; black; age: 9 months; death cause: "unknown"; died: 18 Jun. 1909; record # 31309.

NEAL, Howard H.; age: 2 years and 1 month; death cause: "spinal meningitis"; died: 13 May 1909; record # 31310.

EDWARDS, James H.; age: 64; born: North Carolina; married; death cause: "paralysis"; died: 2 Sep.1908; record # 31311.

MORGAN, Till; female; age: 44; married; death cause: "tuberculosis"; died: (day not stated) Sep.1909; record # 31312.

CUTSHALL, Mary Jane; age: 21 years and 8 days; single death cause: "tuberculosis"; died: 21 Dec. 1908; record # 31313.

REAVES, Major James; age: 84 years, 6 months and 1 day; born: Greene County; married; death cause: "paralysis of lungs"; died: 15 Jul. 1909; record # 31314.

TEAGUE (?), Pauline; age: 1; death cause: "measles"; died: 4 Jul. 1909; record # 31315.

LEONARD, Jake; age: 43; married; death cause: "heart failure"; died: 28 Feb. 1909; record # 31316.

LOWE, Will; age: 32; married; death cause: "heart trouble"; died: 10 May 1909; record # 31317.

JONES, Laura; age: 41; married; death cause: "stomach"; died: 13 Dec. 1908; record # 31318.

WILLHOIT, Ella; age: 9 months; death cause: "stomach"; died: 10 Jun. 1909; record # 31319.

MITCHEL, Caty; age: 5 months; no additional information; record # 31320.

COAL, Naunah R.; age: 41; married; death cause: "consumption"; died: 22 Apr. 1909; record # 31321.

PITT, Mary; age: 26; married; death cause: "nervous prostration"; died: 28 Apr. 1909; record # 31322.

KING, Perrie; male; death cause: "born dead"; died: 4 Sep. 1908; record # 31323.

KING, Ruth; lived 6 hours; death cause: not stated; died: 28 Jun. 1909; record # 31324.

CARTER, Leona; age: 12; death cause: "consumption"; died: 15 Oct. 1908; record # 31325.

SMITH, W.A.; age: 56; married; death cause: "skull fracture"; died: 6 Jan. 1909; record # 31326.

HENSLEY, Cora Belle; age: 1; death cause: "stomach trouble"; died: 20 Aug. 1909; record # 31327.

CAMPBELL, Winfred; age: 17; married; death cause: "typhoid fever"; died: 19 Nov. 1909; record # 31328.

LUTTRELL, Laura; age: 42; married; death cause: illegible; died: 10 Jun. 1910; record # 31329.

MOORE, A.N.; age: 20 years and 8 months; single; death cause: "killed by a ball"; died: 25 Sep. 1909; record # 31330.

STARNES, Melvina; age: 70 years and 1 day; widow; death cause: "chronic disease"; died: 8 Oct. 1909; record # 31332.

SMITH, Mary; black; age: 21; born: Hawkins County; married; death cause: "tuberculosis"; died: 15 Apr. 1910; record # 31332.

WEST (?), John W.F.; age: 26 years and 3 months; single; death cause: "consumption"; died: 28 Jan. 1910; record # 31333.

GARDNER, Olive; age: 7; death cause: "diphtheria"; died: 15 Sep. 1909; record # 31334.

UNIDENTIFIED, Infant; female; lived 2 hours; death cause: "unknown"; died: 15 May 1910; record # 31335.

HOPE, Pash; female; age: 60; married; death cause: "consumption"; died: 7 Feb. 1910; record # 31336.

UNIDENTIFIED, Infant; male; lived one-half hour; death cause: not stated; died: 13 Jun. 1910; record # 31337.

STARNES, Jennie E.; age: 23 years and 4 months; married; death cause: "catarrh of stomach"; died: 20 Oct. 1909; record # 31338.

ARTER, James; black; age: 68; born: South Carolina; single; death cause: "dropsy"; died: 19 Dec. 1909; record # 31339.

GALASPIE, Loreta; black; age: 29; married; death cause: "tuberculosis"; died: 21 Jan. 1910; record # 31340.

WILLSON, Olliver P.; age: 3 years, 7 months and 14 days; death cause: "burn and pneumonia fever"; died: 26 Feb. 1910; record # 31341.

KAHL, Roy; age: 1 year and 7 months; death cause: "pneumonia and flu"; died: 18 Feb. 1910; record # 31342.

JONES, Hazaline; age: 7; death cause: "unknown"; died: 2 Jun. 1910; record # 31343.

JONES, Infant; female; age: not stated; death cause: not stated; died: 19 Apr. 1910; record # 31344.

ROYAL, Ida; age: 25 years, 8 months and 25 days; widow; death cause: "tuberculosis"; died: near Menlor, Kansas on 27 Apr. 1910; record # 31345.

MCGINLEY, Miss N.I.; age: 52; born: Maryville, Blount County; single; death cause: "general breakdown"; died: 3 Jul. 1909; record # 31346.

GLEUDMON, Infant; male; death cause: "born dead"; died: 18 Apr. 1909; record # 31347.

LUTTRELL, Martha; age: 74; widow; death cause: "pneumonia"; died: 29 Dec. 1909; record # 31348.

LOVE, Rote; black; male; age: 54; married; death cause: "dropsy"; died: 5 Jun. 1910; record # 31349.

HARRISON, Elizabeth; black; age: 1 year, 3 months and 15 days; death cause: "croup"; died: 15 Nov. 1909; record # 31350.

JONES, Elmer A.; black; age: 1 year and 4 months; death cause: "idigestion <sic> of brain"; died: 24 Jan. 1910; record # 31351.

CARSON, Garland W.; black; age: 5 months; death cause: "spine trouble"; died: 26 Dec. 1909; record # 31352.

HUX, James; age: 25; married; death cause: illegible; died: 22 Dec. 1909; record # 31353.

BAILEY, J.H.; age: 35; born: Cocke County; married; death cause: "murdered"; died in North Carolina on 24 Feb. 1910; record # 31354.

HANEY, Troy; age: 1 year and 2 months; born: North Carolina; death cause: "cholera"; died: 4 Jun. 1910; record # 31355.

BAILEY, Oscar; lived 5 hours; death cause: not stated; died: 23 Jun. 1910; record # 31356.

GENTRY, Ervin; age: 22; born: North Carolina; married; death cause: "gun shot"; died: 19 Oct. 1910; record # 31357.

MANUEL, Edith; black; age: 2; death cause: "pneumonia"; died: 5 Oct. 1909; record # 31358.

COALMAN; W.T.; age: 67; born: Carter County; married; death cause: not stated; died in Johnson City on 24 Sep. 1909; record # 31359.
JOHNSON, Sarah Van D.; age: 51; born: North Carolina; married; death cause: "heart trouble"; died: 1 Jun. 1910; record # 31360.
BRYANT, Calvin; age: 96 years, 11 months and 7 days; born: North Carolina; married; death cause: "old age"; died: 7 Aug. 1910; record # 31361.
HENRY, James A.; age: 62; married; death cause: "indigestion"; died: 20 Dec. 1908; record # 31362.
MCNEW, Josephine; age: 26 years and 5 months; married; death cause: "typhoid fever"; died: 15 May 1909; record # 31363.
HARTMAN, Myrtle M.; age: 16 years, 3 months and 15 days; death cause: "typhoid fever"; died: 23 May 1909; record # 31363.
SOLOMAN, Lena E.; age: 22 years and 9 months; married; death cause: "typhoid fever"; died: 7 May 1909; record # 31365.
LUTTRELL, George; age: 37 years and 3 months; married; death cause: "complicated spinal and kidney"; died: 11 Jun. 1909; record # 31336.
REED, Chassie; age: 30 years and 1 month; married; death cause: "typhoid fever"; died: 27 May 1909; record # 31367.
WILLIAMSON, Elizabeth C.; age: 56; married; death cause: "spinal disease"; died: 29 Oct. 1910; record # 31368.
REEVE, Fred A.; age: 29; single; death cause: "assassinated by pistol shot"; died: 1 Aug. 1910; record # 31369.
BROYLES, Callie; age: 2; death cause: "diphtheria"; died: 11 Nov. 1910; record # 31370.
BROYLES, Newton A.; age: 73; single; death cause: "diarrhea"; died: 11 Mar.1911; record # 31371.
SEATON, Sallie; age: 89; born: Greene County; single; death cause: illegible; died: 10 May 1911; record # 31372.
DAVIS, Rushia; male; age: 2; death cause: "flux"; died: 25 Jun. 1911; record # 31373.
MORELOCK, Jacob; age: 2; death cause: "flux"; died: 10 Jun. 1911; record # 31374.
WILLHOIT, Dulice; age: 1 year and 6 months; death cause: "flux"; died: 7 Jun. 1911; record # 31375.

GREENE, Anna S.; age: 1 year and 6 months; death cause; "flux"; died: 8 Jun. 1911; record # 31376.
SMITH, Hassie; age: 2; death cause: "flux"; died: 31 May 1911; record # 31377.
SMITH, Amanda; age: 4 days; death cause: "flux"; died: 10 May 1911; record # 31378.
NELSON, Henry F.; age: 71; married; death cause: "rheumatism"; died: 5 Feb. 1911; record # 31379.
LOVE, Ethel; age: 3; death cause: "flux"; died: 26 Jun. 1911; record # 31380.
UNIDENTIFIED, Infant: female; age: 6 days; death cause: "unknown"; died: 30 Feb. 1911; record # 31381.
JOHNSON, Alex; age: 68; married; death cause: "flux"; died: 15 Jun. 1911; record # 31382.
EADS, S.H.; age: 50; born: Arkansas; married; death cause: "paralysis"; died: 4 Jun. 1911; record # 31383.
THOMPSON, Seo; age: 5 months; death cause: "flux"; died: 12 Jun. 1911; record # 31384.
CLICK, Rachel; age: 5; death cause: "membranous croup"; died: 1 Feb. 1911; record # 31385.
HARRISON, S.B.; age: 76; born: Greene County; married; blacksmith; death cause: "Brights disease"; died: 16 Jun. 1911; record # 31386.
PAINTER, Alfred; age: 91; born: Greene County; married; death cause: "paralysis"; died: 23 Sep. 1910; record # 31387.
DOCKERY, George; age: 72; born: Madison County, NC.; married; death cause: "consumption of bowels"; died: 4 Jun. 1911; record # 31388.
HENSLEY, Evert; age: 7; death cause: "measles"; died: 25 Jun. 1911; record # 31389.
COSTLEY, Charles; age: 91; born: Burt County, NC.; married; death cause: "paralysis"; died: 1 May 1911; record # 31390.
CRUM, Beulah; lived 1 day; death cause: "unknown disease"; died: 31 Jul. 1910; record # 31391.
NORTON, Infant; female; lived 1 day; child of G.W. NORTON; death cause: not stated; died: 10 Aug. 1910; record # 31392.

HENSLEY, Infant; male; child of Minnie HENSLEY; death cause: "died same day of birth"; died: 15 Jul. 1910; record # 31393.

JOHNSON, Lucile; age: 2; death cause: "diarrhea"; died: 4 Jun. 1911; record # 31394.

FILLERS, Fanny; age: 19; married; death cause: "pneumonia fever"; died: 28 May 1911; record # 31395.

FILLERS, Bird; male; age: 1; death cause: "flux"; died: 11 Jun. 1911; record # 31396.

FLETCHER, John; age: 31; married; death cause: "rheumatism"; died: 6 May 1911; record # 31396.

GENTRY, Carl; age: 1; death cause: "scrofula"; died: 1 Aug. 1910; record # 31397.

REAVES, Betsey Jane; age: 76; born: Greene County; widow; death cause: "jaundice"; died: 4 Nov. 1910; record # 31399.

BOWMAN, Mary; age: 58; widow; death cause: "heart failure"; died: 20 Nov. 1910; record # 31400.

CRUM, Floy; age: 18; single; death cause: "consumption"; died: 16 Mar.1911; record # 31401.

REAVES, Hurse; male; age: 16; death cause: "typhoid fever"; died: 9 Apr. 1911; record # 31402.

BOWMAN, Nellie; age: 22; single; death cause: "consumption"; died: 30 Apr. 1911; record # 31403.

RICKER, Velma; age: 2; death cause: "scrofula of bowels"; died: 2 Apr. 1911; record # 31404.

NORTON, Ollie; female; age: 30; married; death cause: "giving birth to child"; died: 10 Aug. 1910; record # 31405.

RAMBO, Sallie; age: 80; born: Greene County; widow; death cause: "chronic diarrhea"; died: 8 Oct. 1910; record # 31406.

JONES, Julia; age: 71; born: Greene County; widow; death cause: "flux"; died: 10 May 1911; record # 31407.

BOWMAN, Cecil; age: 14 days; death cause: "bold hives"; died: 17 Dec. 1910; record # 31408.

FANNING, Annie; age: 4 months; death cause: "pneumonia fever"; died: 3 Dec. 1910; record # 31409.

THOMPSON, Ollie; female; age: 1; death cause: "flux"; died: 22 May 1911; record # 31410.

BOWMAN, Myrtle; age: 32; married; death cause: "typhoid fever"; died: 29 Nov. 1910; record # 31411.

BOWMAN, Edna; age: 3; death cause: "flux"; died: 3 Jun. 1911; record # 31412.

MCINTURF, Tilda; age: 67; widow; death cause: "flux"; died: 28 Jun. 1911; record # 31413.

BOWMAN, Infant; male; child of Dora BOWMAN; death cause: "died the same day"; died: 20 Nov. 1910; record # 31414.

MCCOY, James; age: 22; single; death cause: "stomach trouble"; died: 16 Mar.1911; record # 31415.

CHAPMAN, David; age: 2; death cause: "pneumonia"; died: 9 Mar.1911; record # 31416.

TADLOCK, Lewis; age: 87; born: Washington County; single; death cause: "old age"; died: (day not stated) Nov. 1910; record # 31418.

HAYS, Annie; age: 26; single; death cause: "consumption; died: 24 Dec. 1910; record # 31418.

BIBLE, Christian; age: 63; married; death cause: "paralysis"; died: 30 Jan. 1911; record # 31419.

ILLEGIBLE, Nannie; age: 41; married; death cause: "meningitis"; died: 11 Jun. 1911; record # 31420.

CULVER, William; age: 45; married; mail carrier; death cause: "pneumonia"; died: 17 Jan. 1911; record # 31421.

BIBLE, Emma; age: 66; born: Hamblen County near Whitesburg; single; death cause: "Brights disease"; died: (day not stated) Feb. 1911; record # 31422.

DOAK, Dr. Hubert; age: 46; married; farmer and physician; death cause: "pneumonia fever"; died: 5 Feb. 1911; record # 31423.

RANKIN, Margarite; age: 18; single; death cause: "appendicitis"; died: (day not stated) Jul. 1911; record # 31424.

SHENAULT, Harry; age: 32; married; death cause: "consumption"; died: 20 Nov. 1910; record # 31425.

MORROW, Emma; age: 58; married; death cause: "rheumatism"; died: 5 Oct. 1910; record # 31426.

HARRISON, Grover; age: 22; single; death cause: "typhoid fever"; died: 7 Oct. 1911; record # 31427.

GALLIEN, Houston; age: 35; single; invalid; death cause: "epileptic fits"; died: 16 Mar.1911; record # 31428.

BEAMER, Florence; age: 25; born: Hawkins County; invalid; death cause: "syphilis"; died: 20 Jul. 1910; record # 31429.

FANNON, Peggy; age: 75; single; death cause: "rheumatism"; died: 10 Jul. 1910; record # 31430

SMITH, Joseph; age: 77; single; death cause: "old age"; died: 3 Dec. 1910; record # 31431.

CANNON, Samuel; age: 2 years and 6 months; death cause: "flux and measles"; died: 13 Jun. 1911; record # 31432.

BELL, Henry; age: 4; death cause: "pneumonia and fever"; died: 21 Dec. 1910; record # 31433.

SHEPARD, William; age: 61; born: Yancey County, NC.; married; death cause: "locked bowels"; died: 6 Jan. 1911; record # 31434.

SUTHERLAND, Mary; age: 28; married; death cause: "dropsy"; died: 10 Jul. 1911; record # 31435.

SUTHERLAND, Charlie; age: 1 day; death cause: "not known"; died: 10 Jul. 1911; record # 31436.

ILLEGIBLE, Robert; age: 31; born: Jonesboro, TN.; married; death cause: "consumption"; died: 15 Feb. 1911; record # 31437.

COYLES, Major; age: 53; married; death cause: "consumption"; died: 3 Sep. 1910; record # 31438.

GREGORY, Jim; age: 47; death cause: "throat trouble"; died: 28 Mar.1911; record # 31439.

RICKER, Hassie; age: 1; death cause: "pneumonia and fever"; died: (day not given) Feb. 1910; record # 31440.

RUSSELL, Walter; age: 2; death cause: "diphtheria"; died: (day not given) Nov. 1909; record # 31441.

AMOS, Martha E.; age: 56; born: Mountain City, TN.; single; death cause: "dropsy"; died: 6 Jul. 1909; record # 31442.

AMOS, Harry; age: 11; death cause: "consumption"; died: (day not given) Mar.1910; record # 31443.

COOLEY, Hannah; age: 52; married; death cause: "rheumatism"; died: 16 Dec. 1909; record # 31444.

FORTNER, John; age: 26; married; death cause: "typhoid fever"; died: (day not given) Oct. 1909; record # 31445.

COLLIER, Meonie; female; age: 3; death cause: "stomach trouble"; died: (day not given) Jul. 1909; record # 31446.

MORELOCK, Oletha; age: 8 months; death cause: not stated; died: 28 Nov. 1909; record # 31447.

HICKSON, J.R.; age: 74; born: Grainger County; married; death cause: "kidney disease"; died: 9 Aug. 1909; record # 31448.

GUDGER, Anis; black; age: 29; married; death cause: "consumption"; died: (day not given) Apr. 1910; record # 31449.

CLAYTON, Harold; black; age: 18; single; death cause: "consumption"; died: (day not given) Mar.1910; record # 31450.

CARTER, Berry; black; age: 74; born: North Carolina; single; death cause: "old age"; died: (day not given) Apr. 1910; record # 31451.

FILEPS, Gabril; age: 76; married; death cause: "rheumatism"; died: 6 Oct. 1909; record # 31452.

HULL, D.M.; age: 66 (10th day of January); married; death cause: "rheumatism"; died: 19 Apr. 1910; record # 31453.

BIBLE, Mary; age: 3 years and 6 months; death cause: "unknown"; died: 10 Nov. 1909; record # 31454.

BAYLES, Gurtie R.; age: 8 months; death cause: "flux"; died: 10 Sep. 1910; record # 31455.

HARMON, Bessie; age: 10 days; death cause: "bold hives"; died: 27 Feb. 1910; record # 31456.

HARMON, Onie F.; male; age: 7; death cause: "pneumonia fever"; died: 13 Feb. 1910; record # 31457.

GRAHAM, Bessie; age: 6 days; death cause: "spinal trouble"; died: 21 Jan. 1910; record # 31458.

DIXON, Hermon; age: 14 months; death cause: "measles"; died: 16 Jul. 1909; record # 31459.

ILLEGIBLE, Thomas; age: 9 months; death cause: "heart trouble"; died: 27 May 1910; record # 31460.

H__ (illegible), David R.; age: 22 months; death cause: "flux"; died; 10 Jun. 1910; record # 31461.

RITE, Guy; age: 10; death cause: illegible; died: 19 Sep. 1909; record # 31462.

BROOKS, First name illegible; female; age: 70; born: Greene County; married; death cause: "pneumonia fever"; died: 16 May 1910; record # 31463.

UNIDENTIFIED, Infant; female; black; lived 9 hours; death cause: not stated; died: 27 May 1910; record # 31464.

BROOKS, Jake; age: 40; married; death cause: "pneumonia fever"; died: 18 Jun. 1910; record # 31465.

PERS, Marien; black; age: 15; death cause: illegible; died: 3 Oct. 1909; record # 31466.

GASS, Cate; age: 6 months; death cause: "unknown"; died: 7 Jul. 1909; record # 31467.

DIXON, First name illegible; female; age: 42; married; death cause: "heart trouble"; died: 15 Feb. 1910; record # 31468.

CONKIN, Mattie; age: 55; married; death cause: "consumption"; died: 30 Apr. 1910; record # 31469.

HALL, Stanley M.; age: 14 years and 6 months; death cause: "blood poison"; died: 16 Oct. 1909; record # 31470.

RUSH, Martha; age: 47; single; death cause: "garter stone of liver"; died: 25 Jun. 1910; record # 31471.

BALL, Leroy; age: 1; death cause: "unknown"; died: 1 Dec. 1909; record # 31472.

MILLER, Cecil; age: 6; death cause: "burned to death"; died: 9 Dec. 1909; record # 31473.

THORNBURG, Alies; male.; age: 18; born: Sullivan County; single; death cause: "thrown by horse"; died: 29 Feb. 1910; record # 31474.

BRANDON, James; age: 60; married; merchant; death cause: "consumption"; died: 13 May 1910; record # 31475.

DYKES, Jasper; age: 23; single; death cause: "consumption"; died: 30 May 1910; record # 31476.

FOX, Liew (illegible); female; age: 34; born: Scott County, VA.; married; death cause: "dropsy of heart"; died: 7 Jan. 1910; record # 31477.

JACKSON, Jane; age: 45; married; death cause: "consumption"; died: 15 Nov. 1909; record # 31478.

JACKSON, Bettie; age: 35; single; death cause: "consumption"; died: 15 Nov. 1909; record # 31479.

DIXON, Clyde; age: 1 month and 3 days; death cause; illegible; died: 10 Dec. 1909; record # 31480.
TOLIVER, Berthia; age: 23 months; death cause: "blood poison"; died: 30 Jan. 1909; record # 31481.
COLLINS, Johnie; age: 1; death cause: "whooping cough"; died: 10 Nov. 1910; record # 31482.
COLLINS, Nancy; age: 1; death cause: "whooping cough"; died: 20 Jan. 1910; record # 31483.
BOWHIE, Cart; male; age: 32; married; death cause: "consumption"; died: 26 Jun. 1910; record # 31484.
WHITE, Infant; age not given; death cause: "diphtheria"; died: 10 Sep. 1909; record # 31485.
ILLEGIBLE, Doyle; age: 6; death cause: "diphtheria"; died: 30 Sep. 1910; record # 31486.
KILDAY, Mattie; age: 27; married; death cause: "consumption"; died: 27 Feb. 1910; record # 31487.
UNIDENTIFIED; Child; male; age: 2; death cause: illegible; died: 1 Jan. 1910; record # 31488.
CRABTREE, A.B.; age: 71; born: Greene County; married; death cause: "paralysis"; died: 23 Jan. 1910; record # 31489.
MIDDLETON, Rosa; age: 22; married; death cause: "consumption"; died: 30 Jan. 1910; record # 31490.
DUNWOODY, Amanda; age: 44; born: Blount County; married; death cause: "(illegible) acid poisoning"; died: 20 Jan. 1910; record # 31491.
REED, Martha Alice; age: 37; single; death cause: "consumption"; died: 1 Apr. 1910; record # 31492.
COLLET, Child; age: 2; death cause: "brain trouble"; died: 15 Mar.1910; record # 31493.
BASS, Mariane; age: 50; married; death cause: "typhoid fever"; died: 9 Oct. 1909; record # 31494.
UNIDENTIFIED, Female; black; married; death cause: "shot by husband"; died: date not given; death registered: 29 Jul. 1910; record # 31495.
AUSHIE, Brad M.; age 1 week; death cause: "brights disease"; died: 27 Aug. 1910; record # 31496.

HUNT, Elen; age: 23; married; death cause: "pneumonia fever"; died: 14 Feb. 1910; record # 31497.

CROXWELL, Margaret; age: 65; married; death cause: "dropsy"; died: 10 Oct. 1909; record # 31498.

YOUNG, Gertrude; age: 29 years and 10 months; married; death cause: "consumption"; died: 13 Oct. 1910; record # 31499.

RYLER, Alexander; age: 16; death cause: "consumption"; died: 24 Jan. 1910; record # 31500.

MCDONALD, James; age: 67; married; death cause: "pneumonia"; died: 11 May 1910; record # 31501.

MALONEY, George A.; age: 45; married; merchant; death cause: not recorded; died: 8 Nov. 1909; record # 31502.

DYKE, Infant; male; age: "nearly a year"; son of John DYKE; death cause: "stomach trouble"; died: 10 Nov. 1909; record # 31503.

MCABEE, Thomas; age: "about 70"; born: South Carolina; married; death cause: "lagrippe"; died: 30 Nov. 1909; record # 31504.

MOORE, A.J.; age: 51; married; death cause: "rabies or hydrophobia"; died: 17 Dec. 1909; record # 31505.

MYERS, Infant; male; age: "about 1 year"; child of Jim MYERS; death cause: "lagrippe"; died: 15 Jan. 1909; record # 31506.

KELLEY, William; age: "about 62"; married; sawyer; death cause: "pneumonia fever"; died: 8 Feb. 1910; record # 31507.

MYERS, Cora Carter; age: 35; married; death cause: "consumption"; died: 21 Feb. 1910; record # 31508.

CARTER, Sadie; age: 25; single; death cause: "stomach trouble"; died: 10 Mar. 1910; record # 31509.

COX, Mary; age: 77; born: Tennessee; married; death cause: "stomach trouble"; died: 14 Mar.1910; record # 31510.

MCGUIRE, M.F.; age: 54; married; death cause: "consumption"; died: 9 Jun. 1910; record # 31511.

MCKAY, Mrs.; age: "about 70"; "single, had been married"; death cause: "consumption"; died: 22 Mar.1910; record # 31512.

CARTER, Infant; male; lived 2 hours; child of Elec CARTER; death cause: "unknown"; died: 27 Mar.1910; record # 31513.

HARRIS, G.D.; age: "54, born 1 June 1855"; married; death cause: "consumption"; died: 19 Jul. 1909; record # 31514.

SWINDELL, George C.; age: 6 months; death cause: "convulsions"; died: 16 Oct. 1909; record # 31515.

WEST, Lulia Lee; age: 2 months; death cause: not stated; died: 2 Jul. 1908; record # 31516.

BRIT, John; age: "near 80"; born: Virginia; death cause: "old age"; died: 3 May 1909; record # 31517.

BRITTON, M.E.; age: 38; married; death cause: "stroke with paralysis"; died: 21 Sep. 1908; record # 31518.

SMITH, W.H.; age: 42; married; death cause: "gun shot"; died: 9 Oct. 1908; record # 31519.

QUINTON, Leroy; age: 1 year and 4 months; death cause: "flux"; died: 7 Jun. 1909; record # 31520.

MORRISON, Infant; male; lived 1 day; death cause: not stated; died: 5 Jul. 1908; record # 31521.

MORRISON, Martha; age: "about 50"; married; death cause: "dropsy"; died: 15 Jun. 1909; record # 31522.

MALONE, Roy; age: 19; single; death cause: "consumption"; died: 15 May 1909; record # 31523.

NEAL, Hazel; age: 10 months; death cause: "cholera infantum"; died: (day not given) Jun. 1909; record # 31524.

WEBSTER, Eliza; age: "about 30"; married; death cause: "consumption"; died: 29 Nov. 1908; record # 31525.

UNIDENTIFIED, Infant; male; death cause: not stated; died: (day not given) Jan. 1909; record # 31526.

GORDD, Josie I.; age: 18; death cause: not stated; died: 12 Dec. 1908; record # 31527.

COUCH, Poluntine (?); male; age: 87; born: near Romeo, TN.; death cause: "cancer"; died: 7 Jun. 1909; record # 31528.

COUCH, Mary Ann; age: 62; married; death cause: "paralysis"; died: 1 Jun. 1909; record # 31529.

UNIDENTIFIED, Infant; female; lived 2 days; death cause: not stated; died: (day not given) May 1909; record # 31530.

HECK, Maggie; age: 25; born: Hawkins County; single; death cause: "flux"; died: (day not given) Sep. 1908; record # 31531.

CANTER, Samuel; age: 72; born: Baileyton; married; death cause: "pneumonia fever"; died: 26 Nov. 1908; record # 31532.

MCCROSKY, Roxie Leona; age: 3; death cause: not stated; died: (day not given) Nov. 1908; record # 31533.
SELF, S. Harriett; age: 28; married; death cause: "consumption"; died: (day not given) Sep. 1908; record # 31534.
LIGHT, Gilbert; age: 9 months; death cause: "whooping cough"; died: (day not given) Oct. 1908; record # 31535.
COLDWELL, Lee; age: 15 months; death cause: "whooping cough"; died: 6 Jul. 1908; record # 31536.
GARDNER, Infant; lived 1 day; death cause: not stated; died: (day not given) Jul. 1908; record # 31537.
WAITS, Georgia; age: 16; death cause: "typhoid fever"; died: 18 Oct. 1908; record # 31538.
YOKLEY, G.W.; age: "about 69"; born: Hawkins County; married; death cause: "kidney trouble"; died: (day not given) Oct. 1908; record # 31539.
CRUM, Sparkling Janes; male; age: 62; married; death cause: "bronchial asthma"; died: 18 Mar.1911; record # 31540.
CUTSHALL, Virgil; age: 1 month and 10 days; death cause: "unknown"; died: 29 Apr. 1911; record # 31541.
FILLERS, Fanny; age: 18 years, 7 months and 7 days; married; death cause: "pneumonia fever"; died: 28 Mar.1911; record # 31542.
CRUM, Geneva; lived 15 days; death cause: "brain trouble"; died: 14 Dec. 1910; record # 31543.
CARLISLE, Joseph; age: 32 years, 10 months and 27 days; married; death cause: "pneumonia fever"; died: 27 Nov. 1910; record # 31544.
JOHNSON, Infant; male; lived 1 hour; death cause: "unknown"; died: 22 Feb. 1911; record # 31545.
WALLIN, T.J.; age: 63 years and 9 months; born: North Carolina; married; death cause: "pneumonia fever"; died: 9 Jan. 1911; record # 31546.
CRUMLEY, James; age: 23; single; death cause: "fever"; died: 20 Jun. 1909; record # 31547.
CHANDLER, Elbert; age: 5 months; death cause: "whooping cough"; died: (day not stated) Jul. 1910; record # 31548.
MACE, Hannah; age: 35; married; death cause: "consumption"; died: 17 May 1911; record # 31549.

BURGNER, Infant; age: 3 days; death cause: "bled to death"; died: 3 Apr. 1911; record # 31550.
SWATSEL, Ester Mae; death cause: "still born"; died: 26 Oct. 1910; record # 31551.
FARNSWORTH, Catherine; age: 72 years, 5 months and 20 days; born: Tennessee; widow; death cause: "apoplexy"; died: 22 Feb. 1911; record 31552.
CUTSHALL, L.C.; age: 24 years, 6 months and 17 days; single; death cause: "paralysis"; died: 2 Jul. 1910; record # 31553.
EVANS, Perry; age: 77; "native of Greene County"; married; death cause: "pneumonia fever"; died: 10 Dec. 1910; record # 31554.
MASSIE, Rachel; age: 25; born: North Carolina; married; death cause: "heart failure"; died: (day not given) Sep. 1910; record # 31555.
SEXTON, Arthur; age: 1 year and 9 months; death cause: "brain and spinal trouble"; died: 31 May 1911; record # 31556.
SEXTON, J.R.; age: 39; married; death cause: "stomach and heart"; died: 29 Jul. 1910; record # 31557.
HENSLEY, Julia Mae; age: 1 year, 8 months and 27 days; death cause: "paralysis"; died: 20 Aug. 1910; record # 31558.
SEXTON, William; age: 55; married; death cause: "pneumonia fever"; died: 2 Dec. 1910; record # 31559.
SEXTON, Emaline; age: "not known but over 75 years; born: Tennessee; married; death cause: "pneumonia fever"; died: 10 Dec. 1910; record # 31560.
HENSLEY, Joseph; age: 55; married; death cause: "pneumonia fever"; died: 4 Dec. 1910; record # 31561.
MESINGER, John; age: 47; married; death cause: "pneumonia fever"; died: 26 Dec. 1910; record # 31562.
MILLER, Caroline; age: 65; married; death cause: "a bealed foot"; died: 1 Feb. 1911; record # 31563.
MILLER, Sarah; age: 20; single; death cause: "consumption"; died: (day not given) Jan. 1911; record # 31564.
BIBLE, Thomas; age: 29; married; death cause: "pneumonia fever"; died: 31 May 1911; record # 31565.

HARRISON, Catherine E.; age: 74 years and 3 months; born: Greene County; married; death cause: "pneumonia fever"; died: 17 Jan. 1911; record # 31566.

BIRD, Clyde; age: 6 months and 17 days; death cause: "stomach trouble"; died: 17 Jul. 1910; record # 31567.

CONSTABLE, Clarissa; age: 85 years and 9 months; born: North Carolina; widow; death cause: "pneumonia fever"; died: 24 Mar. 1911; record # 31568.

WILLHOIT, John P.; age: 72 years, 9 months and 20 days; born: Tennessee; married; death cause: "dropsy"; died: 1 May 1911; record # 31569.

KENT, Harriet; age: 82; born: North Carolina; widow: death cause: "old age"; died: (day not stated) May 1909; record # 31570.

CASH, Infant; male; lived 1 day; child of William CASH; death cause: "unknown"; died: 13 Jun. 1919; record # 31571.

POE, Infant; male; lived 3 days; child of William POE; death cause: "unknown"; died: (day not given) May 1909; record # 31572.

MCKAY, B.M.; age: "about 67"; married; death cause: "heart disease"; died: (day not given) Apr. 1909; record # 31573.

HULL, Alfred; age: "about 1 year"; death cause: "nervousness"; died: (day not given) Nov. 1908; record # 31574.

LONG, A.B.; male; age: 8 months; death cause: "eczema"; died: (day not given) Dec. 1908; record # 31575.

LONG, J.R.; age: 27; married; death cause: "typhoid fever"; died: (day not given) Jan. 1908; record # 31576.

DAY, William; age: 76; born: Greene County; married; death cause: "heart failure and old age"; died: 8 Dec. 1908; record # 31577.

MCDONAL, Dessie; age: 27; married; death cause: "kidney trouble or Brights disease"; died: 13 Aug. 1908; record # 31576.

UNIDENTIFIED, Infant; female; death cause: "child birth"; died: 12 Aug. 1908; record # 31579.

KNIGHT, R.F.; age: 49; married; death cause: "indigestion"; died: 2 Jun. 1909; record # 31580.

MOORE, Hubert; age: 9 years, 7 months and 8 days; death cause: "heart disease"; died: 15 Sep. 1908; record # 31581.

JEFFERS, D.C.; age: 33; married; death cause: "typhoid fever"; died: 6 Jan. 1909; record # 31582.

MOORE, Taylor F.; age: 29 years, 11 months and 2 days; soldier; single; death cause: "consumption"; died: 2 Mar.1909; record # 31583.

MCPEARSON, Alex; age: 64 years, 11 months and 27 days; married; death cause: "consumption"; died: 28 Feb. 1909; record # 31584.

PIERCE, G.B.; age: 49; married; death cause: "typhoid"; died: 20 Aug. 1908; record # 31585.

BABB, A.B.; age: 70 years, 9 months and 18 days; married; death cause: "cholera"; died: 13 Jun. 1909; record # 31586.

BABB, Mary; age: 64 years, 4 months and 20 days; married; death cause: "typhoid fever"; died: 5 Dec. 1908; record # 31587.

JEFFERS, Lacy Lee; age: 1 year and 1 month; death cause: "whooping cough"; died: 22 Sep. 1908; record # 31588.

ERWIN, Onie; age: 1; death cause: "brain trouble"; died: 25 Jul. 1908; record # 31589.

REATHERFORD, Mary; age: 77; born: Greene County; married; death cause: "consumption"; died: 11 Nov. 1909; record # 31590.

UNIDENTIFIED, Infant; male; age: 4 months; death cause: "diarrhea"; died: 5 Sep. 1908; record # 31591.

UNIDENTIFIED, Infant; male; death cause: "born dead"; died: 4 Apr. 1909; record # 31592.

UNIDENTIFIED, Infant; female; lived 4 hours; death cause: "unknown"; died: 12 Dec. 1908; record # 31593.

SHEFFEY, Leonie; age: 16 months; death cause: "inflammation of bowels"; died: 17 May 1909; record # 31594.

HARRIS, Elen; age: 18; married; death cause: "burned"; died: 16 Jun. 1909; record # 31595.

HUFF, Mrs. Noah; age: 70; married; death cause: "flux"; died: 20 Jun. 1909; record # 31596.

GREGG, Cas; female; age: 70; widow; death cause: "heart trouble"; died: 22 Mar.1909; record # 31597.

BOLES, Virginia; age: 32; married; death cause: "tuberculosis"; died: 22 Jun. 1909; record # 31598.

BOLES, Robert; age: 71 years, 3 months and 20 days; born: Greene County; married; death cause: "paralysis"; died: 6 Dec. 1908; record # 31599.

COLWERS, Elizabeth; age: 83; born: Greene County; widow; death cause: "tuberculosis"; died: 10 Jun. 1909; record # 31690.

LUTTRELL, G.W.; age: 40; married; death cause: "flux"; died: 21 Jun. 1909; record # 31691.

THOMPSON, James; age: 2; death cause: "scarlet fever"; died: 4 Feb. (year not given); record # 31602.

GOOD, Florence; age: 19; single; death cause: "tuberculosis"; died: 18 Mar. 1910; record # 31603.

GOOD, Russell; age: 4; death cause: "accident by fall"; died: 22 Jan. 1910; record # 31604.

DAVENFORT, Hannah; age: 68; married; death cause: "paralysis"; died: 25 Jul. 1909; record # 31605.

BROWN, Margaret; age: 7 weeks; death cause: "brain fever"; died: 28 Aug. 1909; record # 31606.

BULLEN, Mary; age: 28; married; death cause: "double pneumonia"; died: 22 Apr. 1910; record # 31607.

WILLIAMS, Cynthia; age: 38; married; death cause: "tuberculosis"; died: 26 Jun. 1910; record # 31608.

ARMITAGE, Dollie; age: 43; married; death cause: "pellagra"; died: at Ashville, NC. on 1 Apr. 1910; record # 31609.

ANDERSON, Memory; age: 62; married; death cause: "pneumonia"; died: 20 Jan. 1910; record # 31610.

SMITH, Sallie M.; age: 42; married; death cause: "surgical operation"; died: 6 Jun. 1910; record # 31611.

KERBOUGE (?), Martha M.; age: 2; death cause: "meningitis"; died: 1 Apr. (year not given); record # 31612.

JONES, Garret; age: 81; born: North Carolina; single; death cause: "kidney trouble"; died: 7 May 1910; record # 31613.

MITCHELL, Katie; age: 9 months; death cause: "congestion of brain"; died: 26 Nov. 1909; record # 31614.

YOST, James D.; age: 13; death cause: not stated; died: 22 Apr. 1909; record # 31615.

NEAL, Nola; age: 20; single; death cause: "tuberculosis"; died: 21 Apr. 1910; record # 31616.

STOKES, Maynard C.; age: 2 weeks; death cause: "unknown"; died: 22 Jun. 1910; record # 31617.

KNIGHT, Delie E.; age: 45; born: Washington County; married; death cause: "tuberculosis"; died: 16 Mar.1910; record # 31618.

LINK, Caroline; age: 82; born: Washington County; married; death cause: not stated; died: 8 Dec. 1910; record # 31619.

SUSONG, A.E.; age: 81; born: Greene County; married; death cause: "toxincie"; died: 18 Mar.1910; record # 31620.

HARRISON, James; black; age: 30; single; hotel waiter; death cause: "consumption"; died: 22 May 1910; record # 31621.

EASTERLY, Elbert; age: 50; born: Cocke County; married; death cause: "dropsy"; died: 18 Feb. 1910; record # 31622.

DIXON, Bertie; black; age: 28; single; death cause: "heart failure"; died: 3 Jun. 1910; record # 31623.

STEPHENS, A.J. Sr.; age: 67; married; death cause: "apoplexy"; died: 17 Jan. 1910; record # 31624.

JONES, Charles; age: 88; born: Randolph County, NC.; married; death cause: "old age"; died: 12 Jul. 1909; record # 31625.

DEVAULT, Mary E.; age: 58; born: Clover Bottom, Sullivan County; married; death cause: "heart failure"; died in Sullivan County on 7 Apr. 1910; record # 31626.

MILLER, Della; age: 26; married; death cause: "indigestion"; died: 27 Aug. 1908; record # 31627.

UNIDENTIFIED, Child; first name Paul; age: 6; death cause: not stated; died: 12 Nov. 1910; record # 31628.

WHITE, Francis M.; age: 68; married; death cause: "lung trouble"; died: 14 Oct. (year not given); record # 31629.

WHITE, John; age: 83; born: 16th District, Greene County; married; death cause: "dropsy"; died: (day not given) Apr. 1911; record # 31630.

SMITH, Margaret L.; age: 44; born: Washington County; married; death cause: "lung trouble"; died: 3 Jul. 1911; record # 31631.

UNIDENTIFIED, Adult, age: 78; female; married; death cause: "dropsy"; died: 24 May 1911; record # 31632.

DOWNIE, Feletie A.; age: 16; death cause: "fever"; died: 28 Aug. 1910; record # 31633.

MORRISON, Ruste; female; age: 7; death cause: "fever"; died: 29 Jan. 1911; record # 31634.

WILLIAMS, Carl; age: 5; death cause: "pneumonia fever"; died: 15 Nov. 1910; record # 31635.

BRIGHT, Rosa; age: 32; born: Baltimore, MD.; married; death cause: "pneumonia"; died: 12 Feb. 1911; record # 31636.

ILLEGIBLE, Mattie; age: 3; death cause: "pneumonia"; died: 22 Nov. 1910; record # 31637.

ALLEN, Laura; age: 65; married; death cause: "stomach trouble"; died: 17 Mar.1912; record # 31638.

COPLEY, Gertrude; age: 12; death cause: "grippe"; died: 12 Jan. 1912; record # 31639.

SAUSLBERY, Pearl; age: 12; death cause: not stated; died: 19 Apr. 1912; record # 31640.

HUX, Cora; age: 12; death cause: "spinal affliction"; died: 10 Nov. 1911; record # 31641.

HUX, Dovy; age: 6; death cause: "pneumonia fever"; died: 25 Nov. 1911; record # 31642.

SAMONS, William O.; age: 65; married; death cause: "brights disease"; died: 1 Sep. 1911; record # 31643.

HALL, Mrs. Martha J.; age: 68; widow; death cause: "pneumonia"; died: 10 Apr. 1909; record # 31644.

BOSWELL, Luther; age: 1 year and 6 months; death cause: "tuberculosis"; died: 2 Aug. 1908; record # 31645.

EADS, Mrs. Annie; age: 75; born: Greene County; widow; death cause: "consumption"; died: 16 May 1909; record # 31646.

UNIDENTIFIED, Infant; female; age: 2 weeks; death cause: "not matured"; died: 8 Jul. 1908; record # 31647.

WILLIAMS, Warn; black; age: 73; born: Greene County; married; blacksmith; death cause: "tuberculosis; died: 17 Dec. 1908; record # 31648.

HAROLD, Elizabeth; age: 2; death cause: "flux or cholera"; died: 3 Jun. 1909; record # 31649.

ANDERSON, Robert; age: 25; married; death cause: "tuberculosis"; died: 4 Jan. 1909; record # 31650.

PIERCE, Edward; age: 29; single; death cause: "typhoid fever"; died: 19 Jun. 1909; record # 31651.

BARNES, Robert S.; age: 33; born: Bristol, TN.; married; telegraph operator; death cause: "consumption"; died: 3 Sep. 1908; record # 31652.

YOST, Will D.; age: 42; married; death cause: "tuberculosis"; died: 9 Nov. 1908; record # 31653.

WILLSON, Margaret Ann; age: 74; born: Rheatown; married; death cause: "heart trouble and dropsy"; died: 10 Nov. 1908; record # 31654.

RICKLE, Theodore; age: 31; married; death cause: "tuberculosis"; died: 25 Mar.1912; record # 31655.

MARSHALL, Eva Elizabeth; age: 50; married; death cause: "heart failure"; occupation: spinster; died: 20 Aug. 1911; record # 31656.

BIRD, Hugh; age: 49; married; death cause: "brain trouble"; died: 28; Aug. 1911; record # 31657.

SWATSEL, Nellie Bell; age: 22; days; death cause: "heart failure"; died: 28 May 1912; record # 31658.

BURGNER, James; age: 17 years and 6 months; death cause: "pneumonia fever"; died: 7 Jan. 1912; record # 31659.

ARNIE, Mary; age: 12; death cause: "fever"; died: 2 Nov. 1911; record # 31660.

ALLDIED, Dewy; age: 8 days; death cause: "hives"; died: 14 Jan. 1912; record # 31661.

RICKER, Elizabeth; age: 57; married; death cause: "something grew on brain"; died: 4 Mar 1912; record # 31662.

PRICE, Denver; age: 4 years, 1 month and 5 days; death cause: "measles and flux"; died: 31 Jul. 1911; record # 31663.

DIXON, William Tell; age: 1 year and 6 months; death cause: "spinal meningitis"; died: 14 Feb. 1912; record # 31664.

DIXON, Infant; male; death cause: "still born"; died: "winter of 1911 or 1912"; record # 31665.

MITCHELL, Fannie Date; age: 8 months; death cause: "cholera infantum"; died: 4 Jun. 1912; record # 31666.

MCKINNEY, Marshal; age: 54; born: North Carolina; married; death cause: "paralysis"; died: 19 Aug. 1911; record # 31667.

KNIGHT, Joseph; death cause: "born dead"; died: 1 Jul. 1911; record # 31668.

UNIDENTIFIED, Infant; female; death cause: "born dead"; died: (day not given) Apr. 1912; record # 31669.

KIRK, Levina; age: 2; death cause: "flux"; died: 24 Jul. 1911; record # 31670.

HUFF, Levina; age: 5; death cause; "peritonitis"; died: 10 Feb. 1912; record # 31671.

SHEFFEY, Texas; female; age: 65; widow; death cause: "pulmonary tuberculosis"; died: 4 Mar 1912; record # 31672.

CLAUD (?), Sarah; age: 73; married; death cause: "cancer"; died: 5 Feb. 1911; record # 31673.

UNIDENTIFIED, Infant; female; death cause: "still born"; died: 1 Jul. 1910; record # 31674.

WILLIAMS, Infant; male; age: 4 weeks; death cause: not stated; died: 15 Jun. 1911; record # 31675.

HOLLEN, Osker; age: 12; death cause: "measles"; died: 5 Apr. 1911; record # 31676.

UNIDENTIFIED, Female; age: not stated; death cause: not stated; died: 19 Mar 1911; record # 31677.

CHATMAN, Infant; male; age: 2 months; death cause: "bold hives"; died: 10 Apr. 1912; record # 31678.

MARSHAL, Guy; age: 8 months; death cause: "membranous croup"; died: 12 Nov. 1911; record # 31679.

REAVES, Ed; age: 39; married; death cause: "dropsy"; died: 6 Nov. 1911; record # 31680.

REAVES, Polly; age: 91; born: Greene County; widow; death cause: "paralysis"; died: 9 Mar 1912; record # 31681.

FAN, Edgar; age: 18; single; death cause: "spinal disease"; died: 18 Oct. 1911; record # 31682.

DAVIS, Mary; age: 10 weeks; death cause: "not known"; died: 29 Dec. 1911; record # 31683.

FOX, Serence; female; age: 2 weeks; death cause: "bold hives"; died: 7 Apr. 1912; record # 31684.

GRAY, Bunion; male; age: 24; married; death cause: "shot with a gun"; died: 13 Oct. 1911; record # 31685.
FILLERS, Maggie; age: 4 months; death cause: "membranous croup"; died: 19 Jun. 1912; record # 31686.
PRATHER, Onetta; death cause: "born dead"; died: 9 Jun. 1912; record # 31687.
DUNCAN, Ethel; age: 49; born: Carter County; married; death cause: "antiseptic or female trouble"; died: 19 Sep. 1911; record # 31688.
HARTMAN, Enoch; age: 78; born: Greene County; married; death cause: "hardening of arteries"; died: 3 Jun. 1912; record # 31689.
BARYHERD, John A.; age: "28 the 10th of June"; single; death cause: "tuberculosis"; died: 21; Nov. 1911; record # 31690.
SHACKLEFORD, Enoch; age: 28 years and 5 months; death cause: "acute pneumonia"; died: 19 Dec. 1911; record # 31691.
SMELEER (?), William A.; age: 62; married; death cause: "unknown"; died: 21; Aug. 1911; record # 31692.
UNIDENTIFIED, Infant; male; age: "lived only a few minutes"; death cause: "injury to head"; died: 23 Jul. 1911; record # 31693.
HUNT, G.B.; age: 58; born: Sullivan County; married; death cause: "pneumonia"; died: 6 Jan. 1912; record # 31694.
BOWERS, James H.; age: 63; married; death cause: "disease of heart"; died: 8 Jan. 1912; record # 31695.
SUSONG, John Elmer; age: 38; single; death cause: "tuberculosis of bowels"; died: 19 Jul. 1911; record # 31696.
DUNCAN, Anna; age: 3 days; death cause: "unknown"; died: 26 Aug. 1911; record # 31698.
HOGAN, Lola Lee; age: 10; death cause: "pneumonia"; died: 14 Dec. 1911; record # 31698.
CARTER, Lee; age: 12; death cause: "peritonitis"; died: 8 Dec. 1911; record # 31699.
CARTER, Christina; age: 1 month; death cause: "whooping cough"; died: 13 Apr. 1912; record # 31700.
DRAIN, James; age: 55; married; death cause: "heart"; died: 23 Dec. 1911; record # 31701.
MORELOCK, Lucretia; age: 64; married; death cause: "tuberculosis"; died: 3 Nov. 1911; record # 31702.

LUCAS, Callie; age: 29; married; death cause: "tuberculosis"; died: 26 Feb. 1912; record # 31703.

CRUMLY, John; age: 3 months; death cause: "congestion of brain"; died: 25 Apr. 1912; record # 31704.

WEST, Carrie; age: 19; married; death cause: "tuberculosis"; died: 2 Oct. 1911; record # 31705.

HARMON, Martin; age: 63; born: Albany; married; death cause: "tuberculosis"; died: 25 Jul. 1911; record # 31706.

JUSTICE, Donald; age: 3; death cause: "membranous croup"; died: 11 Nov. 1911; record # 31707.

SMITH, Gilbert; age: 25; single; death cause: "septicemia"; died: 7 Dec. 1911; record # 31705.

CARTER, John Biddle; age: 57; married; death cause: "pneumonia"; died: 4 Apr. 1912; record # 31709.

MORRIS, Henry; age: 52; married; death cause: "pneumonia"; died: 27 Mar 1912; record # 31710.

EVERHART, Kathleen; age: 1; death cause: "membranous croup"; died: 12 Nov. 1911; record # 31712.

CARTER, Henry; age: 61; married; death cause: "heart failure"; died: 4 Dec. 1911; record # 31712.

WILLIAMSON, W.T.; age: 52; married; death cause: "blood poison"; died: 18 Apr. 1911; record # 31713.

NEAR, Jacob E.; age: 27 years and 27 days; single; death cause: "typhoid fever"; died: 9 Dec. 1910; record # 31714.

KEYES, Elizabeth; age: 79 years, 6 months and 26 days; born: Cocke County; married; death cause: "nervous and heart disease"; died: 1 Sep. 1910; record # 31715.

GOSNELL, Melenia B.; age: 1 year and 18 days; death cause: "lagrippe"; died: 22 Dec. 1910; record # 31716.

MELTON, James E.; lived 11 hours; death cause: "croup"; died: 20 Dec. 1910; record # 31717.

BOWER, Sallie; age: 90 years, 7 months and 11 days; born: Greene County; married; death cause: "stomach disease"; died: 17 Jul. 1910; record # 31718.

HUMPHREYS, Clarence; age: 1 year, 5 months and 25 days; death cause: "measles and fever"; died: 20 Apr. 1911; record # 31719.

WARD, Elizabeth; age: 20 years and 27 days; single; death cause: "unknown"; died: 30 Jul. 1910; record # 31720.

BARRIER, Robbert; black; age: 51 years, 8 months and 8 days; born: Charleston, S.C.; married; death cause: "heart failure"; died: 11 Oct. 1911; record # 31721.

SLUDER, James; age: 11 months and 26 days; death cause: "spinal meningitis"; died: 9 Mar 1911; record # 31722.

FRANKLIN, Emmaline; age: 46 years, 5 months and 6 days; born: Madison County, N.C.; married; death cause: "consumption"; died: 28 Feb. 1911; record # 31723.

WILLS, Bertha; age: 1 year, 2 months and 1 day; death cause: "flux"; died: 19 Jul. 1910; record # 31724.

CONDUFF, William A.; age: 63 years, 5 months and 10 days; married; death cause: "pneumonia fever"; died: 14 Mar 1911; record # 31725.

CONDUFF, Alvin; age: 2 months and 10 days; death cause: "unknown"; died: 5 Jun. 1911; record # 31726.

CUTSHALL, Frederick; age: 89 years, 2 months and 11 days; born: Greene County; married; death cause: "typhoid fever"; died: 31 Jan. 1911; record # 31727.

BIBLE, Clide; age: 24; married; death cause: "consumption"; died: (day not given) Oct. 1911; record # 31728.

FASCHIR (Fisher ?), Bird; age: 30; married; death cause: "cancer"; died: (day not given); Jan. 1911; record # 31729.

UNIDENTIFIED, Infant; female; age: 1 month; death cause: "hives"; died: (day not given) Feb. 1911; record # 31730.

MYERS, Tommie; age: 32; married; death cause: "diphtheria"; died: (day not given) Oct. 1910; record # 31731.

BROWN, Jinnie; age: 53; married; death cause: "tuberculosis of skin"; died: 23 Jun. 1911; record # 31732.

VAUGHN, T.W.; lived 2 days; death cause: "hurt in birth"; died: 21 Jan. 1911; record # 31733.

BIBLE, Tommie; age: 28; married; death cause: "fever"; died: 31 May 1911; record # 31734.

MALONE, Olive; age: 19 days; death cause: illegible; died: 22 Dec. 1910; record # 31735.

BALLES, Marie E.; age: 56; married; death cause: "diarrhea"; died: (day not given) Oct. 1910; record # 31736.

HENDRY, Lilior; female; age: 5 years and 5 months; death cause: "membranous croup"; died: 28 Oct. 1910; record # 31737.

ROLLENS, G.B.; age: 82; born: Greene County; married; death cause: "old age"; died: (day not given) Oct. 1911; record # 31738.

UNIDENTIFIED, Infant; female; age: 1 day; death cause: "bold hives"; died: 17 Dec. 1910; record # 31739.

BATES, Rece; age: 9 months and 4 days; death cause: "membranous croup"; died: (day not given) Feb. 1911; record # 31740.

BOULS, Infant; age: 15 days; child of Edd BOULS; death cause: "hives"; died: 15 Mar.1911; record # 31741.

HUNYCUT, Henry; age: 9; death cause: "typhoid fever"; died: (day not given) Jun. 1911; record # 31742.

CALLETT, Margaret; age: 16 days; death cause: "diphtheria"; died: 27 Sep. 1910; record # 31743.

JOHNSON, Mary E.; age: 82; born: Greene County; widow; death cause: "paralysis and old age"; died: 31 Jul. 1910; record # 31744.

DAVIS, Joseph A.; age: 46; married; death cause: "fever"; died: 14 Dec. 1908; record # 31745.

FRESHENS, Annie May; age: 3 months and 10 days; death cause: "bold hives"; died: 16 Jun. 1910; record # 31746.

DAVIS, Steller E.; age: 13 years and 11 months; death cause: "female trouble"; died: 7 Jul. 1909; record # 31747.

MYERS, Ella F.; age: 33; born: Washington County; married; death cause: "kidney trouble"; died: 19 Jun. 1910; record # 31748.

PRESLEY, R.B.; age: 61; born: Madison County, N.C.; married; death cause: "lagrippe"; died: 13 Apr. 1910; record # 31749.

HAIR, George; age: 29; married; death cause: "killed - murdered"; died: 9 Jan. 1910; record # 31750.

WILSON, J.H.; age: 45; born: Ashe County, N.C.; married; death cause: "suicide"; died: 23 Jan. 1910; record # 31751.

BOWLAND, Stella; age: 3 months; death cause: "unknown"; died: 11 Dec. 1911; record # 31752.

SOLOMAN, Loeta; born: Jun. 1911; age: 2 years and 8 months; parents: J.M. SOLOMAN and Mary HARTMAN; death cause: "meningitis"; informant: R.J. GAMMON; died: 9 Feb. 1914; record (1914): # 27.

AILSHIE, Infant; male; born: 31 Jan. 1914; parents: William AILSHIE and Flora WAMPLER; death cause: "premature"; informant: Mrs ILSHIE; died: 14 Jan. 1914; record (1914) # 26.

RUSH, Infant: male; born: 3 Nov. 1913; parents: John K. RUSH and Buna FOWLER (born: South Carolina); death cause: "premature birth"; died: 2 Jan. 1914; record (1914) # 25.

LAMBERT, Mary; born: 16 Aug. 1858; parents: "not known"; death cause: "chronic rheumatism and heart failure"; informant: J.A. LAMBERT (Mohawk); died: 18 Jan. 1914; buried: Concord; record (1914) # 24.

ROSS, James; born: 6 Sep. 1837 in Greene County; parents: James ROSS, Sr. and Sallie WEEMS; death cause: "tuberculosis"; died: 28 Jan. 1914; record (1914) # 23.

BOWER, Infant; born: 15 Jan. 1914; parents: Aden BOWER and Lisa CAMPBELL; death cause: "unknown"; died: 15 Jan. 1914; buried: St. James Cemetery; record (1914) # 22.

HENSLEY, Birtha; born: 11 Aug. 1889; married; parents: John CAMPBELL (born: N.C.) and (first name not given) HUX; death cause: not stated; informant: W.M. HENSLEY; died: 23 Jan. 1914; buried: Soloman Cemetery; record (1914) # 21.

OVERHOLSER, John Madison; born: 22 Jan. 1830; married; parents: Christopher OVERHOLSER (born: VA.) and (first name not given) STAFFORD (born: N.C.) death cause: "cancer of right cheek"; informant: Florence JONES; died: 3 Jan. 1914; buried: Woolsey Cemetery; record (1914) # 20.

WILSON, Hazel; born: 15 Feb. 1887; married; parents: S.P. BARDING and Martha WHALOCK; death cause: "tuberculosis of lungs"; informant: father (Mohawk); died: 24 Jan. 1914; buried: Hamblen County; record (1914) # 19.

EASTERLY, Matilda Ann; born: 26 Aug. 1836 in North Carolina; widow; parents: Alexander ROBISON (North Carolina) and Mary PALMER (North Carolina); death cause: "mitral regurgitation and aortic aneurysm"; informant: F.P. EASTERLY (Moshiem); died: 3 Feb. 1914; buried: Cocke County; record (1914) # 18.

DYER, Infant; female; born: 25 Jan. 1914; parents: Charley DYER and Celia CRITTENDON; death cause: "atelectosis"; informant; father (Moshiem); died: 26 Jan. 1914; record (1914) # 17.

SOUTHERLAND, Paul; born: 6 Nov. 1913; parents: Leroy SOUTHERLAND (Unicoi County) and Willy May BARM; death cause: "pneumonia and measles"; informant: father (Afton); died: 13 Jan. 1914; buried: Fairview; record (1914) # 16.

SUTTLES, Infant; male; born: 9 Jan. 1914; parents: father not stated and Berthy SUTTLES; death cause: "unknown"; informant: Charley SUTTLES, grandfather; died: 20 Jan. 1914; buried: Pine Grove; record (1914) # 15.

BOWMAN, Mary Elizabeth; age: 67 years and 21 days; married; parents: Barnie THOMAS (Virginia) and __ BIRD (Virginia); death cause: "influenza"; informant: T.J. BOWMAN (Greeneville); died: 27 Jan. 1914; buried: Mount Zion; record (1914) # 14.

WILLIAMS, Dowell; age: 68 years and 4 days; born: Pulaski County, VA., married; death cause: "valvulor heart disease"; no other information; died: 8 Jan. 1914; record (1914) # 13.

WILSON, Infant; male; born: 15 Jan. 1914; parents: A.G. WILSON (North Carolina) and Mary A. HAWKINS (Johnson County); death cause: "premature birth"; died: 17 Jan. 1914; place of burial: illegible; record (1914) # 12.

HUNT, Sarah Jane; born: 17 Jul. 1843; born: Hawkins County; widow; parents: William MYERS (Hawkins County) and Nettie JONES (Hawkins County); death cause: "heart failure"; informant: Rebecca HUNT (Baileyton); died: 10 Jan. 1914; place of burial: illegible; record (1914) # 11.

BELL, Samuel Allen; born: 23 Dec. 1913; parents: Samuel BELL and Jennie BELL; death cause: not stated; informant: father (Greeneville); died: 3 Jan. 1914; record (1914) # 10.

WILLIAMS, Harriett; black; born: 1 Jan. 1837 in Greene County; parents: unknown; death cause: "paralysis"; informant: J.R. MYERS (Greeneville); died: 9 Jan. 1914; buried: Greeneville; record (1914) # 9.

WAGNER, Buford; born: 18 Mar.1912; parents: John WAGNER and Daisy LISTER; death cause: "diphtheria"; informant: father (Greeneville); died: 22 Jan. 1914; buried: Greeneville; record (1914) # 8.

MCLAIN, Leonard Mitchell; born: 1 Apr. 1830 in Hawkins County; married; parents: unknown; death cause: "old age"; informant: Mrs. Flora CHRISTIAN (Greeneville); died: 28 Jan. 1914; buried: Greeneville; record (1914) # 7.

CAMPBELL, Mae; born: 13 Apr. 1887; married; parents: E. KIDWELL and Jennie PARRY; death cause: "tuberculosis of larynx"; informant: L.P. CAMPBELL (Baileyton); died: 2 Feb. 1914; buried: Salem; record (1914) # 6.

MORELOCK, Charlie B.; age: 51 years, 8 months and 15 days; married; parents: Mike MORELOCK and Marg PHILLIPS; death cause: "cancer of esophagus"; informant: E.B. ELLIS (Chuckey); died: 24 Jan. 1914; buried: Liberty Hill; record (1914) # 5.

BOLES, David J.; born: 27 Feb. 1836 in Tennessee; married; parents: Jacob BOLES (Virginia) and mother's name illegible; mother born: North Carolina; death cause: "mitral regurgitation"; died: 22 Jan. 1914; buried: Pine Grove; record (1914) # 4.

WOLFE, Hettie Maranda; born: 8 Sep. 1853; married; parents: James GARDNER (North Carolina) and Anna MYERS; death cause: "pneumonia fever"; informant: M. RATLIFF (Baileyton); died: 29 Jan. 1914; buried: Van Hill; record (1914) # 3.

JUSTICE, William Elbert; born: 6 Feb. 1858; married; parents: WA. JUSTICE and Jane (not stated); death cause: "lobar pneumonia"; informant: Mary E. JUSTICE (Baileyton); died: 3 Jan. 1914; buried: illegible; record (1914) # 2.

BRADLEY, Infant; male; parents: Wona (?) BRADLEY and Nola PATTERSON; death cause: "still born"; informant: Alison BRADLEY (Moshiem); died: 27 Jan. 1914; record (1914) # 1.

HARKLEROAD, Infant; female; parents: Myrtle J. HARKLEROAD (Sullivan County) and Mary F. PARKER (Sullivan County); death cause: "still born"; informant: J.C. MARSHALL (Chuckey); died: 24 Feb. 1914; record (1914) # 57.

TAYLOR, David; born: 12 Feb. 1830 in Carter County; widower; parents: William TAYLOR (Carter County) and Ella HYDER (Carter

County); death cause: "old age and mitral regurgitation"; informant: J.M. TAYLOR (Greeneville); died: 23 Feb. 1914; buried: 17th District; record (1914) # 56.

GOODMAN, Columbus; born: 30 Jun. 1834 in Catawba County, NC.; married; parents: not stated; death cause: "chronic diarrhea"; informant; M.H. KENT (Moshiem); died: 3 Feb. 1914; buried: Carter's Chapel; record (1914) # 55.

MALONE, William; born: 31 Mar.1832 in Tennessee; widower; parents: Humphrey MALONE and Elizabeth LINEBAUGH; death cause: "heart disease"; informant: G.N. MORRISON (Baileyton); died: 21 Feb. 1914; buried: Zion; record (1914) # 54.

REYNOLDS, Nancie Jane; born: 20 Sep. 1880; married; parents: "William MALONE and Mary Ann MALONE; death cause: "tuberculosis of lungs"; informant: C.E. DAVIS (Greeneville); died: 15 Feb. 1914; buried: illegible; record (1914) # 53.

COATES, Rufus Clide; born: 29 Dec. 1913; parents: C.D. COATES and Lettie SPEN__(illegible) (born: Virginia); death cause: "malnutrition"; informant: Charles COATES (Greeneville); died: 11 Feb. 1914; record (1914) # 52.

WILLS, Nancy Emeline; born: 1 Oct. 1863; married; parents: Price Hiram TAYLOR (Washington County) and Polly RUBLE (Washington County); death cause: "pulmonary tuberculosis"; informant: Thomas Coke WILLS (Greeneville); died: 20 Feb. 1914; buried: Price Cemetery; record (1914) # 51.

MORGAN, Felix Elbert; born: 16 Jul. 1913; parents: father not stated and Laura Myrtle MORGAN; death cause: "unknown"; informant: mother (Greeneville); died: 23 Feb. 1914; buried: Mount Olivet; record (1914) # 50.

FAIR, T.M.; born: 13 Apr. 1895; single; parents: Eli FAIR (North Carolina) and Eliza MOORE; death cause: "inflammation of brain"; died: 21 Feb. 1914; buried: Mt. Carmel; record (1914) # 49.

KELLER, Elizabeth; born; 18 Mar.1836; widow; parents: father's name unknown and Mary WELLES; death cause: illegible; informant: B.F. KELLER (Afton); died: 19 Feb. 1914; buried: Union Chapel; record (1914) # 48.

ROLLINS, Viannie Shelton; age: 59 years; born: North Carolina; widow; parents: Martin SHELTON (North Carolina) and Polly FRANKLIN (North Carolina); death cause: "lobar pneumonia"; informant: Nancy NORTON (Greeneville); died: 31 Jan. 1914; record (1914) # 47.

HAULTY (?) Ada; born: 5 Jun. 1910 in Telford; parents: W.F. (illegible) and Mary OLER; invalid; death cause not stated; informant: J.M. OLER (Greeneville); died: 6 Feb. 1914; buried: Mt. Bethel; record (1914) # 46.

MERCER, Sarah; age: 79 years; widow; parents: Billie JENNINGS and mother's name unknown; death cause: "hemiplegia of left side"; informant: Sherman CHAPMAN (Greeneville); died: 3 Feb. 1914: record (1914) # 45.

RUBLE, Harriett; age: 70 years; married; parents: "unknown"; death cause: not stated; informant: F.C. BROOKS (Greeneville); died: 13 Feb. 1914; buried: Mt. Herbron; record (1914) # 41.

CHAPMAN, Amanda; born: 4 Feb. 1868 in North Carolina; married; parents: Jasper BRADLEY (North Carolina) and mother's name unknown; death cause: "pneumonia"; informant: F.C. CHAPMAN (Greeneville); died: 4 Feb. 1914; record (1914) # 43.

WALLIN, Infant; female; born: 14 Feb. 1914; parents: J.M. WALLIN (North Carolina) and Bessie STANTON (North Carolina); death cause: "8 month child"; informant: father (Greeneville); died: 14 Feb. 1914; buried: Mt. Herbron; record (1914) # 42.

WALLIN, Bessie F.; born: 10 Feb. 1887 in North Carolina; married; parents: Sol STANTON (North Carolina) and Hester TWEED (North Carolina); death cause: illegible; informant: J.M. WALLIN (Greeneville); died: 15 Feb. 1914; buried: Mount Hebron; record # 41.

HILL, Carl King; born: 1 Jan. 1892 in Bristol; single; parents: Hugh Jasper HILL (West Virginia) and Jennie C. BRANSON (Virginia); death cause: "tuberculosis"; informant: H.J. HILL (Greeneville) died: 19 Feb. 1914; record (1914) # 40.

HENARD, Louis C.; born: 3 Sep. 1848 in Hawkins County; single; parents: Madison HENARD (Hawkins County) and Polly TUCKER (Hawkins County); death cause: "epileptic seizure causing a fall and coma"; informant: C.J. MCLAIN (Greeneville); died: 24 Feb. 1914; buried: New Lebanon; record (1914) # 39.

MORRISON, Orville; born: 10 Jan. 1911; parents: J.C. MORRISON and Mary DIXON; death cause: "burn"; informant: James R. MERCER; died: 24 Feb. 1914; buried: Mt. Vernon; record (1914) # 38.

MORRIS, Raymond; born: 22 Sep. 1913; parents: Joe MORRIS (Sweetwater, TN.) and Martha SHORT (Persia, TN.) death cause: "measles, 2 days"; informant: father (Greeneville); died: 25 Feb. 1914; record (1914) # 37.

BASHAM, Lucretia; born: 2 Feb. 1881; married; parents: W.J. FOX and Lena SEXTON; death cause: pulmonary tuberculosis"; informant: Dave BASHAM (Greeneville); died: 26 Feb. 1914; buried: Green Ward; record (1914) # 36.

WILLIAMS, Mary Alice; born: 28 Jun. 1913; parents: Will D. WILLIAMS and Martha NAFF; death cause: "whooping cough"; informant: father (Greeneville); died: 28 Feb. 1914; buried: Oak Grove; record (1914) # 35.

COLLINS, Carson; born: 23 Dec. 1913; parents: father not stated and Martha COLLINS (Washington County); death cause: "broncho pneumonia"; informant: John COLLINS (Jeroldstown); died: 23 Feb. 1914; buried: Lovelace, TN.; record (1914) # 34.

DEZZARN, Nancy Ellen; born: 29 Sep. 1843; widow; parents: Michael HENSLEY and Mary ARNOLD (Hawkins County); death cause: "pulmonary tuberculosis"; informant: Curtis ROBERTS (Jeraldstown); died: 7 Mar.1914; record (1914) # 33.

JENKINS, Sallie; born: 24 Feb. 1869; married; parents: Jackson PINKSTON (North Carolina) and Nancy MEFFORD; death cause: "cancer of uterus and bladder"; informant: J.M. LOYD (Mohawk); died: 24 Feb. 1914; buried: Mt. Hope; record (1914) # 32.

SOLOMAN, George W.; born: __ Feb. 1872; married; parents: Jack SOLOMAN and mother unknown; death cause: "pulmonary tuberculosis"; informant: Fannie SOLOMAN (Greeneville); died: 14 Feb. 1914; buried: St. James; record (1914) # 31.

NERTON, Eliza; born: 15 Jan. 1884 in North Carolina; parents: Henry FRANKLIN (North Carolina) and Emeline GENTRY (North Carolina); death cause: not stated; informant: Henry FRANKLIN (Greeneville); died: 25 Feb. 1914; buried: Cocke County; record (1914) # 30.

BELCHER, Bertha Lucille; born: 20 Jan. 1914 in Cocke County; parents: Thomas BELCHER and Martha WILLET (North Carolina); death cause: "acute nephritis"; informant: Rufus BELCHER (Moshiem); died: 28 Feb. 1914; buried: Loves Memorial; record (1914) # 29.

ARNOLD, Ida Vena; born: 17 Dec. 1862; married; parents: Nat WILSON (South Carolina) and Hariet MOSUER; death cause: "pulmonary tuberculosis"; informant: Robert ARNOLD (Moshiem); died: 7 Feb. 1914; buried: Meadow Creek; record (1914) # 28.

CAMPBELL, ____; adult, male; black; born: 1 Jul. 1832 in North Carolina; parents: Jacob CAMPBELL (North Carolina) and mother's name unknown; death cause: "chronic gastritis"; informant: Hugh CAMPBELL (Chuckey); died: 29 Mar.1914; buried: Rheatown; record (1914) # 92.

GRAY, Ema Elizabeth; born: 14 Jan. 1914; parents: William GRAY and Ethel BRUMLEY; death cause: "unknown"; informant: F.T. CARTER (Greeneville); died: 6 Mar.1914; buried: New Bethel; record (1914): 91.

MCAMIS, Elbert; born: 30 Nov. 1861; married; parents: Isaac MCAMIS and Rhoda SHANKS; death cause: "pulmonary tuberculosis"; died: 15 Mar.1914; buried: English Cemetery; record (1914) # 90.

PULLIAM, Milton M.; born: 2 Mar.1839 in Claiborne County; married; parents: Madison PULLIAM (North Carolina) and mother's name unknown; death cause: "softening of brain"; died: 3 Mar.1914; buried: Lovelace, TN.; record (1914) # 89.

ALEXANDER, John R.; born: 21 Sep. 1835 in Afton, TN.; married; parents: William ALEXANDER (Afton) and Iley JOHNSON (Afton); death cause: "paralysis - cerebral hemorrhage"; informant: C.W. ALEXANDER (Chuckey); died: 23 Mar.1914; buried: Shilo; record (1914) # 88.

NELSON, Lee; born: __ Apr. 1912; parents: William NELSON and Gretie (illegible); death cause: "entero colitis"; informant: S.J. BARRMON (Greeneville); died: 25 Mar.1914; buried: Union Chapel; record (1914) # 87.

ROBERTS, Infant; female; parents: Bruce ROBERTS and Venie BROYLES; death cause: "still born"; informant: Cora ROBERTS (Afton); died: 31 Mar.1914; buried: Union Chapel; record (1914) # 86.

GRAY, Roxe; born: 17 Dec. 1913; parents: father not stated and Eva GRAY; death cause: "heart failure - lived 4 hours"; informant: Walter GRAY (Chuckey); died: 24 Mar.1914; buried: Union Chapel; record (1914) # 85.

BLACK, Infant; female; born: 26 Mar.1914; parents: Jessie BLACK (Cocke County) and Allis BLACK (Cocke County); death cause: "jaundice"; informant: father (Midway); died: 8 Apr. 1914; buried: St. Joseph's Chapel; record (1914) # 84.

BENCH, Infant; female; born: 30 Mar.1914; parents: James S. BENCH and Alpha PITTS; death cause: "unknown"; informant H.C. SEAY (Midway); died: 30 Mar.1914; buried: Moshiem; record (1914) # 83.

GARDNER, Infant; male; born: 13 Mar.1914; parents: Joseph GARDNER and Mary Kate TAYLOR; death cause: not stated; informant: Tom COBBLE (Midway); died: 13 Mar.1914; buried: Bibles Chapel; record (1914) # 82.

ISOM, John Henry; black; born: 17 Dec. 1905; parents: Gordon ISOM and Molly CHESNUT; death cause: "broncho pneumonia"; informant: Mollie ISOM (Mohawk); died: 14 Mar.1914; buried: Whitesburg, TN.; record (1914) # 81.

CULBERTSON, Caswell; born: 17 May 1836 in Greene County; married; parents: William CULBERTSON and Nancy LAUDERDALE (Greene County); death cause: "pulmonary consumption"; informant: Ona KIRK (Midway) died: 23 Feb. 1914; record (1914) # 80.

HAUN, Florence Elizabeth; born: 3 Aug. 1859 at Bulls Gap; married; parents: Peter RADE and Kizih RHEA; death cause: "acute rheumatism"; informant: John HAUN (Mohawk); died: 1 Apr. 1914; buried: Concord Cemetery; record (1914) # 79.

DICKERSON, Mary M.; born: 11 Jun. 1887 in Washington County; married; parents: William E. WALLER and Annie ROGERS; death cause: "erysipelas"; informant: William WALLER (Limestone); died: 16 Mar.1914; record (1914) # 78.

BROYLES, Martha; black; born: 17 Jul. 1895; single; parents: J.F. BROYLES and Hester YOUNG (North Carolina); death cause: "pneumonia"; informant: father (Greeneville) died: 15 Mar.1914; buried: New Hope; record (1914) # 77.

LAMONS, Sallie; born: 16 Jan. 1837 in Greene County; widow; parents: George SEXTON and Mary MILLER; death cause: "pneumonia"; informant: R.A. SWATSELL (Greeneville); died: 17 Mar.1914; buried: Oak Grove; record (1914) # 76.
BAXTER, James M.; born: 11 Jan. 1854; married; parents: John BAXTER and __ BRIGHT; death cause: "tuberculosis of lungs"; informant: Newton MYERS (Greeneville); died: 19 Mar.1914; buried: Mt. Pleasant; record (1914) # 75.
MORRIS, Burton Arnold; born: 24 Jan. 1913; parents: Fred MORRIS (Washington County) and Emma LOWE; death cause: "lobar pneumonia and measles"; informant: father (Greeneville) died: 21 Mar.1914; record (1914) # 74.
WARDON, Flora; born: 5 Jul. 1897; married; parents: Manie ARNOLD and Lizzie BROOKS; death cause: "septicemia, childbirth"; informant: Jess WARDEN (Greeneville); died: 22 Mar.1914; buried: Mt. Bethel; record (1914) # 73.
WADDLE, Feliz; born: 25 Sep. 1891; parents: E.C. WADDLE and Georgia JOHNSON; death cause: "pneumonia"; informant: father (Greeneville) died: 23 Mar.1914; record (1914) # 72.
JOHNSON, Willie D.; born: 22 Mar.1914; parents: John JOHNSON and Lizzie WILKERSON; death cause: illegible; informant: father (Greeneville) died: 27 Mar.1914; record (1914) # 71.
KEELER, John R.; born: 20 Oct. 1862; married; parents: Wash KEELER and Nancy WELLER; death cause: "paralysis of right side"; informant: John BROYLES (Greeneville); died: 11 Mar.1914; buried: Union Chapel; record (1914) # 70.
ENGLE, Sallie; born: 10 Jun. 1886 in North Carolina; married; parents: John LANDRES and Betty NORTON (North Carolina); death cause: "pulmonary tuberculosis"; informant: M.B. MELONE (Chuckey); died: 14 Mar.1914; buried: Cedar Grove; record (1914) # 69.
JUSTICE, Polly Ann; born: 6 Jan. 1836; married; parents: John MALONE and Temple WEEMS; death cause: "diarrhea"; informant: C.P. WEEMS (Baileyton); died: 3 Apr. 1914; buried: 11th District; record (1914) # 68.
KINCHLOW, Birtha; black; born: 12 Mar.1914; parents: father's name not stated and Elizzie KINCHLOW (Hawkins County); death cause:

"born at about 7th month"; died: 14 Mar.1914; buried: Salem; record (1914) # 67.

COFFEE, Mirna Jane; born: 22 Mar.1848 in Hawkins County; married; parents: Dock LONG (Hawkins County) and Mima Jane LONG (Hawkins County); death cause: "abdominal tumor"; informant: J.S. LONG (Bulls Gap); died: 22 Mar.1914; buried: Beech Grove; record (1914) # 66.

MARSHALL, Martha M.; born: 23 Oct. 1841 at Mohawk; widow; parents: Soloman REED (Warrensburg) and Margaret LADY; death cause: "brain fever"; informant: Candice WALL (Mohawk); died: 28 Mar.1914; buried: Mt. Hope; record (1914) # 65.

PITTS, Bettie; born: 2 Apr. 1857; widow; parents: Steve GRIFFEY (North Carolina) and Vina AMBERS; death cause: "infection"; informant: Tom FRY (Greeneville); died: 2 Mar.1914; buried: Mt. Bethel; record (1914) # 64.

SWATSELL, Infant; male; born: 22 Jan. 1914; parents: Bruce SWATSELL (Cocke County) and Lizzie CARTELL; death cause: "lagrippe"; informant: father (Greeneville); died: 3 Mar.1914; buried: Mt. Pleasant; record (1914) # 63.

COOTER, John M.; born: __ Mar.1835; married; parents: Barney COOTER (Greene County) and Mary Ann LOWERY (Greene County); death cause: "old age"; informant: W.T. MITCHELL (Greeneville); died: 5 Mar.1914; buried: Pisgah; record (1914) # 62.

HOUSLEY, Benjamin Franklin; born: 20 Feb. 1840 in Carter County; single; parents: Howell HOUSLEY (Carter County) and Nancy WARDEN (Kentucky); death cause: "cerebral hemorrhage"; informant: Walter HENSLEY (G'ville); died: 10 Mar.1914; record (1914) # 61.

EVANS, James; black; age: 19 years; single; parents: Dave EVANS and Hattie WILKINS; death cause: "pneumonia and Jaundice"; informant: John WOODS (Greeneville); died: 11 Mar.1914; buried: New Hope; record (1914) # 60.

CHAPMAN, John Wesley Emmett; born: 14 Oct. 1910 in Wise County, VA.; parents: G.W. CHAPMAN (Washington County, VA.) and Elsenr WILSON (Washington County, VA.); death cause: "pneumonia and measles"; informant: father (Greeneville); died: 12 Mar.1914; buried: Oak Grove; record (1914) # 59.

BOWMAN, Pearl; born: 27 Feb. 1914; parents: Marion F. BOWMAN and Grace LAWING (Unicoi County); death cause: not stated; informant: Henry FANNON (Greeneville); died: 15 Mar.1914; record (1914) # 58.

SKELTON, George Washington; age: 73 years and 10 days; born: Jefferson County; married; parents: not stated; death cause: "valvulor heart disease"; informant: Mrs. M.E. SKELTON (Moshiem); died: 8 May 1914; buried: Mt. Carmel; record (1914) # 125.

MCNABB, Lula A.; born: 30 Nov. 1891; married; parents: S.E. JEFFERS and; __ JUSTICE; death cause: "pulmonary tuberculosis"; informant: Walter MCNABB (Moshiem); died: 24 Apr. 1914; buried: Carmel; record (1914) # 124.

FOSHIE, William; born: __ Sep. 1847; married; parents: John FOSHIE and Ann FOSTER; death cause: "broncho pneumonia, labrippe"; informant: Mrs. Priscilla FOSHIE (Moshiem); died: 7 Apr. 1914; buried: Mt. Carmel; record (1914) # 123.

CUTSHALL, Elmer Hubert; born: 28 Sep. 1910; parents: Asa CUTSHALL (Paint Creek) and Nora RICKER (Camp Creek); death cause: "cholera infantum"; informant: Ella MONTGOMERY (Greeneville); died: 29 Apr. 1914; buried: Cutshall Cemetery; record (1914) # 122.

BROCKWELL, John R.; born: __ Feb. 1836 in Virginia; married; parents: unknown; death cause: "pulmonary hemorrhage"; informant: Tennessee BROCKWELL (Moshiem); died: 7 Apr. 1914; buried: Moshiem; record (1914) # 121.

PRUITT, Mollie; born: 4 Nov. 1873; married; parents: John BIBLE and Rachel HORTON, death cause: "unknown"; informant: J.M. MYERS (Moshiem); died: 13 Apr. 1914; record (1914) # 120.

MCGEE, Infant; male; born: 20 Apr. 1914; parents: Ed MCGEE and Maggie (illegible); death cause: "premature birth"; informant: father (Moshiem); died: 22 Apr. 1914; buried: Harmon Cemetery; record (1914) # 119.

LINEBARGER, Hobart L.; born: 20 May 1896; single; parents: James A. LINEBARGER (Henson) and Alpha Isabel WALTERS (St. James); death cause: "pulmonary tuberculosis"; informant: Penelope RENNER (Moshiem); died: 9 Apr. 1914; buried: St. James; record (1914) # 118.

BRIGMAN, Sarah; born: 19 Aug. 1874; married; parents: father unknown and Katie PITTS; death cause: "pulmonary tuberculosis"; informant: N.K. BRIGMAN (Parrotsville) died: 17 Apr. 1914; record (1914) # 117.

FINCH, Anna Catherine; born: 23 Apr. 1914; parents: Larance FINCH (Kentucky) and Lizzie MCCLURE (Hawkins County); death cause: "7 month child"; informant: father (Baileyton); died: 23 Apr. 1914; buried: Salem; record (1914) # 116.

WARD, Mollie; born: 21 Apr. 1886; married; parents: James RAMSEY and Martha Jane HANKS; death cause: "pulmonary tuberculosis"; informant: C.A. MORELOCK (Bulls Gap); died: 21 Apr. 1914; buried: Beech Grove; record (1914) # 115.

PIPER, Joe Keebler; born: 23 Aug. 1898; parents: W.F. PIPER (Washington County) and Mary S. KEEBLER; death cause: "hereditary spinal ataxia"; informant: father (Chuckey); died: 27 Apr. 1914; buried: Shilo; record (1914) # 114.

WILSON, William; born: 16 Mar.1844 in Virginia; married; parents: not stated; death cause: "acute gastritis"; informant: Rev. FORT (Greeneville); died: 14 Apr. 1914; buried: Wesley; record (1914) # 113.

JOHNSON, Dora Belle; age: 29 years; married; parents: Martin CUTSHALL and Kittie HOLLAND; death cause: "pulmonary tuberculosis"; informant: C.B. MORGAN (Greeneville); died: 21 Apr. 1914; buried: Red Hill; record (1914) # 112.

SUSONG, Sara; born: 23 Apr. 1834 (age 80) in Greene County; single; parents: John SUSONG (Greene County) and Christy L__ (illegible); death cause: "senility"; informant: W.A. SUSONG (Greeneville) died: 23 Apr. 1914; buried: __ Ridge; record (1914) # 111.

COX, Margaret Eveline; born: 15 Apr. 1862; married; parents: Crawford REYNOLDS and Mary KEE; death cause: "tuberculosis of lungs"; informant: J.M. CASTEEL (Greeneville); died: 25 Apr. 1914; buried: Malone; record (1914) # 110.

GRUEY (?), Laura; age: 50 years; married; parents: Andrew BLAZER and mother unknown; death cause: "tuberculosis"; informant: Ed HARRISON (Greeneville); died: 26 Apr. 1914; buried: Amity; record (1914) # 109.

GASS, John; born: 10 Nov. 1831 in Greene County; married; parents: John GASS (Ireland) and mother unknown; death cause: "cancer"; informant: G.R. GASS (Greeneville); died: 26 Apr. 1914; buried: Kidwell; record (1914) # 108.

JOHNSON, Jadie; female; born: 20 Nov. 1892 in Missouri; parents: J.G. HOUSTON (Virginia) and Meneva HOUSTON (Tennessee); death cause: "tuberculosis"; informant: C.G, JOHNSON (Afton); died: 26 Apr. 1914; record (1914) # 107.

FORTNER, George; born: 16 Jun. 1882; married; parents: George FORTNER, Sr. and Rebecca SCOTT (Virginia); death cause: "tuberculosis"; informant: W.E. FORTNER (Greeneville); died: 28 Apr. 1914; buried: Oak Grove; record (1914) # 106.

MOORE, Belle; born: __ Apr. 1888; single; parents: John MOORE and mother illegible; death cause: "pellagra"; informant: J.W. MORELOCK (Greeneville); died: 28 Apr. 1914; record (1914) # 105.

BROOKS, Henry Allen; born: 9 Dec. 1858; married; parents: William BROOKS and Margaret JOHNSON; death cause: "pellagra"; informant: W.E. JOHNSON (Greeneville); died: 30 Apr. 1914; buried: Pisgah; record (1914) # 104.

PAYNE, Belvin Wheeler; born: 12 Jun. 1872; married; school teacher; parents: George Valentine PAYNE (Sullivan County) and Mary Elizabeth BUSHONG (Sullivan County); death cause: "tuberculosis"; informant: Tennessee Payne HALL (Fall Branch); died: 11 Apr. 1914; buried: Bethesda; record (1914) # 103.

FRY, Martha; born: 11 Nov. 1837 in Greene County; widow; parents: William BACHAM and Polly Ann BOSWELL; death cause: "malignant disease of liver"; informant: T.S. HULL (Greeneville); died: 1 Apr. 1914; buried: Oak Grove; record (1914) # 102.

STURM, Stella; born: 3 Apr. 1876 in Jonesborough; married; parents: Landon MORRIS (Jonesborough) and Mary SMITH; death cause: "uramic __ illegible"; informant: Fred MORRIS (Greeneville); died: 3 Apr. 1914; buried: Oak Grove; record (1914) # 101.

COOTER, Edith; born: 7 Apr. 1858 in Union County, SC.; married; parents: __ WOODS (SC) and mother not stated; death cause: "valvulor heart disease"; informant: J.A. WILHOIT (Greeneville); died: 7 Apr. 1914; buried: Gravel Hill; record (1914) # 100.

JUSTICE, Robert; age: 45 years; born: Carter County; married; parents: L.R. JUSTICE (Carter County) and Sarah JACKSON (Carter County); death cause: "found in Chuckey River on 6 Apr. 1914"; informant: Mrs. R.C. JUSTICE (Greeneville); buried: Oakland; record (1914) # 99.

BOWMAN, Frank M.; born: 26 Sep. 1912; parents: W.F. BOWMAN and Jennie MOCUIER; death cause: illegible; informant: T.J. BOWMAN (Greeneville); died: 9 Apr. 1914; record (1914) # 98.

GADDIS, Rena; age: 58 years; single; parents: Jessie GADDIS (North Carolina) and mother not stated; death cause: "complication of disease - tuberculosis"; informant: John GADDIS (Greeneville); died: 5 Apr. 1914; buried: Gaddis Shed; record (1914) # 97.

RHOADS, Clyde; born: 8 Apr. 1914; parents: Will RHODES and Kittie FREMAN (Smith County, VA.); death cause: "exposure"; informant: mother (Greeneville); died: 9 Apr. 1914; record (1914) # 96.

RHODES, Jeanett; born: 8 Apr. 1914; parents: Will RHODES and Kittie FREMAN (Smith County, VA.) death cause: "exposure"; informant: mother (Greeneville); died: 11 Apr. 1914; buried: Oak Grove; record (1914) # 95.

BOWMAN, Alonzo; born: 24 Dec. 1913; parents: John BOWMAN and Dora B. OWENS; death cause: "pneumonia"; informant: Jacob KINNURY (Greeneville); died: 13 Apr. 1914; buried: Oak Grove; record (1914) # 94.

FOX, Infant; male; age: not stated; parents: Worley FOX and Annie JOHNSON; death cause: "abdominal __ (illegible) of 11 months duration, operation 14 Apr. 1914; buried: Chucky; record (1914) # 93.

JOHNSON, Barbara Elizabeth; born: 15 Mar.1912; parents: Willis JOHNSON and Hazel REYNOLDS; death cause: "carbolic acid poisoning"; informant: father (Greeneville); died: 18 May 1914; buried: Moshiem; record (1914) # 92.

DAVIS, Decatur; black; born: 21 May 1893 in Cocke County; divorced; parents: John DAVIS (Cocke County) and Lizzie DAVIS (Cocke County); death cause: "typhoid fever"; informant: Adam MORRIS (Greeneville); died: 14 May 1914; record (1914) # 151.

CAMPBELL, Marion; black; born: 14 Mar.1896; parents: Sam CAMPBELL and mother unknown; death cause: "drowned accidental"; died: 23 May 1914; buried: Pruetts Hill; record (1914) # 150.

HARRISON, John; black; age: 86 years; single; parents and death cause: not stated; died: 24 May 1914; buried: Mt. Bethel; record (1914) # 149.

MCAFEE, Leonard King; born: 24 May 1858; married; parents: Marion MCAFEE and Polly BRODERICK; death cause: "tubuculer abscess"; informant: Eliza MCAFEE (Greeneville); died: 26 May 1914; buried: Mt. Carmel; record (1914) # 148.

WEEMS, John; age: 64 years; married; parents: unknown; death cause: "pulmonary tuberculosis"; informant: Mrs. J.C. WEEMS (Greeneville); died: 26 Apr. 1914; buried: Pleasant Vale; record (1914) # 147.

CRAWFORD, George; age: 50 years; married; parents: Will CRAWFORD and Sinthey COB; death cause: "pulmonary tuberculosis"; died: 9 May 1914; buried: McCarty Cemetery; record (1914) # 146.

ARMANTROUT, Fred; born: 18 Dec. 1843; married; parents: Jesse ARMENTROUT (Virginia) and Rachel __ (illegible); death cause: "pulmonary tuberculosis"; informant: J.G. ARMENTROUT (Limestone) died: 4 Jun. 1914; record (1914) # 145.

KNIGHT, John; born: 27 Nov. 1854; married; parents: Will KNIGHT (South Carolina) and Mary BALL (South Carolina); death cause: "pulmonary tuberculosis"; informant: Elic JONES (Moshiem); died: 8 Jun. 1914; buried: Whitesburg; record (1914) # 144.

ISELY, Jane; born: 13 Jun. 1842 in Hawkins County; married; parents: Joseph JENKINS and Myra __ ; death cause: "dropsy"; informant: J.M. ISELY (Moshiem); died: 10 May 1914; record (1914) # 143.

MORRISON, Tilda Ann; born: 1 Jan. 1891 in Hawkins County; single; parents: Jacob MORRISON (Hawkins County) and Martha PIERCE; death cause: "lobar pneumonia"; informant: Sam MORRISON (Baileyton); died: 23 May 1914; buried: Jackson Cemetery; record (1914) # 142.

SHAW, Pinkney Monroe; born: 24 Aug. 1848; married; minister; parents: James SHAW (North Carolina) and Edith Johnson RATHDGE (North Carolina); death cause: "chronic nephritis"; informant: T.M. SHAW (Greeneville); died: 18 May 1914; record (1914) # 141.

MASSY, Edward Milburn; born: 20 Sep. 1901; parents: Guder MASSY (North Carolina) and Katherne HUNTER (North Carolina); death cause: "appendicitis, operation, peritonitis"; informant: G.F. MASSY (Greeneville); died: 14 May 1914; record (1914) # 140.

CRAWFORD, Sarah Margaret; born: 20 Jan. 1857; widow; parents: Josiah SMITH and Rebecca SHANKS; death cause: "injury to spinal column caused by a fall"; informant: Margaret A. SMITH (Jeraldstown); died: 7 Jun. 1914; buried: Ratliff Cemetery; record (1914) # 139.

MATTHEWS, Tilda Ann; born: 15 Dec. 1914; parents: S.F. MATHEWS and Ollie OTTINGER; death cause: "spinal meningitis"; informant: O.E. OTTINGER (Mohawk); died: 30 May 1914; buried: J.W. Rights; record (1914) # 138.

MARSHAL, Lendin Vincin; born: 22 Apr. 1914; parents: A.E. MARSHAL and Chassie DOUTHAT; death cause: "whooping cough"; informant: O.E. DOUTHAT (Mohawk); died: 6 Jun. 1914; record (1914) # 137.

KESTERSON, John; age: 53 years; widower; parents: Riley KESTERSON and Rachel HURLEY; death cause: "gastro enteritis"; informant: J.W. REDNOUR (Mohawk); died: 17 May 1914; record (1914) # 136.

BROWN, Lolia May; born: 2 May 1914; parents: G.W. BROWN and Effie MALONE; death cause: "congestion of lungs"; informant: J.A. BROWN (Baileyton); died: 17 May 1914; buried: Wesley Chapel; record (1914) # 135.

PAXTON, Ellen; born: 29 Dec. 1863; single; parents: Alfred PAXTON and Cattie KESLING; death cause: "atrophy of liver, stomach trouble"; informant: _ KIRK (Midway); died: 15 Apr. 1914; buried: Bible Chapel; record (1914) # 134.

SMITH, Florence Lela; born: 11 Feb. 1891; married; parents: Orville KIRK and Mit PAXTON; death cause: "child bearing, adhered placenta"; informant: John MYERS (Moshiem); died: 27 May 1914; buried: Bible Chapel; record (1914) # 133.

JONES, Infant; male; born: 16 May 1914; parents: Sheridan JONES and Sallie CARMICLE; death cause: "premature birth"; informant: R.J. GAMMON (Midway); died: 17 May 1914; buried: Midway; record (1914) # 132.

BALES, Buford; age: 12 years; parents: J.W. BALES and Laura BRUMLEY; death cause: "tuberculosis of lungs"; informant: C.E.

BALES (Greeneville); died: 2 May 1914; buried: Gass Shed; record (1914) # 131.
HAYNES, Mary Elizabeth; age: 59 years; widow; parents: James BRITTON and Hannah BRITTON; death cause: "pellagra"; informant: G.D. BRITTON (Greeneville); died: 23 May 1914; buried: Oak Grove; record (1914) # 130.
LAWING, Elbert Ambros; born: 1 Jun. 1884 in Unicoi County; single; parents: W.W. LAWING (Unicoi County) and Cena MURRAY (Unicoi County); death cause: "epilepsy"; informant: J.F. LAWING (Greeneville); died: 6 May 1914; record (1914) # 129.
GRAY, John Trig; age: 64 years; married; parents: father unknown (born, VA) and Susan LATHEM (Virginia); death cause: "enlarged prostrate and __ (Illegible); informant: Cy GRAY (Greeneville); died: 10 May 1914; buried: Meadow Creek; record (1914) # 128.
LAMB, Bertha Lois; born: 15 Apr. 1911; parents: Earnest LAMB and Nellie MOORE; death cause: illegible; informant: __ KILGORE (Greeneville); died: 11 May 1914; buried: Shilo; record (1914) # 127.
BOWMAN, Ethel; born: 17 May 1914; parents: W.F. BOWMAN and Julia FANNON; death cause: "premature"; informant: father (Greeneville); died: 18 May 1914; buried: Mt. Olive; record (1914) # 126.
MCGUIRE, Limon B.; born: 8 Apr. 1860 in Hawkins County; married; parents: Jonathan MCGUIRE and Catherine LIGHT; death cause: "pneumonia, heart disease"; informant: Mrs. L.B. MCGUIRE (Baileyton); died: 6 Mar. 1914; buried: New Lebanon: record (1914) # 348.
CARTER, Robert Taylor; born: 8 Aug. 1881; single; parents: Henry N. CARTER and Mary L. WRIGHT; death cause: "pulmonary tuberculosis"; informant: M.D. CARTER (Moshiem); died: 13 Feb. 1914; buried: Romeo, TN.; record (1914) # 349.
HAGOOD, Elizabeth; born: 17 Apr. 1831 in Hawkins County; widow; parents: __ COLDWELL (Hawkins County) and mother unknown; death cause: "chronic bronchitis"; informant: W.M. HAGOOD (Baileyton); died: 14 Feb. 1914; buried: Romeo; record (1914) # 350.
BROWN __; adult male; age: 76 years; parents: William BROWN and Margaret BROWN; death cause: "nervous exhaustion, old age"; informant: G.B. TUCKER (Baileyton); died: 25 Feb. 1914; buried: Price Chapel; record (1914) # 351.

OWENS, Melton Glover; born: 7 Jul. 1872; single; parents: Sewell V. OWENS (Sullivan County) and Mary A. ALMAN (Lynchburg, VA.); death cause: "tuberculosis"; died: 4 Jun. 1914; record (1914) # 194.

SMELCER, Martha Jane; age: "about 61 years"; born: North Carolina; married; parents: William HUX (South Carolina) and mother unknown; death cause: "chronic valvulor heart disease"; died: 7 May 1914; buried: Hartman Chapel; record (1914) # 193.

WILBURN, Ben; born: 17 May 1852 in Virginia; married; parents: Benjamin WILBURN (Virginia) and Margaret WILBURN (Virginia); death cause: "abscess of kidneys"; informant: Charles BIBLE (Midway); died: 29 Jun. 1914; buried; Bible Chapel; record (1914) # 192.

KIRK, Lemuel C.; born: 27 Mar.1857; widower; parents: Joseph KIRK and Eliza LAUGHTNER; death cause: "tuberculosis of lungs"; informant: L.V. KIRK (Moshiem); died: 24 Jun. 1914; buried: Bibb Chapel; record (1914) # 191.

STROUD, Sarah Elizabeth; born: 20 Feb. 1863; married; parents: R.W. WILKERSON and Mary OWEN; death cause: "hemiplegia"; informant: James HAUN (Mohawk); died: 20 Jun. 1914; buried: Fairview; record (1914) # 190.

STINES, J.E. Monroe; born: 30 Mar.1914; parents: R.M. STINES and Maggie BIBLE; death cause: "unknown"; informant: father (Moshiem); died: 4 Jul. 1914; record (1914) # 189.

BIBBES, Child; age: 6 year and 6 months; parents: Frank BIBBS and Nancy HANKINS; death cause: "flux"; informant: Kidwell HANKINS (Greeneville); died: 6 Jun. 1914; buried: Fairview; record (1914) # 188.

JONES, Rachel; born: 3 Jun. 1886; married; parents: W.M. LOONEY and Ema JONES; death cause: "pulmonary tuberculosis"; informant: R.E. JONES (Greeneville); died: 12 Jun. 1914; buried: Red Hill; record (1914) # 187.

HARMON, Mary; age: 24 years; married; parents: Joe M. HARMON and Sarah HARMON; death cause: "puerperal __ (illegible"); informant: J.M. HARMON (Greeneville); died: 12 Jun. 1914; buried: Kidwell; record (1914) # 186.

LYNCH, Annie Lytisa; age: 74 years; widow; parents: __ SIMPSON and mother unknown; death cause: "chronic diarrhea"; informant: W.M.

JONES (Greeneville); died: 15 Jun. 1914; buried: Kingsport, TN., record (1914) # 185.

HOLLEY, Helen; born: 21 Dec. 1912; parents: W.M. HOLLEY and Claude STOKES; death cause: "colitis"; informant: father (Greeneville); died: 15 Jun. 1914; buried: Oak Grove; record (1914) # 184.

WHITE, Sylvia Edna; born: 28 Apr. 1913; parents: Floyd H. WHITE (Randolph County, West VA.) and Vernie A. WHITE (Pendleton County, West VA.); death cause: "enteritis"; informant: father (Greeneville); died: 15 Jun. 1914; record (1914) # 183.

HOPE, Helen Leona; born: 2 Jun. 1912; parents: Lon HOPE (Hawkins County) and Annie ANDERSON; death cause: "scald"; informant: father (Greeneville); died: 18 Jun. 1914; buried: Mt. Vernon; record (1914) # 182.

BROWN, Oscar; black; born: 14 Aug. 1900; parents: Mark BROWN (South Carolina) and Vinia DENSMORE; death cause: "tuberculosis and uremia"; informant: Will BROWN (Greeneville); died: 24 Jun. 1914; buried: New Hope; record (1914) # 181.

CRISLEY (?), Emily; born: 4 Jul. 1840; widow; parents: James B__ (Cocke County) and Sallie BURGNON (Cocke County); death cause: "chronic diarrhea"; informant: Mrs. James WADDELL (Greeneville); died: 26 Jun. 1914; buried: Bershiba; record (1914) # 180.

MOWE, Jacob; age: 59 years; born: Hawkins County; married; parents: Jacob MOWE (Hawkins County) and Mandy SMITH (Hawkins County); death cause: "brights disease"; informant: Mrs. Jacob MOWE (Greeneville); died: 27 Jun. 1914; buried: Oak Grove; record #179.

RUSSELL, Sallie; age: 64 years; widow; parents: Humphries WELLS and Mariah EARNEST; death cause: "cancer, uterus and bladder"; informant: Sue RUSSELL (Greeneville); died: 27 Jun. 1914; buried: Johnson Cemetery; record (1914) # 178.

WARDON, Mary Ema; born: 8 Mar.1814; parents: Jess WARDON (Newport) and Flora ARWOOD; death cause: "malnutrition"; informant: father (Greeneville); died: 30 Jun. 1914; record (1914) # 177.

SMITH, Sarah Francis; born: 11 Mar.1862 in Washington County; married; parents: John B. WALKER (Washington County) and Margaret KEYS (Washington County); death cause: "anemia";

SMITH (Jeraldstown); died: 10 Jun. 1914; buried: Oak Grove; record (1914) # 176.
COLLINS, English; age: "about 25 years"; born: Washington County; married; parents: Jacob COLLINS (Virginia) and Ellen SMITH (Sullivan County); death cause: "measles relapse"; informant: John COLLINS (Jeraldstown); died: 23 Jun. 1914; record (1914) # 175.
CARICO, Lucy Alice; born: 17 Oct. 1853 in Sullivan County; widow; parents: unknown; death cause: "pulmonary tuberculosis"; informant: Lena CARICO (Jeraldstown); died: 20 Jun. 1914; buried: Pleasant View; record (1914) # 174.
ROGERS, Charles Newton; born: 6 Oct. 1886; single; parents: James P. ROGERS and Mattie Jane DUGGER; death cause: "lobar pneumonia"; informant: mother (Baileyton); died: 9 Jun. 1914; buried: Oak Grove; record (1914) # 173.
WHITE, Rubie Osibell; born: 22 Jun. 1914; parents: Ross WHITE and Rebecca Liza EASTEP; death cause: "jaundice"; died: 9 Jul. 1914; buried: New Lebanon Cemetery; record (1914) # 172.
DYKES, Lillie Victory; born: 21 Feb. 1910; parents: Thomas DYKES and Effie L. DIZAM; death cause: "something like diphtheria"; informant: mother (Jeroldstown); died: 5 Jul. 1914; buried: Bethany; record (1914) # 171.
NEWMAN, Joel Thomas; born: 24 May 1914; parents: Thomas NEWMAN and Grace KOONTZ; death cause: pulmonary tuberculosis, heart weakness"; informant: Jitt MAUPIN (Chuckey); died: 23 May 1914; record (1914) # 170.
BROYLES, King; black; age: "about 80 years"; born: Greene County; single; parents: Bob ALEXANDER and Mag BROYLES; death cause: "general failure, asthma"; informant: A.J. JOHNSON (Chuckey); died: 27 May 1914; record (1914) # 169.
DIXON, Thelma; born: 21 Jun. 1914; parents: G__ (illegible) DIXON (Virginia) and Ella WILHOIT; death cause: "no medical attention"; informant: P.C. PARMAN (Greeneville); died: 29 Jun. 1914; buried: Cove Creek; record (1914) # 168.
GAMMON, Eliza Ellen; age: 62 years, 2 months and 20 days; born: Cocke County; married; parents: John BLAZER (Cocke County) and Kathern OTTINGER (Cocke County); death cause: "mitral incom-

pency"; informant: L.A. GAMMON (Moshiem); died: 2 Jun. 1914; record (1914) # 167.
OTTINGER, L__ (illegible); born: 3 Mar.1864; married; parents: Jacob OTTINGER and Mary CHAPMAN; death cause: "nephritis"; informant: Essie OTTINGER (Greeneville); died: 24 Jun. 1914; buried: St. James; record (1914) # 166.
TOOMEY, Rachel; black; born: 23 Jul. 1884; single; parents: A.E. TOOMEY and Minnie DIXON; death cause: "tuberculosis, bronchitis"; informant: J.W. KIRK (Greeneville); died: 1 Jun. 1914; buried: West End Cemetery; record (1914) # 165.
WILSON, Elmira; black; born: 22 Oct. 1891; single; school teacher; parents: William Wilson and mother unknown; death cause: "pulmonary tuberculosis"; informant: J.W. KIRK (Greeneville); died: 3 Jun. 1914; buried: West End Cemetery; record (1914) # 164.
CHAPMAN, Sallie; born: 1 Jun. 1900; parents: Ed CHAPMAN and Minnie SEXTON; death cause: "accidental drowning"; informant: E.B. DOBSON (Greeneville); died: 4 Jun. 1914; buried: Shilo; record # 163.
WILLIAMS, Chassie; born: 1 Jun. 1896; married; parents: Ed CHAPMAN and Minnie SEXTON; death cause: "accidental drowning"; informant: E.B. DOBSON (Greeneville); died: 4 Jun. 1914; buried: Shilo; record (1914) # 162.
MCCALL, Louise; born: 2 Jun. 1913 in Knoxville; parents: John MCCALL and mother "unknown"; death cause: "cholera infantum"; informant: James DAVIS (Greeneville); died: 4 Jun. 1914; buried: Oak Grove; record (1914) # 161.
WESTMORELAND, Infant; male; parents: W.H. WEST (Cocke County) and Birtha PHILLIPS; death cause: "brights disease"; informant: father (Mohawk); died: 28 Jun. 1914; record (1914) # 160.
GILDON, John; age: "unknown"; soldier; single; parents: "unknown"; death cause: "organic heart trouble"; informant: J.O. CAPP (Mohawk); died: 29 Jun. 1914; buried: Mt. Hope; record (1914) # 159.
CONWAY, Mrs. Laura; born: 16 Sep. 1859; married; parents: G.B. PRICE and M.J. MALONE; death cause: "pulmonary tuberculosis"; informant: W.A. CARTER (Mohawk); died: 18 Jun. 1914; record # 158.
BROYLES, Claud; born: 6 Jun. 1914; parents: Adam BROYLES and Florence J__ (illegible); death cause: "heart failure"; informant: Robert

HILTON (Afton); died: 12 Jun. 1914; buried: Union Chapel; record (1914) # 157.

GRAY, Andy C.; age: 84 years; born: Greene County; widower; parents: not stated; death cause: "paralysis, left side"; informant: Cecil GRAY (Chuckey); died: 28 Jun. 1914; buried: Pleasant Hill; record # 156.

HILTON, Elizabeth; age: 62 years; born: Carter County; single; parents: father not stated and Elizabeth HILTON; death cause: "cancer"; informant: G.M. MILLER (Chuckey); died: 15 Jun. 1914; buried: Union Chapel; record (1914) # 155.

GRAY, Eva; born: 29 May 1889; divorced; parents: father not stated and Amanda GRAY; death cause: "organic heart trouble"; informant: Walter GRAY (Chuckey); died: 14 Apr. 1914; buried: Union Chapel; record (1914) # 154.

RODGERS, Theodore Roosevelt; black; born: 10 Sep. 1913; parents: William RODGERS and Nellie S. RODGERS; death cause: "membranous croup"; informant: mother (Baileyton); died: 4 Jul. 1914; buried: Zion Cemetery; record (1914) # 153.

BLACK, Robert S.; born: 7 Jan. 1913; parents: Billie BLACK and Corda LAMBERT; death cause: "cholera infantum"; informant: father (Midway); died: 14 Jul. 1914; buried: St. Joseph Chapel; record # 235.

DOUTHAT, Vincin Aster; born: 22 Apr. 1914; parents: Robert Powell DOUTHAT and Nora STROND; death cause: "acute gastritis"; informant: J.W. DYER (Mohawk); died: 17 Jul. 1914; buried: Fairview; record (1914) # 234.

CRUMLEY, Benjamin Douglas; born: 24 Dec. 1866; married; parents: Abraham CRUMLEY and Nancy Ann JUSTIS; death cause: "typhoid fever"; informant: J.S. WHITE (Greeneville); died: 25 Jul. 1914; buried: Gass Shed; record (1914) # 235.

STARNES, Allis; female; born: 8 Jun. 1870; widow; parents: A.B. LOVE and Katherine MCCURRY; death cause: "uterine cancer"; informant: Vern STARNES (Baileyton); died: 5 Jul. 1914; buried: Salem; record (1914) # 232.

DUNN, Susan; age: 63 years; married; parents: William HAUN (Jefferson County) and mother not stated; death cause: "died from shock of daughter's death"; informant: Sam DUNN (Chuckey); died: 18 Jul. 1914; buried: Union Temple; record (1914) # 231.

WAIN (?), Elizabeth; born: 3 Jul. 1950; widow; parents: __ MOON and mother "unknown"; death cause: "cancer of jaw"; informant: J.C. MARSHALL (Chuckey); died: 3 Jul. 1914; buried: Doty Cemetery; record (1914) # 230.

JOHNSON, Lura Anna Cutshall; born: 6 Mar.1887; married; parents: Andrew J. CUTSHALL and Sarah MACE; death cause: not stated; died: 16 Apr. 1914; buried: Cutshall Cemetery; record (1914) # 229.

WALLIN, Anietta; born: 15 Jul. 1914; parents: Ben WALLIN and Gertie PARHAM; death cause: not stated; informant: P.C. PARHAM (Greeneville); died: 15 Jul. 1914; record (1914) # 228.

CUTSHALL, Paulen; female; born: 11 May 1914; parents: Elbert Anderson CUTSHALL and Ella Bell STILL; death cause: "unknown"; informant: Ella MONTGOMERY (Greeneville); died: 30 May 1914; record (1914) # 227.

CUTSHALL, Maudie Pauline; born: 11 May 1914; parents: Elbert Anderson CUTSHALL and Ella Bell STILL; death cause: "unknown"; died: 21 May 1914; record (1914) # 402.

PINKRTON, Mollie; born: 5 Mar.1914; parents: Robert PINKRTON and Lissie WHITE; death cause: "premature birth"; informant: C.W. MCCULLUM (Bulls Gap); died: 5 Mar.1914; buried: Bulls Gap; record (1914) # 226.

CANTRELL, Mary Bell; age: 31 years, 9 months and 12 days; parents: Joseph LYNCH (Hamblen County) and __ CLIMER (Hamblen County); death cause: "puerperal convulsions"; died: 15 Jul. 1914; buried: McCullum Cemetery, Hamblen County; record (1914) # 225.

RADER, Florence Addie; born: 13 Apr. 1914; parents: Uless G. RADER and Susa DAVIS (Cynthia, KY.); death cause: "entero colitis, rickets"; died: 16 Jul. 1914; buried: Bulls Gap; record (1914) # 224.

SMELCER, Kironie N.; male; age: 29 years, 10 months and 7 days; parents: Henry SMELCER and Jane REYNOLDS; death cause: "tuberculosis"; informant: Horton JONES (Moshiem); died: 17 Jul. 1914; buried: Mt. Sinai; record (1914) # 223.

BRIGHT, Eliza; born: 28 Jul. 1869; married; parents: George BURNETT and Eliza JONES; death cause: "pulmonary __ (illegible)"; informant: W.M. BRIGHT (Greeneville); died: 28 Jul. 1914; buried: Greeneville; record (1914) # 222.

LAWS, Infant; black; born: 30 Jul. 1914; parents: Tom LAWS (North Carolina) and Lillie PAYNE; death cause: "premature, 7 month"; informant: father (Greeneville); died: 30 Jul. 1914; buried: Wesley; record (1914) # 221.

BOWMAN, A.J.; born: 19 Jul. 1848; married; parents: William BOWMAN and Margaret HARDIE; death cause: "chronic cystitis"; informant: S.A. BOWMAN (Greeneville); died: 30 Jul. 1914; buried: Mt. Olive; record (1914) # 220.

BABB, Trixie Maud; born: 2 Sep. 1913; parents: Joe BABB and Laura HANKINS; death cause: "dysentery"; informant: J.M. BROWN (Greeneville) died: 31 Jul. 1914; buried: Gass Shed; record # 218.

HUGHES, Grant; born: 14 Feb. 1867; married; dentist; parents: Archibald HUGHES and Deborah HOWS; death cause: illegible; informant: Thomas HUGHES (Jeroldstown); died: 15 Jul. 1914; record (1914) # 218.

HOWARD, Hamilton Baldwin; born: 7 Jul. 1842 in Johnson County; married; parents: Samuel HOWARD (Johnson County) and Lukinsie BOWMAN; death cause: "tuberculosis of lungs and bowels"; informant: Joseph S. HOWARD (Jonesborough); died: 8 Aug. 1914; buried: Mt. Bethel; record (1914) # 217.

PRICE, James Edwin; age: not stated; born: South Carolina; widower; farmer; parents: not stated; death cause: "pneumonia"; died: 31 Jul. 1914; buried: South Carolina; record (1914) # 215.

RICKER, Virtie; female; age: 6 years; parents: Columbus RICKER (North Carolina) and Susan DAVIS; death cause: not stated; informant: C.C. RICKER (Greeneville); died: 8 Jul. 1914; buried: Cove Creek; record (1914) # 214.

KELLER, Bonnie; born: 10 Jan. 1913; parents: J.B. KELLER and Virgie DUNBAR; death cause: illegible; informant: Dailey WILHOIT (Chuckey); died: 21 Jul. 1914; buried: Union Gap; record (1914) # 213.

CLARK, Ellen; age: 74 years; widow; parents: father not stated (Johnson County) and mother not stated; death cause: "chronic dysentery"; informant: Nick SHAW (Afton); died: 1 Aug. 1914; record # 212.

HAMPTON, Margaret; born: 7 Mar.1847; married; parents: W.M. COOLEY and Elender BOWMAN (North Carolina); death cause:

"acute indigestion"; informant: D.W. FILLERS (Greeneville); died: 14 Jun. 1914; buried: Union Chapel; record (1914) # 211.
HENSLEY, Frank Winston; born: 8 Oct. 1912; parents: Thomas H. HENSLEY and Lizzie MITCHELL; death cause: illegible; died: 8 Jun. 1914; buried: Union Chapel; record (1914) # 210.
INGLE, Maud Duncan; born: 21 Jan. 1897 in Sullivan County; single; parents: Ellis B. INGLE (Sullivan County) and Martha HITE (Sullivan County); death cause: "pulmonary tuberculosis"; informant: Crocket FULKERSON (Jeraldstown); died: 12 Jul. 1914; buried: Rock Springs; record (1914) # 209.
LOWE, Alonzo; born: 4 Jan. 1914; parents: George LOWE and Lillie WILLETT; death cause: "gastro entero colitis"; informant: father (Greeneville); died: 1 Jul. 1914; buried: Oak Grove; record # 421.
SAVILLE, Cora N.; born: 21 Sep. 1880; married; parents: John LISTER and Annie GRIGSBY (Hawkins County); death cause: "obstruction of bowels"; informant: W.T. SAVILLE (Bulls Gap); died: 7 Jul. 1914; buried: White Pine; record (1914) # 422.
BARNET, Lottie; born: 10 Mar.1849 in South Carolina; widow; parents: "unknown"; death cause: "chronic diarrhea"; informant: John FOSHIE (Greeneville); died: 14 Jul. 1914; buried: Gass Shed; record # 423.
EVANS, Hillie; black; born: 22 Jul. 1872; married; parents: John SUMMERS (South Carolina) and Winnie GERDUER (South Carolina); death cause: "tuberculosis"; informant: Dave EVANS (Greeneville); died: 15 Jul. 1914; buried: New Hope; record (1914) # 424.
HANNAH, John W.; born: 17 Feb. 1832 in Roanoke, VA.; married; parents: George HANNAH (Roanoke) and Elizabeth STOVER (Roanoke); death cause: "brights disease; informant: Mrs. J.G. MCFERRIN (Bristol); died: 19 Jul. 1914; buried: Shilo; record # 425.
HOLT, Marion; born: __ Mar.1898; parents: Ed HOLT and Ida HARRISON; death cause: "typhoid infection"; informant: Scot HOLT (Greeneville); died: 22 Jul. 1914; buried: Cedar Hill; record # 426.
CARTER, Infant; male; parents: Brolson CARTER and Tenia CARSON; death cause: "born too soon"; informant: J.M. MYSINGER (Greeneville) died: 20 Jul. 1914; buried: Mt. Pleasant; record (1914) # 427.
LEE, Bonnie; black; born: 23 Feb. 1887; married; parents: Rufus VANCE and Hannah BROYLES; death cause: "tuberculosis"; infor-

mant: Loyd FARNSWORTH (Greeneville); died: 23 Jul. 1914; buried: Colored Graveyard; record (1914) # 428.

ELLENBURG, Henry; age: 26 years; widower; parents: John ELLENBURG and Harriett D__ (illegible); death cause: "obstruction of bowels"; informant: L.D. ELLENBURG (Greeneville); died: 24 Jul. 1914; buried: St. James; record (1914) # 429.

SMITH, Hailey; born: 27 Jun. 1906; parents: J.D. SMITH and Addie SLAGLE; death cause: "membranous croup"; informant: father (Greeneville); died: 26 Jul. 1914; record (1914) # 430.

JACKSON, Mary Alice; born: 13 Oct. 1847; married; parents: Andrew J. LOGAN and Mahach LOUDERBACH (Hawkins County); death cause: "post operative abscess, surgery for fibroid tumor"; informant: J.K.P. JACKSON (Jeroldstown); died: 3 Sep. 1914; buried: Bethany; record (1914) # 431.

MORRISON, Infant; female; born: 7 Aug. 1914; parents: father not stated and Francis MORRISON (Hawkins County); death cause: "stillborn"; informant: Alfred HARRIS (Baileyton); died: 7 Aug. 1914; buried: Salem; record (1914) # 432.

HARRIS, Francis Morrison; age: 19 years, 3 months and 18 days; born: Hawkins County; married; parents: Lace BARNET (Hawkins County) and Mary MORRISON (Hawkins County); death cause: "septicemia and typhoid fever"; informant: A.L. HARRISON (Baileyton); died: 18 Aug. 1914; buried: Salem; record (1914) # 433.

IVINS, Alpha Carolina; born: 7 Jan. 1837; widow; parents: Robert REED and Mary REED; death cause: "abscess in lung, tuberculosis probably"; died: 7 Sep. 1914; buried: Liberty Hill; record (1914) # 434.

KILDAY, Willard Lee; born: 13 Aug. 1914; parents: Alexander H. KILDAY and Sarah Maud KENNEY; death cause: "7 month child"; informant: M.H. DAVENPORT (Baileyton); died: 13 Aug. 1914; buried: Mountain Valley; record (1914) # 435.

SHANKS, G.M.D.; born: 1 Nov. 1841; married; parents: Ambrose SHANKS and Sarah FRACKER; death cause: "hemorrhage of lungs"; informant: C.D. KELLER (Afton); died: 13 Aug. 1914; buried: Gass Shed; record (1914) # 436.

JONES, Anna May; born: 15 Feb. 1914; parents: Dave JONES and __ LANE; death cause: "still born"; informant: father (Afton); died: 15 Feb. 1914; buried: Doty Cemetery; record (1914) # 437.

SOLOMAN, Infant; born: 14 May 1914; parents: Huston SOLOMAN and Frankie GENTRY (North Carolina); death cause: "still born"; died: 15 (?) May 1914; buried: Mt. Olivet; record (1914) # 438.

JACK, Melvin Leroy; born: 30 Mar.1854 in New Hampshire; married; furniture factory supervisor; parents: Ira T. JACK (Maine) and Mechitable HASKER (New Hampshire); death cause: "nephritis"; informant: M.L. JACK Jr. (Greeneville); died: 24 Aug. 1914; buried: Pennsylvania; record (1914) # 439.

MOORE, Mary Elizabeth; born: 21 May 1862 in Illinois; married; parents: James DOLTON (Ireland) and Mary YOUNG (Louisville, KY.); death cause: "carcinoma of uterus"; informant: W.P. MOORE (Greeneville); died: 26 Aug. 1914; buried: Oak Grove; record # 440.

SNAPP, Robert J.; age: 70 years; married; merchant; parents: W.M. SNAPP (Cocke County) and Edilene SNAPP (Kingsport); death cause: "nervous exhaustion"; died: 27 Aug. 1914; buried: Oak Grove: record (1914) # 441.

SEATON, Florence; born: 29 Jun. 1914; parents: Sidney SEATON and Florence GIBBS; death cause: "nephritis"; informant: Dave GIBBS (Greeneville); died: 31 Aug. 1914; buried: Cove Creek; record # 442.

BAKER, Nannie E.; born: 16 May 1861; married; parents: Jim RHEA and mother not stated; death cause: "diarrhea believed from malignant tumor"; died: 6 Sep. 1914; buried: Pleasant View; record (1914) # 443.

MITCHELL, William; age: 39 years; married; parents: Edward MITCHELL and Amanda GRAY; death cause: "typhoid fever"; died: 14 Aug. 1914; buried: Mt. Bethel; record (1914) # 444; (note this may be a duplicate of record #447 below).

BARKLY, Infant; black; born: 8 Sep. 1914; parents: George BARKLY and Hattie LOCK; death cause: "premature child"; informant: father (Chuckey); died: 8 Sep. 1914; record (1914) # 445.

EARNEST, Rhoda; born: 2 Mar.1852; widow; parents; __ INMAN and mother unknown; death cause: "apoplexy"; informant: L. ELLIS (Chuckey); died: 22 Aug. 1914; record (1914) # 446.

MITCHELL, William R.; born: 6 Feb. 1875; married; parents: E.B. MITCHELL (Washington County) and Mandy GRAY (Illinois); death cause: "typhoid fever"; informant: Edward PENCE (Limestone); died: 14 Aug. 1914; buried: Mt. Bethel; record (1914) # 447.

HOLT, ___; adult male; born: 16 Mar.1873 in Floyd County, VA.; single; parents: Sparl HOLT (Floyd County, VA.) and Eliza Jane COLLINS (Floyd County, VA.); death cause: "typhoid fever"; informant: father (Afton); died: 21 Sep. 1914; buried: Mt. Zion; record (1914) # 448.

BROWN, Arrie; female; born: 5 Jul. 1863 in Indiana; widow; parents: Joseph A. KIRK and Susanna HARMON; death cause: "chronic ___ (illegible) of bowels"; informant: Kyle BROWN (Midway); died: 10 Aug. 1914; buried: Moshiem; record (1914) # 449.

HAYSE, Paggie; black; age: "about 70 years"; born in South Carolina; widow; parents: "unknown"; death cause: "cerebral apoplexy"; informant: Amon HAYS (Jeraldstown); died: 10 Aug. 1914; buried: Pleasant Vale; record (1914) # 450.

HAYS, Harriett; born: 16 Oct. 1827 in Greene County; widow; parents: Samuel WALKER and Mary GRAY; death cause: "paralysis" died: 23 Aug. 1914; buried: Bethesda; record (1914) # 451.

ALEXANDER, James; black; born: 5 Nov. 1913; parents: Jess ALEXANDER and Chassie WOODFIN; death cause: "pneumonia"; informant: father (Greeneville); died: 2 Aug. 1914; buried: Greeneville; record (1914) # 452.

ASTES (?), Thomas; black; age: 71 years; born: Greeneville, SC.; shoemaker; parents: "unknown"; death cause: "rheumatism, senile debility"; informant: Ike BARNETT (Greeneville); died: 2 Aug. 1914; record (1914) # 453.

SLEDAM, Mae; born: 5 Dec. 1910; parents: father not stated and ___ HENDRIX (Virginia); death cause: "pneumonia"; informant: S.S. KILGORE (Greeneville); died: 7 Aug. 1914; buried: Orphans Home; record (1914) # 454.

SHAW, Thomas Greene; born: 23 Apr. 1847; married; parents: Thomas SHAW and Nellie CANNON (Virginia); death cause: "tuberculosis"; informant: L. SHAW (Greeneville); died: 19 Aug. 1914; record # 455.

HOLT, John; age: 80 years; born: Greene County; widower; parents: Jacob HOLT and mother "unknown"; death cause: "cancer of liver"; informant: Ed HOLT (Greeneville); died: 13 Aug. 1914; buried: Cedar Hill; record (1914) # 456.

BOWMAN, Guy; born: 17 Mar.1913; parents: W.F. BOWMAN and Julia FANNON; death cause: "enteritis"; informant: J.H. JONES (Greeneville); died: 18 Aug. 1914; buried: Red Hill; record # 457.

ANDERSON, Melinda; born: 21 May 1855 in Hawkins County; widow; parents: James HUGHES (Rogersville) and Laura HUGHES (Hawkins County); death cause: "pellagra"; died: 20 Aug. 1914; buried: Oak Grove; record (1914) # 458.

BEASON, H__ (illegible); black; female; born: 14 Oct. 1913; parents: Harry BROWN and Mamie WILLIAMS; death cause: "enteritis"; died: 20 Aug. 1914; record (1914) # 459.

YOUNG, Eliza; age: "about 60 years"; widow; parents: not stated; death cause: "pellagra"; died: 22 Sep. 1914; buried: Poor Farm; record # 460.

PRESNELL, Bertha; born: 29 May 1911; parents: Dave PRESNELL and Prescilla HUDDLESTON; death cause: "pyemia"; informant: father (Greeneville); died: 27 Sep. 1914; buried: Oak Grove; record # 461.

MATHIS, Infant; male; born: 26 Sep. 1914; parents: Wilber MATHIS and Stella BRIGMAN (North Carolina); death cause: "still born"; informant: father (Greeneville); died: 26 Sep. 1914; buried: Mt. Vernon; record (1914) # 462.

GIRDNER, Catherine; age: 50 years; widow; parents: John MARSHALL and mother "unknown"; death cause: "pulmonary tuberculosis"; informant: John GERDNER (Greeneville); died: 26 Sep. 1914; buried: Hebron; record (1914) # 463.

KELLER, Mary Jane; age: 70 years, 4 months and 2 days; widow; parents: Javis KELLEY and Lavona FRESHOUR; death cause: "burn"; informant: Mrs. Birtie HOUSTON (Greeneville); died: 25 Sep. 1914; buried: Bersheba; record (1914) # 464.

COOPER, Rachel; born: __ Feb. 1836 in Greene County; married; parents: Thomas PARK and __ DOBSON; death cause: "rheumatism, acute indigestion"; informant: R.N. COOPER (Greeneville); died: 23 Sep. 1914; buried: Oak Grove; record (1914) # 465.

FREEMAN, Catherine; black; born: 19 Mar.1914; parents: Jim FREEMAN (Knoxville) and Liza ROLLINS; death cause: "tubercular meningitis"; informant: father (Greeneville); died: 22 Sep. 1914; record (1914) # 466.

HARMON, Elizabeth Beatrice; born: 10 Jun. 1914; parents: J.F. HARMON and Mattie C__ (illegible); death cause: not stated; informant: father (Greeneville); died: 19 Sep. 1914; buried: Wells Cemetery; record (1914) # 467.

BROWN, Infant; male; parents: Monroe BROWN (Johnson County) and Nancy MAINES (Hawkins County); death cause: "unknown"; informant: father (Greeneville); died: 7 Sep. 1914; buried: Oak Grove; record (1914) # 468.

DUGGER, J. Paul; born: 7 Oct. 1914; parents: R.R. DUGGER and Nettie KILDAY; death cause: "unknown"; informant: Newt DUGGER (Baileyton); died: 9 Oct. 1914; buried: Lebanon; record (1914) # 469.

PIERCE, Sarah F.; born: 28 Feb. 1845 in Sullivan County; widow; parents: William POWELL (Sullivan County) and Sarah RHINE POWELL (Sullivan County); death cause: "organic heart trouble"; informant: Florence PIERCE (Bulls Gap); died: 4 Oct. 1914; buried: Hawkins; record (1914) # 470.

KENNEY, Colman Campbell; born: 12 Feb. 1847; widower; parents: James KENNEY and Elizabeth WEEMS; death cause: "pellagra"; informant: J.M. KENNEY (Greeneville); died: 24 Sep. 1914; buried: Gass Shed; record (1914) # 471.

WILHOIT, Nancy; age: 96 years; born: Greene County; parents: "unknown"; death cause: not stated; informant: S.C. WARE (Greeneville); died: 18 May 1914; buried: Cove Creek; record # 472.

WHITE, Minnie Kate; born: 9 Aug. 1885; married; parents: Jacob Lafayette MATTHEWS (Warrensburg) and Susan Victoria COURTNEY (Warrensburg); death cause: "chronic diarrhea"; informant: father (Mohawk); died: 5 Sep. 1914; buried: Fairview; record (1914) # 472.

RHODES, Alberta; born: 12 Sep. 1914; parents: James RHODES and Nellie SUSONG; death cause: "memaina"; informant: father (Mohawk); died: 20 Sep. 1914; buried: Hamblen County; record (1914) # 474.

HYBARGER, Infant; male; parents: I.A. HARBARGER and Katherine Josephine SIZEMORE; death cause: "foot presentation"; informant: father (Midway); died: 19 Sep. 1914; buried: Moshiem; record # 475.

MITCHELL, William R.; age: 39 years; married; parents: "unknown"; death cause: "gall stones, typhoid fever"; died: 14 Aug. 1914; buried: Chuckey; record (1914) # 476.

GOOD, Michell W.; born: 11 Jan. 1844; widower; parents: Joseph GOOD and Callie BURKETT; death cause: "diarrhea and pulmonary tuberculosis"; informant: Mrs. Scott SHOWMOR (Limestone); died: 26 Aug. 1914; buried: Oakland Cemetery; record (1914) # 477.

MORRISON, __ (illegible) Ray; male; born: 16 Mar.1913; parents: J.B. MORRISON and Mae LONG (Hawkins County); death cause: "gastro enteritis"; informant: father (Greeneville); died: 30 Sep. 1914; buried: Mt. Vernon; record (1914) # 478.

SMELCER, Alice; born: 4 Apr. 1895; single; parents: "unknown"; death cause: "accidental burning from explosion of oil can, kindling fire"; died: 24 Sep. 1914; record (1914) # 479.

BARNES, Joseph; age: 75 years, 11 months and 2 days; born: Washington College, TN.; married; parents: Mashey BARNES (Washington College) and Elizabeth STEP (Washington County); death cause: "tuberculosis"; informant: Elmer W. BARNES (Chuckey); died: 22 Sep. 1914; buried: Washington County; record (1914) # 480.

GRUBBS, Willie; born: 5 Oct. 1914; parents: Frank GRUBBS and Nellie G__ (illegible); death cause: "pulmonary collapse"; informant: father (Afton); died: 8 Oct. 1914; record (1914) # 266.

STATEN, Lucy Mataline; born: 2 Oct. 1910; parents: Sam STATEN and Jennie WILLIAMS; death cause: "membranous croup"; informant: J.C. MARSHALL (Chuckey); died: 2 Oct. 1914; buried: Liberty Hill; record (1914) # 265.

BOWERS, Eva Nell; born: 8 Feb. 1914; parents: Charles BOWERS and Rhoda FORD (Sullivan County); death cause: "whooping cough"; informant: father (Baileyton); died: 15 Sep. 1914; record (1914) # 264/483.

HECK, Charles; age: 40 years, born: Hawkins County; married; parents: Stewart HECK (Hawkins County) and __ SMITH (Hawkins County);

death cause: "pleurisy"; informant: Mrs. Charles HECK (Baileyton); died: 3 Nov. 1914; buried: County Line; record (1914) # 484.

SMITH, Grace B.; born: __ Jun. 1912; parents: Charles SMITH and __ WILLIS; death cause: "diphtheria"; informant: father (Baileyton); died: 22 Oct. 1914; buried: Price Cemetery; record (1914) # 485.

COLLINS, James; age: 21 (?) years; single, saw miller; parents: Joseph COLLINS and Catherine HOLT; death cause: "falling on saw causing instant death"; died: 9 Oct. 1914; record (1914) # 486.

MORRISON, Elmer; born: 11 Sep. 1904; parents: Mack GADDIS and Anna MORRISON; death cause: "been treated for typhoid fever"; informant: Alex DIXON (Greeneville); died: 13 Sep. 1914; buried: Fairview; record (1914) # 487.

LANE, Katherine; born: 27 Dec. 1847; married; parents: John MCCURRY and Hannah MORELOCK; death cause: "pulmonary hemorrhage"; informant: J.F. LANE (Greeneville); died: 1 Oct. 1914; buried: Gass Shed; record (1914) # 488.

MALONE, Rebecca; born: 19 Sep. 1846 in North Carolina; married; parents: Joseph HOLTSCLAW (North Carolina) and Armentie AUSTIN (North Carolina); death cause: "pneumonia fever"; informant: Elmer NEAL (Baileyton); buried: Gass Shed; record (1914) # 489.

TOMPSON, Marthie; born: 8 Jun. 1836 in Hawkins County; widow; parents: David STUART (Hawkins County) and mother unknown; death cause: "dropsy"; informant: E.P. TOMPSON (Greeneville); died: 9 Oct. 1914; record (1914) # 490.

SHACKLEFORD, Infant; female; parents: John H. SHACKLEFORD and Mary HOLLAND; death cause: "still born"; informant: father (Baileyton); born/died: 16 Oct. 1914; record (1914) # 491.

DUNN, Georgia; born: 31 Jan. 1885; married; parents: George KING and Armenta TERFINE; death cause: "tuberculosis, pregnant"; informant: S.N. DUNN (Chuckey); died: 28 Oct. 1914; buried: Union Temple; record (1914) # 492.

HALL, David E.; born: 22 Apr. 1852; married; parents: John HALL and Catherine CRAWFORD (Hawkins County); death cause: "pulmonary tuberculosis"; informant: Elizabeth ARMSTRONG (Fall Branch); died: 25 Oct. 1914; buried: Lovelace; record (1914) # 493.

BOWLIN, Peter Filmore; born: 8 Mar.1880; single; parents: father not stated and Nancy BOWLIN; death cause: "typhoid fever"; informant: Bell BOWLIN (Baileyton); died: 21 Oct. 1914; buried: Lebanon; record (1914) # 494.

ADAMS, Viola; born: 1 Mar.1894; single; parents: __ (illegible) ADAMS and Mary RUSTON; death cause: "pulmonary tuberculosis"; informant: Frank CRAWFORD (Telford); died: 29 Oct. 1914; record (1914) # 495.

MARION, Lula Bell; born: 23 Jan. 1890; married; parents: R.L. WALTER (North Carolina) and Hannah __ (illegible); death cause: "pulmonary tuberculosis"; informant: Sallie MORRIS (Limestone); died: 28 Sep. 1914; buried: Pleasant Vale; record (1914) # 496.

TRELLORS, Woodrow Wilson; born: 25 Sep. 1913; parents: Byrd TRELLORS and Lotta HOLT; death cause: "no medical attention"; informant: J.S. TRELLORS (Greeneville); died: 1 Oct. 1914; buried: Cove Creek; record (1914) # 497.

CARPER, Walter; black; born: 6 Oct. 1883 in Virginia; married; parents: Moses CARPER (Virginia) and mother unknown; death cause: "alcoholism, nephritis"; informant: Will DUNCAN (Greeneville); died: 8 Oct. 1914; record (1914) # 498.

BAKER, Johnathan Noah; age: 75 years and 8 months; born: "Landon County, VA."; married; minister; parents: not stated; death cause: "angina pectoris"; informant: Mrs. Fannie BAKER (Greeneville); died: 9 Oct. 1914; buried: Fall Branch; record (1914) # 499.

ALL__ (illegible), Alexander; black; born: 17 Apr. 1837 in South Carolina; married; parents: "unknown"; death cause: "tuberculosis"; informant: Carl ALL__ (illegible); died: 12 Oct. 1914; buried: Wesley Cemetery; record (1914) # 500.

CARTER, Liea Anna Ellen; born: 24 Sep. 1914; parents: Berton CARTER and Nona KEY; death cause: "without medical attention"; informant: J.M MYSINGER (Greeneville); died: 13 Oct. 1914; buried: New Bethel; record (1914) # 501.

PIERCE, Floyd; black; born: 24 Jul. 1871; married; parents: Alfred PIERCE and Elizabeth RICHARDSON (Virginia); death cause: "unknown"; informant: Mrs. Floyd PIERCE (Greeneville); died: 22 Oct. 1914; record (1914) # 502.

KYLE, Houston; black; age: "about 60 years"; born in Rogersville; married; parents: "unknown"; death cause: "chronic diarrhea"; informant: G.R. CARTER (Greeneville); died: 30 Oct. 1914; record (1914) # 503.

HARMON, Nannie; born: 27 Jul. 1878; married; parents: J.R. HUISTONON (?) and N.J. DLON (?); death cause: "tuberculosis"; died: 7 Nov. 1914; buried: Drake; record (1914) # 504.

WALKER, Elizabeth Jane; age: 67 years; single; parents: William WALKER and __ WARD; death cause: "tuberculosis and old age"; informant C.W. LONG (Whitesburg); died: 1 Nov. 1914; buried: Mt. Hope; record (1914) # 505.

SMELCER, Infant; male; parents: James Claude SMELCER and Susan Kate HURLEY; death cause: "premature birth"; informant: mother (Midway); born/died: 26 Oct. 1914; buried: Crosby Cemetery; record (1914) # 506.

COLE, Andrew; born: 2 Sep. 1909 in "Dakota"; parents: Robert COLE (Virginia) and Minnie KEICHER; death cause: "overdose of morphine"; informant: Aaron KEICHER (Midway); died: 25 Oct. 1914; buried: Sinking Creek; record (1914) # 507.

KIRK, Ellen; born: 30 May 1831 in Tennessee; widow; parents: Joseph BLACK (Virginia) and Ellen BLACK (Tennessee); death cause: "edema and heart trouble"; died: 24 Oct. 1914; buried: 19th District; record (1914) # 508.

PACK, Infant; male; parents: Noah PACK and Lydia KESS; death cause: "still born"; born/died: 10 Oct. 1914; buried: St. Joseph Chapel; record (1914) # 509.

COOTER, Maggie Mae Ellen; born: 26 Oct. 1914; parents: James E. COOTER and Laura V. KENNEY; death cause: "typhoid fever"; informant: father (Moshiem); died: 26 Oct. 1914; buried: Prices Chapel; record (1914) # 510.

KITE, G.W.; born: 31 Oct. 1856; married; parents: John KITE (Hawkins County) and Polly Ann SMITH; death cause: "epithelioma of bladder"; informant: Robert KITE (Moshiem); died: 15 Oct. 1914; buried: Mt. Carmel; record (1914) # 511.

HENDRIX, Otis; black; age: 18 years; born: Georgia; road laborer; parents: "unknown"; death cause: "gunshot wound"; informant: B.T.

ROBINSON (Moshiem); died: 13 Oct. 1914; buried: Midway; record (1914) # 512.

REYNOLDS, Infant; born: 2 Nov. 1914; parents: John REYNOLDS and Berthy SUTTLES; death cause: "premature birth"; informant: Bettie RICKER (Moshiem); died: 3 Nov. 1914; buried: Pine Grove; record (1914) # 513.

MCNEW, Infant; male; parents: Charley MCNEW (North Carolina) and Maude HUMPHREY; death cause: not stated; informant: C.W. MCNEW; died: 6 Oct. 1914; buried: Hartmans; record (1914) # 514.

GUNTER, Rubie; male; born: 15 Sep. 1900; parents: Caney H. GUNTER (Madison County, NC.) and Sarah A. GIRDNER; death cause: "typhoid fever"; informant: father (Greeneville); died: 22 Oct. 1914; record # 515.

KING, Charles J.; born: 26 Feb. 1894; single; parents: E.S. KING and Nora HAWKINS; death cause: "suicide"; informant: father (Moshiem); died: 26 Jul. 1914; record (1914) # 516.

SELF, Infant; female; parents: Robert M. SELF and Bertha Jane DYER (Washington County); death cause: "premature, 7th month"; informant: father (Bulls Gap); born/died: 9 Oct. 1914; buried: Gap Creek; record (1914) # 517.

RADER, Cornelius; born: 10 Jan. 1868; single; parents: William RADER and Haney RADER; death cause: "pleurisy and pneumonia"; informant: William STEPHENS (Midway); died: 1 Dec. 1914; buried: Timber Ridge; record (1914) # 518.

WILSON, Ollie; born: 21 Dec. 1879; married; parents: Kin JONES and Mary POTTER; death cause: "puerperal peritonitis"; informant: Charley WILSON (Mohawk); died: 4 Dec. 1914; buried: Russleville; record (1914) # 519.

MCCRACKEN, Robert; born: 11 Apr. 1885; single; parents: James MCCRACKEN and Ted (?) GRAY; death cause: "spinal disease"; informant: father (Afton); died: 18 Nov. 1914; record (1914) # 520.

LUSTER, Peter; age: 62 years, 1 month and 29 days; married; parents: James LUSTER and Larinda C. HARMON; death cause: "tuberculosis"; informant: Mrs. Jennie LUSTER (Afton); died: 7 Nov. 1914; buried: Mt. Pleasant; record (1914) # 521.

BROWN, Clara Ruby; born: 2 Dec. 1892; married; parents: Robert

HONEYCUT and Hariet HYDER; death cause: "tuberculosis"; informant; Robert BROWN (Chuckey); died: 29 Nov. 1914; buried: Mt. Zion; record (1914) # 522.

LOVE, Jay; black; age: 14 months; parents: Hube LOVE and Ida WELLS; death cause: "meningitis"; informant: Fred GRAY (Greeneville); died: 1 Nov. 1914; record (1914) # 523.

PAYNE, Charlie; born: __ Sep. 1909; parents: H.M. PAYNE (North Carolina) and Bessie PAYNE; death cause: "scald"; informant: H.C. PAYNE (Greeneville); died: 2 Nov. 1914; buried: Cove Creek; record (1914) # 524.

MCCOY, J.W.; age: 76 years; widower; parents: "unknown"; death cause: "cancer"; informant: H.C. BRITTON (Greeneville); died: 4 Nov. 1914; buried: Mt. Zion; record (1914) # 525.

LANE, Sallie; born: 5 Oct. 1868; married; parents: William HARRIS and Tennie __ (illegible); death cause: "tuberculosis"; informant: Alf LANE (Greeneville); died: 5 Nov. 1914; buried: Oak Grove; record # 526.

DAVIS, Willie; age: 3 years; parents: John DAVIS (Washington County) and Sarah TREADWAY (Washington County); death cause: "no medical attention"; informant: Joe COGDILL (Greeneville); died: 5 Nov. 1914; record (1914) # 527.

BROWN, Sudie Mae; age: 8 years; parents: W.D. BROWN and Lizzie BABB; death cause: "pneumonia fever"; informant: father (Greeneville); died: 11 Nov. 1914; buried: Cross Anchor; record (1914) # 528.

BROOKS, Alfred; born: 30 Sep. 1832 in Virginia; widower; parents: Joseph BROOKS (North Carolina) and Sallie SMITH (North Carolina); death cause: "pneumonia fever"; informant: T.W. BROOKS (Greeneville); died: 12 Nov. 1914; buried: Gass Shed; record (1914) # 529.

AYERS, David Jones; born: 13 Feb. 1872; married; parents: Crofford AYERS and Lila JONES (Cocke County); death cause: "disease of kidney and bladder"; informant: Mrs. David AYERS (Warnsburg); died: 18 Nov. 1914; record (1914) # 530.

LANCASTER, John B.; born: 29 Sep. 1914; parents: Eustis A. LANCASTER (Blacksburg, VA.) and Mamie HOLLOWAY (Knoxville); death cause: "premature birth"; informant: father (Greeneville); died: 19 Nov. 1914; record (1914) # 531.

BOSWELL, Charles Earl; born: 10 Oct. 1913; parents: Elliott BOSWELL and Bessie MCCLAIN; death cause: "pneumonia"; informant: father (Greeneville); died: 17 Nov. 1914; buried: Oak Grove; record (1914) # 532.

BECHAM, Hassie; born: 20 Jun. 1912; parents: Clarence BECHAM and Lillie MCKFFIE; death cause: "diphtheria"; informant: John WILSON (Greeneville); died: 20 Nov. 1914; buried: Shilo; record (1914) # 533.

THOMPSON, Mrs. Mary E.; born: 17 Apr. 1846 in Clear Springs, TN.; widow; parents: John HENRY (Washington County) and Linda HENRY (Washington County); death cause: "pneumonia"; informant: H.E. DOBSON (Greeneville); died: 25 Nov. 1914; buried: Oak Grove; record (1914) # 535.

WILLIAMS, Florence; age: 65 years; married; parents: Anderson WALKER and mother not stated; death cause: "tuberculosis"; informant: Bruce WILLIAMS (Greeneville); died: 27 Nov. 1914; buried: Oak Grove; record (1914) # 536.

PHILLIPS, John; age: "about 35 years"; single; parents: Harvey PHILLIPS and Lucinda MC__ (illegible); death cause: "tubercular pneumonia"; died: 28 Oct. 1914; buried: Bethesda; record (1914) # 537.

CARR, Bazzle Clide; born: 16 Sep. 1913; parents: Charley Edward CARR (Sullivan County) and Effie HALL; death cause: illegible; informant: father (Fall Branch); died: 14 Nov. 1914; buried: Lovelace; record (1914) # 538.

MCDONALD, Mary; born: 15 Oct. 1828 in Tennessee; widow; parents: William DYKES and Jane MOORE; death cause: "carcinoma of face"; informant: David MIDDLETON (Jeroldstown); died: 17 Nov. 1914; buried: Pleasant Hill; record (1914) # 539.

MCAMIS, Nancy Catherine; born: 28 Dec. 1858; widow; parents: __ (illegible) STRONG and Betsie RUSH; death cause: "heart failure"; informant: John STRONG (Jeraldstown); died: 21 Nov. 1914; buried: English Cemetery; record (1914) # 540.

MCMACKINS, Elizabeth; age: 86 years; birthplace: "unknown"; parents: Soloman SMITH and mother's name illegible; death cause: "mitral regurgitation"; informant: John CHASE (Limestone); died: 26 Jul. 1914; record (1914) # 541.

WHITE, Eliza; born: 3 May 1837; widow; parents: Jacob WHITE and mother's name unknown; death cause: "tuberculosis"; informant: Charlie BOWSER (Baileyton); died: 5 Dec. 1914; buried: Union Temple; record (1914) # 542.

TAYLOR, Winnie Ruth; born: 13 Feb. 1914; parents: James N. TAYLOR and Mary J. ARNOLD; death cause: "pneumonia fever"; informant: J.C. MARSHALL (Chuckey); died: 26 Nov. 1914; buried: Union Temple; record (1914) # 543.

HARRISON, Eulalia Margiria; born: 20 Nov. 1914; parents: Caleb A. HARRISON and Gertrude E. HARRISON; death cause: "unknown"; informant: father (Greeneville); died: 30 Nov. 1914; record # 544.

MILLER, Barbe; age: "about 70 years"; single; parents: "unknown"; death cause: "chronic diarrhea"; died: 20 Oct. 1914; buried: Pleasant Hill; record (1914) # 545.

BROYLES, Emory B.; born: 3 Jul. 1842; single; parents: Nathaniel BROYLES and Elendar BROYLES (Washington County); death cause: "liver and kidneys"; informant: Twoney MILLER (Chuckey); died: 9 Jul. 1914; buried: Cedar Grove; record (1914) # 546.

CRUM, John; age: 33 years, 4 months and 13 days; married; parents: William CRUM and Mary E. RICKER; death cause: "tuberculosis of stomach"; died: 30 Nov. 1914; record (1914) # 547.

OTTINGER, Martha Francis; born: 27 Feb. 1842; widow; parents: Charles L. EVANS and Mary PAYNE; death cause: "intestinal nephritis"; informant: W.W. OTTINGER (Moshiem); died: 26 Nov. 1914; record (1914) # 548.

HOUSTON, Martha; age: "about 68 years"; born: North Carolina; married; parents: __ BRIANT (North Carolina) and mother unknown; death cause: "cancer of stomach"; died: 1 Nov. 1914; buried: Meadow Creek; record (1914) # 549

OTTINGER, Eliza Jane; born: 5 Oct. 1866; married; parents: Robert LUTTRELL and Pheba MCMURTY; death cause: "ersipelas, facial"; informant: G.M. OTTINGER (Parrotsville); died: 7 Nov. 1914; buried: Pine Grove; record (1914) # 550.

CASH, Infant; female; parents: Willie CASH and Ida MCCURRY; death cause: "still born"; informant: father (Moshiem); born/died: 28 Nov. 1914; record (1914) # 551.

JOHNSON, Thomas; age: 37 years and 4 months; married; parents: Robert JOHNSON and __ BURKEY; death cause: "lagrippe and pneumonia"; informant: Harrison JOHNSON (Greeneville); died: 30 Dec. 1914; record (1914) # 552.

ALDRED, George Haskell; born: 3 Jun. 1914; parents: W.M. ALDRED (Wake County, NC.) and Laura JOHNSON; death cause: "unknown"; informant: father (Greeneville); death date not recorded; buried: Piney Grove; record (1914) # 553.

JOHNSON, Ervin Emmett; born: 30 Oct. 1914; parents: K.M. JOHNSON and Edna CRUM, death cause: "heart failure"; informant: Amy JOHNSON (Greeneville); died: 14 Nov. 1914; record # 554.

CUTSHALL, Lowell Edward; born: 17 Oct. 1914; parents: B.R. CUTSHALL and Nora Murtel KELEY; death cause: "cerebral hemorrhage"; informant: mother (Greeneville); died: 26 Dec. 1914; buried: Price Cemetery; record (1914) # 555.

WEEMS, Infant; male; born; 1 Dec. 1914; parents: S.J. WEEMS and Mamie JUSTIS; death cause: "respiration could not be established"; informant: father (Greeneville); died: 1 Dec. 1914; buried: Wesley Chapel; record (1914) # 556.

HOGAN, Frank Bell; lived 3 days; parents: Hunley HOGAN and __ (illegible) OTTINGER, death cause: "unknown, found dead in bed"; informant: father (Greeneville); buried: Whittenburg Church; record (1914) # 557.

RADAR, Hugh Vallie; black; born: 14 Oct. 1897; single; parents: James RADER and Harriet SCRUGGS; death cause: "tuberculosis of lungs"; informant: Tulmon SNODDY (Midway); died: 21 Dec. 1914; buried: Warrensburg; record (1914) # 559.

AYERS, Sallie; age: 42 years; single; parents: Samuel O. AYERS and Lucinda MURS; death cause: "tuberculosis of lungs"; informant: L.C.H. AYERS (Midway); died: 21 Dec. 1914; buried: Warrensburg; record (1914) # 558.

MYERS, Miss Eliza; born: 11 May 1851; single; parents: James MYERS and Elizabeth WILLOUGHBY; death cause: "double pneumonia"; informant: C.F. MYERS (Mohawk); died: 22 Dec. 1914; buried: Willoughby Cemetery; record (1914) # 560.

HUNTSMAN, Mrs. N.J.; born: 12 May 1847; widow; parents: James DILON (Virginia) and mother's name illegible; death cause: "senile pneumonia"; informant: J.A. HUNTSMAN (Bulls Gap); died: 16 Dec. 1914; buried: Drakes; record (1914) # 561.

MELTON, Silas; born: 25 Mar.1829 in North Carolina; widower; parents: John MELTON (North Carolina) and Rebecca K__ (illegible) (North Carolina); death cause: "organic heart disease"; informant: John MELTON, Jr. (Bulls Gap); died: 18 Dec. 1914; record (1914) # 562.

MANESS, Alfred Allen; age: 23 years; single; parents: Alfred MANESS and mother's name unknown; death cause: "typhoid fever"; died: 23 Nov. 1914; buried: Zion; record (1914) # 563.

MAULDIN, Will; black; age: 23 years; married; parents: John MAULDIN and Etta WILLIAMS; death cause: "tuberculosis"; died: 7 Dec. 1914; record (1914) # 564.

GASS, Thomas; black; age: 40 years; single; parents: Srigfield GASS and Eliza MCKINNEY (Hawkins County); death cause: "tuberculosis"; informant: John KIRK (Greeneville); died: 7 Dec. 1914; buried: Gass Cemetery; record (1914) # 565.

JONES, Caney; black; born: 10 May 1913; parents: Oscar JONES and Mary BLACK; death cause: "acute bronchitis"; died: 10 Dec. 1914; record (1914) # 566.

FILLERS, Martha Jane; age: 60 years and 2 months; married; parents: James __ (illegible)(North Carolina) and Eliza CRUM; death cause: "chronic nephritis"; died: 19 Dec. 1914; buried: Red Hill; record # 567.

HARROLD, Nancy E. born: 11 Oct. 1850; single; parents: Lewis HARROLD and Annie HORTON; death cause: "tuberculosis"; informant: E.L. HARROLD; died: 19 Dec. 1914; buried: Harrold Cemetery; record (1914) # 568.

BIDDLE, William; born: 19 Feb. 1874; single; parents: John M. BIDDLE and Louise DOBSEN; death cause: "nephritis"; died: 20 Dec. 1914; buried: Oak Grove; record (1914) # 569.

SISK, Toliver; born: 26 Jan. 1871; married; parents: William SISK (Cocke County) and Ellen CHAPMAN (Cocke County); death cause: "tuberculosis"; informant: Mrs. Nattie SISK (Greeneville); died: 26 Dec. 1914; buried: Cedar Hill; record (1914) # 571.

HALL, Mary; born: 30 Jan. 1859; married; parents: Richard MCCURY (Virginia) and Peggy HALL; death cause: "endocarditis, lagrippe"; informant: George FLOWERS (Greeneville); died: 28 Dec. 1914; buried: Oak Grove; record (1914) # 572.

KNIGHT, Homer Price; born: 27 Jun. 1897; parents: W.M. KNIGHT and Addie A. PEARCE; death cause: "dysentery"; informant: father (Moshiem); died: 6 Oct. 1914; buried: Brown Church; record # 573.

COX, William C.; born: 22 Jul. 1838 in North Carolina; widower; parents: William COX and Mary MOODY; death cause: "brights disease"; informant: J.M. COX (Moshiem); died: 25 Nov. 1914; buried: Carter Chapel; record (1914) # 574.

MCGEE, Mary; born: 13 Jul. 1914; parents: R.E. MCGEE and Silvie MORIS; death cause: "capillary bronchitis"; informant: father (Moshiem); died: 25 Nov. 1914; buried: Carter Chapel; record # 575.

PARRIS, Susan S.; born: 24 Feb. 1859 in Buncumb County, NC.; widow; parents: Lorenza BUCKNER (Buncome County) and __ SPRINKLES (Madison County, NC.); death cause: "laryngitis"; informant: Troy PARRIS (Afton); died: 28 Dec. 1914; buried: Union Chapel; record (1914) # 576.

MARSHALL, J.C. (Medical Doctor); born: 1 Mar.1865; married; parents: Robert MARSHALL and Deborah ROBERTSON; death cause: "tubercular meningitis"; informant: Minnie MARSHALL (Chuckey); died: 30 Dec. 1914; buried: Union Temple; record # 577.

GOOD, William W.; born: 2 Feb. 1964; married; parents: Jacob GOOD and Elizabeth MCCALL; death cause: "acute rheumatism"; informant: Charles BAXTER (Jeroldstown); died: 30 Dec. 1914; buried: Bethesda; record (1914) # 578.

BAILEY, Infant; male; "lived about 36 hours"; father not stated and Osa Fern BAILEY; death cause: "died at hands of some person in a violent way"; died: "from 20 - 22 Dec. 1914; record (1914) # 579.

WYAN, Lavina Cathern; born: 24 May 1834 in Greene County; widow; parents: Peter WYAN (North Carolina) and mother not stated; death cause: "yellow atrophy of liver"; died: 5 Aug. 1914; record # 580.

VESTAL, Infant; female; born: 17 Sep. 1914; parents: Paris VESTAL and mother "unknown"; death cause: "unknown"; died: __ Sep. 1914; buried: Mt. Zion; record (1914) # 581.

BERNARD, Laura Cornelia; born: 11 Mar.1859; married; parents: S.H. BALL and Mary LUCAS (Virginia); death cause: "cancer of gall bladder"; informant: F.M. BERNARD (Baileyton); died: 6 Dec. 1914; buried: Zion; record (1914) # 582.

ARNOLD, Susie Ollie; born: 4 Aug. 1895; single; parents: Robert ARNOLD (South Carolina) and Ida WILLSON; death cause: "pulmonary consumption"; informant: Robert ARNOLD (Moshiem); died: 28 Dec. 1914; buried: Meadow Creek; record (1914) # 583.

ARNOLD, Major Henry; born: 3 Apr. 1891; single; parents: Robert ARNOLD (South Carolina) and Ida WILLSON; death cause: "pulmonary tuberculosis"; informant: father (Moshiem); died: 4 Dec. 1914; buried: Meadow Creek; record (1914) # 584.

NEAS, Elma Ruth; age: 4 years, 4 months and 19 days; parents: Tabat C. NEAS and Odessa DAVIS (Cocke County); death cause: "gastro interitis"; informant: J.W. NEAS (Greeneville); died: 3 Dec. 1914; buried: St. James; record (1914) # 585.

HOUSTON, Isaac; age: 29 years; single; parents: James HOUSTON and mother "unknown"; death cause: "assassinated by pistol in hands of Rankin HOUSTON"; informant: J.H. RADER; died: 1 Dec. 1914; record (1914) # 586.

GOSNELL, Katie; age: "about 69 years"; born in North Carolina; married; parents: Oliver COOK (North Carolina) and mother "unknown"; death cause: "paralysis"; informant: Major GOSNELL (Greeneville); died: 2 Dec. 1914; buried: Mt. Olivet; record # 587.

FARLEY, Francis H.; born: 12 Oct. 1839 in Virginia; married; preacher; parents: "unknown"; death cause: "old age and heart failure"; informant: Orville H. HAWS (Midway); died: 17 Dec. 1914; buried: Midway; record (1914) # 588.

LOONEY, Ruben Earl; born: 20 Jun. 1913; parents: Homer LOONEY and Lilly MARSHALL; death cause: "no physician"; informant: Lilly LOONEY (Greeneville); died: 19 Nov. 1914; record (1914) # 120.

SPEER, William King; born: 5 Nov. 1863 in Virginia; married; parents: John R. SPEER (Virginia) and Elizabeth RODDY (Virginia); death cause: "tuberculosis of lungs"; informant: Ottie SPEER (Chuckey); died: 22 Nov. 1914; buried: Pleasant Vale; record (1914) # 121.

FISHER, Mary Elizabeth; born: 11 Dec. 1857; widow; parents: Andy DOBBINS and Honey PICKERING; death cause: "tuberculosis of lungs"; informant: L.H. FISHER (Afton); died: 29 Oct. 1914; buried: Dotson Shanks; record (1914) # 122.

HAMPTON, Nancy; age: 83 years; born in North Carolina; parents: __ NORTON (North Carolina) and mother unknown; death cause: __ (illegible) of kidneys and old age"; informant: D.J. GRAY (Chuckey); died: 18 Dec. 1914; buried: Union Chapel; record (1914) # 123.

FULLINS, Eliza Jane Mullendore; age: 45 years, 8 months and 14 days; married; parents: Newton MULLENDORE (Sevier County) and Margaret CARTER; death cause: "carcinoma of liver and organic heart disease"; informant: J.C. CARTER (Baileyton); died: 5 Jan. 1916 (?); record (1915) # 1.

WILHOIT, Janette Ricker; born: 13 Mar.1875; married; parents: Warren RICKER and Elizabeth MILLER; death cause: "pneumonia and general peritonitis"; informant: Sarah FILLERS (Greeneville); died: 31 Jan. 1915; buried: Cove Creek Church; record (1915) # 2.

WAMPLER, Isaac; born: 14 Oct. 1845; widower; parents: Soloman WAMPLER (Germany) and mother unknown; death cause: "chronic intestinal nephritis": informant: J.M. MYERS (Moshiem); died: 2 Jan. 1915; record (1915) # 3.

MORELOCK, Willie Lee; female; born: 1 Mar.1901; parents: Elbert Alexander MORELOCK and Ida CARTER; death cause: "acute nephritis"; informant: E.A. MORELOCK (Moshiem); died: 7 Jan. 1915; record (1915) # 4.

SEXTON, Infant; female; parents: Bart SEXTON and Vertie SMITH; death cause: "stillborn"; informant: I.B. BROWN (Moshiem); died: 13 Jan. 1915; buried: Brown Church; record (1915) # 5.

LOGAN, Hellen; born: 14 Jan. 1915; parents: M.F. LOGAN and Gussie SAYLOR; death cause: "died without medical attention"; informant: C.E. JONES (Moshiem); died: 19 Jan. 1915; buried: Albany; record (1915) # 6.

CAMPBELL, Margaret; born: 7 Jun. 1835 in Tennessee; widow; parents: John HULL (Tennessee) and Jane LYLE (Tennessee); death cause: "pneumonia fever"; informant: L.P. CAMPBELL (Baileyton); died: 17 Jan. 1915; buried: Salem; record (1915) # 7.

STONESBURY, I.H.; age: 62 years; married; parents: not stated; death cause: "cancer"; informant: Mrs. STONESBURY (Knoxville); died: 30 Jan. 1915; record (1915) # 8.

PAINTER, Sarah Elizabeth; born: 16 dec. 1848; widow; parents: Ira SEATON and Sallie WILLIAMSON; death cause: "pellagra"; informant: C.S. LOVE (Chuckey); died: 29 Jan. 1915; buried: Pleasant Hill; record (1915) # 9.

JACKSON, Sallie; born: 5 May 1863 in Hawkins County; age: 61 years, 8 months and 2 days; married; parents: Thomas BALL (Hawkins County) and Lucinda DYKES (Hawkins County); death cause: "pulmonary tuberculosis"; informant: C.A. JOHNSON (Jeroldstown); died: 7 Jan. 1915; buried: Bethany; record (1915) # 10.

ROBERTS, Fitzhue F.; born: 26 Nov. 1914; parents: William H. ROBERTS (Hawkins) and Ruth DYKES (Scott County, VA.); death cause: "died without medical attention"; informant: Roam BRANDON (Fall Branch); died: 20 Jan. 1915; buried: Lovelace; record (1915) # 11.

TAYLOR, Robert Carson; born: 6 Mar.1914; parents: Frank Garfield TAYLOR (Kingsport) and Lydia May PITT; death cause: "broncho pneumonia"; informant: J. Carson MOORE (Jeroldstown); died: 3 Jan. 1915; buried: Pleasant Hill; record (1915) # 12.

GRAGG, Hannah May; born: 28 Jun. 1913 in Sullivan County; parents: Elbert GRAGG (Hawkins County) and Sallie FULWILER (Sullivan County); death cause: "acute indigestion"; informant: F.J. FEAGINS (Jeroldstown); died: 26 Jan. 1915; buried: Sullivan County; record # 13.

BAXTER, Elizabeth; born: 6 Aug. 1837 in Greene County; widow; parents: James SHANKS and Malinda MAYS; death cause: "tubercular pleurisy"; informant: S.P. BAXTER (Fall Branch); died: 28 Jan. 1915; buried: Cedar Lane; record (1915) # 14.

STONES, Margaret; age: 76 years; divorced; parents: John LANE and mother not stated; death cause: "paralysis"; died at Baileyton on 31 Jan. 1915; buried: Family Cemetery; record (1915) # 15.

RADER, Susan; age: 83 years and 3 months; born: Greene County; widow; parents: not stated; death cause: "infirmities of age"; informant: John M. LUITZ (Greeneville); died: 27 Jan. 1915; buried: St. James; record (1915) # 16.

JONES, Febia; age: 70 years; single; parents: Daniel JONES and mother unknown; death cause: "old age and heart failure"; informant: W.E. JONES (Moshiem); died: 27 Jan. 1915; buried: Pine Grove; record # 17.

HARMON, Moses Piny; born: 26 Aug. 1855; married; parents: John HARMON and Sallie COBBLE; death cause: "heart failure"; informant: J.B. HARMON (Midway); died: 8 Jan. 1915; buried: Harmon Cemetery; record (1915) # 18.

CROSBY, Mary Elizabeth; born: 29 Dec. 1914; parents: William H. CROSBY and Floy MCCORKLE; death cause: "injuries incidental to birth"; informant: father (Mohawk); died: 4 Jan. 1915; record # 19.

CUTSHOWL, Jake; age: "about 48 years"; single; inmate at poor asylum; parents: "unknown"; death cause: "pellagra"; informant: J.M. MORELOCK (Greeneville); died: 2 Jan. 1915; buried: Poor Farm; record (1915) # 20.

MORELOCK, Richard; age: "about 29 years"; married; parents: Richard MORELOCK and Elvira MORELOCK; death cause: "tetanus from gunshot wound in arm"; informant: A.D. GARDNER (Church Hill); died: 7 Jan. 1915; record (1915) # 21.

COX, Lemuel K.; born: 23 Mar.1827 in Tennessee; parents: William COX (Tennessee) and Rachel MIL__ (illegible); death cause: "senile debility"; informant: Frank COX (Greeneville); died: 8 Jan. 1915; buried: Mt. Pleasant; record (1915) # 22.

COLYER, Andrew Jackson; born: 9 Feb. 1878; widower; parents: E.F. COLYER and Fannie ORR; death cause: not stated; informant: Ed COLYER (Greeneville); died: 8 Jan. 1915; buried: Oak Grove; record (1915) # 23.

GLOVER, Infant; male; age: 21 days; parents: Ollie GLOVER and __ POE; death cause: "no medical attention"; informant: W.B. MILLS (Greeneville); died: 8 Jan. 1915; buried: Cedar Hill; record (1915) # 24.

GREGORY, Mrs. Sarah A.; age: 74 years; widow; parents: "unknown"; death cause: illegible; informant: George WINKLE (Greeneville); died: __ Jan. 1914; buried: Cove Creek; record (1915) # 25.

TILSON, Sam Flemings; born: 15 Jan. 1915; parents: Bruce TILSON and Anis H__ (illegible); death cause: "unknown"; informant: father (Greeneville); died: 14 Jan. 1915; buried: Mt. Bethel; record # 26.

FOWLER, William Francis; born: 6 Oct. 1839 in Tennessee; married; dentist; parents: Francis FOWLER and Martha J. MALONEY; death cause: "paralysis"; informant: O.M. DUGGER (Greeneville); died: 14 Jan. 1915; buried: Oak Grove; record (1915) # 27.

WILLIAMS, Francis; born: 17 Dec. 1914; parents: Nat WILLIAMS and Georgia HUNTER; death cause: "pneumonia"; informant: S.H. SELF (Greeneville); died: 17 Jan. 1915; buried: Fairview; record (1915) # 28.

CONN, James; born: 10 May 1844; single; parents: John CONN (Maryland) and Nancie FROST; death cause: "pneumonia"; informant: Robert CONN (Greeneville); died: 25 Jan. 1915; record (1915) # 29.

WILLET, Lillie; age: 35 years; married; parents: R. NELSON and mother unknown; death cause: "tuberculosis of lungs"; informant: Joe WILLET (Greeneville); died: 27 Jan. 1915; buried: New Bethel; record (1915) # 30.

DEARSTONE, William M.; age: 57 years; married; parents: Henry DEARSTONE and __ RUSSELL; death cause: "tuberculosis"; informant: George DEARSTONE (Greeneville); died: 30 Jan. 1915; record (1915) # 31.

MATHES, Cordie; age: "about 26 years"; single; parents: "unknown"; death cause: "pellagra"; informant: James MORELOCK (Greeneville); died: 31 Jan. 1915; buried: Poor Farm; record (1915) # 32.

SHEFFEY, Alfred K.; born: 8 May 1913; parents: Marion SHEFFEY and Minnie BORDEN; death cause: "cholera infantum"; informant: father (Greeneville); died: 6 Jan. 1915; buried: Piney Grove; record (1915) # 33.

BAKER, Oscar Wilds; born: 11 Feb. 1882; single; parents: Wilburn BAKER and Nancy C. DAVIS; death cause: "tumor of brain"; informant: R.R. BAKER (Mohawk); died: 31 Jan. 1915; buried: St. Paul; record (1915) # 34.

BROWN, Emily Elizabeth; born: 25 Jan. 1915; parents: George Peter BROWN and Lula Eudra ROBERTSON; death cause: "stillborn"; died: 25 Jan. 1915; buried: Concord; record (1915) # 35.

WHITTAKER, Mary Ellen; born: 18 Mar.1913; parents: J.T. WHITAKER and Irene DERRIL; death cause: "pneumonia and uremic poison"; informant: J.T. POTTER (Moshiem); died: 18 Jan. 1915; buried: Bewley Chapel; record (1915) # 36.

HALL, Mchoge; age: 88 years; born in Rutherford County, NC.; single; parents: Eliga HALL (McDowell County, NC.) and Ana WILKERSON (Rutherford County, NC.) death cause: "lobar pneumonia"; informant: A.W. HALL (Chuckey); died: 18 Jan. 1915; record (1915) # 37.

HALL, McHoge; age: 88 years; born: Rutherford County, NC.; single; parents: Eliga HALL (McDowell County, NC.) and Ana WILKERSON (Rutherford County, NC.); death cause: "lobar pneumonia"; informant: A.W. HALL (Chuckey); died: 18 Jan. 1915; record (1915) # 37.

WHITE, Elbert Carl; born: 21; Nov. 1896; single; parents: J.R. WHITE (Washington County, VA.) and M.E. GOOD; death cause: "lobar pneumonia"; informant: father (Chuckey); died: 3 Jan. 1915; record (1915) # 38.

GADDIS, Redmon; born: 12 Oct. 1849 in North Carolina; married; parents: Jessie GADDIS (North Carolina) and Winnie PIERCE (North Carolina); death cause: "tuberculosis"; informant: John GADDIS (Greeneville); died: 10 Feb. 1915; buried: Mt. Pleasant; record # 39.

MULLINDON, Jacob Newton; born: 27 Dec. 1839 in Sevier County; widower; parents: David MULLINDON and Catherine EASTERLY; death cause: "impaction of bowels"; informant: Will GORBER (Moshiem); died: 24 Feb. 1915; buried: Price Cemetery; record # 40.

COBBLE, Infant; female; born: 17 Apr. 1914; parents: Allis A. COBBLE and Ethyl S. KELLEY; death cause: "died without medical attention"; informant: A.A. COBBLE (Moshiem); died: 14 Feb. 1915; record # 41.

HUNTSMAN, Ruth Butter; born: 17 Feb. 1915; parents: J.B. HUNTSMAN and Ethel HANIE (?)(Hamblen County); death cause: "suffocation"; informant: father (Bulls Gap); died: 23 Feb. 1915; buried: Drakes; record (1915) # 42.

WHITAKER, Infant; female; parents: John WHITAKER and Alice GREGG; death cause: "still born"; informant: father (Moshiem); born/died: 13 Feb. 1915; record (1915) # 43.

BLACK, Jessie; born: 29 Jun. 1861; married; parents: Thomas BLACK and Polly Ann LAMBERT; death cause: "double pneumonia"; informant: Billie BLACK (Midway); died: 3 Feb. 1914; buried: St. Josephs Chapel; record (1915) # 44.

BLAZER, Eliza Ruth; born: 22 Oct. 1906 in Cocke County; parents: Joe BLAZER and Ellen KILGORE (Cocke County); death cause:

"pulmonary tuberculosis"; informant: father (Moshiem); died: 9 Feb. 1915; buried: Memorial Cocke County; record (1915) # 45.

GLASCOCK, Matilda; born: 4 May 1907; parents: James GLASCOCK and Minnie IRVIN; death cause: "aortic insufficiency"; informant: John WRIGHT (Mohawk); died: 5 Feb. 1915; buried: Fairview Church; record (1915) # 46.

NEILSON, William Huff; born: 19 Aug. 1914; parents: James R. NEILSON and Ella HUFF; death cause: "broncho pneumonia - whooping cough"; informant: Mrs. F.A. MCCORKLE (Mohawk); died: 17 Feb. 1915; record (1915) # 47.

BOUGHARD, Mary Jane; age: 62 years and 8 months; married; parents: James BABB and __ CARTER; death cause: "valvulor heart disease"; informant: W.J. BOUGHARD (Mohawk); died: 22 Feb. 1915; record (1915) # 48.

SMILEY, Samiel; born: 11 Feb. 1846; married; parents: "unknown"; death cause: "pulmonary tuberculosis"; informant: John ESTEP (Jeroldstown); died: 27 Feb. 1915; buried: Rock Spring; record # 49.

THORNBURG, Noah E.; born: 28 Mar.1836 in North Carolina; widower; parents: Leonard THORNBURG (North Carolina) and mother unknown; death cause: "old age and cystitis"; informant: H.E. ENGLISH (Jeroldstown); died: 23 Feb. 1915; buried: Bethany; record (1915) # 50.

SLUDER, Infant; male; parents: William SLUDER and Nancy NELSON; death cause: "still born"; informant: father (Greeneville); died: 21 Feb 1915; buried: Meadow Creek; record (1915) # 51.

OTTINGER, Jacob; born: 24 Nov. 1819 in Cocke County; widower; parents: Henry OTTINGER (Greene County) and Susan NEAS (Greene County); death cause: "intestinal nephritis, mitral heart regurgitation"; informant: C.H. KEYS (Greeneville); died: 14 Feb 1915; buried: St. James; record (1915) # 52.

HARRISON, Jessie; female; age: 24 years; married; parents: __ COLYER and mother not stated; death cause: "tuberculosis of lungs"; informant: Ed HARRISON (Greeneville); died: 1 Feb. 1915; buried: Cedar Hill; record (1915) # 53.

HARROLD, Ann__ (illegible); born: 10 Nov. 1840; widow; parents: J. BROWN and Eliza __; death cause: "gastro enteritis"; informant: Miss

Ella HAROLD (Greeneville); died: 4 Feb. 1915; buried: Oak Grove; record (1915) # 54.

WHITTENBURG, Effie; age: "about 35 years"; single; parents: W.S. WHITTENBURG and Emma HARRISON; death cause: "cancer of uterus"; died: Greeneville, 4 Feb. 1915; buried: Pine Grove; record # 55.

DALLINGER, James Arthur; age: 2 months and 26 days; parents: Spence DALLINGER (North Carolina) and Maud MARROW; death cause: "no medical attention"; informant: father (Greeneville); died: 5 Feb. 1915; buried: Oak Grove; record (1915) # 56.

COX, Bessie; born: 6 Jan. 1895 in Morristown; single; parents: John N. __ (illegible) and Louise CHENY (Morristown); death cause: "pellagra"; died: 8 Feb. 1915; buried: Morristown; record (1915) # 57.

DYKES, John; born: 11 Feb. 1860; widower; parents: Gus DYKES (Virginia) and Lucindy WOODS; death cause: "acute nephritis"; informant: J.A. DYKES (Greeneville); died: 11 Feb. 1915; buried: New Bethel; record (1915) # 58.

PIPER, Charles Wesley; born: 5 Feb. 1844 in Hawkins County; married; parents: Albert M. PIPER and Martha __ (illegible); death cause: "lagrippe"; died: 26 Feb. 1915; buried: Shiloh; record (1915) # 59.

WRIGHT, Lewis; born: 19 Apr. 1957 in Hawkins County; parents: J.T. WRIGHT (Hawkins County) and Nely RAY; death cause: "tubercular meningitis"; informant: T.J. BERRY (Mohawk); died: 2 Feb. 1915; buried: Browns Cemetery; record (1915) # 60.

SHUW, James; born: 24 Mar.1915; parents: Nic A. SHUW and Bonnie Lee ALEXANDER; death cause: "premature birth"; died: 24 Mar.1915; record (1915) # 61.

BARNES, Lucy; black; age: 98 years; widow; parents: "unknown"; death cause: "old age"; informant: John BARNES (Greeneville); died: 4 Mar.1915; buried: Pruits Hill; record (1915) # 62.

STEPHENS, S.J.R.; born: 12 Aug. 1847; miller; parents: Samuel STEPHENS and Jane FARNSWORTH; death cause: "mitral regurgitation"; informant: Alice STEPHENS (Greeneville); died: 14 Mar.1915; record (1915) # 63.

KISER, Infant; male; parents: A.D. KISER Jr. and Grace PIPER; death cause: "child delivery"; informant: C.M. KISER (Greeneville); died: 7 Mar.1915; buried: Oak Grove; record (1915) # 64.

HANKINS, John E.; age: 61 years and 7 months; married; parents: John E. HANKINS Sr. and Elizabeth GASS; death cause: "aortic regurgitation"; died: 1 Mar.1915; buried: Gass Shed; record (1915) # 65.

ROLLINS, Essie Anna; born: 27 Aug. 1874; married; parents: Anderson COLLIER and Florence R__ (illegible); death cause: "acute gastritis"; informant: D.H. ROLLINS (Greeneville); died: 17 Mar.1915; buried: Cove Creek; record (1915) # 66.

RENNER, Infant; male; age: 4 days; parents: Will RENNER and Lula BIBLE; death cause: "no medical attention"; informant: father (Greeneville); died: 17 Mar.1915; buried: Susong Memorial; record (1915) # 67.

CUTSHALL, T.M.; age: 44 years; parents: Andrew CUTSHALL and Cathern HENSLEY; death cause: "pulmonary at__ (illegible)"; informant: N.J. CUTSHALL (Greeneville); died: 20 Mar.1915; buried: Cutshall Cemetery; record (1915) # 68.

COOTER, Mary A.; age: 75 years; born: Greene County; widow; parents: "unknown"; death cause: "pneumonia"; informant: John GRAY (Greeneville); died: 28 Mar.1915; buried: Pisgah; record (1915) # 69.

CRAWFORD, Fred Hale; age: illegible; parents: R.E. CRAWFORD (Hawkins County) and mother unknown; death cause: "no medical attention"; informant: U.A COX (Greeneville); died: 7 Mar.1915; record (1915) # 70.

KELLEY, Martha J.; born: 30 May 1851; divorced; parents: Calvin HANEY and Polly A. MCCOY; death cause: "tuberculosis"; informant: J.C. KELLEY (Greeneville); died: 19 Mar.1915; record (1915) # 71.

RICKER, Roy Roscoe; born: 27 Dec. 1902; parents: James Martin RICKER and Sarah Jane BURGER; death cause: "concussion of brain, thrown and dragged by mule"; informant: Sarah Jane MILLER (Greeneville); died: 2 Mar.1915; record (1915) #72.

HOUSTON, Wayland Lee; born: 22 Nov. 1913; parents: William HOUSTON and Alice ALDRIDGE; death cause: "catarrhal pneumonia"; informant: father (Greeneville); died: 14 Mar.1914; record # 73.

HARRISON, Wade Gahagan; born: 17 Sep. 1912; parents: Francis HARRISON and Lillie FARNSWORTH; death cause: "carcinoma of left jaw"; informant: Charles WILHOIT (Greeneville); died: 17 Mar.1915; buried: Harrrisons; record (1915) # 74.

SWATSELL, Alice; born: 27 Mar. 1875; married; parents: Jack S. KYLES and Salina BROYLES; death cause: "chronic diarrhea"; informant: Dr. LOVE (Chuckey); died: 2 Mar. 1915; buried: Pleasant Hill; record (1915) # 75.

KYLES, Salina S.; born: 10 Oct. __; age: 73 years and 7 months; married; parents: John BROYLES and Mary PAINTER; death cause: "pellagra"; informant: Dr. LOVE (Chuckey); died: 15 Mar.1915; buried: Pleasant Hill; record (1915) # 76.

SCOTT, William C.; born: 17 Aug. 1847; married; blacksmith; parents: Pain SCOTT and __ FILLERS; death cause: "valvulor heart disease and intestinal nephritis"; informant: Lydia SCOTT (Chuckey); died: 17 Mar.1915; record (1915) # 77.

JONES, Jane; age: 76 years, 8 months and 18 days; born: Greene County; widow; parents: Charles LOYD and Paggie RODGERS; death cause: "gastric catarrh and rheumatism"; informant: W.B. LOYD (Chuckey); died: 27 Mar.1915; buried: Pleasant __ (illegible); record (1915) # 78.

HULL, Eula Bell; born: 14 Jan. 1897; single; parents: John M. HULL and Delia BROWN; death cause: "broncho pneumonia"; informant: father (Moshiem); died: 7 Mar.1915; buried: Brown Church; record (1915) # 79.

BROWN, Elmer C.; born: 31 Jul. 1896; parents: Calvin F. BROWN and Eliza J. CARTER; death cause: "rupture of left ventricle of heart"; informant: father (Moshiem); died: 28 Mar.1915; buried: Browns; record (1915) # 89.

DRAKE, James Edgar; born: 4 Mar.1915; parents: William T. DRAKE and Vida V. PIGMON (Kentucky); death cause: "still born"; informant: father (Bulls Gap); died: 4 Mar.1915; record (1915) # 81.

GUTHRIE, Hascal; age: 1 year and 9 months; parents: A.A. GUTHRIE and Lydia STRAND; death cause: "rickets"; informant: James HAUN (Mohawk); died: 21 Mar.1915; buried: Mt. Hope; record (1915) # 82.

HAUN, Orbie Mable; born: 22 Feb. 1915; parents: Charlie H. HAUN and Myrtle CUPP (Hawkins County); death cause: "malformed heart"; informant: father (Bulls Gap); died: 6 Mar.1915; buried: Phillips; record (1915) # 83.

COOK, Anson King; born: 28 Dec. 1903 in Johnson City; parents: E.G. COOK and Fannie KING; death cause: "articular rheumatism, heart lesions"; informant: father (Afton); died: 31 Mar.1915; buried: Bristol, Tennessee; record (1915) # 84.

BEALS, Lydia Emily; born: 17 Jul. 1849; single; parents: Asbery BEALS and Mary ELLIS; death cause: "carcinoma of back of neck"; informant: H.H. BEALS (Afton); died: 28 Mar.1915; buried: Mt. Zion; record (1915) # 85.

GRAGLEY, Chassie E.; age: 8 months; parents: E.F. GREGLEY and __ HYDER (Carter County); death cause: "lobar pneumonia"; informant: father (Afton); died: 18 Mar.1915; record (1915) # 86.

PULLIAM, Margaret J.; born: 25 Sep. 1847 in Russell County, VA.; married; parents: Hugley MITCHELL (Virginia) and Mary C. ARNOLD (Washington County); death cause: "softening of brain, paralysis"; informant: M__ (illegible) PULLIAM (Jeroldstown); died: 9 Mar.1915; buried: Lovelace; record (1915) # 87.

JEFFERS, Joseph Wheeler; born: 17 Dec. 1899; parents: Samuel E. JEFFERS and Elizabeth JUSTICE; death cause: "pulmonary tuberculosis"; informant: father (Moshiem); died: 20 Mar.1915; buried: Mt. Carmel; record (1915) # 88.

LOVE, L__ (illegible) M.; female; born: 11 may 1873; married; parents: John SHIELDS and Harriet OTTINGER; death cause: "pulmonary tuberculosis"; informant: B.W. LOVE (Greeneville); died: 11 Mar.1915; buried: Pine Grove; record (1915) # 89.

MCMYSTIC, Bettie; age: 79 years; born: Greene County; married; parents: __ REEDER and mother not stated; death cause: "pulmonary tuberculosis"; informant: Vol MCMYSTIC (Moshiem); died: 10 Mar.1915; buried: Craft Cemetery; record (1915) # 90.

JONES, Mollie; born: 10 May 1867; parents: James CARTER and Martha BERL, death cause: "pulmonary tuberculosis"; informant: W.C. JONES (Moshiem); died: 3 Mar.1915; buried: Pine Grove; record (1915) # 91.

CAMPBELL, Amanda; born: 26 Dec. 1860; married; parents: James SHANKS and Elizabeth PICKENS; death cause: "complete paralysis"; died: 19 Mar.1915; buried: Salem; record (1915) # 92.

REED, Nellie M.; born: 19 Dec. 1912; parents: John REED and Carrie G. LONG (Hamblen County); death cause: "whooping cough";

informant: father (Mohawk); died: 9 Mar.1915; buried: Concord; record (1915) # 93.

WILKERSON, Richard Thomas; born: 13 Jul. 1841; married; parents: K.T. WILKERSON (North Carolina) and Rettia KISTERSON; death cause: "aortic insufficiency"; informant: J.H. WILKERSON (Knoxville); died: 18 Mar.1915; buried: Concord Church; record (1915) # 94.

ALEXANDER, Margaret Elizabeth; born: 22 Jan. 1912; parents: Charles S. ALEXANDER and Dora B. BOWMAN (record not clear); death cause: "paralysis, pneumonia and meningitis"; informant: father (Greeneville); died: 22 Mar.1915; buried: Timber Ridge; record # 95.

SUNCEMAN, Infant; male; born: 7 Mar.1915; parents: Roy SUNCEMAN and Nora BEACH; death cause: "born before full term"; informant: J.B. BELL (Greeneville); died: 7 Mar.1915; buried: Whittenburg; record (1915) # 96.

SUTHERLAND, S.D.; age: 63 years, born: South Carolina; married; parents: Phillip SOUTHERLAND (South Carolina) and mother not stated; death cause: "cancer of stomach"; died: 14th District, 1 Mar.1915; record (1915) # 97.

HENSLEY, Enoch H.; age: "about 70 years"; born: North Carolina; married; parents: Amos HENSLEY (North Carolina) and Artie NORTON (North Carolina); death cause: "dropsy of chest"; informant: S.H. BROYLES (Chuckey); died: 28 Apr. 1915; buried: Pleasant Hill; record (1915) # 98.

WADDLE, A.W. Justins; age: 74 years and 10 months; born: Greene County; married; parents: "unknown"; death cause: "rheumatism and disease of heart"; informant: Laura E. WADDLE (Greeneville); died: 23 Apr. 1915; buried: Bersheba; record (1915) # 99.

RADER, Emaline; born: 27 Apr. 1849 in Mississippi; widow; parents: Alex HOOD and Sallie __; death cause: not stated; informant: Leona HOOD (Moshiem); died: 27 Apr. 1915; buried: Moshiem; record # 100.

STUART, Anna; born: 5 Apr. 1915; parents: Henry STUART and Lizzie SIMPSON (Hawkins County); death cause: "malnutrition, mother unable to nourish"; informant: Bud STUART (Baileyton); died: 20 Apr. 1915; buried: Price Cemetery; record (1915) # 101.

COOTER, Carrio; female; age: 18 years and 11 months; single; parents: Charles R. COOTER and Bell WAITS; death cause: "tuberculosis of lungs"; informant: John COOTER (Baileyton); died: 22 Apr. 1915; buried: Zion; record (1915) # 102.

HEADWICK, Malinda Jane; born: 12 Nov. 1838 in Tennessee; single; parents: William M. HEADWICK and Katherine E. SMITH; death cause: "nervous prostration"; died: 3 Apr. 1915; buried: Salem; record (1915) # 103.

BRICE, Infant; black; parents: J. BRICE (South Carolina) and mother not stated; death cause: not stated; died: 4 Apr. 1915; record (1915) # 104.

FOX, Eva Cate; age: 2 years, 7 months and 28 days; parents: Clifford FOX and Julia ELLENBURG; death cause: not stated; informant: Harriett ELLENBURG (Greeneville); died: 14 Apr. 1915; buried: St. James; record (1915) # 105.

MORELOCK, Ida Carter; age: 41 years, 10 months and 17 days; born: 11 Jun. 18__; married; parents: W.B. CARTER and Dora POPE; death cause: "acute diarrhea"; informant: E.A. MORELOCK (Moshiem); died: 28 Apr. 1915; record (1915) # 106.

MERCY, Freda Lenore; born: 17 Feb. 1908; parents: Fred L. MERCY (Maine) and Atta TRAVIS; death cause: "poisoned by eating mustard greens"; informant: father (Moshiem); died: 28 Apr. 1915; record # 107.

BROWN, Elizabeth A.; born: 1 Sep. 1834 in Hamblen County; widow; parents: John MCDONALD and __ SELF; death cause: "tuberculosis of __ (illegible) and spine"; informant: John M. HULL (Moshiem); died: 10 Apr. 1915; buried: Brown Church; record (1915) # 108.

GUFFIE, Lee; born: 26 Dec. 1892 in North Carolina; single; parents: father not stated and __ GUFFIE (North Carolina); death cause: "tuberculosis"; informant: W.T. HARMON (Greeneville); died: 19 Apr. 1915; buried: Gass Shed; record (1915) # 109.

BOWMAN, Cora Patten; born: 29 Apr. 1872 married; parents: Samuel FOX and Florence BURGNER; death cause: "lagrippe, heart disease"; died at Chuckey on 12 Apr. 1915; buried: Cedar Grove; record # 110.

TOLLIVER, John Idris; born: 12 Mar.1905; parents: W.D. TOLLIVER and Eveline YOKELY; death cause: "tuberculosis of lungs"; died: 26 Apr. 1915; buried: English Cemetery; record (1915) # 111.

DOBBINS, Berthire; female; age: 76 years and 10 months; widow; parents: "unknown"; death cause: "old age"; informant: E. DOBBINS (Fall Branch); died: 5 Apr. 1915; buried: Lovelace; record (1915) # 112.

MCNEW, W.R.; born: 3 Jan. 1837 in Greene County; married; parents: James MCNEW (Virginia) and Millie GOSWELL; death cause: "old age, mitral regurgitation"; informant: Charles D. MCNEW (Moshiem); died: 4 Apr. 1915; buried: Timber Ridge; record (1915) # 113.

BALES, Mary Adeline; born: 14 Jan. 1846; widow; parents: William PIERCE and Cahtern PIERCE; death cause: "tuberculosis"; died in 20th District, 13 Apr. 1915; buried: Mt. Zion; record (1915) # 114.

HOWARD, Mary Catherine; age: 73 years and 5 days; born: 29 Mar.1843 at Limestone, TN.; widow; parents: Abraham MILLER and Elizabeth BACON; death cause: "broncho pneumonia"; informant: J.F. WILLIAMS (Limestone); died: 3 Apr. 1915; buried: Mt. Bethel; record (1915) # 115.

HARMON, Alice; born: 16 Apr. 1915; parents: Peter HARMON and Della J. MYERS; death cause: "still born"; informant: Pete HARMON (Moshiem); died: 16 Apr. 1915; buried: Pilot Knob; record # 116.

FREEMAN, David; black; age: 75 years; born: North Carolina; married; parents: "unknown"; death cause: "chronic rheumatic endocarditis"; informant: Will FREEMAN (Midway): died: 16 Apr. 1915; record (1915) # 117.

CROSBY, Infant; female; parents: Andrew Jackson CROSBY and Francis Mae SOUTHERN; death cause: "still born"; informant: father (Mohawk); died: 23 Apr. 1915; buried: Concord; record (1915) # 118.

TAYLOR, Alvira Williams; born: 24 Mar.1842 in Ohio; widow; parents: John WILLIAMS (Ohio) and mother unknown; death cause: "heart disease"; died: 1 Apr. 1915; record (1915) # 119.

MCAMIS, Thomas; born: 10 May 1851; married; parents: Thomas MCAMIS, Sr. and mother unknown; death cause: illegible; informant: W.A. MCAMIS (Greeneville); died: 6 Apr. 1915; buried: Fairview; record (1915) # 120.

ALLEN, Daniel C.; born: 13 Jan. 1843 in Greene County; widower; parents: Robert ALLEN and Ganett FARNSWORTH; death cause: "heart failure"; informant: Jones COOTER (Greeneville); died: 16 Apr. 1915; buried: Soloman Cemetery; record (1915) # 121.

BARTLEY, Eliza Jane; age: 67 years; widow; parents: Jack MARSHALL and mother unknown; death cause: "paralysis"; informant:

J.E. BARTLEY (Greeneville); died: 15 Apr. 1915; buried: Pisgah; record (1915) # 122.

PARMAN, Jay; age: 1 year; parents: L.F. PARMAN and Emily FILLERS; death cause: "broncho pneumonia"; died: 11 Apr. 1915; buried: Cove Creek; record (1915) # 123.

ILLEGIBLE, Emily J.; black; born: 30 May 1885; married; parents: "unknown"; death cause: "consumption"; died: 17 Apr. 1915; buried: Wesley; record (1915) # 124.

HARMON, Simon B.; age: 47 years; single; parents: Robert L. HARMON and Mary PICKERING; death cause: "syphilis"; informant: J.L. HARMON (Greeneville); died: 18 Apr. 1915; buried: Mt. Vernon; record (1915) # 125.

RICKER, Silas; age: 65 years; married; parents: Christopher RICKER and mother unknown; death cause: "chronic nephritis"; informant: M.R. JENNINGS; died: 25 Apr. 1915; record (1915) # 126.

ANDERSON, Mrs. William; age: 36 years; parents: J.P. CARTER and __ GUTHRIE; death cause: "childbirth and lagrippe"; died: 27 Apr. 1915; buried: Carter Cemetery; record (1915) # 127.

ELWELL, Joseph W.; age: 47 years; born: North Carolina; married; moving picture show manager; parents: "unknown"; death cause: "heart failure"; died: 28 Apr. 1915; buried: Oak Grove; record (1915) # 128.

PARMAN, Curtis Jay; born: 21 Mar.1914; parents: Lorence PARMAN and Emily FILLERS; death cause: "broncho pneumonia"; informant: mother (Greeneville); died: 17 Apr. 1915; record (1915) # 129.

CUTSHALL, Orpha; age: 73 years; born: Greene County; married; parents: W.M. CUTSHALL and Nancy RICKER; death cause: "asthma and heart failure"; informant: N.J. CUTSHALL (Greeneville); died: 7 Apr. 1915; buried: Price Cemetery; record (1915) # 130.

MCGEE, Lora Anza; born: 11 Feb. 1915; parents: Edd MCGEE and Maggie SMELCER; death cause: "unknown"; informant: father (Moshiem); died: 11 Apr. 1915; record (1915) # 131.

BOLLEW, Sarah J. Bertha; age: 32 years, 6 months and 2 days; married; parents: George TROBAUGH and Mary Jane RADER, death cause: "intestinal paralysis"; informant: J.W. BALEU (Mohawk); died: 1 Apr. 1915; buried: Mt. Hope; record (1915) # 132.

REEVE, Fred Smith; parents: T__ (illegible) Smith REEVE and Daisey E. MORELOCK; death cause: "premature birth"; informant: Roy REEVE (Chuckey); born/died: 3 May 1915; record (1915) # 134.
PACKSTON, Elzie; age: "unknown"; married; parents: father unknown and Ellen PAXTON, death cause: "typhoid fever"; informant: Herman PAXTON (Mohawk); died: 4 Apr. 1915; buried: Bible Chapel; record (1915) # 133.
MOONEYHAM, Orpha; born: 15 Jul. 1900; parents: James A. MOONEYHAM and Sarah GREGG (Cocke County); death cause: "typhoid fever"; informant: Minnis GREGG (Parrotsville, Cocke County) died: 12 May 1915; buried: Mt. Olivet; record (1915) # 135.
WADDLE, Lura S.; born: 14 Nov. 1884; married; parents: John M. JACKSON and Catherine HOLT; death cause: "consumption"; informant: B.E. JACKSON (Concord); died: 11 May 1915; buried: Cove Creek; record (1915) # 136.
VANCE, John C.; born: 15 Jun. 1862; married; parents: Marain B. VANCE and Martha RADER; death cause: "chronic diarrhea"; informant: Bert VANCE (Mohawk); died: 18 May 1915; record # 137.
PATTERSON, David B.; born: 15 Jun. 1834 in Hamblen County; widower; parents: Thomas PATTERSON and Ettie KIDWELL; death cause: "lagrippe, heart disease"; informant: Will PATTERSON (Moshiem); died: 25 May 1915; record (1915) # 138.
ARTER, Gavenor; black; age: "about 40 years"; single; parents: James ARTER and mother unknown; death cause: "cardio hypertrophy"; died: 25 May 1915; record (1915) # 139.
HARRISON, Will; age: 45 years; married; parents: "unknown"; death cause: "angina pectoris"; informant: James JOHNSON (Greeneville); died: 5 May 1915; buried: Wesley Cemetery; record (1915) # 140.
GONAS, Sarah; age: "about 45 years"; single; parents: John GONAS and mother unknown; death cause: "tuberculosis"; died: 3 May 1915; buried: Carter Cemetery; record (1915) # 141.
KELLY, Dana Milburn; born: 26 May 1911; parents: Jeff KELLY and Katie BABB; death cause: "burned"; informant: father (Afton); died: 14 May 1915; buried: Gass Shed; record (1915) # 142.

RANKIN, Richard; born: 4 May 1842; married; parents: Lewis RANKIN and mother unknown; death cause: "uremic poison";; died: 5 May 1915; record (1915) # 143.

CUTSHALL, Ellen Faye; born: 21 Apr. 1915; parents: Sam CUTSHALL and Nancy RADER; death cause: "meningitis"; informant: father (Greeneville); died: 27 May 1915; buried: Greenwood Cemetery; record (1915) # 144.

MOYER, Mary; born: 23 Jan. 1915; parents: E.J. MOYER and Lora HARTMAN; death cause: "found dead in bed"; informant: Louise CAMPBELL (Greeneville); died: 30 May 1915; buried: Greenwood Cemetery; record (1915) # 145.

HUFFAKER, Wanda Deforest; age: 2 days; parents: Robert D. HUFFAKER and Bertham B. HILL; death cause: "heart failure"; informant: father (Chuckey; died: 1 May 1915; record (1915) # 146.

ALEXANDER, King; black; age: 73 years; married; parents: King DIXON and mother unknown; death cause: "tuberculosis of lungs"; informant: J.A. LONGMIRE (Chuckey); died: 28 May 1915; buried: Rheaton; record (1915) # 147.

DUMERON, Infant; male; parents: Moses S. DUMERON (Kentucky) and Laura JOHNSON (Virginia); death cause: "prolapse of cord"; informant: J. Earson MOORE (Jeroldstown); died: 31 May 1915; record (1915) # 148.

WILBURN, Mack; black; age: 53 years; parents: "unknown"; death cause: illegible; died at Midway on 20 May 1915; buried: Bulls Gap; record (1915) # 149.

HARMON, James F.; born: 17 Jul. 1845; married; magistrate; parents: John HARMON and Nancy CAVERN; death cause: "paralysis"; informant: Lillie HARMON (Midway); died: 17 May 1915; record (1915) # 150.

BROWN, Mary Nan Effie; born: 2 Nov. 1883; married; parents: William MALONE and Mary CRUMLEY; death cause: "lagrippe"; informant: J.A. BROWN (Baileyton); died: 3 May 1915; buried: Wesley Chapel; record (1915) # 151.

HARRISON, Infant; female; parents: William B. HARRISON and Ora Bell CROWN; death cause: "still born"; informant: F.C. BRITTON (Greeneville); died: 14 May 1915; record (1915) # 152.

BLEVIN, Infant; female; lived 12 days; parents: Joe BLEVIN and Flora JAMES; death cause: "malnutrition"; informant: Charles COOLER (Greeneville); died: 4 May 1915; buried: Mt. Hebron; record # 153.

REED, Alta Mira; born: 11 Nov. 1888; parents: Daniel B. REED and Sarah A. HARTMAN; death cause: "gastro enteritis"; informant: J.M. REED (Moshiem); died: 15 May 1915; buried: Mt. Pleasant; record (1915) # 154.

MACE, Mary; age: "about 17 years"; parents: George Washington MACE and Hannah RAWLINS; death cause: "tubercular trouble"; died in the 2nd District on __ (date not stated) Jun. 1915, record # 155.

JENKINS, Elizabeth; born: 7 Sep. 1850 in Hawkins County; married; parents: Gabral WALKER and Sarah WALKER; death cause: "astromylitis, toxemia"; informant: Gabral JENKINS, Jr. (Bulls Gap); died: 16 Jun. 1915; buried: Mt. Hope; record (1915) # 156.

EDWARDS, Dicie; black; age: 19 (?) years; single; born: Springfield, TN.; parents: not stated; death cause: "gunshot wound entering right shoulder"; died at Bulls Gap on 1 Jun. 1915; record (1915) # 157 (duplicate record at # 163).

WILLHOIT, Emanuel; born: 14 Nov. 1831 in Greene County; married; parents: Simeon WILLHOIT and Sarah PARMAN; death cause: "brights disease"; informant: J.C. WILHOIT (Greeneville); died: 13 Jun. 1915; record (1915) # 158.

HAWK, Lavina; born: 6 Oct. 1874; married; parents: David RENNER and Susan NEAS; death cause: "pulmonary tuberculosis"; informant: F.A. HAWK (Greeneville); died: 18 Jun. 1915; buried: St. James; record (1915) # 159.

CRUM, John F.; age: "near 44 years"; married; parents: Wes CRUM and mother not stated; death cause: "pulmonary tuberculosis"; informant: J.W. NEAS (Greeneville); died: 3 Jun. 1915; buried: Meadow Creek; record (1915) # 160.

STEEL, Katherine; born: 28 Dec. 1888; single; parents: M.H. STEEL and Nancy HOGAN; death cause: "tuberculosis of lungs"; informant: John LUSTER (Mohawk); died: 17 Jun. 1915; record (1915) # 161.

KITE, Silvis Joe; born: 18 Jun. 1915; parents: Joe KITE and Flora BULLINGTON; death cause: "umbilical hemorrhage"; informant:

Alfred KITE (Bulls Gap); died: 30 Jun. 1915; buried: Phillips; record (1915) # 162.

EDWARDS, Dicie; black; age: 19 years; born: Springfield, TN.; parents: "unknown"; death cause: "gunshot wound, homicide"; informant: Dora RAZER (Bulls Gap); died: 1 Jun. 1915; buried: Springfield, TN., record (1915) # 163.

BIBLE, Josephine; age: 23 months; parents: Truman BIBLE and Cora HUMPHRIES; death cause: "no medical attention"; died: 25 Jun. 1915; buried: Susong; record (1915) # 164.

ROLLINS, Rovena Bell; born: 5 Feb. 1915; parents: D.H. ROLLINS and Ora COLLENS; death cause: not stated; informant: father (Greeneville) died: 27 Jun. 1915; buried: Cove Creek; record (1915) # 165.

BURGNER, Isaac Mitchell; born: 27 Oct. 1840; married; parents: Christian BURGNER and Malinda FULLER; death cause: illegible; informant: J.H. BURGNER (Greeneville); died: 11 Jun. 1915; buried: Shilo; record (1915) # 166.

BOWMAN, Susan; born: 27 May 1855; marital status: not stated; parents: Ben MCCOY and Leda BLAKE; death cause: "tubercular meningitis"; informant: T.M. JONES (Greeneville); died: 24 Jun. 1915; buried: Getsemna; record (1915) # 167.

BABB, Margaret; born: 14 Jan. 1915; parents: Ed BABB and Daisey BABB; death cause: "acute gastro-enteritis"; informant; father (Greeneville) died: 3 Jun. 1915; buried: Oak Grove; record # 167.

THOMPSON, Edward; born: 27 Oct. 1853; married; parents: Henry THOMPSON and Elizabeth VAUGHN; death cause; "tubercular meningitis"; informant: W.H. THOMPSON (Greeneville); died: 6 Jun. 1915; buried: Fairview; record (1915) # 168.

MITCHELL, Lucy; born: 22 Jun. 1913; parents: James MITCHELL and Minnie MCDONALD; death cause: "enteritis"; informant: father (Greeneville); died: 15 Jun. 1915; buried: Oak Grove; record # 169.

OLINGER, Infant; male; parents: Clive OLINGER and Pearl HART; death cause: "hernia"; informant: C.M. HART (Greeneville); died: 16 Jun. 1915; record (1915) # 170.

CLOYD, Larua; born: 19 Jun. 1850; widow; parents: William LAUGHTLIN and Margaret MAUSHLER; death cause: "dysentery";

informant: J.H. LAUHLIN (Greeneville); died: 14 Jun. 1915; buried: Cedar Hill; record (1915) # 171.

LEONARD, Bettie J.; born: 10 May 1837; widow; parents: Pansler SMITH and Nancy MANAR; death cause: "cancer of kidney"; informant: Miss B__ (illegible) LEONARD (Greeneville); died: 25 Jun. 1915; buried: Shilo; record (1915) # 172.

BARNETT, Mabry M.; age: 25 years, 1 month and 3 days; married; parents: W.T. BARNETT and Virginia CUTSHALL; death cause: "pulmonary tuberculosis"; informant: J.H. CUTSHALL (Greeneville); died: 8 Jun. 1915; buried: Oak Grove; record (1915) # 173.

BALES, E.O.; age: 84 years; born: Greene County; widower; parents: Joe BALES and mother unknown; death cause: "fatty degeneration of heart"; informant: J.W. BALES (Greeneville); died: 6 Jun. 1915; buried: Pleasant Vale; record (1915) # 174.

BASKET, Louise E.; born: 31 Jan. 1844; widow; parents: John MCMACKIN and Polly A. BAILEY; death cause: "aneurysm, hemorrhage"; informant: A.B. REED; died in the 15th District on 21 Jun. 1915; buried: Milburntown; record (1915) # 175.

BAYLESS, John Alexander; born: 12 Dec. 1848 in Jonesborough; married; parents: Luke B. BAYLESS and Margarett A. MURKY; death cause: "tuberculosis of throat"; informant: Mrs. J.A. BAYLESS (Limestone); died: 8 Jun. 1915; record (1915) # 176.

MOORE, Bonnie May; born: 4 Jun. 1915; parents: Milburn Ingle MOORE (Hawkins County) and E__ (illegible) LIGHT; death cause: "faulty development"; informant: J. Carson MOORE (Jeroldstown); died: 8 Jun. 1915; buried: Simpson Cemetery, Hawkins County; record (1915) # 177.

STATON, Robert; age: 74 years; born: Washington County; married; parents: John STATON and Eslaine KORTZ; death cause: "cancer"; informant: J. Carson MOORE (Jeroldstown); died: 28 Jun. 1915; buried: Pleasant Hill; record (1915) # 178.

PARENAN (?), Sarah; age: 65 years; widow; parents: not stated; death cause: "chronic gastritis"; informant: Claud PERENANS (?); died: 20 Jun. 1915; buried: Cove Creek; record (1915) # 179.

WILHOIT, Manuel; age: 83 years; born: Greene County; widower; parents: not stated; death cause: not stated; informant: Tom WADDEL (Greeneville); died: 13 Jun. 1915; buried: Cove Creek; record # 180.

PRICE, Mrs. Glen; black; age: 22 years; married; parents: John KINCHLOE and Lizzie LYONS; death cause: "typhoid fever"; informant: Lem PRICE (Baileyton); died: 1 Jul. 1915; record # 181.

MCCOY, David; age: 12 years; parents: Dock MCCOY and __ TAYLOR; death cause: "infection"; informant: John FILLERS (Greeneville); died: 1 Jun. 1915; buried: "Bershebee"; record # 182.

BROYLES, Annie Lee; born: 18 Aug. 1914; parents: Nat H. BROYLES and Georgie GREEN; death cause: "cholera infantum"; informant: John BROYLES (Chuckey); died: 20 Aug. 1915; buried: Union Chapel; record (1915) # 183.

BROWN, Mrs. Hila; age: 83 years; born: Hawkins County; widow; parents: father unknown and __ FIELDS; death cause: "old age, valvulor heart disease"; informant: Carl HECK (Baileyton); died: 24 Jul. 1915; buried: family cemetery; record (1915) # 184.

HARKLEROAD, Infant; male; born: 30 Jul. 1915; parents: M.J. HARKLEROAD and mother "unknown"; death cause: "immaturity"; informant: father (Chuckey); died: 31 Jul. 1915; record (1915) # 185.

REMINE, Darvin Keith; age: 8 years, 11 months; parents: H.C. REMINE and Lizzie SHANKS; death cause: "typhoid fever"; informant: father (Greeneville); died: 18 Jul. 1915; buried: Limestone; record # 186.

DUNBAR, John A.; age: 64 years and 10 months; married; parents: Ben DUNBAR and mother "unknown"; death cause: "heart trouble"; informant: W.C. DUNBAR (Afton); died: 5 Jul. 1915; buried: Liberty Cemetery; record (1915) # 187.

SEXTON, Cordie Elnora; age: 22 years; single; parents: William Henry SEXTON and Mary Elizabeth MYSINGER; death cause: "typhoid fever"; informant: Ed SEXTON (Greeneville); died: 13 Jul. 1915; buried: Price Cemetery; record (1915) # 188.

JOHNSON, Infant; male; parents: T.A. JOHNSON and Lida LEMANS; death cause: "stillborn"; informant: mother (Greeneville); died: 12 Jul. 1915; buried: Harrison Cemetery; record (1915) # 189.

FRESHOUR, Elizabeth; age: "about 60 years"; widow; parents: J. CINDUFF and mother "unknown"; death cause: "heart trouble and paralysis"; informant: Charles FRESHOUR (Greeneville); died: 20 Jul. 1915; buried: Cedar Creek; record (1915) # 190.

JONES, Sarah M.; born: 8 Aug. 1836 in Tennessee; widow; parents: John PICKLE (Tennessee) and Elizabeth PICKLE (Tennessee); death cause: "dysentery"; informant: R. JONES (Mohawk); died: 9 Jul. 1915; buried: Jones Cemetery; record (1915) # 191.

HAUN, Jacob Daniel; born: 19 Oct. 1845; married; parents: Elax HAUN and Elizabeth HAUN; death cause: "tuberculosis and chronic interitis"; informant: J. CANTRELL (Bulls Gap); died: 23 Jul. 1915; buried: Mt. Hope; record (1915) # 192.

CARTER, Eliz Alice; born: 25 Jun. 1898; parents; Joseph E. CARTER and Mary A. EVERHART; death cause: "killed crossing the railroad track"; informant: father (Moshiem); died: 28 Jul. 1915; buried: Everhart Cemetery; record (1915) # 193.

HAUN, Martha Isabell Johnson; born: 10 May 1867; married; parents: Andrew HAUN and Elizabeth DYER; death cause: "tuberculosis of lungs"; informant: W.S. DYER (Mohawk); died: 19 Jul. 1915; buried: Hugans; record (1915) # 194.

GODSEY, Joe; black; age: 7 years; parents: Charles GODSEY and Daisy LOUDERMILK; death cause: "tuberculosis"; informant: William RUSSELL (Bulls Gap); died: 5 Jul. 1915; buried: Drakes Cemetery; record (1915) # 195.

UNKNOWN, Male; age: "about 25 to 30 years; parents: "unknown"; death cause: "killed by Southern Railroad train, found in creek dead"; died: "about 1 Jul. 1915"; buried: Railway right of way; record # 196.

WHITSON, Infant; male; born: 8 Jul. 1915; parents: Will WHITSON and Belle KNIGHT; death cause: "died soon after birth"; informant: father (Greeneville); died: 8 Jul. 1915; buried: Tidwell Church; record (1915) # 197.

HAMMOND, Ruth Evelyn; parents: P.L. HAMMOND and Ruth Maude HIGHT (Texas); death cause: "stillborn"; informant: father (Greeneville); died: 10 Jul. 1915; buried: Oak Grove; record (1915) # 198.

JOHNSON, Lillie; black; born: 6 Mar.1895; single; parents: J.L. JOHNSON and Alfie BILLINGSLY (Georgia); death cause: "tuberculosis"; informant: father (Greeneville); died: 17 Jul. 1915; record (1915) # 199.

RANKIN, Infant; female; parents: E.K. RANKIN and Oline STRAND (Illinois); death cause: "7 month child"; informant: father (Greeneville); died: 20 Jul. 1915; buried: Rankin Cemetery; record (1915) # 200.

CATRON, Zenas; male; born: 27 Jul. 1890; married; parents: J.B. CATRON and Barbara COBBLE; death cause: "typhoid fever"; informant: father (Midway); died: 27 Jul. 1915; buried: Midway; record (1915) # 201.

HARE, John S.; born: 8 May 1830 in Greene County; married; parents: Abram HARE and mother "unknown"; death cause: "tuberculosis"; informant: Lane J. HARE (Greeneville); died: 18 Jul. 1915; buried: Pine Springs; record (1915) # 202.

WILSON, Margaret; age: 56 years; married; parents: "unknown"; death cause: "neurasthenia"; informant: John WILSON (Greeneville); died: 18 Jul. 1915; buried: Mt. Hebron; record (1915) # 202.

ANDERSON, Annie; age: 31(?); married; parents: William KELLER and Jonnie ROSS; death cause: "shock from surgical hysterectomy"; informant: James ANDERSON; died: 31 Jul. 1915; buried: Gass Shed; record (1915) # 203.

SHORES, Joseph; born: 10 Aug. 1914; parents: John SHORES and Carrie L__ (illegible); death cause: "indigestion"; informant: Charles SHORES (Greeneville); died: 2 Jul. 1915; buried: Shilo; record # 204.

BAILES, Lizzie; age: 72 years; single; parents: "unknown"; death cause: "dysentery"; died: 4 Jul. 1915; record (1915) # 205.

CHAPMAN, Laura; born: 5 Jul. 1875 in North Carolina; married; parents: father "unknown" and Lillie RUDE; death cause: "hemorrhage of lungs"; informant: Ed CHAPMAN (Greeneville); died: 5 Jul. 1915; buried: Shilo; record (1915) # 205.

PHILLIPS, Riley; born: 3 Jul. 1888; married; parents: Nathan PHILLIPS and mother not stated (Scott County, VA.); death cause: "drowned in Chucky River"; informant: David PHILLIPS (Afton); died: 14 Jul. 1915; buried: Fairview; record (1915) # 207. (see also record # 210)

PHILLIPS, Doak; age: 16 years; parents: Jim PHILLIPS and mother "unknown"; death cause: "accidental drowning"; informant: Nathan PHILLIPS (Chucky); died: 14 Jul. 1915; buried: Fairview; record (1915) # 208. (see also record # 209)

PHILLIPS, Doak; age: 17 years; parents: Nathan PHILLIPS and mother "unknown"; death cause: "accidental drowning"; informant: Nathan PHILLIPS (Chucky); died: 4 Jul. 1915; buried: Fairview; record # 209.

PHILLIPS, Riley; born: 3 Jul. 1882; married; parents: Nathan PHILLIPS and mother "unknown"; death cause: "accidental drowning"; informant: Nathan PHILLIPS (Chucky); died: 4 Jul. 1915; buried: Fairview; record (1915) # 210.

WHITE, Margaret A.; born: 28 Jun. 1862; widow; parents: James RODGERS and Ellen RODGERS; death cause: "tuberculosis and pneumonia"; informant: Frank RODGERS (Baileyton); died: 31 Jul. 1915; buried: 20th District; record (1915) # 211.

ALLEN, Sam; born: 9 Apr. 1856; widower; parents: Danil ALLEN and mother "unknown"; death cause: "darn fool never had a doctor"; informant: W.R. DOUGLAS (Greeneville); died: 9 Jul. 1915; buried: Meadow Creek; record (1915) # 212.

COLINS, Robert Claud; born: 21 Aug. 1914; parents: Charles COLINS and Laura COLLIT; death cause: "entero colitis"; informant: father (Baileyton); died: 14 Jul. 1915; buried: Pleasant Vale; record # 213.

MCABEE, Susan; age: 76 years; born: North Carolina; widow; parents: __ ROBERTS and mother not stated; death cause: "dysentery"; informant: John MCABEE (Moshiem); died: 17 Jul. 1915; buried: Brown Springs; record (1915) # 214.

SMITH, Ida A.; born: 22 Jan. 1865; married; parents: William RADER and Nancy RADER; death cause: "peritonitis, appendicitis"; informant: James C. SMITH (Moshiem); died: 4 Jul. 1915; buried: Midway; record (1915) # 215.

WILLIAMS, Bruce; born: 5 Dec. 1914; parents: John WILLIAMS and Vinie DAVIS; death cause: "tuberculosis of bowels"; informant: father (Greeneville); died: 5 Aug. 1915; buried: Mt. Bethel; record # 216.

SHACKLEFORD, Mary S.; born: 21 Jun. 1891; married; parents: William H. HOLLAND and Susan REYNOLDS; death cause: "tuberculosis"; informant: John SHACKLEFORD (Baileyton); died: 24 Aug. 1915; buried: Doty Cemetery; record (1915) # 217.

MILLER, Infant; male; black; parents: Joe MILLER and Harriet BEARD; death cause: "7 month infant"; born/died: 5 Aug. 1915; buried: Baileyton; record (1915) # 218.

MOORE, Marlina Hartsell; born: 6 Sep. 1897; single; parents: William Sherwood MOORE and Nirva Francis WATTENBURGER; death cause: "typhoid fever"; died: 5 Aug. 1915; buried: Zion; record # 219.

SMITH, Kyle Vincent; born; 27 Mar.1914; parents: Edgar SMITH and __ (illegible) HOPE; death cause: "enter colitis"; informant: J.F. SMITH (Afton); died: 14 Aug. 1915; buried: Mt. Zion; record (1915) # 220.

SKYLES, John W.; born: 1 Mar.1835 in Tennessee; married; parents: John W. SKYLES and Salina BROYLES; death cause: "intestinal nephritis"; informant: John H. SKYLES (Chucky); died: 20 Aug. 1915; buried: Pleasant Hill; record (1915) # 221.

KIDWELL, Elijah; age: "about 68 years"; married; parents: John KIDWELL and mother "unknown"; death cause: "tuberculosis of bowels"; informant: J.J. MALONEY (Greenvellle); died: 30 Aug. 1915; buried: Gass Shed; record (1915) # 221(duplicate 221)

PATTISON, James W.; age: 42 years; married; parents: David B. PATTISON and Polly Ann COUCH; death cause: "cancer of neck and typhoid fever"; informant: E.T. DAY (Bulls Gap); died: 15 Aug. 1915; buried: Kidwell Cemetery; record (1915) # 222.

RICE, Thomas; born: 2 Aug. 1889; single; parents: John RICE (North Carolina) and Jane GILBERT; death cause: "abscess of liver"; informant: father (Parrotsville); died: 2 Aug. 1915; buried: Parrotsville; record (1915) # 223.

HUX, Gladys; age: 13 months; parents: Charles HUX and Pearl COLYER; death cause: "whooping cough, flux"; informant: father (Greeneville); died: 7 Aug. 1915; buried: Oak Grove; record # 224.

JOHNSON, James; black; born: 23 Aug. 1860; widower; plasterer; parents: James JOHNSON, Sr. and mother "unknown"; death cause: "lagrippe"; informant: Will BRISCOE (Greeneville); died: 23 Aug. 1915; record (1915) # 225.

BRISCOE, Mary; black; born: 21 Dec. __; age: 13 years, 8 months and 2 days; parents: Will BRISCOE and Mary BRISCOE; death cause: "diphtheria"; informant: father (Greeneville); died: 23 Aug. 1915; record (1915) # 226.

BIBLE, Eliza; age: 58 years; widow; parents: John SEXTON and __ DAUKINS; death cause: "heart failure"; informant: Harrison BIBLE (Greeneville); died: 24 Aug. 1915; record (1915) # 227.

METCALF, Absalom; born: 7 Nov. 1831 in Yancey County, NC.; married; parents: Hiram METCALF and Jennie HENSLEY; death cause: "diarrhea and heart disease"; informant: S.E. METCALF (Greeneville); died: 26 Aug. 1915; buried: Mt. Taher; record # 228.

KETRON, John Thomas; age: 2 years, 5 months and 20 days; born: Washington County; parents: A.C. KETRON and Sue R. ROSS; death cause: "gastro enteritis"; informant: father (Chucky); died: 7 Aug. 1915; record (1915) # 229.

SMITH, Mary A.; born: 28 Dec. 1850; married; parents: James T. JACKSON and Sally DALTON; death cause: "pulmonary tuberculosis"; informant: M.H. HENSLEY (Jeroldstown); died: 10 Aug. 1915; buried: Bethany; record (1915) # 230.

BABB, Kittie Deborah; born: 29 Aug. 1887; single; parents: Elbert S. BABB and Mary A. CHASE; death cause: "Hodgkin's disease"; informant: Charles F. CRAWFORD (Fall Branch); died: 4 Aug. 1915; buried: Pleasant Hill; record (1915) # 231.

ISHAM, Marion Franklin; born; 26 Jul. 1915; parents: Jacob ISHAM and Katie EVANS; death cause: "no medical attention"; informant: Harry CONKIN (Jeroldstown); died: 14 Aug. 1915; buried: Liberty Hill; record (1915) # 232.

FINCHER, David B.; born: 23 Oct. 1839 in Greene County; widower; parents: Joseph FINCHER (Tennessee) and Susan STONECIPHER (Tennessee); death cause: "nephritis"; informant: R.B. FINCHER (Fall Branch); died: 7 Aug. 1915; record (1915) # 233.

QUINN, Mabel Ruth; born: 11 Apr. 1914; parents: Walter QUINN and Mary Lou WALKER; death cause: "broncho pneumonia"; informant: father (Moshiem); died: 27 Aug. 1915; buried: Bethel; record # 234.

ETTER, George Alexander; born: 22 Sep. 1841; married; parents: father "unknown" and Vista BIBLE; death cause: "diabetes mellitus"; informant: H.P. MCCARNEY (Mohawk); died: 22 Aug. 1915; buried: Home cemetery; record (1915) # 235.

LUSTER, Robert Noah; born: 31 Jul. 1915; parents: William LUSTER and Lillie MURRAY; death cause: "pneumonia, diphtheria"; informant: father (Mohawk); died: 26 Aug. 1915; buried: Luster Cemetery; record (1915) # 236.

GUTHRIE, William Thomas; born: 25 May 1847 in South Carolina; married; school teacher; parents: William GUTHRIE and Clementine THOMAS; death cause: "heart failure"; informant: Mrs. W.T. GUTHRIE (Midway); died: 24 Aug. 1915; buried: Midway; record (1915) # 237.

HARMON, Cloyd Vernon; born: 22 Apr. 1914; parents: William C. HARMON and Vina MILTON; death cause: "accidental drowning"; informant: father (Midway); died: 13 Aug. 1915; buried: McMillan Chapel; record (1915) # 238.

WAMPLER, William Webb; born: 7 Jan. 1911; parents: Dempsy WAMPLER and Nora AILSHIE; death cause: "dysentery"; informant: father (Midway); died: 1 Aug. 1915; buried: Moshiem; record # 239.

GASS, Howard Clayton; born: 18 May 1914; parents: Henderson GASS and Ida MALONE; death cause: "pneumonia" died at Baileyton on 16 Aug. 1915; buried: Mitchell Cemetery; record (1915) # 240.

FASHIE, Mrs. William; born: 31 Aug. 1855; widow; parents: Emerson REYNOLDS and Margaret BROWN; death cause: "nephritis"; died: 2 Aug. 1915; buried: Mt. Carmel; record (1915) # 241.

PRICE, Henry; born: 4 Jan. 1842 in Washington County; widower; parents: Martin PRICE and Mariann __; death cause: "__ (illegible) heart"; informant: Charles M. PRICE (Afton); died: 6 Sep. 1915; buried: Stone Dam, Tennessee; record (1915) # 242.

CARTER, Irene; age: 14 months; parents: John CARTER and Effa EVANS; death cause: "entero colitis"; died at Moshiem on 4 Sep. 1915; buried: family cemetery; record (1915) # 243.

GUDGON, Walter; black; age: 23 years; single; parents: "unknown"; death cause: "by pistol shot, homicide"; informant: Ed JONES (Moshiem); died: 5 Sep. 1915; record (1915) # 244. (note: record # 252 may be a duplicate)

CAMPBELL, Clyde; born: 10 Feb. 1899; parents: L.P. CAMPBELL and Mae KIDWELL; death cause: "tuberculosis of lungs"; informant: father (Baileyton); died: 5 Sep. 1915; buried: Salem; record (1915) # 245.

HUGHES, Benjamin H.; born: 16 Sep. 1892; single; school teacher; parents: James H. HUGHES and Sarah MCNEESE; death cause: "typhoid fever"; informant: W.P. HUGHES (Baileyton); died: 25 Sep. 1915; buried: Zion; record (1915) # 246.

SMITH, Mabel; born: 23 Jun. 1914 in Cocke County; parents: Claude E. SMITH (Cocke County) and Massie OTINGER (Cocke County); death cause: "sudden, no physician"; informant: father (Mohawk); buried: Cocke County; record (1915) # 247.

HAYS, Elizabeth J.; born: 15 Jan. 1843 in Milburnton, TN.; widow; parents: William M. FRAKER and Susana HARTMAN (Cherry Grove, TN.); death cause: "tuberculosis"; informant: Eugenia HARSHBARGER (Limestone); died: 23 Sep. 1915; buried: Pleasant Grove; record (1915) # 248.

RANDELL, Mary; born: 13 Aug. 1915; parents: John RANDELL (Minton, Michigan) and Sarah CAIN; death cause: illegible; informant: father (Greeneville); died: 1 Sep. 1915; buried: Oak Grove; record (1915) # 249.

MARTIN, Jennie; born: 3 Sep. 1876 in Virginia; married; parents: Felix __ (illegible) and mother "unknown"; death cause: "tuberculosis"; informant: Bob MARTIN (Greeneville); died: 2 Sep. 1915; buried: Oak Grove; record (1915) # 250.

CLEM (?), George Washington; black; born: 10 Nov. 1832 in Washington County; age: 77 years, 10 months and 20 days; married; parents: "unknown"; death cause: "tuberculosis"; informant: Minerva GASS (Greeneville); died: 2 Sep. 1915; record (1915) #251.

GUDGER, George Walter; black; born: 8 Aug. 1892 in North Carolina; single; parents: Steve GUDGER (North Carolina) and Mamie HERMIN (North Carolina); death cause: "homicide, gunshot wound"; informant: mother (Columbus, Ohio); died: 5 Sep. 1915; buried: Watauga; record (1915) # 252.

ANDERSON, Infant; female; born: 27 Apr. 1915; parents: William ANDERSON and Effie CARTER; death cause: "enteritis"; informant: father (Greeneville); died: 7 Sep. 1915; buried: Carter Station; record (1915) # 253.

DAULTON, Ruby; born: 12 Sep. 1873 in Virginia; married; parents: John D__ (illegible)(Virginia) and mother "unknown"; death cause: "blood poison"; informant: J.L. SWARTZ (Greeneville); died: 12 Sep. 1915; buried: Oak Grove; record (1915) # 254.

WILSON, Ed; born: 10 Aug. 1915; parents: Walter RICKER and Gussie WILSON; death cause: "malnutrition"; informant: Mrs. M.L. JACK (Greeneville); died: 17 Sep. 1915; record (1915) # 255.

BRANCH, Harvey; age: 67 years; married; parents: "unknown"; death cause: "paralysis"; informant: Burge BROOKS (Greeneville); died: 25 Sep. 1915; buried: Mt. Hebron; record (1915) # 256.

BOHANAN, William Thomas; age: 77 years; born: North Carolina; married; parents: Simon BOHANAN (North Carolina) and __ GREER (North Carolina); death cause: "gastric hemorrhage"; informant: John BOHANAN (Greeneville); died: 28 Sep. 1915; buried: Mt. Vernon; record (1915) # 257.

EARLY, Elsa; born: 20 Sep. 1914; parents: William EARLY and Mary THOMPSON; death cause: "diphtheria"; informant: James LANE (Baileyton); died: 27 Sep. 1915; buried: Pleasant Vale; record # 258.

DUNN, John; born: 14 Mar.1843 in North Carolina; married; shoemaker; parents: Samuel M. DUNN (North Carolina) and Julia Ann BLANTON (North Carolina); death cause: "tuberculosis"; informant: Sarah DUNN (Afton); died: 16 Sep. 1915; record (1915) # 259.

VAUGHN, Louise; age: 60 years and 3 months; widow; parents: __ MCAMIS and mother "unknown"; death cause: "pulmonary hemorrhage"; informant: Ray VAUGHN (Afton); died: 11 Sep. 1915; record (1915) # 260.

BOLON, Hazel; born: 6 Jun. 1903; parents: John BOLON and Vinia COLLINS; death cause: "pneumonia and typhoid fever"; informant: James COLLINS (Jeroldstown); died: 3 Sep. 1915; buried: Lovelace; record (1915) # 261.

THACKER, Jane; born: 25 Jun. 1838 in Greene County; widow; parents: S.S. HAWKINS and Catherine LINEBAUGH; death cause: "old age"; informant: S.F. ROGERS (Baileyton); died: 27 Sep. 1915; buried: New Lebanon; record (1915) # 262.

MYERS, A. Inell; born: 15 Jun. 1909; parents: C. Festus MYERS and Lida E. MCGUFFIE; death cause: "septicemia"; informant: father (Mohawk); died: 17 Sep. 1915; record (1915) # 263.

BLACK, Pearl Lucile; born: 6 Aug. 1913; parents: Tom BLACK and Alice SMITH; death cause: "diphtheria"; informant: Katie HARRIS (Mohawk); died: 22 Sep. 1915; buried: Mt. Hope; record (1015) # 264.

MAUK, A.H.; age: 69 years, 4 months and 12 days; born: Washington County; married; parents: John MAUK (Washington County) and mother not stated; death cause: "general debility"; informant: W.R. BITNER (Chucky); died: 22 Sep. 1915; buried: Pleasant Hill; record (1915) # 265.

BLACKBURN, Lucinda Alice Kelley; born: 10 Jul. 1852; married; parents: Samuel KELLEY and Elizabeth JENNINGS; death cause: "cardiac dropsy"; informant: Hugh KELLEY (Greeneville); died: 23 Sep. 1915; buried: Harrison Cemetery; record (1915) # 266.

SELF, Dorthy Maxine; born: 6 Dec. 1913; parents: William K. SELF and Ollie Belle HARTMAN; death cause: "meningitis"; informant: W.R. WEEMS (Midway); died: 27 Sep. 1915; record (1915) # 267.

SCRUGGS, Sallie; black; age "unknown"; widow; parents "unknown"; death cause: "tuberculosis of lungs"; informant: Charles SCRUGGS (Midway); died: 4 Sep. 1915; buried: Warrensburg; record # 268.

LINEBARGER, Infant; female; parents: G. Fox LINEBARGER and Lou MARSHALL; death cause: "malformity of mother and large baby"; informant: Fox LINEBARGER (Moshiem); died: 20 Sep. 1915; record (1915) # 269.

HAWKINS, James Willis; age: 20 years, 3 months and 12 days; single; parents: George HAWKINS and Hila J. BROWN; death cause: "poison from drinking cane juice"; informant: father (Baileyton); died: 23 Sep. 1915; buried: Zion; record (1915) # 270.

KENNEY, Daniel; born: 1 Jan. 1825 in Greene County; widower; parents: father not stated and Sarah KENNEY (Tennessee); death cause: "debility of age"; informant: W.A. KENNEY (Baileyton); died: 22 Sep. 1915; buried: Price Chapel; record (1915) # 271.

GEORGE, Luvena; age: 68 years; widow; parents: Isaac FILLERS and mother "unknown"; death cause: "angina pectoris"; died: 5 Oct. 1915; buried: Red Hill; record (1915) # 272.

GAMMON, Doss; born: 29 Dec. 1913; parents: W.R. GAMMON and Card HOLLEN (?); death cause: "illeo colitis"; informant: father (Afton); died: 1 Oct. 1915; record (1915) # 273 - duplicate record.

BIBLE, Thomas Stokely; born: 26 Jul. 1857; married; parents: Ezra BIBLE and Elizabeth DAVIS; death cause: "cerebral embolism"; informant: Mrs. F. BIBLE (Mohawk); died: 1 Oct. 1915; buried: Warrensburg; record (1915) # 273.

SELF, Infant; female; parents: Robert SELF and Bertha DYER; death cause: "stillborn"; informant: father (Bulls Gap); died: 10 Oct. 1915; buried: Gap Creek; record (1915) # 273.

HORTON, Emma; black; age: 31 years; married; parents: George DUNCAN and Vinie LOVE; death cause: "pellagra"; informant: Mart HORTON (Greeneville); died: 4 Oct. 1915; buried: Wesley Chapel; record (1915) # 275.

WILLIAMS, Mary S.; age: 73 years; born: South Carolina; widow; parents: R.W. SIMPSON (South Carolina) and mother "unknown"; death cause: "uremia"; informant: Frank WILLIAMS (Greeneville); died: 2 Oct. 1915; buried: Oak Grove; record (1915) # 276.

COLLINS, Edith; age: 16 months; parents; J.E. COLLINS and __ KELLEY; death cause: "membranous croup"; died: 4 Oct. 1915; buried: Mt. Hebron; record (1915) # 277.

PIPER, James A.; age: 65 years; born: Knox County; single; merchant; parents: Albert M. PIPER (Virginia) and Mariha ALLEN (Virginia); death cause: "influenza"; informant: John PIPER (Greeneville); died: 23 Oct. 1915; buried: Oak Grove; record (1915) # 278.

HUFFMAN, Fannie Maxine; born: 1 Feb. 1900; married; parents: Robert MCCOY and mother "unknown by informant"; death cause: "typhoid fever"; informant: Robert HUFFMAN (Chattanooga) died: 23 Oct. 1915; buried: Pleasant Vale; record (1915) # 279.

MILLER, Mary A.; age: 74 years; born: Saltville, Virginia; widow; parents: Charles FERRELL and __ UDELL; death cause: illegible; informant: W.A. MILLER (Bristol); died: 4 Oct. 1915; buried: Pleasant Vale; record (1915) # 280.

MARSHALL, Edith; born: 7 Dec. 1914; parents: A.E. MARSHALL and Etta FOX; death cause: "martaditis"; informant: father (Midway); died: 2 Nov. 1915; buried: Warrensburg; record (1915) # 281.

KIRK, Mines Ralph; born: 15 Dec. 1905; parents: J.F. KIRK and Daner MCMILLEN; death cause: "diphtheria"; informant: J.T. DYER (Mohawk); died: 20 Oct. 1915; buried: Midway; record (1915) # 282.

LADY, Oneal C.; born: 8 Nov. 1915; parents: Emery LADY (Sullivan County) and Cora LADY (Washington County); death cause: "croup or pneumonia"; died: 2 Oct. 1915; buried: Lovelace; record (1915) # 283.

HAYS, Joseph; born: 24 Nov. 1851; married; parents: John H. HAYS and Margaret EVANS (Kentucky); death cause: "malignant disease of __ (illegible)"; informant: Malisa HAYS (Jeroldstown); died: 24 Oct. 1915; buried: Pleasant Hill; record (1915) # 284.

EVANS, Caroline; born: 29 Feb. 1854; married; parents: William NEAL and Sarah MCPHERSON; death cause: "acute gastro enteritis"; informant: W.R. EVANS (Fall Branch); died: 13 Oct. 1915; buried: Cedar Lane; record (1915) # 285.

MYERS, Hue Orland; born: 13 Aug. 1900; parents: Henry C. MYERS and Stella T. WOODS; death cause: "__ (illegible) of the throat"; informant: father (Moshiem); died: 30 Oct. 1915; buried: Albany; record (1915) # 286.

BLEDSOE, Infant; male; parents: Will BLEDSOE and Alice DEEN; death cause: "born dead"; died: 18 Oct. 1915; buried: Concord; record (1915) # 287.

RADER, Infant; female; parents: Henry RADER and Nora REYNOLDS; death cause: "still born"; informant: father (Midway); died: 29 Oct. 1915; record (1915) # 288.

GUTHRIE, Lindell; female; age: 4 years; parents: Anderson A. GUTHRIE and Lyda STRONDS; death cause: "diphtheria"; informant: G.W. POE (Mohawk); died: 14 Oct. 1915; buried: Mt. Hope; record (1915) # 289.

MILLER, Ruth; black; born: 8 Oct. 1915; parents: Jasper MILLER (North Carolina) and Gertrude SLIGER; death cause: "malformation of heart"; informant: Ernest WOODS (Bulls Gap); died: 10 Oct. 1915; buried: Drakes; record (1915) # 290.

GARBER, Jacob N.; born: 4 May 1859 in Washington County; single; parents: Jacob GARBER (Virginia) and Manervy NOLLINGTON (Virginia); death cause: "pulmonary tuberculosis"; informant: William GARBER (Moshiem); died: 27 Oct. 1915; buried: Mountain Valley; record (1915) # 291.

SUSONG, Gabriel L.; age: 67 years; widower; parents: John SUSONG and __ ROBERTS; death cause: "tuberculosis of lungs"; informant: Carl SUSONG; died: 1 Oct. 1915; buried: Cedar Hill; record # 292.

KING, Elisha S.; born: 8 Mar.1862; married; school teacher; parents: John KING and Margaret A. MARTIN; death cause: "pulmonary tuberculosis"; informant: Margaret A. KING (Moshiem); died: 1 Oct. 1915; buried: Antioch; record (1915) # 293.

DOAIN, Nancy Jane; born: 11 May 1880; married; parents: John WALKER and mother not stated; death cause: "heart disease"; informant: John WALKER; died: 7 Oct. 1915; buried: Doty Cemetery; record (1915) # 294.

JOHNSON, Hester Virginia; born: 25 May 1858 (?) in Virginia; widow; parents: W.C. BLACK (Virginia) and Barbara E. BAIR (Virginia); death cause: "paralysis"; informant: Robert BIRD (Greeneville); buried: Hermon; record (1915) # 295.

WHITE, Sarah Ann; born: 7 Apr. __ in Virginia; age: 85 years, 7 months and 20 days; widow; parents: father "unknown" and Sarah Ann MCINTURFF; death cause: "general break down, old age"; informant: Lake WHITE (Chucky); died: 27 Nov. 1915; buried: Pleasant Hill; record (1915) # 296.

JOHNSON, Rachel; born: 18 Jul. 1915; parents: Henry JOHNSON and Julia DICKSON (?); death cause: "unknown"; informant: Ella MONTGOMERY (Greeneville); died: 18 Nov. 1915; record # 297.

JOHNSON, Ruth; born: 18 Jul. 1915; parents: Henry JOHNSON and Julia DICKSON (?); death cause: "unknown"; informant: Ella MONTGOMERY (Greeneville); died: 18 Nov. 1915; record # 298.

BRUBAKER, Margaret; born: 8 Jan. 1836 in Greene County; widow; parents: Anderson CARTER (Greene County) and Katie SAYLER (Greene County); death cause: "lagrippe"; informant: D.A. BRUEBAKER (Baileyton); died: 16 Nov. 1915; buried: Mountain Valley; record (1915) # 299.

SPEARS, Thelma; born: __ Apr. 1915; parents; Marion SPEARS (Hawkins County) and mother not stated; death cause: "diphtheria"; informant: Will SPEARS (Baileyton); died: 6 Nov. 1915; record # 300.

DAVIS, Thomas A.; age: 69 years; married; parents: Jesse DAVIS and mother "unknown"; death cause: "gastro enteritis"; informant: J. DAVIS (Greeneville); died: 3 Nov. 1915; buried: Shiloh; record (1915) # 301.

DYER, Madlin; born: 25 Dec. 1911; parents: Fred DYER and Cela ALLEN; death cause: "membranous croup"; informant: father (Greeneville); died: 5 Nov. 1915; buried: Oak Grove; record (1915) # 302.

MORGAN, Wiley; age: 75 years; widower; parents: Thomas MORGAN and Rachel C. PRESLEY; death cause: "organic heart disease"; informant: C.B. MORGAN (Greeneville); died: 8 Nov. 1915; buried: Mt. Hope; record (1915) # 303.

PATRICK, Ida; born: 6 Nov. 1893; single; parents: Alfred PARTICK and Martha __ (illegible); death cause: "gastro enteritis"; informant: Alex FULKS (Greeneville); died: 8 Nov. 1915; record (1915) # 304.

BRUMLEY, Charlotte; born: 30 Mar.1901; parents: Ed BRUMLEY and Lea MALONEY; death cause: "leukemia"; informant: Jud BRUMLEY (Greeneville); died: 9 Nov. 1915; buried: Oak Grove; record # 305.

SIMPSON, Peter; born: 5 Sep. 1835 in Greene County; widower; parents: Henry SIMPSON (Tennessee) and Annie CARTER (Tennessee); death cause: "general debility"; informant: H.A. SIMPSON (Greeneville); died: 11 Nov. 1915; record (1915) # 306.

KYKENDALL, Neple; female; born: 12 Feb. 1915; parents: Avery A. KYKENDALL (North Carolina) and Flora KIRK (North Carolina); death cause: "marasmus"; died: 13 Nov. 1915; buried: Union Chapel; record (1915) # 307.

KYKENDALL, Mrs. Flora; born: 13 Oct. 1890 in North Carolina; married; parents: Richard KIRK (North Carolina) and Sarah SHELTON (North Carolina); death cause: "tuberculosis of lungs"; died: 14 Nov. 1915; buried: Union Chapel; record (1915) # 308.

LEMING, Samuel; born: 31 Jul. 1846; married; parents: James LEMING and mother "unknown"; death cause: "diarrhea"; informant: J.F. SMITHSON (Greeneville); died: 17 Nov. 1915; buried: Harrison; record (1915) # 309.

HARTMAN, Charles Morris; born: 1 May 1910; parents: William H. HARTMAN and Neyotte WALKER; death cause: illegible; died: 20 Nov. 1915; buried: Mt. Pleasant; record (1915) # 310.

BARTLEY, Annie Kate; age: 3 years; parents: J.E. BARTLEY and mother not stated; death cause: "membranous croup"; died: 25 Nov. 1915; buried: Pisgah; record (1915) # 311.

JOHNSON, John; age: 78 years; born: Greene County; widower; parents: James JOHNSON (Greene County) and mother "unknown"; death cause: "chronic asthma"; informant: Willie DEWITT (Greeneville); buried: Susong; record (1915) # 312.

MITCHELL, Bruce; age: 17 years; parents: George W. MITCHELL (Jefferson County) and Ida BARHAM (?); death cause: "pulmonary tuberculosis"; informant: father (Greeneville); died: 29 Nov. 1915; buried: Oak Grove; record (1915) # 313.

GREGG, John; born: 13 Feb. 1835 in Tennessee; married; parents: Marshall GREGG and Alpha SHIELDS; death cause: illegible; informant: Bert RUSSELL (Greeneville); died: 30 Nov. 1915; buried: Morristown, TN.; record (1915) # 314.

MCPHERSON, James Robert Alexander; age: not stated; parents: Tailor MCPHERSON and Emma KNIGHT; death cause: "erysipelas, obstruction of bowels"; informant: W.H. BARLOW (Moshiem); died: 17 Nov. 1915; record (1915) # 315.

SITZER, Gertrude; age: 17 years; parents: Jerrie SITZER and Fannie HUSTON; death cause: "typhoid fever"; informant: Ernest WOODS (Bulls Gap); died: 18 Nov. 1915; buried: Drakes; record (1915) # 316.

KITE, Sallie Kate; born: 18 Nov. 1911; parents: Charlie R. KITE and B.S. CUPP (Hawkins County); death cause: "diphtheria and paralysis"; informant: J.B. CUPP (Bulls Gap); died: 6 Nov. 1915; buried: Phillips; record (1915) # 317.

BERGER, Margaret Jane; born: 13 Oct. 1849; married; parents: Miller SEXTON (North Carolina) and Nancy WHITE; death cause: "acute indigestion and heart failure"; informant: John BURGER (Moshiem); died: 4 Nov. 1915; buried: Albany; record (1915) # 318.

KNIGHT, Blaine; born: 13 Jan. 1914; parents: Ambrose KNIGHT and Emaline BIBLE; death cause: "inflammation of brain from falling on a nail which penetrated the skull"; died at Moshiem on 26 Nov. 1915; buried: Whittenburg Church; record (1915) # 319.

MORRISON, Thomas; age: 55 years; single; parents: "unknown"; death cause: "pellagra"; informant: J.C. KELLEY (Greeneville); died: 10 Nov. 1915; record (1915) # 320.
PHILLIPS, Minuard Hampton; born: 30 Nov. 1903 in Ashe County, NC.; parents: W.R. PHILLIPS (Ashe County, NC.) and Ida Victoria CHURCH (Ashe County, NC.); death cause: "purpura hemorrhagia"; informant: father (Greeneville); died: 30 Nov. 1915; buried: Harrison Church; record (1915) # 321.
COLSON, E.A.; born: 21 Oct. 1915; parents: Oscar COLSON and Effie MCDONALD; death cause: "unknown"; informant: Jessie CARMAC (Jeroldstown); died: 26 Nov. 1915; buried: Pleasant Hill; record # 322.
MCNEESE, Francis Marion; born: 25 Feb. 1861; married; teacher; parents: Samuel MCNEESE and Margaret FREEBORN (Ireland); death cause: "nephritis and gastritis"; informant: Mrs. F.M. MCNEESE (Baileyton); died: 11 Nov. 1915; buried: Lebanon; record (1915) # 323.
BROWN, Sarah Elizabeth; age: 61 years, 9 months and 1 day; born: 6 Feb. 1854; married; parents: David L. GIBSON and Kiciah TRIVET; death cause: "pancreatic abscess"; informant: J.E. GIBSON (Fall Branch); died: 7 Nov. 1915; buried: Gass Shed; record (1915) # 324.
CRUM, Donna Elizabeth; born: 24 Jan. 1914; parents: J.F. CRUM and Florence M. YEARWOOD; death cause: "diphtheria"; informant: Bell CRUM (Greeneville); died: 16 Nov. 1915; record (1915) # 325.
COCKERHAM, James F.; black; born: 24 Nov. 1889; married; parents: J.C. COCKERHAM and Selestra HUTCHINGS (Alabama); death cause: "skull fracture"; informant: Gordan ISHAM (Mohawk); died: 2 Nov. 1915; record (1915) # 326.
MCKAY, Arrah W.; female; born: 26 May 1908; parents: Robert MCKAY and Eliza DAVIS; death cause: "tubercular meningitis"; informant: F.H. MCKAY (Chucky); died: 1 Dec. 1915; buried: Pleasant Vale; record (1915) # 327.
JACKSON, Robert; black; age: 49 years, 9 months and 10 days; married; parents: Robert JACKSON (Virginia) and __ RUSH; death cause: "tuberculosis"; died: 10 Dec. 1915; record (1915) # 328.
WEEMS, George Jones; born: 5 Oct. 1838 in Greene County; married; parents: George WEEMS and Matilda KEELE (?); death cause: "heart

failure"; informant: Mrs. G.J. WEEMS (Mohawk); died: 7 Dec. 1915; record (1915) # 329.

ROBINSON, I.V.; born: 14 Feb. 1912; parents: Jess ROBINSON and Lula BRYANT (Hawkins County); death cause: "diphtheria"; informant: Mrs. ROBINSON (Mohawk); died: 11 Dec. 1915: buried: Phillips Cemetery; record (1915) # 330.

BRIGHT, Sarah Etta; born: 2 Dec. 1891; married; parents: Amos SMITH and M.L. BARKELY (Washington County); death cause: "organic heart disease"; informant: Amos SMITH (Baileyton); died: 11 Dec. 1915; buried: Oak Dale Cemetery; record (1915) # 331.

SMITH, William; age: not stated; born: North Carolina; married; parents: "unknown"; death cause: "heart disease, rheumatism"; informant: Taylor RICKER (Greeneville); died: 2 Dec. 1915; buried: Pine Springs; record (1915) # 332.

BIBLE, Thomas; black; age: 90 years; born: Kentucky; single; parents: "unknown"; death cause: "rheumatism and age"; died in the 4th District on 14 Dec. 1915; buried: Warrensburg; record (1915) # 333.

BYERLY, Agnes; born: 9 Nov. 1888 in Brownsboro, TN.; single; parents: W.R. BYERLY (Telford) and S.E. BAYLESS (Brownsboro); death cause: "mitral heart disease"; informant: father (Baileyton); died: 6 Dec. 1915; buried: Zion; record (1915) # 334.

GREGG, Kate; born: 7 Aug. 1901; father: not stated and Julia GREGG; death cause: "diphtheria"; died: 7 Dec. 1915; buried: Fairview; record (1915) # 335.

LILLIAN, Joseph Huff; born: 16 May 1862 in Cocke County; widower; parents: Jacob KILLIAN (North Carolina) and Marth BLESS (North Carolina); death cause: "carditis"; informant: H.S. MCCAMEY (Midway); died: 25 Dec. 1915; buried: Warrensburg; record # 336.

WISECARVE, James; born: 17 Mar.1844; widower; parents; Harmon WISECARVE (Pennsylvania) and Maris HURLEY; death cause: "kidney trouble, uremic poison"; informant: H.M. WISECARVE (Mohawk); died: 11 Dec. 1915; buried; family cemetery; record # 337.

KEY, Albert; born: 25 Jan. 1913; parents; John KEY and Clodie FOSTER; death cause: "whooping cough"; informant: J.S. FOSTER (Greeneville); died: 1 Dec. 1915; buried: Gass Shed; record # 338.

SALES, Lew; black; age: "about 50 years"; married; parents: "unknown"; death cause: "epilepsy"; informant: A.N. SHOUN (Greeneville); died: 1 Dec. 1915; record (1915) # 339.

BRITTON, J.C.; born: 4 Nov. 1915; parents: Kenney BRITTON and Emma BRITTON; death cause: "gastritis"; informant: father (Greeneville); died: 1 Dec. 1915; buried: Gass Shed; record (1915) # 340.

MITCHELL, Minnie; age: 56 years; single; parents: J.J. MITCHELL (Knox County) and Mary Ann BRITTON; death cause: "gastro entiritis, pellagra"; informant: W.T. MITCHELL (Greeneville); died: 2 Dec. 1915; buried: Oak Grove; record (1915) # 341.

HUBBARD, Charlie; age: 60 years; married; parents; "unknown"; death cause: "tuberculosis"; died in the 22nd District on 11 Dec. 1915; buried: Mountain View; record (1915) # 342.

MCGAMERY, Infant; black; male; parents: Clarnce MCGAMERY and Susie CHANDLER (Georgia); death cause: "born dead"; informant: father (Greeneville); born/died: 9 Dec. 1915; record (1919) # 343.

DAVIS, Infant; female; parents: Tom DAVIS and Nellie MORROW (North Carolina); death cause: "stillborn"; informant: father (Greeneville); died: 12 Dec. 1915; buried: Oak Grove; record (1915) # 344.

CRUM, Elmer; born: 1 Aug. 1915; parents: "father unknown" and Mary CRUM; death cause: "diarrhea"; died: 15 Dec. 1915; buried: Oak Grove; record (1915) # 345.

SMITH, Elliott Benjamin; born: 6 Oct. 1838 in Tennessee; widower; doctor of medicine; parents: Jordan SMITH and mother "unknown"; death cause: "uremic poison"; informant: G.H. SMITH (Greeneville); died: 16 Dec. 1915; buried: Oak Grove; record (1915) # 346.

PICKERING (?), Lillie; born: 4 Jan. 1878; parents: R.A. HAINNER (?) and Mattie CHEDESLER (?); death cause: "pellagra"; died: 16 Dec. 1915; buried: Oak Grove; record (1915) # 347.

BALDEN, Ramen; born: 3 Dec. 1912 in McMinn County; parents: Anderson BALDEN (Sesquashie County) and Sallie GREEN (McMinn County); death cause: "enteritis"; informant: father (Greeneville); died: 17 Dec. 1915; buried: Athens, TN.; record (1915) # 348.

TILSON, Ralph; age: 18 years; born: Unicoi County; married; parents: Lee TILSON (Unicoi County) and Sarah TIPTON (Unicoi County);

death cause: "fell from horse, skull fracture"; died: 18 Dec. 1915; buried: New Bethel; record (1915) # 349.

PITT, Wharton Bisson; born: 9 Jul. 1859; single; parents: John PITT and Nettie PITT; death cause: "pneumonia fever"; died: 21 Dec. 1915; buried: Mt. Vernon; record (1915) # 350.

STANTON, Sarah; age: 67 years; born: North Carolina; married; parents: Roderick SHELTON (North Carolina) and mother "unknown"; death cause: "apoplexy"; died: 23 Dec. 1915; buried: Hebron; record (1915) # 351.

JUSTICE, Ruth; born: 20 Mar.1844; widow; parents: Soloman BAILS (Washington County) and __ PHILLIPS (Washington County); death cause: "diarrhea and brights disease"; informant: James JEFFERS (Moshiem); died: 14 Dec. 1915; buried: Mt. Carmel; record # 352.

REYNOLDS, John; age: not stated; married; farmer; parents: not stated; death cause: "tuberculosis of lungs"; died in the 18th District on 20 Dec. 1915; record (1915) # 353.

WHEELER, Henry; born: 11 Dec. 1890; married; parents: Will WHEELER and Mary JONES; death cause: "heart disease"; informant: James JEFFERS (Moshiem); died: 24 Dec. 1915; buried: Pilot Knob; record (1915) # 354.

EVANS, Robert M.; born: 26 Sep. 1913; parents; Samuel EVANS and Cat (?) LUTTRELL; death cause: "accidental burning of clothing"; informant: Belle OLLINGER (Moshiem); died: 12 Dec. 1915; buried: Pine Grove; record (1915) # 355.

SMITH, Infant; female; age: not stated; parents: father "not stated" and Jessie SMITH; death cause: "stillborn"; informant: Alden SMITH (Greeneville); born/died: 10 Dec. 1915; buried: Albany; record # 356.

BLUE/BALLUE, Dollie; black; born: 3 Nov. 1897; single; parents: Peter BLUE/BALLUE and Nancy SWEENEY; death cause: "pneumonia and tonsillitis"; informant: F.S. BUTTER (Moshiem); died: 9 Dec. 1915; buried: Midway; record (1915) # 357.

RAGSDALE, Nyoma Steller; born: 4 Oct. 1913; parents: George RAGSDALE and Lydia MALONE; death cause: "broncho pneumonia"; informant: mother (Greeneville); died: 2 Dec. 1915; buried: Gass Shed; record (1915) # 358.

HENDRY, Alma Modene; born: 19 Jan. 1914; parents: S.A. HENDRY and Florence DODD; death cause: "broncho pneumonia"; informant: W.B. HENDRY (Baileyton); died: 6 Dec. 1915; buried: Gass Shed; record (1915) # 359.

CASTIEL, William; born: 9 Jun. 1856; married; parents: Jerimiah CASTEEL and Susan WILTIE; death cause: "organic heart disease"; informant: J.M. CASTEEL (Greeneville); died: 13 Dec. 1915; buried: Gass Shed; record (1915) # 360.

MCCOY, Shafter; age: 18 years; single; parents: George W. MCCOY and Maggie JONES; death cause: "epilepsy"; informant: Elis MCCOY (Greeneville); died: 24 Dec. 1915; buried: Gethseminie; record # 361.

COLYER, Etta; age: 2 years, 7 months and 6 days; parents: Charles COLYER and Chassie BROWCH; death cause: "pneumonia"; informant: John COLYER (Greeneville); death date: not recorded; buried: Mt. Hebron; record (1915) # 362.

HOLT, Luther; age: 3 years; parents: Scott HOLT and Florence TEAGUE; death cause: "typhoid fever"; informant: George FARNSWORTH (Greeneville); died: 26 Dec. 1915; buried: Cedar Hill; record (1915) # 363.

BROOKINS, Levenia; black; born: 31 Jul. 1915; parents: Ike BROOKINS and Maggie SCOTT; death cause: "catarral croup"; informant: father (Greeneville); died: 31 Dec. 1915; record # 364.

EVANS, Child; male; age: "about 3 years"; parents: Samuel EVANS and Ota LUTTRELL; death cause: "burn, child fell in fire"; informant: J.S. KIKER (Moshiem); died: 14 Dec. 1915; record (1915) # 365.

WHITE, Infant; female; parents: William E. WHITE and Ettie SHIPLEY (Washington County); death cause: "stillborn"; died: 25 Dec. 1915; buried: Pleasant Hill; record (1915) # 366.

ROSS, George E.; born: 10 Dec. 1827 in Greene County; married; parents: "unknown"; death cause: "died suddenly, no medical attention"; informant: D.O. ROSS (Greeneville); died: 14 Dec. 1915; buried: Gass Shed; record (1915) # 367.

MELTON, Martin Columbus; born: 3 Jul. 1879; single; parents: Lewis E. MELTON (North Carolina) and Louise SANDERS (South Carolina); death cause: "pulmonary tuberculosis"; informant: L.E. MELTON (Greeneville); died: 23 Dec. 1915; buried: Timber Ridge; record # 368.

OWENS, Samuel Robert; born: 9 Jun. 1904; parents: James OWENS (Unicoi County) and Sallie FULKS; death cause: "injury to left side"; informant: father (Afton); died: 24 Dec. 1915; buried: Union Chapel; record (1915) # 369.

NEWSOM, Infant; female; parents: A.F. NEWSOM (Davidson County) and Georgia BEBBER; death cause: "stillborn"; informant: father (Greeneville); died: 3 Jan. 1916; buried: Upchurch; record (1916) # 1.

MOONEYHAM, Samuel; born: __ Mar.1854 in Cocke County; married; parents: William MOONEYHAM (Cocke County) and Tildy COGDALE; death cause: "acute bronchitis"; informant: Orphy MOONEYHAM (Greeneville); died: 12 Jan. 1916; buried: St. James; record (1916) # 2.

CARTER, Willie Ross; born: 4 Sep. 1900; parents: J. Mc CARTER and Cordelie BROWN; death cause: "croupous pneumonia"; informant: father (Moshiem); died: 27 Jan. 1916; buried: Albany; record # 3.

KNIGHT, Infant; parents: G.W. KNIGHT and Adie MCGUFFIE; death cause: "heard labor"; informant: father (Moshiem); born/died: 31 Jan. 1916; buried: Guthrie; record (1916) # 4.

BOWERS, Sarie; born: 17 Oct. 1837 in Greene County; married; parents: Jacob BIBLE and mother not stated; death cause: "bronchitis and rheumatism"; informant: Alvin BIBLE (Midway); died: 29 Jan. 1916; buried: Timber Ridge; record (1916) # 5.

MARSHALL, Annie; born: 2 Feb. 1855; married; parents: Ezekiel ADAMS and Rebecca SCULLY; death cause: "neuralgia of heart"; informant: Bettie ROBINSON (Midway); died: 6 Jan. 1916; buried: Warrensburg; record (1916) # 6.

KIRK, Martha Florence; born: 8 Apr. 1863; married; parents: Thomas KESTERSON and Caroline HURLEY; death cause: "tuberculosis of lungs"; informant: Andrew KIRK (Midway); died: 14 Jan. 1916; record (1916) # 7.

BIBLE, Marllia; born: 1 Jan. 1839; widow; parents: Samuel NEURMAN and Mary ELRNESS (?); death cause: "brights disease"; informant: Mrs. Jess BAKER (Mohawk); died: 25 Jan. 1916; buried: family cemetery; record (1916) # 8.

UNIDENTIFIED, Adult; female; widow; parents: Willison HENSHAW (North Carolina) and Roda PARSON; death cause: "hemorrhage purpura"; informant: Collie MURR (Greeneville); died: 9 Jan. 1916; buried: Whitenburg Cemetery; record (1916) # 9.

MELTON, Willie Ardell; born: 15 Nov. 1915; parents: Sam MELTON and Carrie CARTER; death cause: "found dead in bed, unknown"; informant: R.A. WARD (Bulls Gap); died: 23 Jan. 1916; buried: Willoughbys; record (1916) # 10.

GUTHRIE, Mrs. Mollie; born: 4 Nov. 1854; widow; parents: Taylor POPE and Susan BYERS; death cause: not stated; informant; Mrs. Carter (Moshiem); died: 4 Jan. 1916; buried: Midway; record # 11.

BROWN, Serenie; born: 20 Dec. 1840 in Greene County; married; parents: Barnet BAXTER and Moliss HAYS; death cause: "malignant disease of stomach"; informant: J. Carson MOORE (Jeroldstown); died: 15 Jan. 1916; buried: Pleasant Hill; record (1916) # 12.

GARDNER, Henry Lorenza; born: 12 Mar.1863; married; parents: Alfred GARDNER and Martha MYERS (Hawkins County); death cause: "typhoid fever"; informant: Belle MCCURRY (Baileyton); died: 1 Jan. 1916, record (1916) # 13.

TAYLOR, Bula Clide; born: 29 Jan. 1916; parents: James N. TAYLOR and Mary Jane ARNOLD; death cause: "prematurity"; died: 29 Jan. 1916; record (1916) # 14.

LOWE, Joseph; age: 48 years; married; parents: Frank LOWE and Mary COUCH; death cause: "hepatic abscess, gall stones"; informant: R.A. BERRY (Baileyton); died: 15 Jan. 1916; buried: County Line; record (1916) # 15.

ELLIS, Nancy; born: 19; May 1865; married; parents: John LINEBAUGH and __ MALONE; death cause: "pellagra, bronchitis"; informant: M.D. ELLIS (Baileyton); died: 10 Jan. 1916; buried: Zion; record (1916) # 16.

LAWS, Jack; born: 19 Jul. 1908; parents: Dave LAWS and Effie JENNINGS; death cause: "pneumonia"; informant: J.E. REAVES (Greeneville); died: 19 Jan. 1916; buried: Gethsemine; record # 17.

HOLT, Eveline; age: 12 years; parents: Scott HOLT and Mattie INSCORE; death cause: "typhoid fever"; informant: Tom FARNSWORTH (Greeneville); died: 20 Jan. 1916; buried: Cedar Hill; record (1916) # 18.

MCCLAIN, Mary; age: 80 years; born: Greene County; widow; parents: James JEFFRIES (Greene County) and Sarah KELLER (Greene County); death cause: "heart failure"; informant: Mrs. Morgan C__ (illegible)(Greeneville); died: 20 Jan. 1916; buried: Oak Grove; record (1916) # 19.

L__ (illegible), Alex; age: 54 years; widower; parents: "unknown"; death cause: "no medical attention, unknown"; informant: Will TULLACK; died: 21 Jan. 1916; buried: Oak Grove; record (1916) # 20.

CARSON, Lizzie; black; age: 43 years; married; parents: Peter DAVIS and Nancy GOOD; death cause: "uremia"; informant: Nancy GOOD (Greeneville); died: 21 Jan. 1916; buried: Wesley; record (1916) # 21.

RICKER, James W.; age: 70 years; married; parents: "unknown"; death cause: "heart disease and nephritis"; informant: R.E. RICKER (Greeneville); died: 22 Jan. 1916; buried: Mt. Hebron; record (1916) # 22.

ALEXANDER, Bonnie; born: 20 Jan. 1914; parents: Frank ALEXANDER and Bertie BRIGHT; death cause: "morphine poisoning"; informant: A.J. ALEXANDER (Greeneville); died: 27 Jan. 1916; buried: Mt. Hebron; record (1916) # 24.

WILLARD, Eliza; born: 20 Jan. 1852; married; parents: "unknown"; death cause: "ulcer and cancer of stomach"; died: 22 Jan. 1916; buried: Susong Church; record (1916) # 23.

SHELTON, Brown; born: 2 Oct. 1864 in North Carolina; married; parents: Baxter SHELTON (North Carolina) and Margaret A. SHELTON (North Carolina); death cause: "lobar pneumonia"; informant: Jacob NORTON (Chucky); died: 28 Jan. 1916; buried: Cedar Grove; record (1916) # 25.

HUNNICUT, Lizzie; born: 18 Dec. 1898; parents: Robert HUNNICUT and Harriett HYDER; death cause: "pulmonary tuberculosis"; died at Afton on 20 Jan. 1916; record (1916) #26.

MALINE, John D.; born: 30 May 1842; widower; parents: John MALINE and Patsie CARTER; death cause: "lagrippe and heart disease"; informant: H.B. MALINE (Afton); died: 17 Jan. 1916; buried: Gass Shed; record (1916) # 27.

PAINTER, Mary Jane; age: 78 years, 4 months and 6 days; born: Washington County; widow; parents: John WALKER and Rebecca KUKER;

death cause: "paralysis and heart failure"; informant: W.M. PAINTER (Limestone); died: 14 Jan. 1916; record (1916) # 28.

BOHANNON, C__ (illegible) P.; age: 31 years; divorced; parents: John BOHANNAN and Catherine HARMON; death cause: "tuberculosis and rheumatism"; informant: Neal BOHANNAN (Greeneville); died: 31 Jan. 1916; record (1916) # 29.

LEGARD, Helen; age: 4 years, 8 months and 28 days; parents: C.W. LEGARD and Nannie Kate SNAPP; death cause: "intestinal obstruction and peritonitis"; informant: father (Greeneville); died: 4 Jan. 1916; buried: Cove Creek; record (1916) # 30.

GOSSETT, Infant; black; female; born: 19 Dec. 1915; parents: __ (illegible) GOSSETT and Mattie GOOD; death cause: "malnutrition"; informant: John GOOD (Greeneville); died: 5 Jan. 1916; buried: Wesley; record (1916) # 31.

LISTER, Hattie Virginia; age: 26 years; single; parents: George LISTER and Callie LEONARD; death cause: "tuberculosis"; informant: Charles GREENLEE (Greeneville); died: 5 Jan. 1916; buried: Mt. Hebron; record (1916) # 32.

CARTER, Infant; male; age: 21 days; parents: R.B. CARTER and __ FOSTER; death cause: "no medical attention"; informant: Robert FOSTER (Greeneville); died: 6 Jan. 1916; buried: Harmons; record (1916) # 33.

CLEM (?), Sindy; age: "about 65 years"; parents: "unknown"; death cause: "tuberculosis"; died at the Poor Farm on 8 Jan. 1916; buried: Poor Farm; record (1916) # 34.

DEVATI, Pearl Ruth; age: 10 months and 10 days; parents: Clark DEVATI and mother not recorded; death cause: "broncho pneumonia"; informant: William DEVATI (Greeneville); died: 10 Jan. 1916; buried: Cedar Hill; record (1916) # 35.

BROYLES, Horace; born: 11 Jan. 1916; parents: Arthur G. BROYLES and Mabel E. MAYS (Virginia); death cause: "fracture of skull, forceps"; died: 11 Jan. 1916; buried: Cedar Creek; record (1916) # 36.

RICKER, Richard; born: 14 Oct. 1915; parents: father "unknown" and Lania RICKER; death cause: "lack of nourishment"; died: 14 Jan. 1916; buried: County Farm; record (1916) # 37.

WILLIAMS, Jennie; born: 10 Jan. 1851; widow; parents: "unknown"; death cause: "no medical attention"; died in 10th District on 15 Jan. 1916; record (1916) # 38.

BASHOR, Peter; born: 6 Feb. 1823 in Virginia; widower; parents: Ben BASHOR (Virginia) and Nancy SNIDER (Virginia); death cause: "no medical attention"; informant: A.M. MILLER (Greeneville); died: 17 Jan. 1916; buried: Moore Cemetery; record (1916) # 39.

SWINEY, Rebecca; age: 81 years; born: Carter County; married; parents: Isaac LACEY (Carter County) and mother "unknown"; death cause: "pneumonia"; informant: J.I. SWINEY; died: 18 Jan. 1916; buried: Fairview; record (1916) # 40.

CHASE, Pauline; born: 9 Feb. 1916; parents; Sam CHASE and Estelle BASKET; death cause: "purpura hemorrgica"; informant: father (Limestone); died: 24 Feb. 1916; buried: Milburton, TN.; record (1916) # 41.

MASSEY, Julia A.; born: 31 May 1877 in Virginia; married; parents: Robert SAMS (Virginia) and mother "unknown" death cause: "cancer of uterus"; informant: G.F. MASSEY (Greeneville); died: 16 Feb. 1916; buried: Cedar Hill; record (1916) # 42.

MILLER, Susan; born: 15 Jul. 1837 in Tennessee; single; parents: "unknown"; death cause: "arterio schlorosis"; informant: D.C. MASON (Greeneville); died: 18 Feb. 1916; buried: Oak Grove; record # 43.

MALONE, Mary; born: __ Sep. 1911; parents: Charlie MALONE and Nan __ (illegible); death cause: "lobar pneumonia"; informant: Dick ANDERSON (Greeneville); died: 24 Feb. 1916; buried: Gass Shed; record (1916) # 44.

BOLINGER, Henrietta Catherine; born: 13 May 1831 in Virginia; widow; parents: Jacob BOWERS (Virginia) and mother not stated; death cause: "influenza and bronchitis"; informant: J.H. MYERS (Chucky); died: 2 Feb. 1916; buried: Rheatown; record (1916) # 45.

LILLY, S. Walter; born: 11 Jun. 1871; married; parents: Warren LILLY (North Carolina) and Martha JAMES (North Carolina); death cause: "lobar pneumonia"; informant: J.H. MYERS (Chucky); died: 1 Feb. 1916; buried: Rheatown; record (1916) # 46.

KEYS, Aaron Jr.; born: 5 Jun. 1839 in Washington County; married; parents: Aaron KEYS and Mary HARTMAN; death cause: "heart failure";

informant: N.A. KEYS (Limestone); died: 17 Feb. 1916; record (1916) # 47.

JONES, Ross; parents: J.L. JONES and Ethel JENNINGS; death cause: "stillborn"; informant: father (Afton); died: 28 Feb. 1916; record # 48.

MALONE, Martha Jane Keller; born: 6 Feb. 1852 in North Carolina; married; parents: father "unknown" and Ellen KELLER (Virginia); death cause: "pneumonia"; informant: C.A. MALONE (Afton); died: 22 Feb. 1916; buried: Gass Shed; record (1916) # 49.

BROMLEY, Sarah Elizabeth; born: 10 Oct. 1863; widow; parents: James ROSS and Margaret E. __ (illegible); death cause: "tuberculosis of lungs"; informant: J.O. YOUNG (Baileyton); died: 12 Feb. 1916; buried: Gass Shed; record (1916) # 50.

LASTER, Laura Annie; born: 4 Mar.1915; parents: H. Dave LASTER and E. Ellen JOHNSON; death cause: "pneumonia fever"; informant: H. Dave LUSTER (Moshiem); died: 11 Feb. 1916; record (1916) # 51.

LASTER, William Edward; born: 16 Mar.1893; single; parents: Ham LASTER and Adaline RICHARDS; death cause: "lobar pneumonia"; informant: Sarah RICHARDS (Moshiem); died: 28 Feb. 9116; record (1916) # 52.

DAY, James R.; born: 1 Oct. 1842; married; parents: John DAY (North Carolina) and Sinie WILLIAMS, death cause: "bulbar paralysis"; informant: J.F. DAY (Mohawk); died: 14 Feb. 1916; buried: Fairview; record (1916) # 53.

DAVIS, Willie James; born: 4 Feb. 1916; parents: William Abner Center DAVIS and Sarah Adaline KESTERSON; death cause: "premature birth"; informant: father (Mohawk); died: 15 Feb. 1916; record # 54.

ELLER, Manila; born: 26 Jul. 1856; widow; parents: Milton HALE and Virginia EASTERLY; death cause: "rheumatism and endo carditis"; informant: H.P. MCCAMEY (Midway); died: 20 Feb. 1916; buried: Hale Cemetery; record (1916) # 55.

KESTERLING, Fred; born: 12 Aug. 1913; parents: R.N. KESTERLING and Myrtle CRAFT; death cause: "gastro enteritis"; informant: father (Midway); died: 1 Feb. 1916; record (1916) # 56.

CROAKER, Mrs. Mirann; age: 75 years; born: South Carolina; widow; parents: William GUTHRIE and Clementine THOMAS; death cause: "pneumonia"; died: 5 Feb. 1916; buried: Midway; record (1916) # 57.

JOHNSON, Andrew; age: 56 years; married; parents: William JOHNSON and Nancy L__ (illegible); death cause: "brain abscess and syphilis"; informant: Scott LAFOLLETT (Greeneville); died: 24 Feb. 1916; buried: Red Hill; record (1916) # 58.

BIBLE, Capt John; born: 22 Mar.1840; married; parents: Jacob BIBLE and Elizabeth WILLSON, death cause: "bronchitis and old age"; informant: Charles JACKSON (Moshiem); died: 26 Feb. 1916; buried: Timber Ridge; record (1916) # 59.

COOTER, Henry; born: 28 Dec. 1851; married; parents: John COOTER and mother "unknown"; death cause: "chronic rheumatism"; informant: J.W. COOTER (Baileyton); died: 13 Feb. 1916; buried: Walker Town; record (1916) # 60.

MCNEESE, Wiley; parents: Wiley MCNEESE and Gertrude MILLER (Jonesborough, TN.); death cause: "stillborn, mother falling"; died: 15 Nov. 1915; record (1916) # 61.

DEATHRIDGE, William M.; born: 12 Aug. 1854; married; parents: Andy DEATHRIDGE and mother not stated; death cause: "intestinal nephritis"; informant: J. Carson MOORE (Jeroldstown); died: 24 Feb. 1916; buried: Bethany; record (1916) # 62.

STRAUD, James Sentre; born: 21 Aug. 1834 in Greene County; married; parents: Thomas STRAUD (North Carolina) and Miss HURLEY (Greene County); death cause: "lagrippe and old age": informant: James STRAUD, Jr. (Mohawk); buried: Straud Cemetery; record (1916) # 63.

RADER, Mary Tennessee; born: __ Mar.1844 in Greene County; single; parents: Martin RADER (Tennessee) and Polly LADY (Tennessee); death cause: "lagrippe"; informant: Rinda RADER (Mohawk); died: 18 Feb. 1916; buried: Mt. Hope; record (1916) # 64.

SKEEN, Penington; born: 18 Feb. 1916; parents: James B. SKEEN (Virginia) and Zoed PENNINGTON (Virginia); death cause: "premature birth"; informant: father (Orlinger, VA.); died 18 Feb. 1916; buried: Mohawk; record (1916) # 65.

KITE, Pauline; born: 1 Oct. 1914; parents: D.L. KITE and Zona BARLOW; death cause: "cholera infantum"; informant: C.H. NICLEY (Mohawk); died: 12 Feb. 1916; buried: Pilot Knob; record (1916) # 66.

DOUD, James; born: 27 Oct. 1847 in Greene County; widower; parents: Patrick DOUD (Ireland) and Elizabeth BROTHERTON (North

Carolina); death cause: "nephritis"; informant: E. DOUD (Bulls Gap); died: 18 Feb. 1916; record (1916) # 67.

SETZER, Infant; sex: not stated; parents: L.B. SETZER and Lee PARMAN; death cause: "undeveloped head"; informant: Joe GIBBS (Greeneville); born/died: 10 Feb. 1916; buried: Cove Creek; record # 68.

SEATON, Margaret M.; born: 23 Apr. 1846; marital status: not stated; parents: John BIRD and Sue C__ (illegible); death cause: "pulmonary tuberculosis"; informant: D.S. BOWMAN (Greeneville); died: 1 Feb. 1916; buried: Gethseminie; record (1916) # 69.

SEWLCER, Miss Martha; age: 32 years; single; parents: William SEWLCER and mother not stated; death cause: "sarcoma of __ (illegible) glands"; informant: Charles SEWLCER (Greeneville); died: 10 Feb. 1916; buried: Pine Grove; record (1916) # 70.

PARMAN, Infant; male; parents: William PARMAN and Addie MCDADE; death cause: "premature labor"; informant: P.C. PARMAN; died: 3 Feb. 1916; buried: Flag Branch; record (1916) # 71.

YOUNG, James H.; born: 19 Sep. 1856; married; parents: Crockett YOUNG and Katy PETERS; death cause: "cystitis and nephritis"; informant: J.B. FORD (Chucky); died: 4 Feb. 1916; record (1916) # 72.

BAILES, Lizzie; age: 7 years and 7 months; parents: Charlie BAILES and Pearl COOTER; death cause: "pneumonia fever"; informant: Wice BAILES (Greeneville); died: 7 Mar.1916; buried: Cross Anchor; record (1916) # 73.

DAVIS, Infant; male; parents: Charles M. DAVIS and Minnie HENSLEY; death cause: "premature birth, stillborn"; informant: father (Greeneville; born/died: 30 Mar.1916; buried: Cove Creek; record # 74.

WOOD, William; born: 2 Feb. 1854 in North Carolina; married; parents: __ WOOD (North Carolina) and __ MCAFERS (North Carolina); death cause: illegible; informant: __ (illegible) WOOD (Chucky); died: 6 Mar.1916; record (1916) # 75.

MOORE, Pearl; born: 17 Jul. 1882; married; parents: Peter BURGNER and Frana PAINTER; death cause: "__ (illegible) of brain"; informant: W.C. MOORE (Chucky); died: 2 Mar.1916; buried: Pleasant Hill; record (1916) # 76.

SHAW, Clyde; born: 1 Mar.1916; parents: Rick A. SHAW and Bonnie __ (illegible); death cause: "no physician"; informant: father (Afton) died: 1 Mar.1916; buried: Herman; record (1916) # 77.

MATIABURGER, Haley; female; born: 1 Jan. 1840; widow; parents: Henry CRABTREE (Washington County) and mother not stated; death cause: "paralysis"; informant: John CRABTREE (Baileyton); died: 13 Mar.1916; buried: 20th District; record (1916) # 78.

POE, Infant; male; parents: John POE (Hawkins County) and Elizze BALL; death cause: "stillborn"; died: 19 Mar.1916; buried: Salem; record (1916) # 79.

RADER, J.L.; age: 62 years; married; parents: Henry RADER and Mary BOWERS; death cause: "tubercular inflammation"; informant: A. RADER (Greeneville); died: 23 Mar.1916; buried: Timber Ridge; record (1916) # 80.

GABY, Artie Mintie Couch; born: 13 May 1858; married; parents: Valentine COUCH and Elizabeth HALE (Hawkins County); death cause: "pulmonary tuberculosis"; informant: William GABY (Baileyton); died: 11 Mar.1916; buried: Mountain Valley; record # 81.

JANES, Andrew Jackson; born: 8 Mar.1872; married; parents: John JANES and Sana WADDLE; death cause: "heart failure"; informant: Mrs. G.W. CLICK (Greeneville); died: 3 Mar.1916; buried: Pisgah; record (1916) # 83.

SPEARS, Eliza Jane; born: 27 Feb. 1915 in Hawkins County; parents: William SPEARS (Hawkins County) and Virgia WHITESIDES (Hawkins County); death cause: "capillary bronchitis"; informant: Jerome SPEARS (Persia, TN.); died: 2 Mar.1916; buried: Needmore; record (1916) # 82.

CUTSHALL, Nanie; born: 27 Aug. 1877; married; parents: Daniel RADER and Susan BARNES; death cause: "intestinal obstruction"; informant: Sam CUTSHALL (Greeneville); died: 8 Mar.1916; buried: Timber Ridge; record (1916) # 83.

KEEBLER, Sana; born: 5 Jun. 1824 in Tennessee; widow; parents: Peter ETTER and Pheba MIKLE; death cause: "uremia"; informant: James ARMITAGE (Greeneville); died: 8 Mar.1916; buried: Midway; record (1916) # 85.

HAINS, Ray; born: 23 Jun. 1914; parents: John MCCLURE and mother "unknown"; death cause: "gastro enteritis"; informant: M.J. WISOR (Greeneville); died: 11 Mar.1916; buried: Oak Grove; record # 86.

CRUMM, Mary Ella; age: 36 years; single; parents: Tom CRUM and Elizabeth __ (illegible); death cause: "pulmonary tuberculosis"; informant: James SMITHSON (Greeneville); died: 11 Mar.1916; buried: Red Hill; record (1916) # 87.

HAMLIN, Per__ (illegible); age: 90 years; born: North Carolina; widow; parents: "unknown"; death cause: "senility"; informant: W.R. YONES (Rogersville, TN.); died: 19 Mar.1916; buried: Rogersville; record (1916) # 88.

HARTMAN, William; age: 70 years; widower; parents: Marshall HARTMAN and Sarah RADER; death cause: "sudden death, unknown"; informant: J.P. HARTMAN (Greeneville); died: 19 Mar.1916; buried: Mt. Pleasant; record (1916) # 89.

FILLERS, Wilber Cleveland; born: 14 Feb. 1916; parents: Tom FILLERS and Josie FILLERS; death cause: "no medical attention, unknown"; informant: father (Greeneville); died: 20 Mar.1916; buried: Red Hill; record (1916) # 90.

BOWMAN, Dora B.; born: 18 Feb. 1889; married; parents: Thomas OWENS and Lou C. TITTLE; death cause: "tuberculosis of bowels"; informant: John BOWMAN (Greeneville); died: 21 Mar.1916; buried: Zion Church; record (1916) # 91.

BIBLE, Infant; male; lived 7 days; parents: D.D. BIBLE and Dula COLIER; death cause: "unknown"; died: 22 Mar.1916; buried: Mt. Pleasant; record (1916) # 92.

GUNTER, Oliver Moses; age: 1 year; parents: G.W. GUNTER and __ RUBBLE; death cause: "bronchitis"; informant: B.B. BROOKS (Greeneville); died: 29 Mar.1916; buried: Red Hill; record (1916) # 93.

MOORELOCK, James; parents: Royon MOORELOCK and Annie WOOD; death cause: "born dead"; informant: father (Greeneville); born/died: 29 Mar.1916; buried: Oak Grove; record (1916) # 94.

LOONEY, Infant; female; parents: Michael E. LOONEY and Julia JOHNSON; death cause: "still born"; informant: father (Greeneville); died: 30 Mar.1916; record (1916) # 95.

SMITHSON, L.W.; age: 70 years; born in North Carolina; married; parents: George SMITHSON (North Carolina) and Elizabeth WHITE (North Carolina); death cause: "organic heart disease"; informant: James SMITHSON (Greeneville); died: 31 Mar.1916; buried: Red Hill; record (1916) # 96.

GRUBB, John William; born: 23 Sep. 1914; parents: Alexander GRUBB and Nora WHEELER; death cause: "cholera infantum"; died: 30 Mar.1916; buried: Oak Dale; record (1916) # 97.

JACKSON, James K. Polk; born: 15 Sep. 1847; widower; parents: Taylor JACKSON and Millie DALTON (Hawkins County); death cause: "heart failure"; informant: H.N. JACKSON (Jeroldstown); died: 18 Mar.1916; buried: Bethany; record (1916) # 98.

BROWN, Nancy G.; born: 12 Mar.1840; widow; parents: George HAYS and Sarah RIGERS; death cause: "old age"; informant: Marion HAYS; died in the 17th District on 18 Mar.1916; record (1916) # 99.

JONES, Infant; female; born: 16 Mar.1916; parents: Horton JONES and Alpha ISLEY; death cause: "unknown, no medical attention"; informant: father (Moshiem); died: 17 Mar.1916; buried: Mt. Sini; record # 100.

CARTER, William M. Brown; born: 15 Apr. 1845; widower; parents: Daniel CARTER and Sallie __ (illegible); death cause: "brights of kidney"; informant: Alfred CARTER (Moshiem); died: 26 Mar.1916; buried: Albany; record (1916) # 101.

BROWN, Mary A.; born: 18 Apr. 1841; widow; parents: Milton HULL and Nancy MYERS; death cause: "croupous pneumonia"; died: 26 Mar.1916; buried: Brown Springs, Moshiem; record (1916) # 102.

HONEYCUT, Infant; male; parents: W. Bruce HONEYCUT and Lulo O. BOYD; death cause: "asphyxiation"; informant: father (Moshiem); born/died: 26 Mar.1916; buried: Brown Springs; record (1916) # 103.

LASTER, Martha Lelah; born: 23 Oct. 1914; parents: Andrew J. LASTER and Sarah J. RICHARDS; death cause: "scarletina"; informant: father (Moshiem); died: 30 Mar.1916; record (1916) # 104.

MCPHERSON, Joe Jr.; born: 26 Mar.1916; parents: L__ (illegible) MCPHERSON and Daisy H__ (illegible); death cause: "unknown"; died: 29 Mar.1916; buried; Phillips; record (1916) # 105.

LOLLER, Etta Eva; black; born: 19 Mar.1912; parents: William LOLLER and Otha Lee JACKSON; death cause: "gangrene of mouth"; died: 30 Mar.1916; buried: Bulls Gap; record (1916) # 106.
MOORE, Parley; age: 10 years; parents: Andy MOORE and Florence MCC__ (illegible); death cause: "diabetes"; informant: Joe HARMON (Bulls Gap); died: 4 Mar.1916; record (1916) # 107.
COFFEE, Richard A.; age: "about 63 years"; born: Hawkins County; married; parents: __ COFFEE (Hawkins County) and mother not stated; death cause: "organic heart disease"; informant: Ed COFFEE (Bulls Gap); died: 4 Mar.1916; record (1916) # 108.
MATTHEWS, John Thomas; born: 4 Jul. 1884; age: 30 years, 4 months and 6 days; single; parents: E.W. MATTHEWS and Martha S. STROUD; death cause: "lobar pneumonia"; informant: father (Mohawk); died: 21 Mar.1916; buried: Fairview; record (1916) # 109.
MORRISON, Martha; parents: J.R. MORRISON and Della MALONE; death cause: "still born"; born/died: 31 Mar.1916; record (1916) # 110.
MAHONEY, Wesley; born: 25 Feb. 1859; married; parents: John MAHONEY and Hannah ROBERTS; death cause: "lagrippe"; informant: W.F. MAHONEY (Bristol); died: 9 Mar.1916; buried: Milburton, TN., record (1916) # 111.
MAHONEY, Belle; born: 2 May 1842 in Kentucky; married; parents: George SMITH (Kentucky) and Martha SMITH (Kentucky); death cause: "grippe and pneumonia"; informant: W.F. MAHONEY (Bristol); died: 9 Mar.1916; buried: Milburton, TN.; record (1916) # 112.
POE, Infant; male; parents: J.W. POE and Effie BIBLE; death cause: "suppose to be asphyxia"; informant: father (Moshiem); born/died: 23 Apr. 1916; buried: Brown Springs; record (1916) # 113.
PICKERING, Clarence Weaver; born: 26 Feb. 1892; parents: Albert D. PICKERING and Emma BATTAN (Virginia); death cause: "heart and bright disease"; informant: father (Chucky); died: 5 Apr. 1916; record (1916) # 114.
SHEFFEY, Annie Vister; married; marked "duplicate record" -see also record # 129; death cause: "pulmonary tuberculosis"; died: 29 Apr. 1916; buried: Pine Grove; record (1916) # 115.
PRUETT, Dollie; black; born: 16 Aug. 1889; married; parents: Huse SCRUGGS and Susan SCRUGGS; death cause: "pneumonia";

informant: John FREEMAN (Midway); died: 5 Apr. 1916; buried: Warrensburg; record (1916) # 116.

BIBLE, Andra; born: 18 Oct. 1898; single; parents: William S. BIBLE and Clara HENDRY; death cause: "phthisis pulmonary"; died: 11 Apr. 1916; buried: Mt. Pleasant; record (1916) # 117.

COLLINS, Lucinda Francis; born: 10 Mar.1861; married; parents: Andrew RENNER and Mary BOWERS; death cause: "apoplexy"; informant: C.W. LEGEND (Greeneville); died: 13 Apr. 1916; buried: Cove Creek; record (1916) # 118.

FANNON or FREEMAN, John; age: 60 years; married; parents; Nathan FREEMAN and mother "unknown"; death cause: "died suddenly, unknown"; informant: Charles FREEMAN (Greeneville); died: __ (date not recorded) Apr. 1916; buried: Mt. Hebron; record (1916) # 119.

CHAMBERLAIN, Infant; male; parents: Gene CHAMBERLAIN and Nevil WILLIAMS; death cause: "still born"; born/died: 25 Apr. 1916; buried: Oak Grove; record (1916) # 121.

NELSON, J.W.; born: 20 Mar.1857 in Smith County, VA.; married; parents: J.F. NELSON (Virginia) and Catherine WILLIAMS (Virginia); death cause: "myacarlites"; died: 29 Apr. 1916; buried: Oak Grove; record (1916) # 121.

KNUCKLES, Moses Isaik; black; born: 18 Apr. 1916; parents: Ed KNUCKLES (South Carolina) and Gussie WILLS; death cause: not stated; died: 18 Apr. 1916; buried: Pruitts Hill; record (1916) # 122.

GENTRY, Cloyd R.; born: 24 Mar.1916; parents: Thomas GENTRY and Ethel CONDUFF; death cause: "umbilical perni_ (illegible)"; informant: father (Greeneville); died: 10 Apr. 1916; buried: Mt. Olivet; record (1916) # 123.

MIDDLETON, Abagill Hays; age: 73 years, 8 months and 21 days; married; parents: John S. HAYS and Sarah ENGLISH; death cause: "gastro intestinal toxemia"; died: 25 Apr. 1916; buried: Pleasant Hill; record (1916) # 124.

MURRELL, James A.; born: 24 Jan. 1890; single; parents: father not stated and Sarah Ann MURRELL (Washington County); death cause: "pulmonary tuberculosis"; informant: Aaron HAYS (Jeroldstown); died: 19 Apr. 1916; buried: Pleasant Hill; record (1916) # 125.

WHITE, Joseph; born: 5 Sep. 1878; married; parents: John WHITE and Elisa WHITE; death cause: "pulmonary tuberculosis"; informant: Sarah WHITE (Jeroldstown); died: 5 Apr. 1916; buried: Oak Dale; record (1916) # 126.

SHANKS, Infant; female; parents: James SHANKS and Cordie THACKER; death cause: "still born"; died in the 17th District on 30 Apr. 1916; buried: Oakdale; record (1916) # 127.

BALL, John Franklin Charlie; born: 15 Dec. 1915; parents: Rufus BALL and Lee TURNELL (Hawkins County); death cause: "diphtheria"; informant: father (Baileyton); died: 20 Apr. 1916; buried: Greene and Hawkins Line; record (1916) # 128.

SHEFFEY, Annie Vistie; born: 1 Apr. 1874; married; parents: David H__ (illegible) and Mary M__ (illegible); death cause: "pulmonary tuberculosis"; informant: T.K. SHEFFEY (Greeneville); died: 29 Apr. 1916; buried: Pine Grove; record (1916) # 129.

YOKLEY, Mollie; age: 19 years, 4 months and 29 days; married; parents: A.L. SMITH and Sallie KITE; death cause: "tuberculosis of lungs"; informant: G.A. YOKLEY (Baileyton); died: 5 Apr. 1916; buried: Zion; record (1916) # 130.

COOTER, John Alexander; born: 28 Sep. 1857; married; parents: James R. COOTER and Nancy BROWN; death cause: "diabetes"; informant: Roy K. COOTER (Baileyton); died: 27 Apr. 1916; buried: Zion; record (1916) # 131.

RADER, Bula Louisa; born: 14 Mar.1916; parents: P.E. RADER and Mary GREGORY; death cause: "dead in bed"; informant: father (Greeneville); died: 18 Apr. 1916; buried: Salem; record (1916) # 132.

MCNEW, Infant; male; born: 22 Apr. 1916; parents: Charley D. MCNEW and Maud HUMPHRIES; death cause: "without medical attention"; informant: Garfield MCNEW (Moshiem); died: 23 Apr. 1916; buried: Hartman Chapel; record (1916) # 133.

RADER, Sarah; born: 17 Mar.1916; parents: Roy Frank RADER and Mary BOWERS; death cause: "convulsions"; died: 1 Apr. 1916; buried: Timber Ridge; record (1916) # 134.

REYNOLDS, Infant; male; born: 23 Apr. 1916; parents: John REYNOLDS and Blanche HOSHBERGER; death cause: "non development"; informant: father (Afton); died: 23 Apr. 1916; buried: Mt. Zion; record (1916) # 135.

MONK, Rolie; born: 27 Jun. 1907 in Virginia; parents: Whittny MONK (Russell County, VA.) and Serry __ (illegible); death cause: "lobar pneumonia"; informant: father (Chucky); died: 15 Apr. 1916; buried: Quaker Knob; record (1916) # 136.

HARMON, Lydia; age: 65 years; widow; parents: Christopher BIBLE and mother "unknown"; death cause: "tuberculosis of lungs"; informant: Clark RADER (Midway); died: 6 Apr. 1916; buried: Moshiem; record (1916) # 137.

DEBURK, Martha; born: 8 Apr. 1837; widow; parents: Andrew ANDIES and mother "unknown"; death cause: "broncho pneumonia"; informant: E.S. SMELCER (Midway); died: 18 Apr. 1916; buried: Pine Grove; record (1916) # 138.

HAUN, James; born: 10 Mar.1899; single; parents: Jim HAUN and Annie DUNCAN; death cause: "injury to spine and abdomen by piece of timber"; informant: G.F. HURLEY (Midway); died: 29 Apr. 1916; buried: Crosby Cemetery; record (1916) # 139.

LIEBS, Letha May; born: 8 Mar.1894; single; invalid; parents: J.H. LIEBS and Fannie PETERS; death cause: "osteromylitis and deformity"; informant: father (Chucky); died: 11 Apr. 1916; buried: Pleasant Hill; record (1916) # 140.

KNIGHT, Nancy M.; age: 83 years; born in North Carolina; widow; parents: "unknown"; death cause: "senility"; informant: George KNIGHT (Greeneville); died: 14 Apr. 1916; buried: Fairview; record (1916) # 141.

GREENE, George W.; born: 14 Jun. 1855; married; parents: Enos GREENE and Jane CANON; death cause: "log rolling on him"; informant: Martha G. GREENE (Chucky); died: 19 Apr. 1916; buried: Shilow Cemetery; record (1916) # 142.

LOWRY, Cahterine; age: 65 years; married; parents: Abraham C__ (illegible) and Sallie HARRISON; death cause: "pellagra"; informant: Joe SEATON (Greeneville); died: 1 Apr. 1916; buried: Cove Creek; record (1916) # 143.

HARMON, Charles Elbert; age: 60 years, 2 months and 8 days; married; parents: Mordica HARMON and Elizabeth ROSS; death cause:

"tuberculosis"; informant: D.W. HARMON (Greeneville); died: 3 Apr. 1916; buried: Harmon Cemetery; record (1916) # 144.

COBBLE, James; born: 13 Aug. 1839; widower; parents: father "unknown" and __ RADER; death cause: "organic heart disease"; informant: C.G. BIBLE (Bulls Gap); died: 13 May 1916; buried: Mt. Hope; record (1916) # 145.

DAUD, Manda; born: 23 Nov. 1857; married; parents: Kenric SPEARS and Betsie HICKS; death cause: "myocarditis, heart disease"; informant: Mrs. John KERBAUGH (Greeneville); died: 14 May 1916; buried: Pilot Knob; record (1916) # 146.

T__ (illegible), Sada; age: 53 years; married; parents: Cart TAYLOR and mother "unknown"; death cause: "apoplexy"; informant: Sylvester BLAKE (Greeneville); died: 18 May 1916; record (1916) # 147.

FRESHOUR, Infant; male; parents: Scott FRESHOUR and Adilia MACE; death cause: "stillborn"; born/died: 6 May 1916; buried: Whittenburg; record (1916) # 148.

MITCHELL, Willie Kate; born: 30 Jan. 1883; age: 32 years, 3 months and 8 days; widow; parents; Thomas MITCHELL (Washington County) and Elizabeth PEARSON (Washington County); death cause: "chronic stomach trouble"; informant: father (Chucky); died: 8 May 1916; buried: Philadelphia, Washington County; record (1916) # 149.

BOWSER, Bertha; born: 28 Apr. 1916; parents: Charles BOWSER and Dolly FORD; death cause: "immaturity"; died: 2 May 1916; record (1916) # 150.

OVERHOLSER, James William; born: 30 May 1916; parents: J.C. OVERHOLSER and Bonnie HARRISON, death cause: "__ (illegible) heart"; informant: father (Greeneville); died: 31 May 1916; record (1916) # 151.

BOOKER, Larie; born: 27 Apr. 1916; parents: William BOOKER and Charlie DAVENPORT, death cause: "without medical attention"; informant: father (Baileyton); died: 4 May 1916; buried: Price Chapel; record (1916) # 152.

TULLOCK, Smith Reave; born: 29 Feb. 1832 in Greene County; married; parents: Davie TULLOCK (Scotland) and __ FRAICAR; death cause: "senility"; informant: J.W. TULLOCK (Greeneville); died: 22 May 1916; record (1916) # 153.

COLLETT, Jane; age: 85 years; born in North Carolina; widow; parents: father "unknown" and Mary RHEA; death cause: "intestinal nephritis"; informant: Lizzie MAYEST (Chucky); died: 11 May 1916; buried: Rheatown; record (1916) # 154.

HUNTSMAN, Gay Nell; born: 19 May 1916; parents: James B. HUNTSMAN and Ethel HAUN (Hamblen County); death cause: "premature"; informant: L.A. MCPHERSON (Bulls Gap); died: 19 May 1916; buried: Drakes; record (1916) # 156.

GUDGEN, Infant; black; female; parents: __ (illegible) GUDGEN (South Carolina) and Emeline HAMINTON (?); death cause: "stillborn"; informant: Richard BASKETT (Limestone); died: 28 May 1916; record (1916) # 155.

JONES, William Manerd; born: 13 May 1915; parents: Alex JONES and Bertie KNIGHT, death cause: "pulmonary tuberculosis"; informant: father (Bulls Gap); died: 19 May 1916; record (1916) # 157.

SNYDER, Truman; age: 12 years and 11 months; parents: Darius SNYDER and Dona LIVINGSTONE, death cause: "drowned bathing in creek"; informant: Elmer DAVIS (Midway); died: 27 May 1916; buried: Crosby Cemetery; record (1916) # 158.

MCCULLUM, Jasper; born: 1 Aug. 1856; married; parents: John MCCULLUM and Elizabeth BRIGHT; death cause: "indigestion with heart failure"; informant: Mack DOWNY (Chucky); died: 18 May 1916; buried: Gass Shed; record (1916) # 159.

COLLET, Mary Emma; born: 25 May 1916; parents; John COLLET and Winie TAYLOR; death cause: "stillborn"; informant: James TAYLOR (Chucky); died: 25 May 1916; buried: Union Temple; record # 160.

LUTTRELL, Katherine Lou; born: 26 Aug. 1858; married; parents: James CARTER (Georgia) and Martha BURRELL; death cause: "lobar pneumonia and systemic infection"; informant: J.H. LUTTRELL (Mohawk); died: 6 May 1916; buried: Pine Grove; record (1916) # 161.

BROWN, Lila; born: 27 Feb. 1912; parents: C.F. BROWN and Eliza J. CARTER; death cause: "enteritis and pneumonia"; informant: father (Moshiem); died: 27 May 1916; buried: Brown Springs; record # 162.

LONG, Otha; born: 10 Mar 1914; parents: Ira LONG and Minnie BULLINGTON; death cause: "dysentery"; informant: John

HENDERION (Moshiem); died: 27 May 1916; buried: Willoughbys; record (1916) # 163.
KENT, Martha Jane; born: 11 Mar. 1852; married; parents: not stated; death cause: "bronchial asthma"; died near Moshiem on 31 May 1916; buried: Carters Chapel; record (1916) # 164.
HENSLEY, Mary; age: 45 years; married; parents: father "unknown" and Sue STILLS; death cause: "tuberculosis"; died: 11 May 1916; buried: Pine Grove; record (1916) # 165.
BROYLES, Sam; age: 67 years; single; parents: Jack BROYLES and mother "unknown"; death cause: "esophigal cancer"; informant: R.A. BROWN (Greeneville); died: 27 May 1916; buried: Shiloh; record (1916) # 166.
REAVES, Infant; male; age: 8 months; born: Blount County; parents: E.S. REAVES and Lillie FANNON; death cause: "tubercular dia__ (illegible)"; informant: Charles FANNON (Greeneville); died: 25 May 1916; buried: Mt. Hebron; record (1916) # 167.
CHANDLER, Laura; black; age: 28 years; married; parents: George DUNCAN and Vice LOVE; death cause: "burn"; informant: Jess CHANDLER (Greeneville); died: 22 May 1916; buried: Wesley; record (1916) # 168.
BRYANT, Martha C.; age: 72 years; widow; parents: Alex HARRISON and Manerva FOWLER; death cause: "diabetes"; informant: A.M. BRYANT (Greeneville); died: 21 May 1916; buried: Cedar Hill; record (1916) # 169.
WYKLE, Myrtle; age: 33 years; single; parents: W.D. WYKLE (Hawkins County) and mother not stated; death cause: "pulmonary tuberculosis"; died: 21 May 1916; buried: Mt. Hebron; record # 170.
H__ (illegible), Clara; born: 26 May 1911; parents: "unknown"; death cause: "__ (illegible) and chicken pox"; informant: M.J. WISOR (Greeneville); died: 27 May 1916; buried: Mascot, TN.; record # 171.
SMITH, Infant; male; parents: Will SMITH and Rachel HUMBERT; death cause: "premature birth"; informant: Ross SMITH (Greeneville); born/died: 27 May 1916; buried: Kidwell Cemetery; record # 172.
FORTNER, Lucy; born: 25 May 1886; widow; parents: L.C. BOYD and Mary JOHNSON; death cause: "tubercular pentom__ (illegible)"; died: 26 May 1916; buried: Oak Grove; record (1916) # 173.

MCCLAIN, Louise; born: 18 May 1915; parents: Dan MCCLAIN and Florence MCFARLAND; death cause: "whooping cough"; died: 26 May 1916; buried: Oak Grove; record (1916) # 174.

JONES, Ada; born: 16 May 1916; parents: Charles P. JONES and Florence QUINTON; death cause: illegible; informant: father (Greeneville); died: 17 May 1916; buried: Herman Cemetery; record (1916) # 175.

JONES, Bertha; born: 16 May 1916; parents: Charles P. JONES and Florence QUINTON; death cause: "stillborn"; informant: father (Greeneville); died: 16 May 1916; buried: Herman Cemetery; record (1916) # 176.

ELLIS, Joseph; age: 72 years; married; parents: "unknown"; death cause: "sun stroke"; informant: Jake SOUTHERLAND (Greeneville); died: 16 May 1916; buried: Fairview; record (1916) # 177.

BOHANNON, Martha J.; born: 4 Nov.1854; widow; parents: Sparkling B. HARMON and Katie CARTER; death cause: "pellagra"; informant: S.J.P. BOHANNON (Greeneville); died: 10 May 1916; buried: Mt. Vernon; record (1916) # 178.

BALL, Infant; male; parents: Charles BALL and Eva MCAMIS (Sullivan County); death cause: "stillborn"; informant: father (Baileyton); died: 13 May 1916; buried: Zion; record (1916) # 179.

LOYD, Thomas; born: 15 Oct. 1851; married; parents: John LOYD and Elizabeth SMITH; death cause: "typhoid fever"; informant: Allis LOYD (Baileyton); died: 17 May 1916; buried: English Cemetery; record (1916) # 180.

DUDLEY, Eliza Jane; born: 28 Mar. 1842; widow; parents: "unknown"; death cause: "consumption"; informant: Andrew FRESHOUR (Greeneville); died: 2 May 1916; record (1916) # 181.

ELLENBURG, Mary; age: "near 68 years"; single; parents: Adam ELLENBURG (South Carolina) and Tildy TAYLOR; death cause: "diarrhea"; informant: John ELLENBURG (Greeneville); died: 15 May 1916; buried: St. James; record (1916) # 182.

BARKLEY, Edith Josephine; born: 29 Apr. 1916; parents: George BARKLEY and mother's name illegible; death cause: "perhaps meningitis"; informant: father (Chucky); died: 24 May 1916; record # 183.

ROBERTS, Cora; age: 53 years; married; parents: A.N. BROYLES and Jane NELSON; death cause: "tuberculosis of lungs"; informant: Robert HELTON (Chucky); died: 15 May 1916; buried: Union Chapel; record (1916) # 184.

WILLIAMS, Mary E.; age: 60; married; parents: B__ (illegible) BODWELL and mother "unknown"; death cause: "gastric ulcer"; informant: Joe WILLIAMS (Greeneville); died: 3 May 1916; buried: Fariview; record (1916) # 185.

HYDER, Opal; born: 3 Oct. 1912; parents: John T. HYDER and Mary WHITE; death cause: "membranous croup"; informant: father (Chucky); died: 23 May 1916; buried: Quaker Knob; record (1916) # 186.

LAND, Manda; born: 11 Nov.1851; married; parents: Kenric SPEARS and Betsie HICKS; death cause: "organic heart disease"; informant: Mrs. James KERBOUGH (Greeneville); died: 14 May 1916; buried: Pilot Knob; record (1916) # 187.

WHITE, Floyd; born: 12 Mar. 1908; parents: J.R. WHITE (Locust Springs, TN.) and Mary MALONE; death cause: "kicked by mule, ruptured intestine"; informant: father (Afton); died: 20 May 1916; record (1916) # 188.

FANN, Gennie E.; female; born: 11 Sep. 1901; parents: Fred FANN and Martha A. NICHOLS; death cause: "ascites"; informant: father (Greeneville); died: 28 Jun. 1916; buried: Burnett Chapel; record # 189.

CARTER, Hassie; age: 23 years; married; parents: John SCOTT and mother "unknown"; death cause: "pulmonary tuberculosis"; informant: Roy SCOTT (Greeneville); died: 1 Jun. 1916; buried: Fairview; record (1916) # 190.

SHELTON, Elizabeth; born: 30 Nov. 1868 in North Carolina; married; parents: John TWEED (North Carolina) and Mary CANTER (North Carolina); death cause: "hypertrophy of heart"; died: 13 Jun. 1916; record (1916) # 191.

HAUN, Lewis Cosmo; born: 9 Aug. 1877; married; parents: John R. HAUN and Catherine M. HARMON; death cause: "chronic esatrtis"; informant: J.H. HAUN (Mohawk); died: 26 Jun. 1916; buried: Mt. Hope; record (1916) # 192.

LOWE, Delia Alice; born: 13 Oct. 1861; married; parents: J.W. MARKS and Elizabeth COLLINS; death cause: "endo carditis"; informant: Tom LOWE (Greeneville); buried: Oak Grove; record (1916) # 193.

WHITSON, Infant; female; parents: William WHITSON and Edith KNIGHT; death cause: "premature birth"; informant: father (Greeneville); born/died: 1 Jun. 1916; buried: Kidwell; record # 194.

SWATSELL, Lucy F.; born: 2 Apr. 1914; parents: Robert SWATSELL and Lidie WHITSON; death cause: "dysentery"; informant: father (Greeneville); died: 3 Jun. 1916; buried: Mt. Pleasant; record # 195.

ARNOLD, Richard; black; born: 7 Aug. 1914; parents: Newt ARNOLD and Belle DUNCAN; death cause: "infantile paralysis"; informant: J.E. BIDDLE (Greeneville); died: 16 Jun. 1916; record (1916) # 197.

ALEXANDER, Frank; born: 13 Jun. 1878; married; parents: Andy ALEXANDER and mother "unknown"; death cause: "pulmonary tuberculosis"; informant: Ed ALEXANDER (Greeneville); died: 13 Jun. 1916; record (1916) # 196.

SMITH, William Alexander; born: 16 Jun. 1863; married; parents: William SMITH and Isabelle JONES; death cause: "acute monia"; informant: Mrs. Stella SMITH (Greeneville); died: 19 Jun. 1916; buried: Harrisons; record (1916) # 198.

BRUMLY, Infant; female; parents: S. BRUMLEY and Lilly Maud STAMER (?); death cause: "prolapsed cord"; informant: father (Greeneville); died: 25 Jun. 1916; record (1916) # 199.

RABY, Mamie; born: 29 May 1886; married; parents: C.D. WILLIS and Flora GASS; death cause: "pernicious anemia"; informant: W.W. WILLIS (Greeneville); died: 29 Jun. 1916; buried: Oak Grove; record (1916) # 200.

WRIGHT, E.M.; age: 68 years; born: Washington County; married; parents: not stated; death cause: "general paralysis"; informant: W.T. MITCHELL (Greeneville); died: 2 Jun. 1916; buried: Mt. Hebron; record (1916) # 201.

FITZGERALD, William A.; age: 64 years; single; parents: William FITZGERALD (Virginia) and Annie RUMBO; death cause: "cerebral hemorrhage"; informant: George FITZGERALD (Greeneville); died: 12 Jun. 1916; buried: Oak Grove; record (1916) # 202.

STURM, Alphonso; age: 8 months and 28 days; parents: John W. STURM and Dona JAMES; death cause: "malnutrition"; informant: father (Greeneville); died: 23 Jun. 1916; buried: Oak Grove; record (1916) # 203.

BLEVINS, Mary M.; age: 62 years; born: Anderson County; widow; parents: John SARTIN and _ OVERTON (Anderson County); death cause: "chronic asthma"; informant: J.S. BLEVINS (Greeneville); died: 29 Jun. 1916; buried: Mt. Hebron; record (1916) # 204.

BIBLE, Bettie; age: 71 years; married; parents: Philip COBBLE and Sally STULTZ; death cause: "tuberculosis of lungs"; informant: J.L. COBBLE (Midway); died: 1 Jun. 1916; buried: Sinking Springs; record (1916) # 205.

COCHRAN, Lilie Belle; born: 24 Apr. 1916; parents: John COCHRAN and Mary BOLES; death cause: "unknown"; informant: father (Limestone); died: 3 Jun. 1916; buried: Dixon Chapel; record # 206.

FAIR, George Washington; born: 4 Mar.1915; parents: Bud FAIR and Ruth LAWSON (Hancock County); death cause: "gastro enteritis"; informant: father (Moshiem); died: 17 Jun. 1916; record (1916) # 207.

THOMASON, James; born: 21 Aug. 1882; married; parents: William S. THOMASON and Margaret JONES; death cause: "pulmonary tuberculosis"; died in 14th District on 20 Jun. 1916; record # 208.

LOWERY, Infant; male; parents: William LOWERY and Nomie DAVIS; death cause: "premature, stillborn"; born/died: 3 Jun. 1916; buried: Wesley Chapel; record (1916) # 209.

BROTHERTON, Empress; born: 30 Apr. 1863; married; parents: Shadrack BABB and Licindy JONES; death cause: "bronchitis and arthritis"; informant: Mrs. S.H. MCLAIN (Moshiem); died: 30 Jun. 1916; buried: Prices Chapel; record (1916) # 210.

STARNES, Landon C.; born: 9 May 1889; married; parents: Marion STARNES and Martha SMITH (Hawkins County); death cause: "perforation of bowels"; informant: father (Baileyton); died: 29 Jun. 1916; buried: Brown Mountain; record (1916) # 211.

YOUNG, William K.; born: 26 Apr. 1848; married; parents: Crocket YOUNG and Katie PETERS; death cause: "tuberculosis"; informant: A.M. SPEER (Chucky); died: 15 Jun. 1916; buried: Mt. Zion; record (1916) # 212.

COIN, May; born: 15 Jun. 1836 in Milburnton, TN.; widow; parents: Joseph F. MILBURN and May MILBURN; death cause: "mitral regurgitation"; informant: J.J. MILBURN (Limestone); died: 25 Jun. 1916; buried: Milburnton; record (1916) # 213.

RIGGS, Infant; female; parents: Elbert RIGGS (Carter County) and Jimie MURR; death cause: "stillborn"; died in 17th District, 18 Jun. 1916; record (1916) # 214.

SMITH, James N.; born: 21 Sep. 1866; married; parents: Cornelius SMITH and Sarah A. BONSALL; death cause: "appendicitis"; informant: Hiram STARNES (Baileyton); died: 17 Jun. 1916; buried: New Lebanon; record (1916) # 215.

LEMONS, Samuel; born: 25 Oct. 1844; married; parents: Wesley LEMONS and Sarah SEXTON; death cause: "anasarca"; informant: Ella MONTGOMERY (Greeneville); died: 9 Jun. 1916; buried: Paint Creek; record (1916) # 216.

HALE, Infant; male; parents: H.H. HALE and Lidie BOWERS; death cause: "premature labor"; informant: father (Midway); born/died: 1 Jun. 1916; record (1916) # 217.

WELLS, Mary; black; born: 25 May 1916; parents: Sid WELLS and Mable LOVE; death cause: illegible; informant: father (Bulls Gap); died: 2 Jun. 1916; buried: Drakes; record (1916) # 218.

STRONG, Kate; born: 20 Nov. 1858; married; parents: Steward HICK (Hawkins County) and Mandy HICK (Hawkins County); death cause: "gall stone disease"; informant: Robert MCCOY (Chucky); died: 7 Jun. 1916; record (1916) # 219.

VOILES, James; born: 8 Sep. 1850; married; parents: James VAILES and Clearly HURLEY; death cause: "apoplexy"; died: 24 Jul. 1916; record (1916) # 220.

KELLER, James K.P.; born: 27 Dec. 1845; widower; parents: Phillip KELLER and Rebecca PETTY (Jefferson County); death cause: "organic heart disease"; informant: John WHITE (Greeneville); died: 18 Jul. 1916; buried: Zion; record (1916) # 221.

GASS, Zola; born: 2 May 1900; parents: Joseph GASS and Elizabeth RAGSDALE; death cause: "typhoid fever"; informant: S.W. DOTY (Afton); died: 17 Jul. 1916; record (1916) # 222.

MONTUTH, S__ (illegible); born: 4 Jun. 1854; married; parents: Henry MATHES and Rebeca J. SMITH; death cause: "fatty degeneration of heart"; informant: Bob MATHES (Jeroldstown); died: 13 Jul. 1916; buried: Pleasant Hill; record (1916) # 223.

CURTIS, Gladys Geneva; born: 26 Sep. 1915; parents: Val CURTIS and |Abi FRAZIER; death cause: "organic heart trouble"; died: 5 Jul. 1916; record (1916) # 224.

BRANDON, Edgar Mason; born: 14 Jan. 1916; parents: S.D. BRANDON and Ollie CRAWFORD; death cause: "pneumonia and whooping cough"; died in 17th District, 23 Jul. 1916; buried: Lovelace Cemetery; record (1916) # 225.

PETERS, Nancy Emmaline; born: 18 May 1851; widow; parents: James BAXTER and Catherine MALTSBERGER; death cause: "tuberculosis"; informant: Ernest BABB (Chucky); died: 28 Jul. 1916; buried: Pleasant Hill; record (1916) # 226.

MALONE, Lizzie; born: 1 Jan. 1844; married; parents: Wallas BRITTON and Sallie WICKER; death cause: "general debility"; informant; Perry CRUMLEY (Baileyton); died: 19 Jul. 1916; buried: Babb Cemetery; record (1916) # 227.

JUSTIS, Jacob; born: 9 Feb. 1851; married; parents: Jonnie JUSTIS and Betsy CARTER, death cause: "tuberculosis of lungs"; died: 14 Jul. 1916; buried: Gass Shed; record (1916) # 228.

GASS, Elizabeth; born: 8 Aug. 1835 in Greene County; widow; parents: Joseph MALONE and __ GRAYHAM; death cause: "senility"; informant: Don MALONE (Afton); died: 16 Jul. 1916; buried: Gass Shed; record (1916) # 229.

BLAZER, Lawe Ellen; born: 27 Dec. 187_; age: 37 years, 7 months and 16 days; married; parents: Benjamin LAFOLETT and Maglin WALLY; death cause: "pulmonary tuberculosis"; died: 8 Jul. 1916; buried: Salem; record (1916) # 230.

SMITH, Infant; female; parents: Crofford SMITH and Florence KESTERSON; death cause: "premature labor"; informant: Seth BIBLE (Midway); born/died: 12 Jul. 1916; record (1916) # 231.

YOKLEY, Cars Millon; born: 30 Jul. 1916; parents: Anderw J. YOKLEY and Ida Bell BLACK; death cause: "stillborn"; informant: Dr.

PENNINGTON (Mohawk); died: 30 Jul. 1916; buried: "in garden"; record (1916) # 232.

SNOWDEN, Newton; age: 64 years; born: North Carolina; widower; parents: Tom SNOWDEN (North Carolina) and __ PRUETT (North Carolina); death cause: "pulmonary tuberculosis"; informant: Dewey SNOWDEN (Greeneville); died: 27 Jul. 1916; buried: Wills Cemetery; record (1916) # 233.

GILLIAND, Gwen; male; age: 54 years; born: North Carolina; parents: father not stated and Mattie CHANDLER; death cause: "bloody dysentery"; informant: Will SEWELL (Greeneville); died: 18 Jul. 1916; record (1916) # 234.

RADER, Infant; male; parents: Charles RADER and Sarah MYSINGER; death cause: "stillborn"; informant: S.R. RADER (Greeneville); born/died: 18 Jul. 1916; buried: Mt. Pleasant; record (1916) # 235.

VESTAL, Infant; female; born: 14 Jul. 1916; parents: W.P. VESTAL (Virginia) and Elizabeth KENIERY (Virginia); death cause: "lack of vitality"; died: 16 Jul. 1916; buried: Mt. Zion; record (1916) # 236.

VESTAL, Infant; female; born: 14 Jul. 1916; parents: W.P. VESTAL (Virginia) and Elizabeth KENIERY (Virginia); death cause: "lack of vitality"; died: 15 Jul. 1916; buried: Mt. Zion; record (1916) # 237.

BROWN, Mary; black; age: 70 years; single; parents: not stated; death cause: "senile debility"; informant: Bob CARSON (Greeneville); died: 10 Jul. 1916; buried: Wesley Cemetery; record (1916) # 238.

STONE, Sam; age: 17 years; single; parents: John STONE (Virginia) and Kate KRUNKELTON (Virginia); death cause: "typhoid fever"; informant: Ebb BOWMAN (Greeneville); died: 3 Jul. 1916; record # 239.

JONES, Glena; born: 24 Mar. 1916; parents: Fred JONES and Hattie BROUGHS; death cause: "pellagra contracted from mother"; informant: father (Greeneville); died: 3 Jul. 1916; buried: Oak Grove; record # 240.

WILHOIT, Samuel S.; age: 83 years and 2 months; born: Greene County; married; parents: John WILHOIT and mother not stated; death cause: "__ (illegible" of heart"; informant: W.T. MITCHELL (Greeneville); died: 9 Jul. 1916; record (1916) # 241.

COOTER, Mattie; born: 29 Aug. 1866; widow; parents: Enoch Baker WATTENBERGER and __ MCCURRY; death cause: "tuberculosis of bowels"; informant: I.P. CARTER (Baileyton); died: 28 Jul. 1916; buried: Zion; record (1916) # 242.

WHITE, George W.; born: 3 Sep. 1857; married; parents: John WHITE and Cathern MALTSBARGER; death cause: "pellagra"; informant: Julia A. WHITE (Baileyton); died: 17 Jul. 1916; buried: Zion; record (1916) # 243.

COOTER, Gladys Aline; age: 9 months; parents: Charles R. COOTER and Belle WAITS; death cause: "entero colitis"; informant: C.R. COOTER (Baileyton); died: 23 Jul. 1916; buried: Zion; record # 244.

GASS, Infant; black; female; parents: William GASS and Bessie BIERD; death cause: "stillborn"; informant: father (Baileyton); born/died: 28 Jul. 1916; buried: Salem; record (1916) # 245.

OSBORNE, Pearl; black; age: 32 years; married; parents: Al RILES and Amanda W__ (illegible); death cause: "tuberculosis of lungs"; died: 2 Jul. 1916; buried: Zion ME Church, Baileyton; record (1916) # 246.

WILSON, M.T.; born: 2 Jan. 1847 in Johnson County; married; parents: Joel WILSON (Johnson County) and __ BLEVINS; death cause: "angina pectoris"; informant: R.F. WILSON (Baileyton); died: 1 Jul. 1916; buried: Salem; record (1916) # 247.

RUDDER, Matilda Bales; born: 27 Feb. 1876; married; parents: Jessie BALES and Mary RIDNOUR; death cause: "indigestion and diarrhea"; informant: R.G. RUDDER (Moshiem); died: 1 Jul. 1916; buried: Mt. Carmel; record (1916) # 248.

BROWN, Wilson B.; born: 24 Aug. 1839; widower; parents: Peter BROWN and Marguarate COLLETT; death cause: illegible; informant: J.C. KELTON (Moshiem); died: 1 Jul. 1916; buried: Browns Springs; record (1916) # 249.

SELF, Ethel Irene; born: 30 May 1877; married; parents: Samuel T. RUSSELL and Sallie A. HOOD; death cause: "pulmonary tuberculosis"; informant: Thomas A. RUSSELL (Greeneville); died: 31 Jul. 1916; buried: Moshiem; record (1916) # 250.

RUDDER, Andy T.; born: 13 Apr. 1857; married; parents: Johnson RUDDER and Mollie DAY; death cause: "miliary tuberculosis"; informant: Robert SHEFFEY (Bulls Gap); died: 18 Jul. 1916; buried: Pilot Knob; record (1916) # 251.

DOKE, Sue V.; born: 14 Apr. 1848; single; parents: Alexander M. DOKE and Elizabeth MCCLURE; death cause: "cancer of breast"; informant: Doke WILLS (Bulls Gap); died: 25 Jul. 1916; buried: Antiock; record (1916) # 252.

CROFT, William P.; born: 2 Feb. 1843; married; parents: William CROFT and Margaret REYNOLD; death cause: "valvulor insufficiency, arterio sclerosis"; informant: Joe CROFT (Moshiem); died: 11 Jul. 1916; buried: Mt. Sinai; record (1916) # 253.

GRAY, Mrs. Mary; born: 28 Jul. 1844; married; parents: Bernet WEEMS and Rebecca HARDIN; death cause: "heart disease, dropsy"; informant: V.S. GRAY (Afton); died: 15 Jul. 1916; buried: Mt. Zion; record (1916) # 254.

BALES, Luther; born: 20 Dec. 1895; single; parents: Francis A. BALES and Julie WHITE; death cause: "knife stab of neck (accidental)"; informant: A.B. CRABTREE (Chucky); died: 2 Jul. 1916; buried: Mt. Zion; record (1916) # 255.

RANDLES, Infant; female; parents: father "unknown" and Cary RANDLES; death cause: "born dead"; died: 20 Aug. 1916; buried; Oak Grove Cemetery; record (1916) # 256.

UNKNOWN, Male; black; age and parents "unknown"; death cause: "killed by train, east of Mohawk"; died: 12 Aug. 1916; buried: Drake Cemetery; record (1916) # 257.

SEATON, Edna Helen; born: 4 Jun. 1916; parents: Henry SEATON and Lydia Kate SEATON; death cause: "intestinal __ (illegible)"; informant: Sam BELL; died: 1 Aug. 1916; buried: Pisgah; record (1916) # 258.

JOHNSON, Other; age: 17 years; single; parents: Jim JOHNSON and mother not stated; death cause: "accidental gunshot wound to chest by himself"; informant: Elbert WATSON (Moshiem); died; 27 Aug. 1916; buried: Curtis Chapel; record (1916) # 259.

PATTON, William P.; born: 12 Jun. 1847; married; parents: Thomas PATTON and mother "unknown"; death cause: "cerebral hemorrhage"; informant: Roy R. PATTEN (Moshiem); died: 30 Aug. 1916; buried: Big Springs; record (1916) # 260.

GUTHRIE, Andrew; age: 72 years; married; parents: Andrew GUTHRIE and Isabel RADER; death cause: "paralysis"; informant: Joseph K.

GUTHRIE (Bulls Gap); died: 20 Aug. 1916; buried: Mt. Hope; record (1916) # 261.
JENNINGS, Samuel; age: 30 years; married; parents: Roy JENNINGS and __ BROYLES; death cause: "tuberculosis"; died: 5 Aug. 1916; buried: Union Chapel; record (1916) # 262.
BROTHERTON, Joseph Homer; born: 15 Nov. 1915; parents: Tilman A. BROTHERTON and Nancy __ (illegible); death cause: "tonsillitis and abscess"; died: 26 Aug. 1916; buried: Pilot Knob; record (1916) # 263.
DINSMORE, Infant; female; age: 1 month; parents: S.G. DINSMORE and Sarah JONES; death cause: not recorded; informant: W.G. GRACEY (Greeneville); died: 6 Aug. 1916; buried: Pisgah; record (1916) # 264.
SWATSELL, Amanda; age: 66 years; widow; parents: Jacob WILHOIT and Polly BAYSINGER; death cause: "dysentery"; informant: Rhote SWATSELL (Greeneville); died: 6 Aug. 1916; buried: New Bethel; record (1916) # 265.
MORRISON, Louise; born: 22 Sep. 1915 in Hamblen County; parents: Roy A. MORRISON and Georgia LAMONS; death cause; "pertussis and pneumonia"; informant: father (Greeneville); died: 12 Aug. 1916; record (1916) # 266.
SWATSELL, Ray; born: 11 Aug. 1915; parents: Brad SWATSELL and Licy CASTELL; death cause: "pneumonia"; informant: Roy WILLETT (Greeneville); died: 12 Aug. 1916; buried: Mt. Pleasant; record # 267.
HARTMAN, Fannie L.; born: 2 May 1903; parents: T.C. HARTMAN and Lacy MYERS; death cause: "rheumatic fever"; died: 14 Aug. 1916; buried: Mt. Pleasant; record (1916) # 268.
CLAYTON, Elsie; black; born: 17 Aug. 1900; parents: Haney CLAYTON and mother "unknown"; death cause: "tuberculosis"; informant: J.D. CAMPBELL (Greeneville); died: 18 May 1916; buried: New Hope; record (1916) # 269.
ELKHART, Belle; born: 15 Jun. 1886; married; parents: D.C. WILSON and Fannie ARWOOD; death cause: "enteritis"; informant: J.B. WILSON (Greeneville); died: 18 Aug. 1916; buried: Mt. Hebron; record (1916) # 270.
WILLIAMS, Hannah; born: 20 Jan. 1856; married; parents: Henry THOMPSON and Hannah GASS; death cause: "dysentery"; informant:

W.H. THOMPSON (Greeneville); died: 20 Aug. 1916; buried: Oak Grove; record (1916) # 271.

RANDLES, Cary; age: "about 16 years"; parents: E.B. RANDLES and mother "unknown"; death cause: illegible; died: 20 Aug. 1916; buried: Oak Grove; record (1916) # 272.

GASS, Elzie; age: 93 years; born: Hawkins County; widow; parents: not stated; death cause: "senility"; informant: Robert HANKINS (Greeneville); died: 23 Aug. 1916; buried: Gass Cemetery; record (1916) # 273.

MCNEAL, Mattie; age: 38 years; born: Hancock County; widow; parents: George HARRISON (North Carolina) and __ HOLLAND (Hancock County); death cause: "uterine cancer"; died: 25 Aug. 1916; buried: Hancock County; record (1916) # 274.

BROWN, Rebecca Jane; age: 77 years; single; parents: Robert BROWN and Annie BABB; death cause: "aortic regurgitation"; informant: R.A. BROWN (Greeneville); died: 26 Aug. 1916; buried: Gass Shed; record (1916) # 275.

LONES, Margaret; born: 29 Jul. 1852 in North Carolina; widow; parents: A.J. LONES and Margaret HASS; death cause: "intestinal __ (illegible)"; informant: Tom LONES (Greeneville); died; 30 Aug. 1916; buried: Price Cemetery; record (1916) # 276.

DINKINS, William J.; born: 30 Mar. 1848 in Virginia; married; parents: William DINKINS (Virginia) and Sarrah __ (illegible)(Virginia); death cause: "tuberculosis"; informant: Danil DINKINS (__ Kentucky); died: 30 Aug. 1916; buried: Oak Grove; record (1916) # 277.

ELLIS, Infant; female; born: 30 Aug. 1916; parents: Bill ELLIS (North Carolina) and Vesta Anna REEVES; death cause: "pneumonia"; informant: J.C. REEVES (Greeneville); died: 31 Aug. 1916; record # 273.

CRABTREE, Mamie Ruth; born: 23 Nov. 1915; parents: Thomas E. CRABTREE and Mary Caroline MARSHALL; death cause: "injury from fall"; informant: Willis KILGORE (Afton); died: 18 Aug. 1916; buried: Doty Cemetery; record (1916) # 279.

BRANDON, Martha Christina; born: 24 Jul. 1852 in Carter County; widow; parents: William TAYLOR (Carter County) and Amy WAGONER (North Carolina); death cause: "gastric cancer"; informant:

Thomas G. BRADNON (Fall Branch); died: 8 Aug. 1916; buried: Lovelace; record (1916) # 280.

COLLIER, Alma Thelma; born: 22 Apr. 1916; parents: Henry COLLIER and Ethel DAUGHERTY; death cause: "tubercular meningitis"; informant: father (Fall Branch); died: 22 Aug. 1916; record # 281.

WALTERS, Fouler; born: 22 Jul. 1898; single; parents: G.A. WALTERS and Emma LINTZ; death cause: "pulmonary tuberculosis"; died at Moshiem on 10 Aug. 1916; buried: Pine Grove; record (1916) # 282.

IDELL, John Clyde; born: 15 Aug. 1916; parents: Henry IDELL and Pearl Sue LOWRY; death cause: "premature birth"; informant: H.V. LOWRY (Moshiem); died: 17 Aug. 1916; buried: Midway; record (1916) # 283.

DEAN, Emma Lee; born: 13 Jul. 1916; parents: Andy DEAN and Anna DEAN; death cause: "organic heart failure"; informant: father (Bulls Gap); died: 1 Aug. 1916; record (1916) # 284.

COATNEY, Maggie; age: 48 years; married; parents: James MALONEY and Briney JEFFERS; death cause: "miliary tuberculosis"; informant; Robert COATNEY (Moshiem); died: 7 Sep. 1916; buried; Mt. Carmel; record (1916) # 285.

PARK, Dalphus Alexander; born: 30 Sep. 1862; married; parents: David F. PARK and Martha WHITE; death cause: "enteritis"; informant: Anson J. PARK (Bulls Gap); died: 12 Aug. 1916; buried: Pilot Knob; record (1916) # 286.

HARRISON, Benjamin W.; born: 15 Sep. 1829 in Greene County; married; parents: Jeremiah HARRISON and Betsey JONES; death cause: "croupous pneumonia"; informant: D.P. HARRISON (Greeneville); died: 21 Aug. 1916; buried: Harrison Cemetery; record (1916) # 287.

CASTEEL, Chassis; born: 6 Sep. 1901; parents: W.W. CASTEEL and Lou MALONE; death cause: "typhoid fever"; died: 23 Aug. 1916; buried: Gass Shed; record (1916) # 288.

BROWN, Roy Donal; born: 29 Jan. 1916; parents: John D. BROWN and Nettie C. CASTEEL; death cause: "marasmus"; informant: J.O. YOUNG (Baileyton); died: 19 Aug. 1916; record (1916) # 289.

LANE, Charles Lonzo; born: 5 Jun. 1916; parents: S.C. LANE and Nancy L. KENNEY; death cause: "congenital heart disease"; died: 12 Aug. 1916; record (1916) # 290.

POWELL, Maggie; born: 9 Feb. 1889 (record shows age, 53); parents: Cane POWELL and Eliza HAYS; death cause: "intestinal tuberculosis"; informant: father (Limestone); died: 14 Aug. 1916; record (1916) # 291.

FRY, James Soloman; born: 9 Nov. 1844 in Tennessee; married; parents: Henry FRY (South Carolina) and Barbara WAMPLER; death cause: "uremia, brights disease"; informant: Mrs. E.F. FRY (Moshiem); died: 6 Aug. 1916; buried: Mt. Sinai; record (1916) # 292.

BLACK, Barbara; age: 78 years; born: Virginia; widow; parents: father's name illegible and May BLACK (Virginia); death cause: "paralysis"; died: 29 Aug. 1916; buried: Chucky; record (1916) # 293.

KEIFER, Bersheba; born: 3 Dec. 1846; widow; parents: James M. KEIFER and Bersheba CAMBEL; death cause: "pulmonary tuberculosis"; informant: Melvin HOLT (Midway); died: 30 Aug. 1916; buried: Sinking Springs; record (1916) # 294.

RADER, Eva; parents: Frank Lee RADER and Cleo HARMAN; death cause: "born dead"; born/died: 1 Aug. 1916; buried: Willoughbys; record (1916) # 295.

EADS, Julia; born: 23 Jan. 1892; single; parents: L.H. EADS and Mollie SKYLES; death cause: "typhoid fever"; informant: G.W. ROBERTS (Chucky); died: 19 Sep. 1916; record (1916) # 296.

LOVE, J.; age: 4 years; parents: James L. LOVE and Bell LINTZ; death cause: "diphtheria"; informant: A.T. ALEXANDER (Greeneville); died: 24 Sep. 1916; buried: St. James; record (1916) # 297.

MALONE, Gurtie; born: 18 Oct. 1909; parents: Andy MALONE and Lydia BAILEY; death cause: "epileptic fit"; informant: A.B. MALONE (Baileyton); died: 25 Sep. 1916; buried: Zion; record (1916) # 298.

PATTON, J.D. Ralph; born: 5 Aug. 1916; parents: James A. PATTON and Lula V. LEE; death cause: "pneumonia"; informant: father (Moshiem); died: 12 Sep. 1916; buried: Antioc Church; record # 299.

RAGSDELL, Sarah; born: __ Sep. 1852; widow; parents: John MILLIGAN and Catherine RUSH; death cause: "hemorrhage of lungs"; informant: W.E. MILLIGAN (Baileyton); died: 2 Sep. 1916; buried: Doty Cemetery; record (1916) # 300.

POE, Rosa B.; born: 13 Aug. 1850 in Virginia; widow; parents: John POE and Patience CARTER; death cause: "gall stones with infection";

informant: Robert POE (Baileyton); died: 3 Sep. 1916; buried: Locust Springs; record (1916) # 301.

PACK, Carl; born: 2 Dec. 1915; parents: Tom E. PACK and Lelia MARKWOOD; death cause: "abscess of brain"; informant: Henry LUSTER (Midway); died: 2 Sep. 1916; record (1916) # 302.

RECTOR, Eugene; born: 12 Apr. 1913; parents: Carl RECTOR and Pearl WOLF; death cause: "injury from burn"; informant: father (Limestone); died: 30 Sep. 1916; buried: Dixon Chapel; record # 303.

MOODY, Elizabeth; born: 12 May 1844 in Virginia; widow; parents: Joseph __ (illegible) and Elizabeth __ (illegible); death cause: "intestinal tuberculosis"; informant: J. MOODY (Chucky); died: 25 Sep. 1916; buried: Rheatown; record (1916) # 304.

SHIPLEY, George E.; born: 20 Jun. 1878; married; parents: John SHIPLEY and Mary ROBINSON; death cause: "appendicitis"; informant: J.C. SHIPLEY (Midway); died: 4 Sep. 1916; buried: Cedar Grove; record (1916) # 305.

MILIGAN, James; age: not stated; parents: not stated; death cause: "carcinoma of stomach"; died: 12 Sep. 1916; buried: Hartman Chapel; record (1916) # 306.

DUNN, Glenna; born: 12 Mar. 1907; parents: S.M. DUNN and Jennie SWATSEL; death cause: "drowning"; informant: father (Afton); died: 4 Sep. 1916; buried: Weems Chapel; record (1916) # 307.

RUSSELL, Mary Jane; born: 3 Mar. 1916; parents: A.E. RUSSELL and Glennie DAVIS; death cause: "cholera infantum"; informant: father (Greeneville); died: 3 Sep. 1916; buried: Oak Grove; record # 308.

LOWRY, Sallie; age: 21 years; single; parents: Jessie LOWRY and Catherine CAMRON; death cause: "typhoid fever"; died: 7 Sep. 1916; buried: Cove Creek; record (1916) # 309.

GRAHAM, William A.; born: 4 Nov. 1836 in Tennessee; married; parents: George GRAHAM and mother "unknown"; death cause: "senility"; informant: J.M. SHANKS (Greeneville); died: 8 Sep. 1916; buried: Gass Shed; record (1916) # 310.

EDWARDS, Callie; age: 61 years; marital status: not stated; parents: Will NELSON and mother "unknown"; death cause: "tuberculosis"; informant: J.M. JENKINS (Greeneville); died: 8 Sep. 1916; buried: Cedar Hill; record (1916) # 311.

LOWRY, Charlie; age: 27 years; single; parents: Jessie LOWRY and Catherine CAMRON; death cause: "typhoid fever"; died: 7 Sep. 1916; buried: Cove Creek; record (1916) # 312.

HENDRIX, Sarah; age: 72 years; born: Carter County; widow; parents: __ BOWMAN and mother not stated; death cause: "uremia"; informant: J.R. DODD (Greeneville); died: 11 Sep. 1916; buried: Shiloh; record (1916) # 313.

WRIGHT, Harral; born: 3 Jul. 1916; parents: George WRIGHT and Sue WADDLE; death cause: illegible; informant: father (Greeneville); died: 13 Sep. 1916; buried: Mt. Pleasant; record (1916) # 314.

HUMPHRIES, Annie Lucy; age: 24 years; single; parents: S.H. HUMPHRIES and Mollie MITCHELL; death cause: "epilepsy"; informant: father (Greeneville); died: 14 Sep. 1916; buried: Oak Grove; record (1916) # 315.

SEATON, Cora May; age: 17 days; parents: John SEATON and Nellie TAYLOR; death cause: "malnutrition"; informant: Joe SEATON (Greeneville); died: 23 Sep. 1916; buried: Cove Creek; record # 316.

HUMPHRIES; Mrs. J.T.; age: 76 years; born: Virginia; married; parents: not stated; death cause: "pulmonary tuberculosis"; informant: S.H. HUMPHRIES (Greeneville); died: 24 Sep. 1916; buried: Moshiem; record (1916) # 317.

HARRISON, Melvin; black; born: 2 Apr. 1916; parents: Joe HARRISON and Savana SHARP; death cause: "no medical attention"; informant: father (Greeneville); died: 10 Sep. 1916; record (1916) # 318.

FINCHER, John E.; born: 28 Aug. 1853; married; parents: not stated; death cause: "gastro enteritis and tuberculosis"; died: 3 Sep. 1916; buried: Hartman Cemetery; record (1916) # 320.

LAWSON, George; born: 24 Mar. 1915; parents: George LAWSON and mother "unknown"; death cause: "no medical attention"; informant: J.A. LAWSON (Greeneville); died: 10 Sep. 1916; buried: Harmon Church; record (1916) # 319.

BRUMLY, Kenneth Ray; born: 20 May 1897; single; parents: father not stated and Birthy BRUMLY; death cause: "appendicitis"; died: 8 Sep. 1916; record (1916) # 321.

ANDERSON, Infant; male; born: 15 Sep. 1916; parents: J.B. ANDERSON and Sallie GRAHAM; death cause: "infantile convulsions"; informant: father (Greeneville); died: _ Sep. 1916; buried; Albany; record (1916) # 322.

FILLERS, Hazel Rovina; born: 24 Sep. 1916; parents: Junior FILLERS and Pearl CRUM; death cause: "born dead"; informant: D.H. FILLERS (Greeneville); died: 24 Sep. 1916; buried: Cove Creek; record # 323.

HIXSON, William H.; parents: Grover C. HIXSON and Gladys SHOUN; death cause: "stillborn"; informant: Thomas D. CLOYD (Moshiem); died: 3 Sep. 1916; record (1916) # 324.

BORDEN, Virginia; age: "about 6 years"; parents: Henry BORDEN and mother "unknown"; death cause: "diphtheria"; informant: Mrs. L.A. RADER (Greeneville); died: 18 Oct. 1916; record (1916) # 325.

HOGAN, Sarah Cobble; born: 26 Sep. 1857; married; parents: Nathaniel COBBLE and Elizabeth SMITH; death cause: "chronic nephritis"; informant: J.L. COBBLE (Midway); died: 26 Oct. 1916; buried: Pine Grove; record (1916) # 326.

COURTNEY, Floyd Raymond; born: 23 Nov. 1913; parents: James COURTNEY (Iowa) and Sophroina COURTNEY (Hamblen County); death cause: "diphtheria"; informant: J.L. COURTNEY (Mohawk); died: 29 Oct. 1916; buried: Mt. Hope; record (1916) # 327.

CUPP, Laurie May; born: 8 Nov. 1910; parents: Alfred Allen CUPP (Hawkins County) and Nellie Margarette WARNER; death cause: "diphtheria"; informant: Mrs. M.A. WARNER (Mohawk); died: 20 Cot 1916; buried: Phillipi; record (1916) # 328.

JONES, Cathern; age: 80 years; born: Tennessee; single; parents: Elax SUSONG and Sallie SUSONG; death cause: "inflammation of bladder"; informant: James WHEELER (Bulls Gap); died: 10 Oct. 1916; buried: Mt. Hope; record (1916) # 329.

REDNOUR, Mary; age: "supposed 88 years"; single; parents: unknown; death cause: "senility"; informant: W.A. HALL (Moshiem); died: 19 Oct. 1916; buried: Salem; record (1916) # 330.

PERSON, Mose; black; age: 103 years; born: North Carolina; married; parents: unknown; death cause: "senility and gangrene of left foot"; died at Moshiem, 16 Oct. 1916; record (1916) # 331.

HAYS, Evret W.; born: 20 Sep. 1911; parents: John W. HAYS and Martha A. BROWN; death cause: "small cell sarcoma, left hand"; informant: father (Moshiem); died: 16 Oct. 1916; buried: Saini; record (1916) # 332.

JOHNSON, Della N.; born: 4 Aug. 1891; married; parents: father illegible and __ REYNOLDS; death cause: "tuberculosis of lungs"; informant: Lee JOHNSON (Moshiem); died: 11 Oct. 1916; buried: Albany; record (1916) # 333.

HARMON, Inez; born: 8 Jan. 1909; parents: Isaac D. HARMON and Della HARMON; death cause: "carcinom oris"; informant: father (Moshiem); died: 10 Oct. 1916; record (1916) # 334.

CARSON, Samuel L.; age: 58 years; born: Washington County; married; lawyer; parents: John R. CARSON (Washington County) and mother not stated; death cause: "pulmonary tuberculosis"; informant: Roy CARSON (Greeneville); died: 30 Oct. 1916; buried: Oak Grove; record (1916) # 335.

M__ (illegible), Susan; black; age: 70 years; born: North Carolina; married; parents: Bob RHEA (North Carolina) and mother "unknown"; death cause: "heart failure and acute indigestion"; informant: George M__ (illegible)(Greeneville); died: 22 Oct. 1916; record (1916) # 336.

LOVE, William E.; born: 5 Feb. 1846; married; parents: J.C. LOVE and Martha SMITH; death cause: "chronic diarrhea"; informant: Oscar LOVE (Greeneville); died: 21 Oct. 1916; buried: Oak Grove; record (1916) # 337.

SEDGMYTON, Infant; male; parents: father not stated and May SEDGMYTON, death cause: "premature birth"; informant: A.J. SEDGMYTON (Greeneville); born/died: 15 Oct. 1916; buried: Oak Grove; record (1916) # 338.

SUSONG, Nicholas A.; age: 43 years; married; parents: A.E. SUSONG and Esther GREGG, death cause: "pneumonia"; informant: D.S. SUSONG (Greeneville); died: 11 Oct. 1916; buried: Susong Memorial; record (1916) # 339.

CREASMAN, Infant; sex not stated; born: 3 Sep. 1916; parents: Ben CREASMAN and Mattie, LOWRY; death cause: "meningitis"; informant: father (Greeneville); died: 10 Oct. 1916; buried: Oak Grove; record (1916) # 340.

ANDERSON, William; age: 40 years; widower; parents: Ben ANDERSON and Margaret RUSS; death cause: "typhoid fever"; informant: James ANDERSON (Greeneville); died: 9 Oct. 1916; buried: Carter Station; record (1916) # 341.

NAIL, Eugene; born: 26 Mar. 1905; parents: John NAIL and Kate CARTER; death cause: "burn"; informant: L. ARMITAGE (Greeneville); died: 6 Oct. 1916; buried: Harmons Chapel; record (1916) # 342.

WILLIS, J.W.; age: 62 years, 6 months and 26 days; married; banker; parents: John WILLIS and Elizabeth MCCORD; death cause: "nephritis"; informant: Lyle WILLIS (Greeneville); died: 3 Oct. 1916; buried: Oak Grove; record (1916) # 343.

FELLERS, Lucy; born: 29 Jun. 1889; single; parents: Joseph FILLERS and Josephine LYNCH; death cause: "pulmonary tuberculosis"; informant: J.J. FRASIER (Afton); died: 2 Oct. 1916; buried: Stone Dam; record (1916) # 344.

LISTER, Julia; age: 4 years; parents: Sam LISTER and Fannie MATHES; death cause: "diphtheria"; informant: J.B. MATHES; died: 1 Oct. 1916; buried: Mt. Vernon; record (1916) # 345.

DOTSON, Samuel Rhuben; born: 17 May 1868; married; blacksmith; parents: James DOTSON and Mary AUSTIN; death cause: "heart failure"; informant: U.T. DOTSON (Limestone); died: 12 Oct. 1916; buried: Pleasant View; record (1916) # 346.

BENNETT, Bessie Naome; born: 6 Aug. 1915; parents: David A. BENNETT and Mattie SPEARS; death cause: "spasmodic croup"; informant: J.B. FORD (Chucky); died: 27 Oct. 1916; buried: Pleasant Vale; record (1916) # 347.

SQUIBB, Clifford; born: 30 Sep. 1916; parents: Hugh Paul SQUIBB and Loretta Estelle DOTSON; death cause: "purpura hemor__ (illegible)"; informant: A.J. SQUIBB (Limestone); died: 31 Oct. 1916; record # 348.

WILHOIT, Sarah; born: 24 Oct. 1870; married; parents: John BROYLES and M. BROYLES; death cause: "chronic diarrhea"; died: 10 Oct. 1916; buried: Cedar Grove; record (1916) # 349.

WILLIAMS, James W.; born: 20 Jan. 1853; widower; parents: Allen WILLIAMS and Pop LINEBAUGH; death cause: "diarrhea and enteritis"; informant: J.W. WILLIAMS (Greeneville); died: 22 Oct. 1916; buried: Wesley Chapel; record (1916) # 350.

KENNEY, Willie Good; female; born: 4 Jul. 1892; married; parents: Josiah F. SELF (Hawkins County) and Francis A. WRIGHT (Hawkins

County); death cause: "uremia"; informant: S.L. PENNINGTON (Bulls Gap); died: 14 Oct. 1916; buried: Pilot Knob; record (1916) # 351.

HENDRY, Joseph; born: __ Jun. 1848; age: 68 years and 5 months; married; parents: Bill HENDRY and Massie CARTER; death cause: "gunshot wound by unknown hand, died instantly"; informant: Mrs. Jo HENDRY (Moshiem); died: 4 Oct. 1916;; record (1916) # 352.

DAVIS, Jesse Emerson; born: 28 May 1852; married; parents: Jesse DAVIS and Elizabeth SHANKS; death cause: "gastro enteritis"; informant: W.S. DAVIS (Greeneville); died: 14 Oct. 1916; buried: Gass Shed; record (1916) # 353.

HARRISON, Margaret; age: 60 years; married; parents: not stated; death cause: "pulmonary tuberculosis"; died: 28 Oct. 1916; buried: Hartman Church; record (1916) # 354.

JOHNSON, Elmer; born: 2 Apr. 1912; parents: G__ (illegible) JOHNSON and Callie HURST (Virginia); death cause: "croup"; informant: G.W. JOHNSON (Baileyton); died: 7 Oct. 1916; buried: Pleasant Vale; record (1916) # 355.

HOLLAND, Montie Maud; born: 2 Aug. 1914; widow; parents: Bruce HOLLAND and Lulu B. GAMMONS; death cause: illegible; informant: Omer HOLLAND (Afton); died: 28 Oct. 1916; buried: Doty Cemetery; record (1916) # 356.

HARTMAN, Vern; born: 17 Nov. 1915; parents: J.T. HARTMAN and Nannie WHITE; death cause: "diphtheria"; informant: father (Baileyton); died: 23 Oct. 1916; buried: Union Chapel; record # 357.

GIBBS, Daniel Fox; age: 59 years; married; parents; William R. GIBBS and Mary PARMAN; death cause: "fractured skull sustained in fall"; informant: Joe GIBBS (Greeneville); died: 3 Oct. 1916; buried: Cove Creek; record (1916) # 358.

MELTON, Charlie; born: 30 Mar. 1867; married; parents: John MELTON and Manda WARD; death cause: "suicide, gun shot wound in side of head"; informant: Doke WELLS (Bulls Gap); died: 5 Oct. 1916; buried: Browns; record (1916) # 359.

BROWN, Flora C.; born: 9 Nov. 1881; married; parents: R.A. HAYS and June MCDONALD; death cause: "pulmonary tuberculosis"; died in 17th District, 27 Oct. 1916; buried: Pleasant Hill; record (1916) # 360.

LAZENBERY, Eldridge Hausel; born: 4 Jun. 1916 in Iowa; parents: George LAZENBERY and Alice Leone MCAMIS; death cause: "double pneumonia"; died: 23 Oct. 1916; buried: Fall Branch; record # 361.

PEIRCE, Virginia; born: 25 Aug. 1854; widow; parents: J.M. FULKERSON (Sullivan County) and Nancy MORGAN (Washington County); death cause: "pulmonary tuberculosis"; died in 17th District, 22 Oct. 1916; buried: Bethany; record (1916) # 362.

RYAN, Mattie Jeniva; born: 23 Oct. 1916; parents: William P. RYAN and Fannie DEZARN; death cause: "found dead in bed"; informant: father (Jeroldstown); died: 28 Oct. 1916; buried: Lovelace; record (1916) # 363.

BABB, Lavada; age: 42 years, 5 months and 3 days; widow; parents: Blumfield RIPLY and mother not stated; death cause: "heart disease"; informant: William BABB (Chucky); died: 12 Oct. 1916; buried: Stone Dam Church; record (1916) # 364.

REEL, Infant; female; parents: W.E. REEL and Moe FRAZIER; death cause: "stillborn"; informant: father (Afton); died: 8 Oct. 1916; buried: Stone Dam Church; record (1916) # 365.

JOHNSON, Infant; sex not stated; parents: Fred JOHNSON and Lucusa OWENS; death cause: "infant born dead"; informant: James OWENS (Greeneville); born/died: 17 Oct. 1916; buried: Kenedy; record # 366.

KENNEY, Infant; male; parents: L.K. KENNEY and Willie G. SELF; death cause: "stillborn"; informant: father (Bulls Gap); born/died: 11 Oct. 1916; buried: Pilot Knob; record (1916) # 367.

BOYD, Edgar; born: 10 Jan. 1913; parents: John BOYD AND E_ (illegible) BOYD; death cause: "membranous croup"; informant: father (Moshiem); died: 12 Nov. 1916; buried: Craft Cemetery; record # 368.

CARMAC, Infant; male; parents: Jessie J. CARMAC and Lela COX, death cause: "stillborn"; born/died: 29 Nov. 1916; record (1916) # 369.

MORGAN, James Abel; age: 67 years; widower; parents: White MORGAN and Catherine NOELL; death cause: "tuberculosis"; informant: Robert MORGAN (Greeneville); died: day illegible Nov. 1916; record (1916) # 370.

TINE, Lizzie; age: 69 years; widow; parents: __ KELLER and mother not stated; death cause: illegible; died: 9 Nov. 1916; buried: Pine Springs; record (1916) # 371.

REYNOLDS, Georgia; born: 30 Mar. 1911; parents: Crocket REYNOLDS and Cordie LYNCH; death cause: "diphtheria"; died: 26 Nov. 1916; record (1916) # 372.

PETERS, Cecil; born: 19 Oct. 1916; parents: B.F. PETERS and Eula HENSLEY; death cause: "gastro enteritis"; died: 22 Nov. 1916; record (1916) # 373.

DOWNEY, Martha Jane; born: 29 Jul. 1865; married; parents: George W. EARLY and __ HUTCHINSON; death cause: "cancer of uterus"; died in the 15th District, 27 Nov. 1916; buried: Pleasant Vale; record (1916) # 374.

LEMONS, Mercia Elizabeth; born: 3 Sep. 1871 in North Carolina; marital status: not stated; parents: Abner TWEED (North Carolina) and mother not stated; death cause: "heart leakage"; died in the 2nd District, 19 Nov. 1916; buried: Paint Creek; record (1916) # 375.

DICKSON, Lola Vernel; born: 11 Sep. 1915; parents: William Blaine DICKSON and Sarah Ann CUTSHALL; death cause: "double pneumonia"; died: 29 Nov. 1916; buried: Paint Creek; record # 376.

BROOKS, Harrison; born: 10 Nov. 1914; parents: William BROOKS (Sullivan County) and Francis ARWOOD; death cause: "unknown"; informant: father (Greeneville); died: 11 Nov. 1916; record 377.

HUMBARD, Meldrid; age: 4 years; parents: Bob HUMBARD and E__ (illegible) LAMONS; death cause: "diphtheria"; informant: George BRITTAN (Greeneville); died: 1 Nov. 1916; buried: Gass Shed; record (1916) # 378.

STARNES, Infant; female; parents: Luna STARNES and Dora BRITTON; death cause: "premature"; died in the 12th district, 5 Nov. 1916; record (1916) # 379.

MONTGOMERY, Ransom; black; "born in slavery"; age: 77 years; born: South Carolina; married; parents: not stated; death cause: "senility"; informant: Will MONTGOMERY (Greeneville); died: 9 Nov. 1916; buried: Wesley Cemetery; record (1916) # 380.

BROWN, Infant; sex: not stated; parents: C.S. BROWN and Cora HARDIN death cause: "stillborn"; informant: William H. JOHNSON (Greeneville); died: 13 Nov. 1916; buried: Gass Shed; record # 381.

HARMON, Robert; age: 71 years; marital status: not stated; parents: John HARMON and Ann MONGER (Jefferson County); death cause:

"pulmonary tuberculosis"; informant: Miss Tenie HARMON (Greeneville); died: 14 Nov. 1916; buried: Harmon Cemetery; record # 382.

STROND, Lula; born: 8 Jul. 1884; married; parents: Joseph TILSON and Fannie PATE; death cause: "septic peritonitis"; informant: Fred STROND (Greeneville); died: 17 Nov. 1916; record (1916) # 383.

FARBY, Green; black; age: 52 years; married; parents: Green FARBY and mother not stated; death cause: "tuberculosis"; informant: Charles M. BOWMAN (Greeneville); died: 17 Nov. 1916; buried: Wesley Cemetery; record (1916) # 384.

CHAPMAN, Archibald; born: 21 Jul. 1888; married; parents: E.C. CHAPMAN (North Carolina) and Hannah MERCER; death cause: "accident, head crushed between logs"; informant: J.W. JORDAN (Greeneville); died: 25 Nov. 1916; record (1916) # 385.

GOODIN, Ruth Inell; born: 6 Oct. 1915; parents: Charles H. GOODIN and Mamie Lee RADER; death cause: "without medical attention"; informant: father (Moshiem); died: 24 Nov. 1916; record (1916) # 386.

WRIGHT, Ellen; born: 18 Feb. 1862; widow; parents: Noah L. PACK and Sarah GREGG; death cause: "neuralgia of heart"; informant: N.L. PACK (Midway); died: 15 Nov. 1916; buried: St. Josephs Chapel; record (1916) # 387.

POE, Pery; age: 42 years, 11 months and 20 days; marital status: not stated; parents: Henry POE (Virginia) and Elizabeth BATES; death cause: "pulmonary tuberculosis"; informant: J.D. CARTER (Moshiem); died: 23 Nov. 1916; buried: Browns Springs; record (1916) # 388.

KNICELY, Lanise; born: 8 Nov. 1916; parents: Charley KNICELY (Hawkins County) and Mary Virginia RILEY; death cause: "stillborn, womb disease of mother"; informant: father (Mohawk); died: 8 Nov. 1916; buried: Drake Cemetery; record (1916) # 389.

COOTER, Nora Alice; born: 18 May 1902; parents: Jasper C. COOTER and Elizabeth F. MALONE; death cause: "nephritis"; informant: Gilbert M. MORRISON (Baileyton); died: 1 Nov. 1916; buried: Zion; record (1916) # 390.

JUSTIS, James Eugene French; born: 27 Nov. 1914; parents: Jacob JUSTIS and Loura GASS; death cause: "meningitis"; informant: S.M. GASS (Greeneville); died: 9 Nov. 1916; buried: Gass Shed; record (1916) # 391.

MCAMIS, George D.; born: 17 Mar. 1867 (?); age: 65 years, 7 months and 27 days; married; parents: Alfred MCAMIS and Melvina LOYD; death cause: "nephritis"; informant: Jennie BROTHERTON (Baileyton); died: 13 Nov. 1916; buried: Gass Shed; record (1916) # 392.

PETERS, Cecil Cloid; born: 20 Oct. 1916; parents: B.F. PETERS and Eula HENSLEY; death cause: not stated; informant: father (Greeneville); died: 20 Nov. 1916; buried: St. James; record (1916) # 393.

JACKSON, Infant; male; parents: Charles JACKSON and Ena KELLER; death cause: "stillborn"; born/died: 13 Nov. 1916; buried: Bethany Cemetery; record (1916) # 394.

CHARLTON, Elizabeth; born: 30 Sep. 1830 in Hawkins County; widow; parents: George RUTH and mother "unknown"; death cause: "cancer and heart disease"; informant: L.B. CHARLTON (Jeroldstown); died: 30 Nov. 1916; buried: Bethany Cemetery; record (1916) # 395.

JACKSON, Thomas; age: "about 70 years"; married; parents: James T. JACKSON and Elizabeth DALTON; death cause: "pneumonia"; informant: H.C. JACKSON (Jeroldstown); died: 25 Nov. 1916; buried: Bethany Cemetery; record (1916) # 396.

NESS, Infant; male; parents: Albert H. NESS and Ada B. LINEBERGER; death cause: not recorded; born/died: 13 Nov. 1916; buried: St. James; record (1916) # 397.

BROYLES, Infant; male; parents: John S. BROYLES and Jennie I. REAVES; death cause: "stillborn"; informant: O.S. BROYLES (Greeneville); died: 3 Nov. 1916; buried: Mountain View; record # 398.

EDINGTON, Infant, female; born: 29 Jan. 1912; parents: Eric EDINGTON (Cocke County) and Mary DAVENPORT (Marietta, GA.); death cause: "diphtheria"; informant: J.A. HOOD (Midway); died: 3 Nov. 1916; buried: Pine Grove; record (1916) # 399.

HOUSTON, Emily; age: 84 years; born: Greene County; widow; parents: James MCNEW (Virginia) and __ NEAS; death cause; "fracture of skull"; informant: Charles MCNEW (Moshiem); died: 29 Nov. 1916; buried: Marshall, North Carolina; record (1916) # 400.

RADER, Daniel; born: 6 Nov. 1846; married; parents: John RADER and mother not stated; death cause: "Potts disease"; died: 29 Nov. 1916; buried: Timber Ridge; record (1916) # 401.

ALDRICH, Alma Lee; born: 31 Oct. 1916; parents: Henry Martin ALDRICH and Flora CUTSHALL; death cause: "unknown"; died in the 2nd District, 29 Dec. 1916; record (1916) # 402.

MCNABB, Walter; born: 4 Aug. 1890; married; parents: W.A. MCNABB and Margaret FOSHEE; death cause: "tuberculosis, probable cause"; informant: father (Moshiem); died: 25 Dec. 1916; buried: Carter Cemetery; record (1916) # 403.

ELENBURG, John; born: 2 Dec. 1854; married; parents: Adam ELENBURG and Matilda TAYLOR; death cause: "intestinal nephritis"; died in 3rd District, 14 Dec. 1916; record (1916) # 404.

MASSEY, Emma C.; born: 14 Oct. 1916; parents: James MASSEY (North Carolina) and Ada BUCHANAN (North Carolina); death cause: "gastro enteritis"; informant: J.B. MASSEY (Greeneville); died: 15 Dec. 1916; record (1916) # 405.

BIBLE, Francis Elizabeth; born: 16 Sep. 1862; widow; parents: Daniel MOSIER and Elizabeth BRAKEBILL; death cause: "croupous pneumonia"; informant: Miss Mabel BIBLE (Mohawk); died: 7 Dec. 1916; buried: Warrensburg; record (1916) # 406.

GLASSCOCK, Granville Jackson; born: 26 Apr. 1854; married; parents: James GLASSCOCK and Susan FRY; death cause: "valvulor heart disease"; informant: James F. GLASSCOCK (Mohawk); died: 4 Dec. 1916; buried: Concord; record (1916) # 407.

KELLIM, Mona; born: 6 Dec. 1889; single; parents: Milburn KELLIM (North Carolina) and Lou MCMILLAN; death cause: "burn"; informant: Robert KELLIM (Midway); died: 4 Dec. 1916; buried: Warrensburg; record (1916) # 408.

WRIGHT, Mary; born: 16 May 1851; married; parents: Washington CRITTENDEN and B_ (illegible) HURLEY; death cause: "probably apoplexy"; died in the 4th District, 3 Dec. 1916; record (1916) # 409.

SCRUGGS, Sarrah; born: 1 Apr. 1844; married; parents: Hamilton EVANS and Melissie SMITH; death cause: "valvulor heart trouble"; informant: E.C. SCRUGGS (Warrensburg, TN.); died: 2 Dec. 1916; buried: Jarnigan Cemetery; record (1916) # 410.

KNOWLES, Henry Washington; born: 17 May 1845 in Virginia; widower; parents: George KNOWLES (North Carolina) and mother not stated; death cause: "pericarditis, paralysis"; informant: William KNOWLES (Baileyton); died: 8 Dec. 1916; record (1916) # 411.

SNAPP, Thomas; age: 74 years; widower; parents: Sam SNAPP and mother not stated; death cause: "senility"; informant: W.T. MITCHELL (Greeneville); died: 10 Dec. 1916; buried: Mt. Zion; record # 412.

WILKISON, Infant; female; born: 6 Dec. 1916; parents: Charles C. WILKISON and Tola RADNOUR; death cause: "unknown"; informant: father (Moshiem); died: 12 Dec. 1916; buried: Carters Chapel; record (1916) # 413.

RIPLEY, Infant; male; born: 5 Dec. 1916; parents: David S. RIPLEY and Minnie DEERSTONE; death cause: "premature delivery"; informant: father (Afton); died: 23 Dec. 1916; buried: Stone Dam; record # 414.

ELLENBURG, John; born: 12 Dec. 1852; married; parents: Adam ELLENBURG and Matilda TAYLOR; death cause: not stated; died: 22 Dec. 1916; buried: St. James; record (1916) # 415.

MASSEY, Emma Carter; born: 14 Oct. 1916; parents: James B. MASSEY (Madison County, NC.) and Ada BUCHANAN (Yancey County, NC.); death cause: not stated; informant: father (Greeneville); died: 22 Dec. 1916; buried: Caney Branch; record (1916) # 416.

BURGNER, Peter; born: 13 Feb. 1854; married; parents: Christian BURGNER and Malinda FULLER; death cause: "malignant condition of stomach and liver"; informant: Mrs. Peter BURGNER (Chucky); died: 8 Dec. 1916; buried: Pleasant Hill; record (1916) # 417.

THOMASON, Joseph M.; born: 13 Mar. 1879; married; parents: John P. THOMASON and Mary J. BROYLES; death cause: "epilepsy"; informant: James WADDLE (Chucky); died: 15 Dec. 1915; buried: Pleasant Hill; record (1916) # 418.

JOHNSON, Pauline Ruth; born: 24 Aug. 1916; parents: John JOHNSON and Lena HAMMER; death cause: "meningitis"; informant: father (Greeneville); died: 24 Dec. 1916; buried: Herman Cemetery; record (1916) # 419.

REYNOLDS, Martha; born: 30 Mar. 1850; widow; parents: J.G. BROBECK and Ellen BRANON; death cause: "tuberculosis of lungs"; informant: J.C. BROBECK (Greeneville); died: 20 Dec. 1916; buried: Oak Grove; record (1916) # 420.

STARNES, Charity Victoria; born: 13 Jul. 1841 in North Carolina; widow; parents: Bill MYERS and N__ (illegible) JONES, death cause: "senility"; informant: Joe HARMON (Greeneville); died: 13 Dec. 1916; buried: Prices Chapel; record (1916) # 421.

MYSINGER, Gussie; born: 19 Mar. 1914; parents: A.H. MYSINGER and Lula REED; death cause: "croup and diphtheria"; died: 7 Dec. 1916; buried: Mt. Pleasant; record (1916) # 422.

EALEY, Rebeca; born: 2 Oct. 1835 in Greene County; married; parents: John RECTOR and Bartia DEARSTONE; death cause: not stated; informant: Joe EALEY (Greeneville); died: 2 Dec. 1916; buried: Cedar Hill; record (1916) # 423.

FAIR, Mandy; age: "about 55 years; parents: "unknown"; death cause: "asthma and bronchitis"; died: 2 Dec. 1916; buried: County Farm; record (1916) # 424.

HARMON, Harrison C.; born: 19 Aug. 1834 in Greene County; married; parents: John HARMON and Sallie COBBLE; death cause: "asthma"; informant: R.P. HARMON (Mohawk); died: 18 Dec. 1916; buried: Harmon Cemetery; record (1916) # 425.

SIPE, James; born: "about 1853"; age: 63 years; married; parents: father "unknown" and Linie KINSER; death cause: "paralysis"; informant: Corbett SIPE (Mohawk); died: 13 Dec. 1916; buried: Phillipi Cemetery; record (1916) # 426.

HARMON, Jacob Luther; born: 12 Dec. 1844; married; parents: John HARMON and __ COBBLE; death cause: "artoro scl__ (illegible) and bronchitis"; informant: Mrs. J.S. HARMON (Midway); died: 18 Dec. 1916; buried: Harmon Cemetery; record (1916) # 427.

LOWE, Grover Lafayette; born: 7 Aug. 1916; parents: E.R. LOWE and Sula WRIGHT; death cause: "auto intoxication"; informant: A.L. WRIGHT (Midway); died: 4 Dec. 1916; record (1916) # 428.

SELF, Sarah Eveline; age: 50 years; married; parents: John W. LIVINGSTONE and Drucilla HYDER; death cause: "tuberculosis of lungs"; died: 29 Dec. 1916; buried: Bibles Chapel; record (1916) # 429.

LOYD, Alice; born: 4 Aug. 1865; widow; parents: E__ (illegible) RECTOR and mother's name illegible; death cause: "pulmonary tuberculosis"; informant: W. JEFFERS (Baileyton); died: 12 Dec. 1916; buried: Lebanon; record (1916) # 430.

WEEMS, Ula F.; born: 23 Nov. 1913; parents: J.E. WEEMS and Callie STRONG; death cause: "diabetes"; informant: father (Baileyton); died: 6 Dec. 1916; buried: Zion; record (1916) # 431.

BROYLES, Mary Edna; parents: Max F. BROYLES and Dora B. JOHNSON; death cause: "premature birth"; informant: father (Afton); born/died: 15 Dec. 1916; buried: Hermon Cemetery; record # 432.

BITNER, Dosser; born: 31 Mar. 1914; parents: Ben BITNER and Birtie PAINTER; death cause: "measles"; informant: Blevins WADDLE (Chucky); died: 9 Dec. 1916; buried: Pleasant Hill; record (1916) # 433.

MCCORKLE, Catherine; born: 11 Nov. 1841; widow; parents: James WEBB and mother's name illegible; death cause: "paralysis"; died in the 14th District, 2 Dec. 1916; buried: Stone Dam; record (1916) # 434.

COX, Daisy; born: 12 Apr. 1916; listed as parents: George COX and Essie HOPE; death cause: "whooping cough"; informant: George COX, father (Moshiem); died: 28 Jan. 1917; buried: Mt. Carmel; record (1917) # 1.

ERVIN, Elbert E.; born: 24 Feb. 1853; married; parents: James ERVIN and Mary SUSONG; death cause: "tuberculosis"; informant: T.A. BIBLE (Moshiem); died: 9 Jan. 1917; buried: Brown Springs; record (1917) # 2.

CARTER, Ezekiel; born: 3 Feb. 1855; married; parents: William CARTER and Eliza HARMON; death cause: "apoplexy"; informant: J.D. CARTER (Moshiem); died: 4 Jan. 1917; record (1917) # 3.

BIBLE, James Charles; born: 14 Nov. 1916; parents: Hobert BIBLE and Hessie STEPHENS; death cause: "pneumonia"; informant: father (Mohawk); died: 30 Jan. 1917; buried: Crosby Cem.; record (1917) # 4

MERCER, Martha Ann; born: 8 Feb. 1849; widow; parents: Samuel KENNEDY and Louise MORELOCK; death cause: "nephritis, brights disease"; informant: Mrs. J.L. ARMSTRONG (Limestone); died: 25 Jan. 1917; buried: Providence; record (1917) # 5.

JONES, Elizabeth; age: "about 63 years; single; parents: David JONES and __ HARRIS; death cause: "organic heart disease"; informant: William JONES (Limestone); died: 16 Jan. 1917; record (1917) # 6.

BRADLEY, James; born: 22 Sep. 1916; parents: William Lawrence BRADLEY (North Carolina) and Carrie Rita WHITE; death cause:

"miliary tuberculosis"; informant: W.L. BRADLEY (Chucky); died: 28 Jan. 1917; buried: Pleasant Hill; record (1917) # 7.

MILLER, Frank; born: __ Nov. 1883; single; parents: father "unknown" and Sallie MILLER; death cause: "strangulated hernia"; informant: Henry HAIRE (Chucky); died: 4 Jan. 1917; buried: Pleasant Hill; record (1917) # 8.

PETERS, Paul; born: 18 Dec. 1916; parents: Wesley PETERS and Lula BOWERS; death cause: "unknown"; informant: father (Greeneville); died: 3 Jan. 1917; buried: St. James; record (1917) # 9.

ROGERS, Mollie; born: 10 Nov. 1869; divorced; parents: Manson ROGERS and Sarah BURNETT; death cause: "heart failure"; informant: Mrs. Jane BIBLE (Midway); died: 5 Jan. 1917; record (1917) # 10.

KILLIAN, Martha Diana; born: 28 Mar. 1841 in North Carolina; widow; parents: John SHEPPARD (North Carolina) and Malinda BLUE (North Carolina); death cause: "chronic bronchitis"; informant: W.G. KILLIAN (Midway); died: 11 Jan. 1917; buried: Warrensburg; record # 11.

DECK, L.V.; black; born: 22 Aug. 1903; parents: Rome DECK (North Carolina) and Caroline SWATSEL; death cause: "epilepsy, grand mal seizure"; informant: father (Mohawk); died: 12 Jan. 1917; buried: Warrensburg; record (1917) # 12.

PINKSTON, Sousan; born: 29 Oct. 1820 in Cocke County; parents: John RICKER (Indiana) and Catherine MYSINGER (Indiana); death cause: "tuberculosis of bowels"; informant: John JENKINS (Bulls Gap); died: 3 Jan. 1917; buried: Mt. Hope; record (1917) # 13.

BABB, Cora; born: 11 Feb. 1889; married; parents: Eli HAUN and Eliza WILLOUGHBY; death cause: "catarrh of bowels"; informant: D.A. MORELOCK (Bulls Gap); died: 17 Jan. 1917; buried: Willoughbys; record (1917) # 14.

TURNER, William; born: 12 Jul. 1838 in Tennessee; married; parents: Maltrie TURNER and mother "unknown"; death cause: "sarcoma of stomach"; informant: S.P. SENEKER (Moshiem); died: 19 Jan. 1917; buried: Harmon Cemetery; record (1917) # 15.

COX, Lewis; born: 21 May 1848 in North Carolina; married; parents: Silas COX (North Carolina) and Mary __; death cause: "chronic nephritis"; informant: William COX (Bulls Gap); died: 13 Jan. 1917; buried: Mt. Carmel; record (1917) # 16.

POE, Pauline; born: 12 Jul. 1915; parents: Percy POE and Nancy BULLINGTON; death cause: "bronchial pneumonia"; informant: J.H. POE; died at Bulls Gap, 24 Jan. 1917; buried: Brown Cemetery; record (1917) # 17.

WARDEN, Clyde; age: 5 years, 11 months and 16 days; parents: John WARDEN and Nancy NAUGHTY; death cause: "crushed skull, fell out of bed"; informant: B.F. GOSNELL (Greeneville); died: 18 Jan. 1917; buried: Red Hill Church; record (1917) # 18.

BLAKE, Lou; age: 97 years; born: Greene County; married; parents: Simon BIRD and mother not stated; death cause: "lagrippe"; informant: Dave SHAW (Greeneville); died: 18 Jan. 1917; buried: Harrisons; record (1917) # 19.

CUTSHALL, Stanley Hugh; born: 7 Nov. 1914; parents: William M. CUTSHALL and Jennie Elizabeth CUTSHALL; death cause: "bold hives, lagrippe"; informant: father; died: 2nd District, 16 Jan. 1917; buried: Sexton Cemetery; record (1917) # 20.

POE. Lizzie Kate; born: 4 Dec. 1911; parents: Robert POE and Mary MORRISON; death cause: "acute gastritis"; informant: Rufus MORRISON (Baileyton); died: 21 Jan. 1917; buried: Locust Springs; record (1917) # 21.

MCNABB, Earle; born: 2 Jan. 1917; parents: William A. MCNABB and Rhoda E. MORRIS; death cause: "unknown"; informant: father (Moshiem); died: 16 Jan. 1917; buried: Carter Cemetery; record (1917) # 22.

KENNEY, Infant; male; parents: Elmer KENNEY and Carrie MOORE; death cause: "stillborn"; died: 21 Jan. 1917; buried: Gass Shed; record (1917) # 23.

ALLEN, Henry Clay; born: 9 Oct. 1916; parents: Phillip ALLEN and Oma WARD; death cause: "unknown"; informant: father (Baileyton); died: 14 Jan. 1917; buried: Lebanon; record (1917) # 24.

LANE, Crocket W.; age: 4 years; parents: W.E. LANE and Flora GRAY; death cause: "burn, clothing caught fire"; informant: W.G. GRAY (Greeneville); died: 5 Jan. 1917; buried: Oak Grove; record (1917) # 25.

BIBLE, Bessie; age: 5 years; parents: John BIBLE and Bertie CRUCY death cause: "unknown, found dead in bed"; informant: father (Greeneville); died: 15 Jan. 1917; buried: White Church; record (1917) # 26.

HARTSELL, Charles C.; age: 80 years; born: Washington County; married; parents: Abraham HARTSELL and mother not stated; death cause: "chronic myocarditis"; informant: J.S. HARTSELL (Greeneville); died: 15 Jan. 1917; buried: Pisgah; record (1917) # 27.

LISTER, Mrs. Mary; age: 77 years; widow; parents: __ RUSSELL and mother not stated; death cause: "senility"; informant: W.C. GIBSON (Greeneville); died: 17 Jan. 1917; buried: Cedar Hill; record # 28.

EVANS, Robert; age: 60 years; widower; parents: Calvin EVANS and Caroline REED; death cause: "pneumonia"; informant: Mary JENKINS (Greeneville); died: 20 Jan. 1917; buried: Brights Cemetery; record (1917) # 29.

OWENS, Marion; age: 30 years; marital status: not stated; parents: not stated; death cause: "suddenly, cause not stated"; informant: Michael FRESHOUR (Cedar Creek); died: 20 Jan. 1917; record (1917) # 30.

MCCOY, Mrs. Mollie; age: 35 years; married; parents: A. TAYLOR and Darous CUTSHALL; death cause: "cerebral hemorrhage"; died: 23 Jan. 1917; buried: Bersheba; record (1917) # 31.

BANKS, Kizzie Lee; age: 3 months; parents: Sam BANKS and Kizzie HILTON; death cause: "heart failure"; informant: father (Greeneville); died: 20 Jan. 1917; buried: River Hill; record (1917) # 32.

HARMON, William Z.; age: 66 years; married; manufacturer; parents: Keneda HARMON and Margaret HARMON; death cause: "tubercular spine and kidneys; informant: L.V. HARMON (Moshiem); died: 27 Jan. 1917; buried: Oak Grove; record (1917) # 33.

LOWERY, Dalie May; born: 23 Jan. 1917; parents: Clarence LOWERY (North Carolina) and Harriett BURELL (North Carolina); death cause: "unknown, without medical attention"; died: 28 Jan. 1917; buried: Mt. Pleasant; record (1917) # 34.

BIBLE, Bertie Mae; born: 14 May 1892; married; parents: William BIBLE and Ester RADER; death cause: "pulmonary tuberculosis" informant: Cart BIBLE (Myers); died: 28 Jan. 1917; buried: Mt. Pleasant; record (1917) # 35.

CANNON, Lafayette; black; age: 1 month; parents: Mallome CANNON and Daisy DENTON; death cause: "pneumonia"; informant: Daisy DENTON (Greeneville); buried: Colored Cemetery; record (1917) # 36.

PALMER, Herman; black; age: 24 years, 2 months and 16 days; single; parents: Gabe PALMER and Etta RILES; death cause: "pulmonary tuberculosis"; informant: James RILES (Greeneville); died: 29 Jan. 1917; buried: Wesley Cemetery; record (1917) # 37.

JONES, Irene F.; born: 24 Dec. 1905; parents: J. Marion JONES and Nellie PRESNELL; death cause: "tuberculosis"; informant: J.M. JONES (Greeneville); died: 30 Jan. 1917; buried: Oak Grove; record # 38.

WEEMS, Callie; born: 2 Feb. 1848; widow; parents: John BYRD and Susana CLICK; death cause: "brights disease"; informant: C.R. BYRD (Greeneville); died: 31 Jan. 1917; buried: Herman Church; record #39.

CLIPHAUT, Hannah; age: 73 years; born: Greene County; marital status: not stated; parents: James CLIPHAUT and Margaret DODD; death cause: "gall stones"; died: 31 Jan. 1917; buried: Mt. Hebron; record (1917) # 40.

HOMER, John; born: 13 Mar. 1832 in Pennsylvania; single; Civil War Veteran; parents: "unknown"; death cause: "mitral regurgitation"; informant: A.L. TAYLOR (Fall Branch); died: 21 Jan. 1917; buried: Lovelace; record (1917) # 41.

BOWSER. John; age: 17 years; single; parents: Charles BOWSER and Marilu MOON; death cause: "streptococci and epilepsy"; died: in the 17th District, 10 Jan. 1917; buried: Oakdale; record (1917) # 42.

TOLLIVER, Nancy Jane; age: 83 years; born: Greene County; widow; parents: Louis RUSH and Mary OLINGER; death cause: "paralyzed for 18 years and old age"; informant: Jessie JACKSON (Jeroldstown); died: 8 Jan. 1917; buried; Union Temple; record (1917) # 43.

BROYLES, William A.; born: 1 Jul. 1847; married; parents: Micher BROYLES and Elizabeth FRENCH; death cause: "heart failure"; informant: Bruce ROBERTS (Chucky); died: 21 Jan. 1917; buried: Pleasant Hill; record (1917) # 44.

BAILS/BALES, Rebecca Jane; born: 21 Sep. 1846; married; parents: Alfred KITE and Mary KITE (North Carolina); death cause: "apoplexy, paralysis"; informant: H.H. BALES (Afton); died: 4 Jan. 1917; buried: Quaker __; record (1917) # 45.

BROYLES, William A.; (duplicate record of record 44 above) this record (1917) # 46.

NORTON, George Arnold; born: 17 Oct. 1916; parents: George NORTON (North Carolina) and Callie BYRD; death cause: "found dead in bed"; informant: C.R. BYRD (Greeneville); died: 4 Feb. 1917; buried: Herman Church; record (1917) # 47.

PEARSON, Mable E.; born: 23 Mar. 1915; parents: S.D. PEARSON and Mollie DAIRS; death cause: "infant paralysis"; informant: father (White Pine); died: 8 Feb. 1917; record (1917) # 48.

COOTER, Harley; born: 19 Feb. 1915; parents: Barney COOTER and Nettie UNDERHILL; death cause: "broncho pneumonia"; informant: father (Baileyton); died: 24 Feb. 1917; buried: Zion; record (1917) # 49.

FREEMAN, Jennie; black; age: "approximately 75 years"; widow; parents: Jerry MCKINNEY and Jennie MCKINNEY; death cause: "fibroid tumor"; informant: Will MCKINNEY (Mohawk); died; 20 Feb. 1917; record (1917) # 50.

MERCY, Fred L.; born: 8 Sep. 1880 in Maine; married; parents: Mikel MERCER and Mary Ellen __; death cause: "pneumonia croupous"; informant: Sidney TRAVIS (Moshiem); died; 8 Feb. 1917; record # 51.

MALONE, James H.; born: 9 Sep. 1901; parents: Duncan D. MALONE and Kisa FOSHIE; death cause: "killed by falling tree, cutting timber"; informant: John WILEY (Baileyton); died: 23 Feb. 1917; buried: family cemetery; record (1917) # 52.

HUNT, Susan; age: 74 years; born: North Carolina; widow; parents: father "unknown" and Mary SALES (North Carolina); death cause: "pulmonary tuberculosis"; informant: J.M. JARRELL (Moshiem); died: 24 Feb. 1917; record (1917) # 53.

FRAKER, Rethiah Jane; born: 23 Dec. 1830 in Greene County; widow; parents: Joseph P. MILBURN (Washington County, VA.) and Mary MILBURN; death cause: "senile gangrene on left foot"; informant: T.T.M. FRAKER (Limestone); died: 22 Feb. 1917; buried: Milburnton; record 91917) # 54.

JUSTIC, Sarah J.; born: 3 Sep. 1862; widow; parents: Oliver BROWN and Margaret E. DUGGER; death cause: "tuberculosis of lungs"; informant: C.E. DAVIS (Greeneville); died: 22 Feb. 1917; buried: Gass Shed; record (1917) # 55.

WOODS, Polly; black; born: 2 Mar. 1834 in North Carolina; married; parents: Will PAYNE (North Carolina) and Nancy BUNCH (North

Carolina); death cause: "clothing caught fire, burned to death"; informant: John WOODS (Greeneville); died: 3 Feb. 1917; buried: Wesley; record (1917) # 56.

JONES, S.D.; born: 28 Oct. 1848; married; parents: Samuel JONES and Rachel CASTEEL; death cause: "measles"; informant: I.B. BROWN (Moshiem); died: 24 Feb. 1917; buried: Browns Springs; record # 57.

MCGHEE, Walter; black; age: 24 years; single; parents: William MCGHEE and Dora JOHNSON; death cause: "pulmonary tuberculosis"; informant: Adriane MCGHEE (Greeneville); died: 4 Feb. 1917; buried: Wesley; record (1917) # 58.

WADDLE, J.H.; born: 11 Dec. 1878; married; parents: Green WADDLE and mother not stated; death cause: "tuberculosis"; died: 5 Feb. 1917; buried: Cove Creek; record (1917) # 59.

DOUTHAT, Jessie; age: 4 years; parents: R.P. DOUTHAT and Nora STROND; death cause: "ruptured appendix"; informant: father (Greeneville); died: 6 Feb. 1917; buried: Mohawk; record (1917) # 60.

RIDDLE, Laura; age: 3 months; born: Morristown; parents: George RIDDLE (North Carolina) and Laura HAROLD; death cause: "tubercular meningitis"; informant: father (Greeneville); buried: Harold's Cemetery; record (1917) # 61.

BRABSON, E.D.; born: __ Mar. 1850; widower; parents: Alexander BRABSON (Virginia) and __ STEVENS (Virginia); death cause: "cystitis"; informant: L.E. BRABSON (Telford); died: 8 Feb. 1917; buried: Oakland; record (1917) # 62.

SMITH, Infant; male; born: 4 Feb. 1917; parents: Will SMITH and Lyde RAGSDALE; death cause: "heart disease"; informant: R.L. BROWN (Greeneville); died: 10 Feb. 1917; buried: Gass Shed; record # 63.

TOME, Clarissa; born: 5 Dec. 1851; single; parents: father "unknown" and Oma TOME; death cause: "paralysis"; informant: James BEBBER (Greeneville); died; 11 Feb. 1917; buried: Fairview; record (1917) # 64.

DUNCAN, Aaron; black; born: 7 Aug. 1916; parents: John DUNCAN and Louisa DUNCAN; death cause: "pneumonia"; informant: mother (Greeneville); died: 13 Feb. 1917; buried: Colored Cemetery; record (1917) # 65.

FOLKS, Leonard; age: 17 years; parents: F.O. FOLKS and Abbical CRADLOCK; death cause: "appendicitis"; informant: J.C. HARDIN (Greeneville); died: 6 Feb. 1917; buried: Hardin Chapel; record # 66.
HAYSE, Fannie Jerrels; born: 21 Feb. 1868; married; parents: M.F. JERRELS (Kentucky) and Nancie BLACKBURN; death cause: "cancer of liver"; informant: G.S. HAYSE (Greeneville); died: 22 Feb. 1917; buried: Oak Grove; record (1917) # 67.
PICKERING, Mary F.; born: 8 Aug. 1843; married; parents: Edwin PRICE and Caroline PRICE; death cause: "cerebral hemorrhage"; informant: T.B. PICKERING (Greeneville); died: 22 Feb. 1917; buried: Oak Grove; record (1917) # 68.
SOWERS, James B.; born: 18 Oct. 1841 in Virginia; married; parents: Jacob SOWERS (Virginia) and Mary EPPERSON (Virginia); death cause: illegible; informant: Ida SOWERS (Greeneville); died: 23 Feb. 1917; buried: Oak Grove; record (1917) # 69.
JANES, Jack Bernard; age: 3 days; parents: C.J. JANES and Louise BOLLINGER; death cause: "unknown"; informant: father (Greeneville); died: 24 Feb. 1917; buried: Oak Grove; record (1917) # 70.
PATTERSON, Cleta; black; age: 3 years; parents: Bruce PATTERSON and Lucy IRVING; death cause: "pneumonia"; informant: father (Greeneville); died: 26 Feb. 1917; buried: Wesley; record (1917) # 71.
DOBSON, John; born: 24 Oct. 1843; age: 73 years; widower; parents: Calvin DOBSON and mother "unknown"; death cause: "cancer of liver"; informant: D.D. ALEXANDER (Greeneville); died: 27 Feb. 1917; buried: Shilo; record (1917) # 72.
MACE, Emmie Evalyon; age: "about 87 years"; born: North Carolina; widow; parents: Basil ELKINS (North Carolina) and Celia MCFALLS (North Carolina); death cause: "old age, lagrippe"; died in the 2nd District, 1 Feb. 1917; buried: Sexton Cemetery; record (1917) # 73.
WEST, James Hesekiah; born: 7 Feb. 1850 in North Carolina; married; parents: James WEST and Betty __; death cause: "cancer"; informant: Mrs. WEST; died: 5 Feb. 1917; buried: Lamb Cemetery; record # 74.
DICKSON, Logan; born: 25 Nov. 1899; single; parents: James DICKSON and Mary Jane TWEED; death cause: "accidental gunshot wound on 23 Dec. 1916"; died: 6 Feb. 1917; buried: Sexton Cemetery; record (1917) # 75.

MOORE, S.W.; age: 74 years; parents: not stated; death cause: "chronic diarrhea"; died in the 14th District, 8 Feb. 1917; buried: Stone Dam; record (1917) # 76.

ENGLISH, A.J.; age: 72 years; widower; parents: Milton ENGLISH and A__ (illegible) ENGLISH; death cause: "apoplexy"; died in the 14th District, 18 Feb. 1917; buried: Pleasant Hill; record (1917) # 77.

MCALLISTER, Lee; black; parents: Lee MCALLISTER (Virginia) and Mary WOODS; death cause: "stillborn"; informant: Willie WOODS (Bulls Gap); died: 4 Feb. 1917; buried: Drake; record (1917) # 78.

CUPP, Infant; female; parents: Will CUPP and Etta LAWSON; death cause: "miscarriage"; informant: father (Mohawk); born/died: 18 Feb. 1917; buried: Kirks Cemetery; record (1917) # 79.

CUPP, Infant; female; (duplicate record); record (1917) # 80.

HIXON, Ina Ruth; born: 5 Mar. 1917; parents: Arthur HIXON and Mary ENGLISH; death cause: "croupous pneumonia"; informant: Andy HIXON (Midway); died: 23 Mar. 1917; record (1917) # 81.

CUPP, Joseph Campbell; born: 23 Feb. 1917; parents: Leroy CUPP and Leona G. HAUN; death cause: "unknown"; informant: Bert CUPP (Mohawk); died: 21 Mar. 1917; record (1917) # 82.

JUSTICE, Margaret Ann; born: 5 Aug. 1855; single; parents: Daniel K. JUSTICE and Barbary SMITH; death cause: "bronchitis, probably tuberculosis"; informant: James H. JEFFERS (Moshiem); died: 14 Mar. 1917; buried: Mt. Carmel; record (1917) # 83.

COATNEY, Dana; male; born: 9 Jun. 1902; parents: Yank COATNEY and Maggie JEFFERS; death cause: "unknown, had blisters on his skin"; informant: John JEFFERS (Moshiem); died: 27 Mar. 1917; buried: Mt. Carmel; record (1917) # 84.

BIDDLE, Dorothy; age: 11 months; parents: J.E. BIDDLE (Jefferson County) and Estella CHAPMAN (Chattanooga); death cause: "la-grippe"; informant: father (Greeneville); died: 22 Mar. 1917; buried: Oak Grove; record (1917) # 85.

RADER, Andrew J.; born: 15 Mar. 1852; married; parents: Andrew J. RADER, Sr. and mother "unknown"; death cause: "intestinal nephritis"; died in the 19th District, 11 Mar. 1917; buried: Pine Grove; record (1917) # 86.

BOHANNAN, Mrs. Katherine; age: 74 years; widow; parents: John HARMON and mother not stated; death cause: "lagrippe"; informant: Neal BOHANNAN (Greeneville); died: 20 Mar. 1917; buried: Harmons Cemetery; record (1917) # 87.

TEMPLE, Julia; born: 10 Mar. 1856; married; parents: James RANKINS and Margaret MC__ (illegible); death cause: "cancer of kidneys"; informant; M.J. TEMPLE (Greeneville); died: 17 Mar. 1917; buried: Oak Grove; record (1917) # 88.

CARDON, Dennis; age: 22 years; single; parents: "unknown"; death cause: "pulmonary consumption"; informant: J. MORELOCK (Greeneville); died: 16 Mar. 1917; buried: Fairview; record (1917) # 89.

BENNETT, David; age: 51 years; married; parents: David BENNETT and mother not stated; death cause: "pulmonary tuberculosis"; informant: H.M.E. BENNETT (Chucky); died: 1 Mar. 1917; buried: Pleasant Vale; record (1917) # 90.

PAINTER, Frank G.; born: 19 Dec. 1916 in Illinois; parents: George PAINTER and Pearl BAILEY; death cause: "bronchitis"; informant: father (Baileyton); died: 6 Mar. 1917; buried: Zion; record (1917) # 91.

PATTON, John Earnest; born: 3 Mar. 1917; parents: J.N. PATTON (California) and Kate EARNEST; death cause: "convulsions"; informant: father (Chucky); died: 24 Mar. 1917; buried: Cedar Grove; record (1917) # 92.

LOWE, John Robinson; born: __ Apr. 1839 in Tennessee; widower; parents: "unknown"; death cause: "heart failure"; informant: J.C. LOWE (Greeneville); died: 13 Mar. 1917; buried: Mt. Bethel; record # 93.

BECK, Sarah Elizabeth; born: 11 Oct. 1911; parents: Henry C. BECK and Mattie E. SOUTHERLAND; death cause: "croupous pneumonia"; informant: H.C. BECK (Moshiem); died: 11 Mar. 1917; buried: Big Springs; record (1917) # 94.

HART, Tilman A.; born: 2 Mar. 1917; parents: Elmer COMES and Bell HART; death cause: "hemorrhage __ (illegible)"; informant: C.M. HART (Greeneville); died: 4 Mar. 1917; buried: Cedar Hill; record (1917) # 95.

CAMPBELL, Lula Elizabeth; born: 11 Jun. 1879 in Jonesborough, TN.; widow; parents: father "unknown" and Marry HELTON (Carter

County); death cause: "cancer of uterus"; informant: J.W. CHANDLER (Chucky); died: 23 Mar. 1917; buried: Jonesborough; record # 96.

DUNN, Bert C.; female; born: 7 Nov. 1891; single; parents: John DUNN (North Carolina) and S. Jane SWATZEL (?); death cause: "tuberculosis"; informant: Nina J. DUNN (Afton); died: 27 Mar. 1917; record (1917) # 97.

BECK, Georgia Lee; born: 8 Jan. 1910; parents; Henry C. BECK and Mattie E. SOUTHERLAND; death cause: "lobar pneumonia"; informant: father (Moshiem); died: 5 Mar. 1917; buried: Big Springs; record (1917) # 98.

MCGEE, Clara Lee; born: 28 Feb. 1917; parents: Edd MCGEE and Maggie D. SMELCER; death cause: not stated; informant: father (Moshiem); died: 3 Mar. 1917; buried: Harmons Cemetery; record (1917) # 99.

PATTON, Sallie Seneker; born: 8 Oct. 1836; widow; parents: Clayton SELF and Margarette FRAZIER; death cause: "rheumatism and valvulor insufficiency"; informant: S.P. SENEKER; died: 2 Mar. 1917; buried: Weems Chapel; record (1917) # 100.

JONES, Mrs. Marion; born: 16 Dec. 1884; married; parents: John PRESNELL and Phoebe WHITSON; death cause: "tuberculosis"; informant: J.M. JONES (Greeneville); died: 6 Mar. 1917; buried: Oak Grove; record (1917) # 101.

BROOKINS, Pauline; black; born: 2 Apr. 1903; parents: Isaac BROOKINS and Maggie SCOTT; death cause: "organic heart leison"; informant: father (Greeneville); died: 7 Mar. 1917; buried: Colored Cemetery; record (1917) # 102.

CRUM, Margaret J.; born: 17 Dec. 1848; widow; parents: John HARMON and Nancy CAVENDER; death cause: "organic heart disease"; informant: Jacob BROYLES (Greeneville); died: 20 Mar. 1917; buried: Harrisons Cemetery; record (1917) # 103.

TUCKER, Nathan B.; born: 14 Feb. 1841 in Hawkins County; widower; parents: Alexander TUCKER and Sallie BALL; death cause: "pneumonia fever"; informant: G.R. WALTERS (Baileyton); died: 22 Mar. 1917; buried: Zion; record (1917) # 104.

BROWN, J. Bradley; born: 3 Apr. 1852 in Hawkins County; married; parents: James C. BROWN and Lousian BAILEY (Hawkins County);

death cause: "lobar pneumonia"; informant: Percie YOKLEY (Baileyton); died: 23 Mar. 1917; buried; Browns Mountain; record (1917) # 105.

BROWN, William Alexander; born: 21 Aug. 1832 in Greene County; widower; parents: John BROWN (Virginia) and Cahterine CRUMLEY (VA); death cause: "pneumonia and senility"; informant: D.T. CASTIEL (Greeneville); died: 24 Mar. 1917; buried: Gass Shed; record # 106.

INGLE, Ellis B.; born: 6 Feb. 1845 in Hawkins County; married; parents: Thomas INGLE and Cenith INGLE; death cause: "pneumonia"; informant: Ola CARR (Fall Branch); died: 10 Mar. 1917; buried: Rock Springs; record (1917) # 107.

WHITAKER, Sarah; born: 14 Apr. 1839 in Washington County; widow; parents: __ ENGLE and mother not stated; death cause: "obstruction of bowel"; died: 12 Mar. 1917; buried: Pleasant Hill; record (1917) # 108.

HENSLEY, Blanch Gladen; born: 30 Jun. 1895; married; parents: John CHARLTON and Mary MCCAMY; death cause: "epileptic fits, fell in fire and burned to death"; informant: J.D. FOX (Jeroldstown); died: 24 Mar. 1917; buried: Bethany; record (1917) # 109.

WADDLE, Dana Lyle; born: 4 Dec. 1916; parents: __ (illegible) WADDLE and Dezzie BROYLES; death cause: "unknown, found dead in bed"; informant: J.B. WADDLE (Chucky); died: 5 Mar. 1917; buried: Cedar Grove; record (1917) # 110.

MOORE, John R.; born: 9 Apr. 1834 in Greene County; married; parents: Edward MOORE (North Carolina) and Nancy MORRIS (North Carolina); death cause: "heart disease"; informant: Mrs. John R. MOORE (Moshiem); died: 5 Mar. 1917; buried: Mt. Carmel; record (1917) # 111.

ELKINS, Sarah E.; born: 26 Aug. 1837; single; parents: father not stated and Rachel SMITH; death cause: "fatty degeneration of heart"; informant: Rice ELKINS (Midway); died: 12 Mar. 1917; buried: Bewley Cemetery; record (1917) # 112.

MORELOCK, Virginia Preston; born: 23 Jun. 1863; married; parents: Oliver M. BROYLES and Sarah KING; death cause: "tuberculosis of lungs"; informant: S.F. MORELOCK (Chucky); died: 21 Mar. 1917; buried: Herman; record (1917) # 113.

MANESS, Charley; born: 20 Mar. 1917; parents: Alfred A. MANESS and Mollie WEEMS; death cause: "premature birth"; informant: A.A. MANESS (Baileyton); died: 20 Mar. 1917; buried: Zion; record # 114.

SHOWMAN, Sallie; born: 16 Sep. 1889; married; parents: J.A. BROWN (Washington County) and Emma SWATZELL; death cause: "pulmonary tuberculosis"; died in the 16th District, 7 Mar. 1917; record (1917) # 115.

JONES, Infant; sex: not stated; parents: Gass JONES and Ida CASTEEL; death cause: "premature"; informant: R.G. GRAHAM (Greeneville); died: 28 Mar. 1917; buried: Casteel Cemetery; record (1917) # 116.

HUGHES, J. Lafayette; born: 27 May 1867; married; parents: Hiram B. HUGHES and Martha LINTIAUM (Virginia); death cause: "lobar pneumonia"; informant: Adbry BATES (Baileyton); died at Afton on 6 Apr. 1917; record (1917) # 117.

BALES, Zella May; born: 27 Jul. 1889; married; parents: J.M. LAWSON and mother not stated; death cause: "paralysis"; informant: R.R. BALES (Moshiem); died: 2 Apr. 1917; buried: Mt. Carmel; record (1917) # 118.

SMITH, James Alexander; born: 17 Feb. 1907; parents: Isaac SMITH and Susan BACON; death cause: "pneumonia and epileptic convulsions"; informant: father (Midway); died: 1 Apr. 1917; buried: Bewley Cemetery; record (1917) # 119.

REDMON, Nancy; age: "about 87 years"; born: Tennessee; widow; parents: Peter EISENHOUR and mother not stated; death cause: "hemorrhage of brain"; died in 3rd District, 13 Apr. 1917; buried: Caney Branch; record (1917) # 120.

JACKSON, Emeline; born: 30 May 1835 in Tennessee; widow; parents: Steve JACKSON and mother not stated; death cause: "aortic stenosis"; informant: James SOUTHERLAND (Parrotsville); died in 2nd District, 14 Apr. 1917; record (1917) # 121.

MCQUEEN, Bert R.; born: 23 Sep. 1893; married; parents: H.O. MCQUEEN and Alice PACKER; death cause: "heart trouble"; informant: father (Greeneville); died: 27 Apr. 1917; buried: Shilo; record (1917) # 122.

BIDDLE, William J.; born: 20 Apr. 1896; single; parents: William BIDDLE and Mollie JONES; death cause: "tuberculosis"; informant:

Brabson JONES (Greeneville); died: 24 Apr. 1917; buried: Oak Grove; record (1917) # 123.

DAVIS, Susan T.; age: 72 years; born: Sullivan County; widow; parents: Joseph MCCRARY and mother not stated; death cause: "mitral heart disease"; informant: Gena DAVIS (Greeneville); died: 23 Apr. 1917; buried: Shilo; record (1917) # 124.

HOLLEY, Laura; age: 68 years; married; parents: not stated; death cause: "uremic poison"; died in 24th District, 18 Apr. 1917; buried: River Hill; record (1917) # 125.

DAVIS, Miss Mary Alice; born: 26 Mar. 1849; single; parents: S.W. DAVIS and Eliza REED; death cause: "brights disease"; informant: W.S. MOORE (Afton); died: 10 Apr. 1917; record (1917) # 126.

SEAVERS, Ida Fox; born: 8 Apr. 1881; married; parents: James FOX and Tempa LEMING; death cause: "self inflicted pistol wound in head"; informant: W.A. HURST (Greeneville); died: 9 Apr. 1917; buried: Shilo; record (1917) # 127.

KYKENDALL, Neavele; born: 11 Feb. 1915; parents: Avery KYKENDALL (Madison County, NC.); and Flory KIRK (North Carolina); death cause: "measles and croup"; informant: H.D. ALEXANDER (Chucky); died: 6 Apr. 1917; buried: Union Chapel; record # 128.

WILHOIT, Mary Blair; born: 30 Dec. 1840; married; parents: John W. WILHOIT and Mary BROYLES; death cause: "heart trouble and bronchitis"; informant: J.S.J. WILHOIT (Afton); died: 4 Apr. 1917; buried: Hermon; record (1917) # 129.

MCNEW, Irene; age: 6 years; parents: Charles MCNEW and Mande HUMPHRIES; death cause: "measles and pneumonia"; informant: J.B. BELL (Greeneville); died: 6 Apr. 1917; buried: Moshiem; record # 130.

SEAY, Sarah; born: 5 May 1863; married; parents: William COCHRAN and Neriva SHEFFEY; death cause: "lobar pneumonia"; died in the 25th District, 29 May 1917; buried: Pine Grove; record (1917) # 131.

PRUITT, Newt; born: 16 Dec. 1896; parents: J.A. PRUITT and Mary BIBLE; death cause: "double pneumonia"; died: 5 Apr. 1917; buried: Hartmans; record (1917) # 132.

SHANKS, Mary A.; born: 13 Nov. 1841; widow; parents: father not stated and Mary FERGUSON; death cause: "paralysis caused by blood clot"; informant: James R. SHANKS (Afton); died: 20 Apr. 1917; record (1917) # 133.

HENSLEY, Mary Edith; born: 7 May 1916; parents: Garfield HENSLEY and Alice Belle SMITH; death cause: "whooping cough, pneumonia"; died: 27 Apr. 1917; buried: Bethany; record (1917) # 134.

LADY, Orval D.; born: 10 Apr. 1916; parents: Emory LADY (Sullivan County) and Cora LADY (Sullivan County); death cause: "whooping cough"; informant: Emory LADY (Fall Branch); died: 6 Apr. 1917; buried: Lovelace Cemetery; record (1917) # 135.

CONKIN, M. Eveate; born: 2 Sep.1880; married; parents: S.B. CONKIN and Mattie PHILLIPS; death cause: "septic infection"; informant: Dr. MOORE (Jeroldstown); died: 10 Apr. 1917; buried: Pleasant Hill; record (1917) # 136.

PATTON, Infant; male; parents: Roy R. PATTON and Cora B. FINCHUM; death cause: not stated; informant: father (Moshiem); born/died: 3 Apr. 1917; buried: Big Springs; record (1917) # 137.

BROWN, William A.; born: 17 Aug. 1846; married; parents: Peter BROWN and Mary COLLETT; death cause: "intestinal nephritis"; informant: C.F. BROWN (Moshiem); died: 27 Apr. 1917; buried: Big Springs; record (1917) # 138.

CASTEEL, William; born: 29 Mar.1846; widower; parents: John CASTEEL and Lydia; STINKER (?); death cause: "double pneumonia"; informant: R.T. CASTEEL (Greeneville); died: 2 Apr. 1917; buried: Gass Shed; record (1917) # 139.

THOMPSON, James; born: 18 Jun. 1841; widower; parents: Alex THOMPSON and Kizziah LANE; death cause: "brights disease"; informant: C.E. DAVIS (Greeneville); died: 1 Apr. 1917; buried: Gass Shed; record (1917) # 140.

DUGGER, Edd; born: 7 Apr. 1877; married; parents: A. TUCKER and Lucinda DUGGER; death cause: "tuberculosis of lungs"; informant: M.E. DUGGER; died: 29 Apr. 1917; buried: Union Temple; record (1917) # 141.

CRUMLEY, Lavie Pauline; born: 19 Feb. 1917; parents: Jerome CRUMLEY and Vida MALONE; death cause: "unknown"; informant: Hobert HATLEY (Baileyton); died: 1 Apr. 1917; buried: Wesley Chapel; record (1917) # 142.

WEBSTER, Rebecca Sayler; born: 23 Nov. 1845; married; Parents: John SAYLER and Mary FINK (Washington County); death cause: "carcinoma of uterus"; informant: J.K.P. SAYLER (Moshiem); died: 14 Apr. 1917; buried: Price Cemetery; record (1917) # 143.

ANDERSON, Hull B.; black; born: 10 Jun. 1859; single; parents: "unknown"; death cause: "unknown, found dead in a chair"; informant: R.P. HARMON (Mohawk); died: 21 Apr. 1917; buried: Drake Cemetery; record (1917) # 144.

PITTS, Infant; male; lived 6 hours; parents: Andrew PITTS and Maude SATTERFIELD; death cause: "blue baby"; born/died: 7 Apr. 1917; buried: Midway; record (1917) # 145.

COUCH, Opal; born: 5 Apr. 1904; parents: Jode COUCH and Cordie GRIGSBY (Hawkins County); death cause: "bronchial pneumonia"; informant: R.F. SHEFFEY (Bulls Gap); died: 28 Apr. 1917; buried: Pilot Knob; record (1917) # 146.

BLAZER, Franklin; age: "about 73 years and 6 months; married; parents: "unknown"; death cause: "hemorrhage of brain"; informant: Blaine REINER; died in the 3rd District, 12 Apr. 1917; record (1917) # 147.

GRAY, Caroline; born: 10 Nov. 1845; married; parents: Mart WADDLE and Jane S. ALEXANDER; death cause: "bronco pneumonia"; informant: William WADDLE (Chucky); died: 28 Apr. 1917; buried: Union Chapel; record (1917) # 148.

DYKE, Chassie Carter; born: 20 Dec. 1882; married; parents: Stringfield CARTER and Sis CARTER; death cause: "measles and broncho pneumonia"; died at Moshiem, 22 Apr. 1917; buried; Albany; record (1917) # 149.

CANNON, Infant; male; parents: Grant CANNON and Lucy PITTS; death cause: "stillborn"; died: 1 Apr. 1917; buried: Oak Grove; record (1917) # 150.

DYAL, Infant; female; parents: John DYAL (Cumberland County) and Dollie C__ (illegible); death cause: "stillborn"; informant: father (Greeneville); died: 16 Apr. 1917; buried: Oak Grove; record # 151.

BOWER, Infant; male; parents: Frank BOWER and Vici CONDUFF; death cause: "stillborn"; died: 28 Apr. 1917; buried: Cedar Creek; record (1917) # 152.

POE, Thassa; age: "about 70 years; born: North Carolina; widow; parents: ___ GARRETT (North Carolina) and mother "unknown"; death cause: not stated; informant: John BROWN (Bulls Gap); died: 8 May 1917; buried: Antioc; record (1917) # 153.

JOHNSON, Rufus; born: 16 Aug. 1910; parents: K.M. JOHNSON and Edna CRUM; death cause: "measles"; informant: father (Greeneville); died: 6 May 1917; buried: Harrison Cemetery; record (1917) # 154.

MAROK, Nancy Jane; born: 23 Mar.1844; widow; parents: S.J. PAINTER and Marsha JOHNSON; death cause: "pneumonia"; informant: S.J. PAINTER (Chucky); died: 4 May 1917; buried: Pleasant Hill; record (1917) # 155.

LANE, Grayson; born: 14 Jul. 1896; single; parents: Joe LANE and Mary J. FRY; death cause: "potts disease"; informant: Mary J. LANE (Moshiem); died: 25 May 1917; record (1917) # 156.

ARNOLD, Robert; age: "about 57 years; born: South Carolina; widower; parents: John ARNOLD (South Carolina) and Emma SALTERS (South Carolina); death cause: "tuberculosis and emphysema"; informant: James TINSLEY (Greeneville); died: 28 May 1917; buried: Meaders Creek; record (1917) # 157.

MATHES, Chester Lee; born: 5 Nov. 1915; parents: Wilbur MATHIS and Stella BRIGMAN (North Carolina); death cause: "gastro enteritis"; died at Caney Branch, 1 May 1917; record (1917) # 158.

ARNOLD, Robert; age: "about 21 years"; married; parents: Robert ARNOLD (South Carolina) and Ida RENNER; death cause: "pulmonary tuberculosis"; died: 2 May 1917; buried: Meadow Creek; record (1917) # 159.

HOOK, Lawrence Norman; born: 28 Jun. 1887 in South Carolina; single; parents: S.L. HOOK (South Carolina) and Francis HOLTSWANGER (South Carolina); death cause: "pulmonary tuberculosis"; informant: father (Jeroldstown); died: 21 May 1917; buried: Pleasant Hill; record (1917) # 160.

HALL, Mary Cecil; born: 18 Nov. 1899; single; parents: David HALL and Matilda BASKETT; death cause: "miliary tuberculosis"; informant: W.M. HALL (Bulls Gap); died: 6 May 1917; buried: Lovelace; record (1917) # 161.

DYKES, Isham; age: 58 years; married; parents: James DYKES and Loucinda PEARSON; death cause: "pulmonary tuberculosis"; informant: H.C. COMPTON (Jeroldstown); died: 4 May 1917; buried: Chimney Top; record (1917) # 162.

BURNS, William Carter; born: 2 Feb. 1873; married; parents: John E. BURNS (Hawkins County) and Anna CARTER; death cause: "cancer of liver"; informant: J.C. BURNS (Moshiem); died: 16 May 1917; buried: Price Cemetery; record (1917) # 173.

FOSTER, Nora; born: 20 Aug. 1891; married; parents: W.B. ADAMS (Washington County) and Mary RUSTON; death cause: "pulmonary tuberculosis"; informant: W.F. PLEASANT (Limestone); died: 16 May 1917; buried: Providence; record (1917) # 164.

BORDEN, Henry S.; age: 76 years; widower; medical doctor; parents: Elijah BORDEN and Polly SHIELDS; death cause: "nephritis"; informant: W.M. BORDEN (Greeneville); died: 5 May 1917; buried: Meadow Creek; record (1917) # 165.

MERCER, Charles; age: 35 years; single; parents: J.D. MERCER and Mary JONES; death cause: "epilepsy"; informant: D.W. JENNINGS (Greeneville); died: 17 May 1917; buried: Gethseminia; record # 166.

NOEL, Margaret E.; born: 11 Feb. 1832; widow; parents: Daniel ALLEN and Mary BAKER; death cause: "uremic poison"; informant: J.A. NOEL (Greeneville); died: 30 May 1917; buried: family cemetery; record (1917) # 167.

STEVENS, Jack; born: 28 Feb. 1915; parents: J.N. STEVENS and Bessie EDMONS; death cause: "dysentery"; informant: father (Greeneville); died: 28 May 1917; buried: Oak Grove; record (1917) # 168.

JONES, Mrs. H.O.; born: 1 Jan. 1852; parents: Jerre BOYD (Virginia) and Mary FITZSIMMONS (Virginia); death cause: "pellagra"; informant: L.C. BOYD (Greeneville); died: 15 May 1917; buried: Oak Grove; record (1917) # 169.

SMITH, Margarette E.; born: 20 Aug. 1850 in Washington County; widow; parents: Joseph ROGERS and mother not stated; death cause: "cancer"; informant: H.D. KELLER (Afton); died: 10 May 1917; buried: Mt. Hermans; record (1917) # 170.

DENTON, George R.; black; age: 1 year and 6 months; parents: father "unknown" and Pauline DENTON; death cause: "measles"; informant: Jennie DENTON (Greeneville); died: 10 May 1917; record # 171.

DOBSON, Infant; female; parents: E.B. DOBSON and mother's name illegible; death cause: "heart failed to act normally"; died: 8 May 1917; buried: Shilo; record (1917) # 172.

FRANKLIN, Layruth; born: 7 Apr. 1916; parents: James FRANKLIN and Grace BIBLE; death cause: "unknown, found dead in bed"; informant: W.A. RENNER (9th District); died: 8 May 1917; buried: Franklin Cemetery; record (1917) # 173.

VANCE, Fannie; black; age: 41 years; married; parents: Riley BROOKINS and Venie LOVE; death cause: "brights disease"; informant: William VANCE (Greeneville); died: 7 May 1917; buried: Wesley Cemetery; record (1917) # 174.

WHITE, Viviane; black; age: 19 years; married; parents: Frank LOUGHLEY (Virginia) and Annie CANNON; death cause: "pulmonary tuberculosis"; informant: Jerold WHITE (Chattanooga); died: 5 May 1917; buried: Wesley; record (1917) # 175.

LAWSON, John A.; age: 53 years; born: Hawkins County; married; parents: not stated; death cause: "tuberculosis of bowels"; informant: Sherman LAWSON (Greeneville); died: 5 May 1917; buried: Harmon; record (1917) # 176.

DIXON, Etta Mae; age: 19 years; married; parents: W.C. WILHOIT and Dora __ (illegible); death cause: "pneumonia, probably measles"; informant: H.G. DIXON (Greeneville); died: 2 May 1917; buried: Cove Creek; record (1917) # 177.

HARDIN, John; age: 78 years; married; parents: Neal HARDIN and Annie COX; death cause: "brights disease"; informant: Charles HARDIN (Greeneville); died: 7 May 1917; buried: Oak Grove; record (1917) # 178.

SAUCEMAN (?), Infant; female; parents: Wilbur SAUCEMAN (?) and Mae CLINE; death cause: "premature"; informant: J.B. BELL (Greeneville); born/died: 16 May 1917; record (1917) # 179.

DENNY, Lucy A.; born: 18 Jan. 1825 in North Carolina; widow; parents: Gullum MADISON (North Carolina) and Fanny MCDANIEL (North

Carolina); death cause: "digestive failure"; died in the 14th District, 27 May 1917; buried: Stone Dam; record (1917) # 180.

DEAN, Thomas; age: "about 60 years; born: Hawkins County; married; parents: Henry DEAN and Sallie DEAN (Hawkins County); death cause: "congestion of lungs"; informant: Andy DEAN (Bulls Gap); buried; Dean Cemetery; record (1917) # 181.

FARRIS, E. Campbell; born: 28 Jan. 1860 in Hawkins County; married; parents: Samuel FARRIS and mother "unknown"; death cause: "unknown"; informant: Sherman PRESSLEY (Baileyton); died: 25 May 1917; record (1917) # 182.

BROTHERTON, Odie Elizabeth; born: 10 Feb. 1874; married; parents: James EVERHART (Hawkins County) and Agnes SMITH; death cause: "pulmonary tuberculosis"; informant: James EVERHART (Baileyton); died: 26 May 1917; buried: Price Cemetery; record (1917) # 183.

WILHOIT, Anis; born: 20 May 1917; parents: David WILHOIT and Mande SHELTON; death cause: "heart failure, undeveloped heart"; informant: George WILHOIT (Afton); died: 21 May 1917; buried; Cedar Grove; record (1917) # 184.

GENTRY, Gracie; born: 17 Jan. 1917; parents: Thomas GENTRY (North Carolina) and Ethel CONDUFF; death cause: "diphtheria"; died: 8 May 1917; buried: Mt. Olivet; record (1917) # 185.

BALLEW, Ernest; black; born: 9 Feb. 1916; parents: Peter BALLEW and Nancy S__ (illegible); death cause: not stated; informant: father (Moshiem); died: 25 May 1917; buried: Midway; record (1917) # 186.

ARNOLD, William; age: "about 20 years"; married; parents: Robert ARNOLD and Ida RENNER; death cause: "pulmonary tuberculosis"; informant: J.M. LENTZ (Greeneville); died: 1 May 1917; buried: Meadow Creek; record (1917) # 187.

BROYLES, Infant; female; parents: Russell BROYLES and Birdie SHIPLEY; death cause: "stillborn"; informant: L.M. BROYLES (Greeneville); died: 12 May 1917; buried: Harrison Cemetery; record (1917) # 188.

MORELOCK, Infant; female; parents: Charlie A. MORELOCK and Maggie __ (illegible); death cause: "stillborn"; informant: father (Bulls Gap); died: 2 May 1917; buried: Willoughbys; record (1917) # 189.

KYKENDALL, Infant; female; parents: Price KYKENDALL and Loura LAWS; death cause: "stillborn"; informant: Clarence KYKENDALL (Greeneville); died: 22 May 1917; buried: Red Hill; record # 190.

CRASY, Infant; female; parents: R.A. CRASY (North Carolina) and Edith GILBRATH; death cause: "stillborn"; informant: J.W. GILBRAITH (Greeneville); died: 6 May 1917; buried: Hermons; record (1917) # 191.

NUNNELLY, Bonnie C.; born: 28 May 1917; parents: Corbet NUNNELLY and Millie WHITE; death cause: "acute indigestion"; died: 10 Jun. 1917; buried: Lovelace Cemetery; record (1917) # 192.

BLACK, James; born: 30 Dec. 1916; parents: Pery BLACK and Azylda JOHNSON; death cause: "complication of measles"; informant: Jim JOHNSON (Myers); died: 18 Jun. 1917; buried; Moshiem; record (1917) # 193.

GUNTER, Marietta; age: "about 30 years"; married; parents: Alexander ROCK (?) and Hannah MORGAN; death cause: "pellagra"; died: 28 Jun. 1917; buried: Price Cemetery; record (1917) # 194.

TAYLOR, Sadie Christiana; born: 27 Jun. 1897; married; parents: Thomas ELKINS and Mary GILLIAM; death cause: "tuberculosis"; informant: father (Midway); died: 10 Jun. 1917; record (1917) # 195.

STATON, Elizabeth D.; born: 18 Sep 1843 in Virginia; single; parents: Hugh STATON (Virginia) and Eviline KERTZ (Washington County); death cause: "tuberculosis"; died in the 17th District, 4 Jun. 1917; buried: Cedar Lane; record (1917) # 196.

COOTER, Phillip; age: 79 years, 11 months and 1 day; born: Greene County; parents: Barney COOTER and __ JONES; death cause: "brights disease"; informant: C.C. COOTER (Greeneville); died: 15 Jun. 1917; buried: River Hill; record (1917) # 197.

FOX, Rubie; age: 2 years; parents: Frank FOX and Dovie LOWRY; death cause: "pneumonia"; informant: Pink FOX (Greeneville); died: 6 Jun. 1917; buried: Oak Grove; record (1917) # 198.

BAYLESS, John H.; born: 4 Oct. 1862; married; parents: Robert R. BAYLESS and Anna MULKIE; death cause: "brights disease"; informant: E.R. BAYLESS (Johnson City); died: 4 Jun. 1917; buried: Johnson City; record (1917) # 199.

GASSETT, Elizabeth; black; born: 17 Jan. 1917; parents: Estel GASSETT and Mattie GASSETT; death cause: "syphilis"; informant: John GOODE (Greeneville); died: 6 Jun. 1917; record (1917) # 200.

BABB, Etta V.; born: 18 Nov. 1894; single; parents: S.H. BABB and Mary __ (illegible); death cause: "breast cancer"; informant: John KENNEY (Greeneville); died: 11 Jun. 1917; buried: Oak Grove; record (1917) # 201.

CLARK, Al__ (illegible); black; female; born: 11 Apr. 1911; parents: W.C. CLARK and Katie BENTON; death cause: "pneumonia, measles"; informant: father (Greeneville); died: 11 Jun. 1917; buried: Colored Cemetery; record (1917) # 202.

RUSSELL, Jennie; born: 12 Apr. 1905 in Kansas; parents: Finley RUSSELL and Anna RUSS (Illinois); death cause: "appendicitis, peritonitis"; informant: father (Greeneville); died: 11 Jun. 1917; buried: Cedar Hill; record (1917) # 203.

SMOKER, Mrs. Bell; age: 46 years; married; parents: J.G. REAVES and Harriett FARNSWORTH; death cause: "pregnancy, nephritis"; informant: John SMOKER (Greeneville); died: 19 Jun. 1917; buried: Oak Grove; record (1917) # 204.

SEA, W.D.; born: 24 Jun. 1855; married; parents: James SEA and Sarrah ELENBURG; death cause: "pellagra, etc."; informant: Amanda SEA (Greeneville); buried: Oak Grove; record (1917) # 205.

KELLEY, Luke; age: 19 years; parents: J.J. KELLEY and Martha KELTON; death cause: "accidental gunshot wound"; informant: Thomas FARNSWORTH (Greeneville); died: 8 Jun. 1917; buried: Mt. Pleasant; record (1917) # 206.

SALTS, Andrew J.; age: "about 50 years"; married; parents: Allen SALTS and mother "unknown"; death cause: "cholera"; died in the 15th District, 17 Jun. 1917; buried: Milburnton; record (1917) # 207.

GRIERS, Robert Gray; born: 10 Jul. 1854; married; parents: Hiram GRIERS and Louiza SHANKS; death cause: "probably apoplexy"; informant: J.W. GOOD (Limestone); died: 6 Jun. 1917; buried: Mt. Bethel; record (1917) # 208.

KIRK, Joseph Granville; born: 1 Aug. 1912; parents: Elbert KIRK and Nannie ALLEN; death cause: "measles"; informant: father (Midway); died: 5 Jun. 1917; record (1917) # 209.

PACK, Noah L., Sr.; born: 1 Oct. 1837 in Tennessee; married; federal soldier; parents: "unknown"; death cause: "unknown"; informant: Noah L. PACK, Jr. (Midway); died: 12 Jun. 1917; record (1917) # 210.

MURDOCK, Angeline; age: 65 years; married; parents: Joseph HENDRY and __ DODD; death cause: "acute indigestion"; died: 27 Jun. 1917; buried: Prices Cemetery; record (1917) # 211.

GASS, Sarah; born: 28 Feb. 1843 in Tennessee; widow; parents: James WHITE and Becky THOMPSON; death cause: "tuberculosis and paralysis"; informant: G.H. GASS (Baileyton); died: 28 Jun. 1917; buried: Gass Shed; record (1917) # 212.

REYNOLDS, Elizabeth; born: 27 Jun. 1849; widow; parents: William DUGGER and Lucinda BRABSON; death cause: "pneumonia and senility"; informant: Rufus MORRISON (Baileyton); died: 8 Jun. 1917; buried: Gass Shed; record (1917) # 213.

HOLLAND, Luley Bell; born: 16 Aug. 1888; married; parents: George W. GAMMONS and Julia K. HUFF; death cause: "tuberculosis"; informant: W.H. HOLLAND (Afton); died: 17 Jun. 1917; buried: Doty Cemetery; record (1917) # 214.

WALLIN, Benjamin Fox; born: 18 Sep 1892; married; parents: Thomas J. WALLIN (North Carolina) and Rachel C. WALLIN; death cause: "pellagra"; died in 2nd District, 2 Jun. 1917; buried: Pisgah; record (1917) # 215.

RADER, Sarah Angeline; born: 26 Feb. 1844; widow; parents: Andrew BRADFORD (North Carolina) and Susan LOTH__ (illegible)(Pennsylvania); death cause: "spinal __ (illegible); informant: Mrs. W.F. BAYLESS (Morristown); died: 19 Jun. 1917; record (1917) # 216.

HARMON, Taylor; born: 15 Apr. 1847; married; parents: Jacob HARMON and Malinda SELF; death cause: "tuberculosis"; informant: J.W. HARMON (Bulls Gap); died: 26 Jun. 1917; buried: Willoughbys; record (1917) # 217.

LUSTER, William; born: 1 Apr. 1892 in Hawkins County; married; parents: Clinton LUSTER (Hawkins County) and Bettie RICHARDS (Hawkins County); death cause: "cholera"; informant: G.C. PAYNE (Baileyton); died: 7 Jun. 1917; buried: Hawkins County; record # 218.

FINK, George W.; born: 23 Nov. 1847; single; parents: William P. FINK and Sarah WATTENBURGER; death cause: "asthma"; died in 11th District, 15 Jun. 1917; buried: Zion; record (1917) # 219.

TINSLEY, Velma Ruth; born: 6 Jun. 1917; parents: Charles TINSLEY and O'dell SAULS; death cause: "unknown, found dead in bed"; died: 24 Jun. 1917; buried: Pine Grove; record (1917) # 220.

MITCHELL, James C.; born: 26 Nov. 1841; married; parents: John J. MITCHELL and Mary A. BRITON; death cause: "unknown, found dead in bed"; informant: Will K. MITCHELL (Moshiem); died: 28 Jun. 1917; record (1917) # 221.

BROWN, Elsie; born: 22 May 1882; married; parents: James W. WILLIAMS and Malinda BOLTON (Virginia); death cause: "nervous exhaustion, auto toxemia"; died: 20 Jun. 1917; buried: Logans Chapel; record (1917) # 222.

SHANKS, Lucille; born: 9 Nov. 1916; parents: W.R. SHANKS and Lucille BRANDON; death cause: "gastro enteritis"; died in the 17th District, 24 Jun. 1917; buried: Pleasant Hill; record (1917) # 223.

NUNLEY, Bennie Crede; born 28 May 1917; parents: Corlie Lea NUNLEY (Virginia) and Willie WHITE; death cause: "bold hives"; informant: Willie WHITE (Jeroldstown); died: 10 Jun. 1917; buried: Lovelace Cemetery; record (1917) # 224.

DYER, James Luther; born: 22 Nov. 1886; married; parents: James DYER and Celia CLIMER; death cause: "tuberculosis of lungs"; died in the 6th District, 2 Jun. 1917; record (1917) # 225.

BRIGMAN, James Orval Lee; born: 3 Jun. 1906; parents: Nathaniel K. BRIGMAN (North Carolina) and Sarah AIKEN; death cause: "catarrh of stomach"; died in the 3rd District, 6 Jun. 1917; record (1917) # 226.

LIVINGSTON, Lena Belle; born: 16 Jun. 1917; parents: Lonnie LIVINGSTON and Mandie OTTINGER; death cause: not stated; informant: Essie OTTINGER; died in the 3rd District, 23 Jun. 1917; buried: St. James; record (1917) # 227.

PITTS, Infant; female; born: 22 Jun. 1917; parents: Fern PITTS and Bertha COBBLE; death cause: not stated; informant: father (Midway); died: 24 Jun. 1917; record (1917) # 228.

MALONE, George; born: 4 Jun. 1833 in Tennessee; widower; parents: John MALONE and Mirah EDMONS (South Carolina); death cause:

not stated; informant: W.H. MALONE (Afton); died: 11 Jun. 1917; record (1917) # 229.

HENSHAW, Louisah; born: 11 Jan. 1859; single; parents: William HENSHAW (North Carolina) and Nancy REYNOLDS; death cause: "cerebra spinal fever"; informant: John PIERCE; died: 28 Jun. 1917; buried: Mt. Carmel; record (1917) # 230.

BROWN, Infant; male; born: 18 Jun. 1917; parents: G.P. BROWN and Lula ROBESON; death cause: "general debility"; informant: father (Mohawk); died: 20 Jun. 1917; record (1917) # 231.

KIRK, Dorothy; parents: Buford KIRK and Pearl Josephine REEVES; death cause: "stillborn"; informant: father (Mohawk); born/died in the 6th District, 24 Jun. 1917; record (1917) # 232.

LOONEY, Mary Eveline; born: 25 Nov. 1840; married; parents: Henry JONES and Nancy JOHNSON; death cause: "chronic diarrhea"; informant: N. HARRISON (Greeneville); died in the 22nd District, 1 Jul. 1917; record (1917) # 234.

WHITE, Pauline; born: 22 Nov. 1916; parents: Jake WHITE and Dus__ (illegible) FRENCH; death cause: "acute dysentery"; informant: John BOWMAN; died: 2 Jul. 1917; buried: Gethseminie; record # 235.

COX, Infant; female; parents: Charles R. COX and Bertha U. BIBLE; death cause: "unknown"; informant: father (Moshiem); died: 3 Jul. 1917; buried: Mt. Carmel; record (1917) # 236.

FOULKS, Mildred Vivian; born: 4 Jun. 1917; parents: J.F. FOULKS and Mary E. ANDERSON; death cause: illegible; informant: father (Greeneville); died: 3 Jul. 1917; buried: Harden Chapel; record (1917) # 237.

HASH, Callie; born: 24 Mar. 1869 in North Carolina; married; parents: Anderw E__ (illegible)(North Carolina) and mother's name illegible; death cause: "cancer of scalp"; informant: William HASH (Chucky); died: 3 Jul. 1917; buried: Stone Dam; record (1917) # 238.

LAWS, Nola; black; age: 18 years; married; parents: Bill BRIGHT and Eliza __; death cause: "typhoid fever"; informant: Thomas LAWS; died: 4 Jul. 1917; buried: Wesley; record (1917) # 239.

SWENEY, Clarence Alden; born: 26 May 1915; parents: Lowel Edgar SWENEY and Ada Maud RICKER Sweney; death cause: "infantile spinal paralysis"; informant: F.A. REEVES (Limestone); died: 6 Jul. 1917; buried: Rheatown; record (1917) # 240.

STARNES, Sarah; age: 84 years; born: Tennessee; widow; parents: John SELLERS and mother "unknown"; death cause: "nephritis and dysentery"; informant: W.A. STARNES (Baileyton); died: 6 Jul. 1917; buried: Zion; record (1917) # 241.

COOPER, James M.; born: 2 Aug. 1895 in Globe, North Carolina; married; parents: Robert COOPER and __ COOK (North Carolina); death cause: "pulmonary tuberculosis"; informant: Bonnie COOPER (Greeneville); died: 6 Jul. 1917; buried: Mt. Hebron; record # 242.

RADER, Lena Blanch; born: 1 May 1917; parents: Dave RADER and mother "unknown"; death cause: "cholera infantum"; died: 8 Jul. 1917; buried: Mt. Pleasant; record (1917) # 243.

GRIFFIN, Dixie Mae; born: 25 Jun. 1916 in Pennsylvania; parents: Robert W. GRIFFIN (Ohio) and Rettie M__ (illegible); death cause: "colitis"; informant: father (Philadelphia, PA.); died: 9 Jul. 1917; buried: Oak Grove; record (1917) # 244.

RUDDER, James Alexander; born: 28 Sep 1855; married; parents: Johnson RUDDER and Jane MCDONALD; death cause: "dropped dead in the road"; informant: Mrs. J.A. RUDDER (Moshiem); died: 10 Jul. 1917; buried: Rudder Cemetery; record (1917) # 245.

HUNTSMAN, J. Butler, Jr.; born: 11 Jul. 1917; parents: J.B. HUNTSMAN and Ethel HOUSE (Hamblen County); death cause: not stated; informant: father (Bulls Gap); died: 11 Jul. 1917; buried: Phillips Cemetery; record (1917) # 246.

HULL, Isaac Bonham; born: 19 Mar. 1843; married; parents: John M. HULL and Nancy MYERS; death cause: "paralysis"; informant: J.M. HULL (Moshiem); died: 13 Jul. 1917; buried: Brown Springs; record (1917) # 247.

COX, Dallis Paul; born: 24 Jun. 1917; parents: Charles A. COX and Effie PARKER; death cause: "erysipelas"; died: 13 Jul. 1917; buried: Pleasant Hill; record (1917) # 248.

LYNCH, Sarah Jane; born: 14 Mar. 1839; widow; parents: Gale RADER and Poly LADY; death cause: "aortic regurgitation"; informant: George W. LYNCH (Mohawk); died: 13 Jul. 1917; record (1917) # 249.

LAUDERDALE, Benjamin Franklin; born: 1 Jun. 1860; married; parents: George LAUDERDALE and Elizabeth COGBURN; death cause:

"tuberculosis of throat and lungs"; informant: Angeline LAUDERDALE (Moshiem); died: 13 Jul. 1917; buried: Bewleys Chapel; record # 250.

GRAHAM, Roy; age: 22 years; single; parents: James GRAHAM and Isabel ARMITAGE; death cause: "typhoid fever"; informant: father (Greeneville); died: 13 Jul. 1917; buried: Harmons; record (1917) # 251.

INSCORE, Edgar; age: 2 months; parents: Joe INSCORE and __ ASHLEY; death cause: "unknown, found dead in bed"; informant: Joe ASHLEY (Greeneville); died: 15 Jul. 1917; buried: Red Hill; record (1917) # 253.

DAVIS, Belle; age: 27 years; widow; parents: Mark DAVIS and Tildy JONES; death cause: "septicemia, puerperal"; informant: Mark DAVIS (Greeneville); died: 17 Jul. 1917; buried: Oak Grove; record # 253.

BROOKINS, Thidore; black; born: 12 Oct. 1905; parents: Ike BROOKINS and Maggie SCOTT; death cause: "tuberculosis"; informant: father (Greeneville); died: 17 Jul. 1917; record (1917) # 254.

BULLINGTON, Edna; born: 27 Aug. 1916; parents: Jessie BULLINGTON and Dollie MELTON; death cause: "gastro enteritis"; informant: Jack EVANS (Bulls Gap); died: 18 Jul. 1917; buried: Willoughbys; record (1917) # 255.

SELF, J.B.; born: 20 Mar. 1889; married; parents: M.L. SELF and S.J. GRIGSBY; death cause: "pulmonary tuberculosis"; informant: B.A. CUPP (Moshiem); died: 19 Jul. 1917; buried: Weems Chapel; record (1917) # 256.

SWATZELL, Clara Elizabeth; born: 28 Apr. 1917; parents: Charles SWATZELL and Lillie M. WILLIAMS; death cause: "colitis"; informant: father (Chucky); died: 22 Jul. 1917; buried: Cedar Grove; record (1917) # 257.

MORGAN, Frank; age: 67 years; widower; parents: "unknown"; death cause: "heart disease"; informant: F.C. BRITTON (Greeneville); died: 23 Jul. 1917; buried: "Gethseminie"; record (1917) # 258.

KENNEY, Eliza Jane; born: 12 Nov. 1846; married; parents: Valentine D. SMITH and Lucinda CARTER; death cause: "bronchial asthma"; informant: L.D. KENNEY (Baileyton); died: 24 Jul. 1917; buried: County Line; record (1917) # 259.

MYERS, Anna Lee; age: 3 Months; parents: Clinton MYERS and Edith JONES; death cause: "cholera infantum"; informant: M.C. JONES (Greeneville); died: 24 Jul. 1917; buried: Mt. Zion; record (1917) # 260.

COOPER, Landon; born: 2 Jun. 1837 in Carter County; widower; parents: Nathaniel COOPER (Carter County) and mother "unknown"; death cause: "tuberculosis"; informant: Robert COOPER (Greeneville); died: 24 Jul. 1917; buried: Oak Grove; record (1917) # 261.

KIDWELL, Alice; age: 45 years; married; parents: "unknown"; death cause: "pulmonary tuberculosis"; informant: Charles DIXON (Greeneville); died: 4 Jul. 1917; buried: Kidwell Chapel; record (1917) # 262.

OWEN, David Webster; born: 27 Feb. 1860 in Hawkins County; married; medical doctor; parents: William OWEN (Hawkins County) and Jennie JONES (Hawkins County); death cause: illegible; informant: Mrs. D.W. OWEN (Moshiem); died: 25 Jul. 1917; buried: Prices Cemetery; record (1917) # 263.

MORGAN, Rebecca Malinda; born: 6 Feb. 1845 in South Carolina; married; parents: J.B. BLANTON (North Carolina) and mother not stated; death cause: "unknown"; informant: W.E. BLANTON (Moshiem); died: 26 Jul. 1917; buried: Browns Spring; record (1917) # 264.

WHITE, Mary; born: 29 Jul. 1837; married; parents: Elija COLSON (Pennsylvania) and Mary PIERCE; death cause: "pulmonary tuberculosis"; informant: J.H. WHITE (Chucky); died: 26 Jul. 1917; buried: Union Temple; record (1917) # 265.

LANE, Sarah Jane; born: 6 Dec. 1849; married; parents: William HUNT and Susan G__ (illegible); death cause: "indigestion, died suddenly"; informant: William LANE (Afton); died: 27 Jul. 1917; buried: Stone Dam; record (1917) # 266.

HUX, Rosa Mae; born; 18 May 1917; parents: Edd HUX and Lizzie KNIGHT; death cause: "marasmus"; informant: father (Greeneville); died: 27 Jul. 1917; buried: Oak Grove; record (1917) # 267.

FOX, Benjamin Marion; born: 5 May 1916; parents: Robert L. FOX and Fannie JENNINGS; death cause: "cholera infantum and meningitis"; informant: Ben FOX (Limestone); died: 28 Jul. 1917; buried: Cedar Grove; record (1917) # 268.

BARLOW, Nancy; black; age: 40; single; parents: "unknown"; death cause: "brights disease and heart lesion"; informant: J.W. MORELOCK (Greeneville); died: 29 Jul. 1917; buried: Poor Farm; record # 269.

BIBLE, Cordie; age: "about 25 years"; single; parents: "unknown"; death cause: "uterine cancer"; died: 30 Jul. 1917; buried: Poor Farm; record (1917) # 270.

MCCAMPBELL, Edward; age: 61 years; married; parents: John MCCAMPBELL and __ FARNSWORTH; death cause: "pulmonary tuberculosis"; died in the 9th District, 30 Jul. 1917; buried: Cedar Hill; record (1917) # 271.

CUTSHAWL, Evie; born: 20 Feb. 1880 in South Carolina; marital status: not stated; parents: illegible; death cause: "post partum hemorrhage"; died in the 22nd District 30 Jul. 1917; record (1917) # 272.

GILGON, Virgie; age: 45 years; single; parents: not stated; death cause: "paralysis"; informant: R.L. NAVE (Tusculum); died: 31 Jul. 1917; buried: Shiloh; record (1917) # 273.

BOUGHARD, Infant; male; parents: Robert BOUGHARD and Eula M. SMELLER; death cause: "second child of twins, born without __ (illegible)"; informant: father (Moshiem); died: 31 Jul. 1917; record (1917) # 274.

PAINTER, Infant; male; parents: Charles PAINTER and Minnie LINEBAUGH, death cause: "stillborn"; informant: mother (Baileyton); died: 23 Jul. 1917; buried: Oak Dale; record (1917) # 275.

LINTZ, Infant; male; parents: Dewey LINTZ and Laura BRIGMAN (North Carolina); death cause: "stillborn"; informant: father (Parrotsville); died: 12 Jul. 1917; record (1917) # 276.

WAIN, Cordie; born: 30 Jul. 1917; parents: George W. WAIN and Mattie MORRIS; death cause: "suffocation in bed"; died in the 16th District, 1 Aug. 1917; buried: Ratliff Cemetery; record (1917) # 277.

KOHL, James; age: 50 years; married; parents: not stated; death cause: "pulmonary tuberculosis"; informant: John WILSON (Greeneville); died: 4 Aug. 1917; buried: Mt. Bethel; record (1917) # 278.

GASS, James Edwin; born: 29 May 1895; married; parents: J.B. GASS and Susan WARNER; death cause: "typhoid fever"; informant: Willard GASS (Greeneville); died: 4 Aug. 1917; buried: Gass Shed; record (1917) # 279.

DAVIS, John; born: 29 May 1917; parents: John HENRY and Belle DAVIS; death cause: "mal-nutrition"; informant: Mark DAVIS (Greeneville); died: 6 Aug. 1917; buried: Oak Grove; record (1917) # 280.

DEAN, Alonzo; born: 6 Aug. 1917; parents: Andy DEAN and Suda BROWN; death cause: "organic heart trouble"; died at Bulls Gap, 8 Aug. 1917; buried: Willoughbys; record (1917) # 281.

COFFEE, Infant; male; born: 21 Jul. 1915 in North Carolina; parents: Willard COFFEE (North Carolina) and Alice COFFEE (North Carolina); death cause: "diarrhea"; informant: father (Greeneville); died: 9 Aug. 1917; buried: Red Hill; record (1917) # 282.

WILHOIT, Dorthe E.; born: 24 Apr. 1917; parents: D.C. WILHOIT and Bessie WADDLE; death cause: "colitis"; informant: father (Greeneville); died: 9 Aug. 1917; buried: Oak Grove; record (1917) # 283.

JONES, L. Clark; age: 40 years; married; parents: James JONES (Cocke County) and mother not stated; death cause: "gastro enteritis"; informant: W.E. JONES (Moshiem); died: 12 Aug. 1917; buried: Pine Grove; record (1917) # 284.

WOODS, Essie; age: 3 years and 10 months; parents: R.F. WOODS and Sarah MORRIS; death cause: illegible; informant: father (Greeneville); died: 13 Aug. 1917; buried: Oak Grove; record (1917) # 285.

HAYS, Tilda; born: 7 Feb. 1915; parents: Marion HAYS and Donna HALL; death cause: "illio colitis"; informant: father (Jeroldstown); died: 16 Aug. 1917; buried: Lovelace Cemetery; record (1917) # 286.

CRADIC, Herman E.; born: 7 Sep.1916 in Sullivan County; parents: Kyle CRADIC and Fannie DEZORN; death cause: "pertussis"; informant: father (Jeroldstown); died: 18 Aug. 1917; buried: Bethany; record (1917) # 287.

CONDUFF, John; age: 59 years; married; parents: Matt CONDUFF and Vennie FRESHOUR; death cause: "typhoid fever"; informant: C.W. FRESHOUR (Greeneville); died: 19 Aug. 1917; buried: Cedar Creek; record (1917) # 288.

LOVELL, Sallie; born: 20 May 1867; married; parents: John M. COOTER and Mary L__ (illegible); death cause: "typhoid fever"; informant: John LOVELL (Greeneville); died: 21 Aug. 1917; buried: Pisgah; record (1917) # 289.

JUSTIS, Margaret Elizabeth; born: 22 Feb. 1890; married; parents: Anderson JUSTIS and Sarah J. BROWN; death cause: "tuberculosis"; informant: C.E. DAVIS (Greeneville); died: 22 Aug. 1917; buried: Gass Shed; record (1917) # 290.

CARSON, George; black; born: 11 May 1916; parents: Bob CARSON and Flora LAWS; death cause: "typhoid fever"; informant: G.W. LAWS (Greeneville); died: 22 Aug. 1917; record (1917) # 291.

WADDLE, James; born: 3 Jan. 1846; married; parents: Rufus K. WADDLE and Sallie MCAFEE; death cause: "intestinal intoxication"; died in the 10th District, 23 Aug. 1917; buried: Bersheba; record # 292.

EAKIN, Kathrin; born: 14 Feb. 1847; widow; parents: Dawson PITT and Mary HARMON; death cause: "paralysis"; died in the 10th District, 23 Aug. 1917; buried: Mt. Vernon; record (1917) # 293.

BAUGHARD, Cora Bell; born: 30 Apr. 1870; married; parents: G.G. GASS and E__ (illegible) RUSSELL; death cause: "pulmonary tuberculosis"; informant: J.A. BAUGHARD (Greeneville); buried: Moshiem; record (1917) # 294.

BROWN, John; age: 80 years; married; parents: Robert BROWN and Annie BABB; death cause: "heart disease"; informant: W.D. BROWN (Greeneville); died: 25 Aug. 1917; buried: Gass Shed; record # 295.

GARBER, Josie Carter; born: 9 Apr. 1878; married; parents: Dot CARTER and Susan COX; death cause: "pellagra"; informant: Charlie GARBER (Moshiem); died: 25 Aug. 1917; buried: Price Cemetery; record (1917) # 296.

BABB, Infant; female; born: 13 Aug. 1917; parents: Edd BABB and Daisy BABB, death cause: "unknown"; informant: father (Greeneville); died: 25 Aug. 1917; buried: Oak Grove; record (1917) # 297.

MALONE, William; born: 28 Sep.1842; widower; parents: John MALONE and Martha EDMONS; death cause: "aortic stenosis"; informant: C.E. DAVIS (Greeneville); buried: Gass Shed; record # 298.

BABB, Sallie; age: 53 years; married; parents: John HAWKINS and Elizabeth GASS; death cause: "pulmonary tuberculosis"; informant: G.S. HAWKINS (Greeneville); died: 26 Aug. 1917; buried: Gass Shed; record (1917) # 299.

PRICE, Bettie; born: 24 Sep.1840 in Virginia; widow; parents: T.B. PINKNEY (Virginia) and Elizabeth DOBBS (Virginia); death cause:

"old age"; died in the 10th District, 27 Aug. 1917; buried: Oak Grove; record (1917) # 300.

BLAIN, Josephine; black; born: 1 Jun. 1916; parents: Hugh BLAIN and Ada JOHNSON; death cause: "whooping cough"; informant: mother (Chucky); died: 29 Aug. 1917; record (1917) # 301.

COX, James Franklin; born: 8 Dec. 1913; parents: Charles N. COX and Olive BRUMLEY; death cause: "entero colitis"; died in the 17th District, 31 Aug. 1917; buried: Double Springs; record (1917) # 302.

JOHNSON, Infant; male; parents: Charles M. JOHNSON and Debora HAYS; death cause: "stillborn"; died at Jeroldstown, 29 Aug. 1917; buried: Pleasant Hill; record (1917) # 303.

CARTER, Infant; sex: not stated; parents: Zack CARTER and Rubie MYERS; death cause: "stillborn"; informant: B.F. CARTER (Greeneville); died: 26 Aug. 1917; buried: Harrisons; record (1917) # 304.

CARTER, Martha M.; born: 16 May 1830 in Greene County; widow; parents: Jacob SAYLER and __ MCFARLAND; death cause: "heart disease"; informant: Nat M. CARTER (Greeneville); died: 1 Sep.1917; record (1917) # 305.

HENARD, Naoma Jane; born: 17 Oct. 1844; married; parents: William THOMAS (Virginia) and Anna CLEMANS (Virginia); death cause: "tuberculosis"; informant: RC. HENARD (Baileyton); died: 2 Sep.1917; buried: Zion; record (1917) # 306.

WELLS, Moses; black; age: "about 75 years"; married; parents: not stated; death cause: "heart trouble"; died in the 3rd District, 3 Sep.1917; buried: Pruitts Hill; record (1917) # 307.

JOBE, Lessie; age: 2 months and 7 days; parents: Can JOBE and Bonnie BELL; death cause: "unknown, found dead in bed"; informant: father (Greeneville); died: 4 Sep.1917; buried: Hebron; record (1917) # 308.

CRUM, Bell; born: 23 Aug. 1917; parents: William J. CRUM and Nancy J. JOHNSON; death cause: not stated; informant: father (Jeroldstown); buried: Mt. Olivet; record (1917) # 309.

DEVAULT, John A.; born: 11 Oct. 1841; widower; parents: David DEVAULT (Washington County) and Maxie COX; death cause: "gastric ulcer"; informant: Mrs. J.N. TUCKER (Greeneville); died in the 9th District, 5 Sep.1917; record (1917) # 310.

TINSLEY, Major; born: 5 Oct. 1916; parents: James TINSLEY and Rhena THOMAS; death cause: "tuberculosis"; informant: father (Greeneville); died: 7 Sep.1917; buried: Meadow Creek; record # 311.

PHILLIPS, Annie; age: 44 years; married; parents: Manuel BEBBER and Bettie CHAPMAN; death cause: "tuberculosis of lungs"; informant: Dave PHILLIPS (Greeneville); died: 9 Sep.1917; buried: Mt. Zion; record (1917) # 312.

C__ (illegible), Ellen; black; age: 52 years; widow; parents: George BALLARD and Mary __; death cause: "uremia"; informant: Charles C__ (illegible); died: 9 Sep.1917; buried: Wesley Cemetery; record (1917) # 313.

HOLLAND, William Howard; born: 5 May 1916; parents: W. Bruce HOLLAND and Lou GAMMONS; death cause: "unknown"; informant: Claud HOLLAND (Afton); died: 10 Sep.1917; buried: Doty Cemetery; record (1917) # 314.

ISAM, Arther; born: 5 Mar.1900; single; parents: Jake ISAM and Kate ISAM; death cause: "appendicitis"; informant: father (Greeneville); died: 11 Sep.1917; buried: Liberty Hill; record (1917) # 315.

COLLETT, Ottie Berthold; born: 7 Feb. 1916; parents: W.S. COLLETT and Letha M. MCCURRY (Washington County); death cause: "intestinal infection"; informant: Samuel COLLETT (Limestone); died: 11 Sep.1917; buried: Rheatown; record (1917) # 316.

CLICK, Gussie; born: 1 Nov. 1905; parents: Patton CLICK and Lena VESTAL; death cause: illegible; died in the 22nd District, 11 Sep.1917; buried: Hermon; record (1917) # 317.

COLEMAN, Loneta I.; born: 4 Oct. 1915; parents: O.L. COLEMAN and Essie M. ELROD; death cause: "colitis"; informant: father (Greeneville); died: 13 Sep.1917; buried: Oak Grove; record (1917) # 318.

HARROLD, Mary A.; age: 46 years; married; parents: S.B. HARMON and Kate CARTER; death cause: "typhoid fever"; informant: E.L. HARROLD (Greeneville); died: 13 Sep.1917; buried: Harrold Cemetery; record (1917) # 319.

HAUN, Hannah E.; born: 23 Jan. 1844 in North Carolina; widow; parents: Wyley CHANEY (North Carolina) and mother "unknown"; death cause: "paralysis"; informant: J.M. PINKSTON (Mohawk); died: 14 Sep.1917; buried: Bent Creek; record (1917) # 320.

DAVIS, Powell; born: 13 Sep.1913; parents: T.E.R. DAVIS and Bess SQUIBB; death cause: "premature birth"; informant: father (Greeneville); died: 15 Sep.1917; buried: Stone Dam; record (1917) # 321.
DEARSTONE, Grant; age: 53 years; widower; parents: Jacob DEARSTONE and mother not stated; death cause: "tuberculosis"; informant: Bob DEARSTONE (Greeneville); died: 15 Sep.1917; buried: Cedar Hill; record (1917) # 322.
RHEA, Hettie; born: 19 Oct. 1891 in North Carolina; married; parents: J.A. BOLDING (North Carolina) and Rachel HAYNES (North Carolina); death cause: "__ (illegible) of pregnancy, artificial abortion"; informant: E.N. RHEA (Chucky); died: 15 Sep.1917; record # 323.
MORRISON, Mary Evaline; born: 4 Jul. 1909; parents: Benson MORRISON and Martha C. MCAMIS; death cause: "meningitis"; informant: Rufus MORRISON (Baileyton); died: 17 Sep.1917; buried: Locust Spring; record (1917) # 324.
REED, Susan; born: __ Jul. 1843; widow; parents: Grovenor MCNEESE and Mary BALES; death cause: "pulmonary tuberculosis"; informant: J.F. REED (Limestone); died: 19 Sep.1917; buried: Quaker Knob; record (1917) # 325.
WILSON, Maynard B.; born: 15 Aug. 1915; parents: Ben WILSON and Mary LOWERY; death cause: "colitis"; informant: father (Greeneville); died: 22 Sep.1917; buried: Cedar Hill; record (1917) # 326.
WHITE, Loura E.; born: 1 Apr. 1869; married; parents: William WAIN and mother "unknown"; death cause: "articular and muscular rheumatism"; informant: Jacob WHITE (Baileyton); died: 23 Sep.1917; buried: Union Temple; record (1917) # 327.
DYKES, Charley; born: 10 Sep.1917 in Sullivan County; parents: Thomas DYKES and Effie DEZORN; death cause: "colic"; informant: James DEZORN (Jeroldstown); died: 25 Sep.1917; buried: Bethany; record (1917) # 328.
BURGNER, Ralph; born: 15 Aug. 1911; parents: D.W. BURGNER and Dora WILLISON; death cause: "heart disease"; informant: T.S. REEVE (Chucky); died: 25 Sep.1917; record (1917) # 329.
BRYANT, Infant; male; parents: D.M. BRYANT (North Carolina) and Frankie TIPTON (North Carolina); death cause: "premature birth";

informant: father (Greeneville); died: 26 Sep.1917; buried: Oak Grove; record (1917) # 330.

HAWK, Penelope J.; age: 64 years, 3 months and 10 days; married; parents: not stated; death cause: "cancer of bladder and uterus"; died in the 3rd District, 26 Sep.1917; buried: Meadow Creek; record # 331.

REED, Carrie Bell; age: 46 years, 6 months and 10 days; born: Hamblen County; married; parents: E.L. LONG (Hamblen County); and Carrie Bell LONG; death cause: "consumption"; informant: John REED (Mohawk); died: 26 Sep.1917; record (1917) # 332.

BROOKINS, Willis; black; born: 25 Sep.1887; single; parents: Riley BROOKINS and Luven M. LOVE; death cause: "dropsy"; informant: Ike BROOKINS (Greeneville); died: 27 Sep.1917; record (1917) # 333.

HILL, Jimmie G.; female; age: 71 years; born: Virginia; widow; parents: Earl GRAY (Virginia) and Susan LATHAM (Virginia); death cause: "rheumatism"; informant: Fred GRAY (Greeneville); died: 24 Sep.1917; buried: Knoxville; record (1917) # 334.

KELLEY, Ettie; born: 15 Jun. 1882; single; parents: John KELLEY and Jane LUCAS; death cause: "intestinal nephritis"; informant: R.T. KELLEY (Baileyton); died: 29 Sep.1917; buried: Zion; record # 335.

NUNLEY, Vernie; born: 28 May 1917; parents: Corbet NUNLEY and Willie WHITE; death cause: "croup"; informant: Taylor NUNLEY (Fall Branch); died: 30 Sep.1917; buried: Lovelace; record (1917) # 336.

HASHBARGER, William Alexander; born: 17 Apr. 1856; married; parents: Z.S. HASHBARGER (Washington County) and Margaret TELLER (Washington County); death cause: "intestinal tuberculosis"; informant: Julia GOURLEY (Limestone); died: 30 Sep.1917; buried: Milburnton; record (1917) # 337.

BIBLE, J.C.; born: 10 Apr. 1917; parents: Enoch M. BIBLE and Bessie SOLOMAN; death cause: "stillborn"; informant: E.M. BIBLE (Midway); died: 10 Sep.1917; record (1917) # 338.

HENRY Ben A.; born: 26 Jan. 1891; married; parents: B.F. HENRY and Florence DEBURK; death cause: "typhoid"; informant: L.M. COBBLE (Midway); died: 1 Oct. 1917; buried: Pine Grove; record (1917) # 339.

HAWK, William; age: 79 years; married; parents: John HAWK and mother "unknown"; death cause: "brain concussion, fell six feet from verandah"; died in the 3rd District, 1 Oct. 1917; buried: Meadow Creek; record (1917) 340.

DOTY, Infant; female; parents: Allen DOTY and Pearl WEEMS; death cause: "premature birth"; informant: father (Baileyton); died: 3 Oct. 1917; buried: New Lebanon; record (1917) # 341.

SOUTHERLAND, Rossie Pearl; born: 28 __ 1883; age: 34 years and 8 months; married; parents: James BASWELL (Virginia) and Leona BASWELL (Virginia); death cause: "tuberculosis"; informant: father (Greeneville); died: 4 Oct. 1917; buried: Fairview; record (1917) # 342.

BRITTON, Alice; age: "about 73 years"; single; parents: James BRITTON and mother not stated; death cause: "chronic diarrhea"; informant: W.T. MITCHELL (Greeneville); died: 6 Oct. 1917; buried: Oak Grove; record (1917) # 343.

WILHOIT, Nina; age: 2 years; parents: Harry WILHOIT and Lara BROYLES; death cause: "diphtheria"; informant: J.B. WADDLE (Chucky); died: 8 Oct. 1917; buried: Hermon; record (1917) # 344.

WILKERSON, R.S.; born: 28 Jun. 1871; single; parents: R.T. WILKERSON and Mary OWENS; death cause: "apoplexy"; informant: Jack LUSTER (Mohawk); died: 8 Oct. 1917; buried: Concord; record (1917) # 345.

RUPERT, Infant; male; parents: William RUPERT and Minnie CAMPBELL; death cause: "unknown, lived 1 hour"; died in the 3rd District, 10 Oct. 1917; buried: Meadow Creek; record (1917) # 346.

HARRIS, Willie Kate; born: 16 Oct. 1916; parents: R.D HARRIS and Hattie T. SMITH; death cause: "cholera infantum"; informant: father (Parrotsville); died: 12 Oct. 1917; buried: Salem; record (1917) # 347.

HUMBERD, Hazel; age: 16 years; parents: I.W. HUMBERD and Mary MORRISON; death cause: "typhoid fever"; informant: father (Greeneville); died: 12 Oct. 1917; buried: Gass Shed; record (1917) # 348.

BAXLEY, William; age: 90 years; married; parents: "unknown"; death cause: "unknown"; informant: L.P. SENEKER (Moshiem); died: 14 Oct. 1917; buried: Mt. Sinai; record (1917) # 349.

DENWIDDLE, Vera; born: 27 Dec. 1903; parents: J.M. DENWIDDLE and M__ (illegible) DAVIS; death cause: "typhoid, meningitis"; informant: mother (Afton); died: 14 Oct. 1917; buried: Shilo; record (1917) # 350.

MORGAN, William; age: 60 years; single; parents: "unknown"; death cause: "unknown"; died in the 10th District, 15 Oct. 1917; buried: Mt. Vernon; record (1917) # 351.

DEARSTONE, James Kennith; born: 31 Jan. 1917; parents: J.A. DEARSTONE and H.L. MORELOCK; death cause: "bronco pneumonia"; informant: father (Baileyton); died: 17 Oct. 1917; buried: Mt. Pleasant; record: (1917) 352.

BURGNER, William Gipson; born: 14 Nov. 1850; married; parents: Christian BURGNER and Malinda FULLER; death cause: "carcinoma of liver"; informant: Florence BURGNER (Chucky); died: 15 Oct. 1917; record (1917) # 353.

PATTON, Willie J.; age: 2 years; parents: Melvin D. PATTON and Nola BALES; death cause: "diphtheria"; informant: father (Moshiem); died: 17 Oct. 1917; buried: Mt. Carmel; record (1917) # 354.

MILLER, Thomas; black; born: 1 Aug. 1844 in South Carolina; married; parents: Thomas MILLER (South Carolina) and mother "unknown"; death cause: "toxemia, kidney and bladder hemorrhage"; informant: R.J. CROSBY (Mohawk); died: 18 Oct. 1917; buried: near Mt. Hope; record (1917) # 355.

COX, Susan C.; born: 25 Dec. __; age: 71 years, 8 months and 18 days; married; parents: Enoch MOORE and Malinda WELLS; death cause: "brights disease"; informant: G.W. COX (Midway); died: 18 Oct. 1917; buried: Mt. Carmel; record (1917) # 356.

CHANDLER, Mary Ann; born: 17 Jun. 1852 in North Carolina; married; parents: Elijah GARLAND (suppose, Ireland) and Mary CHANDLER (North Carolina); death cause: "heart leakage"; informant: Daniel CHANDLER (Greeneville); died: 19 Oct. 1917; buried: Paint Creek; record (1917) # 357.

ROGERS, Glennie; born: 1 Jan. 1897 at Indian Spring, Sullivan County; single; parents: H.F. ROGERS (Sullivan County) and Ella WATKINS (Sullivan County); death cause: "tuberculosis"; informant: father (Chucky); died: 20 Oct. 1917; buried: Rheatown; record (1917) # 358.

GLASS, Daniel Sherman; born: 4 Aug. 1876 in Unicoi County; married; parents: Smith GLASS (Unicoi County) and Emaline WHITE (Unicoi County); death cause: "tuberculosis"; informant: John S. CLICK (Afton); died: 21 Oct. 1917; buried: Hermons; record (1917) # 359.

HENSLEY, Andrew; born: 24 Apr. 1883 in North Carolina; married; parents: Jesie HENSLEY (North Carolina) and Josephine HENSLEY (North Carolina); death cause: "intestinal obstruction"; informant: G.H. HENSLEY (Greeneville); died: 24 Oct. 1917; buried: Chappel Church; record (1917) # 360.

BABB, Willie Paul; parents: Clarence BABB and Mattie GASS; death cause: illegible; born/died: 24 Oct. 1917; died in the 15th District; record (1917) # 361.

REYNOLDS, Brazelton; born: 25 Nov. 1875; married; parents: James REYNOLDS and Elizabeth DUGGER; death cause: "tubercular meningitis, typhoid"; informant: Bert REYNOLDS (Baileyton); died: 25 Oct. 1917; buried: Gass Shed; record (1917) # 362.

WALDROP, Willie; born: 7 Oct. 1917; parents: Francis Marion WALDROP and Mattie May RICKER; death cause: "unknown"; informant: father (Greeneville); died: 25 Oct. 1917; buried: Pisgah; record (1917) # 363.

OTTINGER, P.C.; born: 7 Aug. 1857 in Cocke County; married; parents: Christian OTTINGER and Eva EISENHOUR; death cause: "cancer of bladder"; informant: F.M. OTTINGER (Washington, D.C.); died: 27 Oct. 1917; buried: Knoxville; record (1917) # 364.

BAILEY, Andrew Jackson; born: 10 Feb. 1839; single; parents: Andrew BAILEY and Nancy BALL (Hawkins County); death cause: "angina pectoris"; informant: Sam SMITH (Baileyton); died: 28 Oct. 1917; buried: Caney Creek; record (1917) # 365.

HIGGINS, Albert; born: 10 Jun. 1862 in North Carolina; married; parents: Irvin HIGGINS (North Carolina) and Sallie SHELTON (North Carolina); death cause: not stated; informant: John NORTON (Chucky); died: 28 Oct. 1917; buried: Cedar Grove; record (1917) # 366.

YOUNG, Samuel Lee; born: 9 Sep.1917; parents: B.A. YOUNG and Rebecca MANIS; death cause: "enteritis"; informant: mother (Greeneville); died: 29 Oct. 1917; buried; Oak Grove; record (1917) # 367.

BROWN, William Bruce; born: 9 Jul. 1900; single; parents: J.D. BROWN, Esquire and Catherine HUNT; death cause: "pneumonia"; informant: father (Baileyton); died: 29 Oct. 1917; buried: Gass Shed; record (1917) # 368.

PATY, Infant; female; parents: Allen PATY and Pearl WEEMS; death cause: "premature birth"; informant: father (Baileyton); died: 3 Oct. 1917; buried: New Lebanon; record (1917) # 369.

MATHIS, Infant; male; parents: W.H. MATHIS and Stella May BRIGMAN; death cause: "premature birth"; informant: father (Greeneville); born/died: 7 Oct. 1917; record (1917) # 370.

WILLIS, Mary; parents: Worley WILLIS and Mary CLOYD; death cause: "stillborn"; died in the 13th District, 31 Oct. 1917; record # 371.

CAMON, Infant; female; black; parents: father "unknown" and Olivia CAMON; death cause: "stillborn"; died in the 10th District, 31 Oct. 1917; record (1917) # 372.

CRUSY, Infant; male; parents: Sol CRUSY and Caroline COPLEY; death cause: "stillborn"; informant: father (Moshiem); died: 13 Oct. 1917; buried: Brown Springs; record (1917) # 373.

RUDDER, Infant; female; born: 22 Nov. 1917; parents: Ernest H. RUDDER and Lura BARLOW; death cause: "unknown"; informant: C.H. RUDDER (Moshiem); died: 25 Nov. 1917; buried: Mt. Sinai; record (1917) # 374.

ROBERTS, Infant; female; parents: Bruce ROBERTS and Virgie BROYLES; death cause: "stillborn"; informant: father (Chucky); died: 27 Nov. 1917; buried: Union Chapel; record (1917) # 375.

MALONE, Annie Elizabeth; born: 4 Feb. 1870; married; parents: David A. GASS and Rhoda A. BROWN; death cause: "cancer of gall bladder and liver"; informant: Samuel E. MALONE (Afton); died: 2 Nov. 1917; record (1917) # 376.

JEFFERS, Emma; born: 2 Aug. 1866; divorced; parents: Jack BROWN and Elizabeth BOWMAN; death cause: "__ (illegible) of liver"; died at Baileyton, 3 Nov. 1917; buried: Zion; record (1917) # 377.

SMITH, Elizabeth; born: 8 Sep.1840 in Hawkins County; widow; parents: Harry SMITH and Nannie REDNOUR; death cause: "paralysis"; informant: L.E. SMITH (Moshiem); died: 2 Nov. 1917; buried: Price Cemetery; record (1917) # 378.

DOTSON, Frank; age: 70 years; single; parents: "unknown"; death cause: "paralysis"; informant: J.F. ST JOHN (Afton); died: 2 Nov. 1917; buried: Rheatown; record (1917) # 379.

BOLDING, Howard; born: 23 Feb. 1915; parents: Mark BOLDING (North Carolina) and Retty JOHNSON; death cause: "diphtheria"; died at Chucky, 4 Nov. 1917; record (1917) # 380.

DAVIS, Ella; age: 43 years; single; parents: William DAVIS and mother not stated; death cause: "pulmonary tuberculosis"; informant: William DAVIS (Greeneville); died: 5 Nov. 1917; buried: Shiloh; record # 381.

KIDWELL, Cecil Paul; born: 19 Jul. 1895; single; parents: George W. KIDWELL and Martha SWEENY; death cause: "tuberculosis"; informant: mother (Greeneville); died: 5 Nov. 1917; buried: Fairview; record (1917) # 382.

EASTERLY, William A. Clark; born: 5 Sep.1848; married; parents: Reuben EASTERLY and __ TROBAUGH; death cause: "pulmonary tuberculosis"; informant: Reuben EASTERLY (Moshiem); died: 5 Nov. 1917; buried: Bewley Chapel; record (1917) # 383.

REEVE, Pauline; born: 18 Aug. 1917; parents: Horace REEVE and Eunice PRATHER; death cause: illegible; informant: father (Chucky); died: 6 Nov. 1917; buried; Pleasant Hill; record (1917) # 384.

BRYAN, Mary G.; born: 10 Sep.1876; divorced; parents: J.M. BRYAN (Virginia) and Elizabeth LOWE; death cause: "unknown"; informant: J.B. WILSON (Greeneville); died: 10 Nov. 1917; buried: Oak Grove; record (1917) # 385.

MORELOCK, Mary Elizabeth; born: 10 Nov. 1917; parents: E.A. MORELOCK and Kate ROBINSON; death cause: "detain in labor"; died in the 19th District, 11 Nov. 1917; record (1917) # 386.

PATRICK, Nancy; age: "suppose near 88 years"; widow; parents; Abraham CURD and Leo BROOKS; death cause: "acute bronchitis"; informant: William PATRICK (Chucky); died: 9 Nov. 1917; buried: Fairview; record (1917) # 387.

LUTTRELL, Mrs. T.J.; age: 48 years; married; parents: John M. CLICK and Jane MORELOCK; death cause: "gall stones"; informant: T.J. LUTTRELL (Greeneville); died: 11 Nov. 1917; buried: Oak Grove; record (1917) # 388.

DICKSON, Irene; born: 2 Oct. 1917; parents: father "not known" and Mary DICKSON; death cause: "unknown, found dead in bed"; died: 15 Nov. 1917; buried: Paint Creek; record (1917) # 389.

MALONE, Margaret; born: 22 Jun. 1869; married; parents: Joe GASS and Sarah WALKER; death cause: "uterine cancer"; informant: William GAMMON (Afton); died: 16 Nov. 1917; buried: 12th District; record (1917) # 390.

CRABTREE, Sarah Florence; born: 5 Sep.1853; married; parents: David L. WOOD (North Carolina) and Harriet MORRIS; death cause: "intestinal tuberculosis"; informant: S.P. CRABTREE (Limestone); died: 17 Nov. 1917; buried: Mt. Bethel; record (1917) # 391.

GUSNELL, Hester; age: "about 15 years"; parents: Dock GUSNELL (North Carolina) and M_ TWEED; death cause: "unknown"; died: 17 Nov. 1917; buried: Mt. Olivet; record (1917) # 392.

REYNOLDS, Sarah; parents: Jack REYNOLDS and Callie THORNBURG; death cause: "mal-formation"; informant: Samuel RENNELS (Fall Branch); died: 20 Nov. 1917; record (1917) # 393.

LEWIS, Martha L.; age: 56 years, 10 months and 12 days; born: Mercer County, Virginia); married; parents: Mark L. SCOTT (Virginia) and Susan A. BOSWELL (Virginia); death cause: "heart disease, rheumatism"; informant: Noel LEWIS (Greeneville); died: 21 Nov. 1917; record (1917) # 394.

GREENE, James Walter; born: 6 Jul. 1879; single; regular soldier; parents: W.H. GREENE and __ GRUBBS (Washington County); death cause: "consumption"; informant: father (Greeneville); died: 24 Nov. 1917; buried: Mt. Hebron; record (1917) # 395.

FARNSWORTH, Thomas J.; born: 23 Dec. 1852; married; parents: John FARNSWORTH and Elizabeth PARMAN; death cause: "brights disease"; informant: Joe FARNSWORTH (Greeneville); died: 24 Nov. 1917; buried: Harrisons; record (1917) # 396.

WADDLE, William; born: 25 Nov. 1914; parents: Sam WADDLE and Bess WILSON; death cause: "lagrippe"; informant: father (Greeneville); died: 25 Nov. 1917; buried: Oak Grove; record (1917) # 397.

MCMACKIN, John L.; born: 14 Mar.1883; married; parents: R.F. MCMACKIN and Mary WALKER; death cause: "illegible"; informant: J.J. WILBURN (Limestone); died: 26 Nov. 1917; buried: Milburnton; record (1917) # 398.

DUNCAN, Alfred; black; born: 10 Sep.1838; married; parents: Alfred DUNCAN and mother "unknown"; death cause: "rheumatism and endo carditis"; informant: Will DUNCAN (Greeneville); died: 27 Nov. 1917; record (1917) # 399.

COUCH, Sallie; born: 15 Mar.__; age: 24 years, 8 months and 8 days; single; parents: Arch COUCH and Francis HALL; death cause: "apoplexy"; informant: father (Moshiem); died: 29 Nov. 1917; buried: Pilot Knob; record (1917) # 400.

HENSLEY, John, Sr.; born: 14 Apr. 1842; married; parents: Benjamin HENSLEY (Virginia) and Mary A. MCDAVID (Virginia); death cause: "mitral insufficiency"; informant: M.M. STALL (Fall Branch); died: 30 Nov. 1917; buried: Lovelace; record (1917) # 401.

THACKER, Infant; male; parents: S.D. THACKER and Minnie MCCURRY; death cause: "premature birth"; informant: father (Baileyton); died: 18 Nov. 1917; buried: Zion; record (1917) # 402.

BEECH, Infant; male; parents: John BEECH (North Carolina) and mother not stated; death cause: "stillborn"; informant: father (Midway); born/died: 8 Nov. 1917; record (1917) # 403.

MCDONALD, Infant; male; parents: father not stated and Davis L. MCDONALD; death cause: "stillborn"; informant: Charles WYATT (Moshiem); born/died: 26 Nov. 1917; record (1917) # 404.

BOWERS, Infant; sex not stated; parents: Wesley BOWERS and Florence CORNWELL; death cause: "stillborn"; born/died: 17 Nov. 1917; buried: St. James; record (1917) # 405.

SCOTT, William Thomas Lacey; born: 30 Dec. 1836; widower; federal soldier; parents: "unknown"; death cause: "brights disease"; informant: Minnie WILLIAMS (Afton); died in the 14th District, 2 Dec. 1917; record (1917) # 406.

GREENE, Clyde; age: "about 35 years"; married; parents: "unknown"; death cause: "believed heart failure"; died: 1 Dec. 1917; buried: Morristown; record (1917) # 407.

OWENS, Panthe E.; born: 5 Dec. 1889; married; parents: Thomas JAYNES and Nellie ERVIN (North Carolina); death cause: "croupous pneumonia"; informant: John OWENS (Mohawk); died: 2 Dec. 1917; buried: Fairview; record (1917) # 408.

CUTSHALL, James; age: 77 years; married; parents: William CUTSHALL and Nancy RICKER; death cause: "organic heart trouble";

informant: John CUTSHALL (Greeneville); died: 3 Dec. 1917; buried: Cove Creek; record (1917) # 409.

LANE, Virginia Viola; born: 25 Jan. 1917; parents: Patton LANE (Virginia) and Mary ESTEP (Virginia); death cause: "croup"; informant: father (Fall Branch); died: 3 Dec. 1917; record (1917) # 410.

HALE, Gladys Robal; born: 20 Dec. 1916 in White County; (this is a Grundy County record filed with Greene County); record (1917) # 411.

HENSLEY, Bonnie; born: 1 Jun. 1916; father not stated and Eliza HENSLEY (North Carolina); death cause: "croup"; informant: G.H. HENSLEY (Chucky); died: 4 Dec. 1917; record (1917) # 412.

GREENE, Stewart; born: 29 Oct. 1917; parents: Mathes GREENE and Roxie KEENER; death cause: illegible; died: 4 Dec. 1917; buried: Shilo; record (1917) # 413.

GIBSON, Andrew J.; born: 11 Oct. 1890; married; parents: John GIBSON and Hallie SUSONG; death cause: "pulmonary tuberculosis"; informant: Mrs. Eva GIBSON (Greeneville); died: 3 Dec. 1917; buried: Cedar Hill; record (1917) # 414.

JONES, Mrs. __ (illegible); born: 19; Dec. 1871 in Virginia; parents: Benjamin MCCRAVY (Virginia) and mother "unknown"; death cause: "tuberculosis of lungs"; informant: Y.J. JONES (Afton); died: 16 Dec. 1917; buried: Stone Dam; record (1917) # 415.

CARSON, Thomas; black; age: "about 40 years"; widower; parents: "unknown"; death cause: "syphilis"; informant: J.W. MORELOCK (Greeneville); died: 8 Dec. 1917; buried: Poor Farm; record # 416.

BICKERSTAFF, Mary Magdalene; black; age: "suppose more than 100 years"; born: North Carolina; widow; parents: "unknown"; death cause: "apoplexy"; informant: M.L. BICKERSTAFF (Midway); died: 9 Dec. 1917; record (1917) # 417.

TAYLOR, Mary; age: 70 years; widow; parents: Fred DEWITT and mother "unknown"; death cause: "unknown"; informant: Ed REAVES (Greeneville); died: 9 Dec. 1917; buried; Red Hill; record # 418.

STACY, David L.; age: 28 years and 2 months; single; parents: G.C. STACY and Sarah MILLER; death cause: "pulmonary tuberculosis"; informant: father (Greeneville); died: 11 Dec. 1917; buried: Chucky; record (1917) # 419.

CHANDLEY, Margaret; age: 45 years; born: North Carolina; married; parents: John STANTON (North Carolina) and Sarah SHELTON (North Carolina); death cause: "cancer of womb"; informant: Horace CHANDLEY; died: 13 Dec. 1917; buried: Hebron; record # 420.

LANE, William; born: 5 Mar. 1914; parents: Sam C. LANE and Nancy KENNEY; death cause: "meningitis"; died in the 21st District, 14 Dec. 1917; buried: Locust Springs; record (1917) # 421.

KAHL, Alice; age: 51 years; widow; parents: John BROOKS and mother "unknown"; death cause: "apoplexy"; informant: Mrs. Roy EAKIN (Greeneville); died: 14 Dec. 1917; buried: New Bethel; record # 422.

COWARD, Amanda Melvina; age: 56 years; widow; parents: James ARNETT and Elizabeth DURHAM; death cause: "embolism"; informant: J.E. COWARD (Johnson City); died: 15 Dec. 1917; buried: Oak Grove; record (1917) # 423.

LYLE, William; age: "about 84 years"; widower; parents: Robert LYLE and Edie WILSON; death cause: "chronic bronchitis"; informant: William LYLE (Mohawk); died: 16 Dec. 1917; record (1917) # 424.

GRAHAM, Synthia; age: "about 80 years"; married; parents: "unknown"; death cause: "pneumonia fever"; informant: J.W. BALES (Greeneville); died: 17 Dec. 1917; buried: Harmons; record (1917) # 425.

BROOKS, Pearl; age: "about 25 years"; born: North Carolina; married; parents: W.A. HOUSTON and __ BRYANT; death cause: "pneumonia fever"; died: 18 Dec. 1917; record (1917) # 426.

BROOKS, Pearl B.; born: 23 Sep. 1887 in North Carolina; married; parents: W.A. HUSTON and S. BRYANT (North Carolina); death cause: "cerebral hemorrhage"; informant: J.A. BROOKS (Greeneville); died: 19 Dec. 1917; buried: Oak Grove; record (1917) # 427.

WILHOIT, Henry; age: 36 years; single; parents: "unknown"; death cause: "epilepsy"; died: 19 Dec. 1917; buried: Poor Farm; record # 428.

PEARCE, Joel N.; born: 18 Nov. 1882; married; parents: H.M. PEARCE and Matilda HEN__ (illegible); death cause: "septic infection, cut on finger"; informant: W.M. GARGER (Moshiem); died: 20 Dec. 1917; buried: Mt. Carmel; record (1917) # 429.

GRAHAM, Mattie; age: 49 years; married; parents: Thomas DUNCAN and mother "unknown"; death cause: "tuberculosis"; informant: Brooks

DUNCAN (Greeneville); died: 20 Dec. 1917; buried: Gass Shed; record (1917) # 430.

HENSLEY, Eva; born: 22 May 1827 in Greene County; widow; parents: John CUTSHALL (Pennsylvania) and __ SMOTHERS (Pennsylvania); death cause: "heart disease and asthma"; informant: G.W. HENSLEY (Greeneville); died: 20 Dec. 1917; buried: Mt. Tabor; record # 431.

HAYS, Essie Caldonia; born: 6 May 1879; married; parents: David E. HALL and Matilda BASKETT; death cause: "pulmonary tuberculosis"; informant: W.M. HALL (Fall Branch); died: 21 Dec. 1917; buried: Lovelace; record (1917) # 432.

TARLTON, Infant; female; parents: Worley TARLTON and Flora REAVES; death cause: "acute indigestion"; informant: O.M. REAVES (Greeneville); died; 22 Dec. 1917; buried: Mt. Tabor; record # 432.

MOOR (?), Ricina; born: 3 Aug. 1844; widow; parents: Samuel P. MCCURRY and Elizabeth LEWIS; death cause: "cerebral hemorrhage"; informant: J.H. MCCURRY (Moshiem); died: 22 Dec. 1917; buried; Mt. Sinai; record (1917) # 434.

WELLS, M.H.; born: 3 Mar. 1846 in South Carolina; parents: F.W. WELLS and Ann BARRON; death cause: "paralysis"; informant: W.H. WELLS (Moshiem); died: 22 Dec. 1917; buried: Antioc; record # 435.

WEBBER, George; age: "about 71 years"; single; parents: "unknown"; death cause: "paralysis"; died: 23 Dec. 1917; buried: Poor Farm; record (1917) # 436.

FOREMAN, Nancy; age: "about 73 years"; born: North Carolina; widow; parents: John FOREMAN (North Carolina) and mother not stated; death cause: "heart trouble"; died: 27 Dec. 1917; buried: Hot Springs, North Carolina; record (1917) # 437.

IDELL, Iny Mae; born: 26 Sep. 1917; parents: Henry IDELL and Pearl L. LAWRY; death cause: "jaundice"; informant: H.V. LAURY (Midway); died: 28 Dec. 1917; record (1917) # 438.

GOOD, James K. Polk; born: 12 Mar. 1855 in Washington County; married; parents: John GOOD (Virginia) and Elizabeth HUMPHRIES (Washington County); death cause: "pellagra"; informant: Maggie GOOD (Chucky); died: 30 Dec. 1917; buried: Oak Dale; record # 439.

SWANGER, Annie; born: 11 Jan. 1914; parents: Robert SWANGER (North Carolina) and Mollie KING (North Carolina); death cause: "pneumonia"; died: 30 Dec. 1917; record (1917) # 440.

WILSON, Infant; male; parents: A.G. WILSON (North Carolina) and E. HANKINS (North Carolina); death cause: not stated; informant: father (Afton); died: 25 Dec. 1917; record (1917) # 441.

TAYLOR, Infant; female; parents: Dave TAYLOR and Dollie CARMON; death cause: "stillborn"; born/died: 27 Dec. 1917; buried: Fairview; record (1917(# 442.

CUTSHALL, Ana Ruth; parents: Newton J. CUTSHALL and Martha J. SEATON; death cause: "stillborn"; informant: father (Greeneville); born/died: 28 Dec. 1917; buried: Price Cemetery; record (1917) # 443.

MCCAMEY, Kenneth; parents: Joe MCCAMEY and Nannie RADER; death cause: "mal-formation of heart"; informant: father (Midway); born/died: 22 Dec. 1917; buried: Moshiem; record (1917) # 443

FORTNER, Oma May; born: 1 Jan. 1887; single; parents: G.F. FORTNER and B__ (illegible) SCOTT; death cause: "heart disease"; informant: father (Greeneville); died: 3 Jan. 1918; buried: Fairview Cemetery; record (1918) # 1.

EAST, George T.; born: 3 Jul. 1849 in Virginia; married; parents: Thomas EAST (Virginia) and __ CLOUD (Virginia; death cause: "cerebral hemorrhage"; informant: G.M. HOWELL (Roanoke, Virginia); died: 3 Jan. 1916; buried: Oak Grove; record (1918) # 2.

EMMETT, Andy; born: 25 Jun. 1917; parents: Charles EMMETT (Pennsylvania) and Ema LAUGHLIN; death cause: "pneumonia fever"; informant: J. EMMETT (Greeneville); died: 4 Jan. 1918; buried: Shilo Cemetery; record (1918) # 3.

MURDOCK, Samuel Hobart; born: 5 Dec. 1917; parents: Crumley MURDOCK and Lena CASTEEL; death cause: "enteritis"; informant: Dick ANDERSON (Greeneville); died: 5 Jan. 1918; buried: Harrison Cemetery; record (1918) # 4.

ROBERTS, Sarah J.; born: 30 Dec. 1835 in Buncombe County, North Carolina; widow; parents: Thomas O. ROBERTS (Buncombe County) and Synthia FOX (Buncombe County); death cause: "natural causes, age"; informant: A.A. ROBERTS (Greeneville); died: 5 Jan. 1918; buried: Pine Grove; record (1918) # 5.

SMITHTON, Infant; male; born: 2 Jan. 1918; parents: T.H. SMITHTON and mother's name illegible; death cause: "heart valve, no closure"; informant: father (Greeneville); died: 6 Jan. 1918; buried: Oak Grove; record (1918) # 6.

SAULS, Martha; age: 70 years; widow; parents: not stated; death cause: "tuberculosis"; informant: H.T. EASTERLY (Greeneville); died: 7 Jan. 1918; buried: Whittenburg; record (1918) # 7.

GOODMAN, Minerva; born: 11 May 1873; married; parents: Robert __ (illegible) and Elizabeth __ (illegible); death cause: "pulmonary tuberculosis"; informant: T.E. GOODMAN (Greeneville); died: 10 Jan. 1918; buried: Oak Grove; record (1918) # 8.

SEATON, Clarence; age: 3 years and 6 months; parents: Monroe SEATON and Edna BOWMAN; death cause: "rheumatism"; informant: D.E. RUSSELL (Greeneville); died: 10 Jan. 1918; buried: Pisgah; record (1918) # 9.

MCGEE, Daniel; born: 4 Jan. 1918; parents: Clide MCGEE and Emily JORDAN; death cause: "unknown, found dead in bed"; informant: father (Chucky); died: 11 Jan. 1918; buried: Ebeneezer; record (1918) # 10.

SAULTS, Alice; born: 17 May 1855; widow; parents: Jessie WHITAKER and Sarah WHITAKER; death cause: "mitral insufficiency and bronchitis"; informant: Mary A. SMITH (Chucky); died: 11 Jan. 1918; buried: Milburnton; record (1918) # 11.

RUTLEDGE, Lee Andrew King; black; age: 89 years; born: Sullivan County; married; parents: not stated; death cause: "senility"; informant: Ed RUTLEDGE (Greeneville); died: 12 Jan. 1918; buried: Wesley; record (1918) # 12.

RADER, Charley; born: 8 Jan. 1875; married; parents: James RADER and Sarah RADER; death cause: "pneumonia fever"; informant: Sarah RADER (Greeneville); died: 13 Jan. 1918; buried: Mt. Pleasant; record (1918) # 13.

WAINE, George; age: 31 years; married; parents: William WAINE and mother "unknown"; death cause: "lobar pneumonia"; informant: Cordie RIGGINS (Baileyton); died: 15 Jan. 1918; buried: Ratliff Cemetery; record (1918) # 14.

DURMAN, William Francis; born: 23 Nov. 1857; single; parents: William DURMAN (Virginia) and Margaret __ (illegible)(Virginia);

death cause: "heart disease"; died in the 21st District, 15 Jan. 1918; buried: Gass Shed; record (1918) # 15.

CARTER, Verdie; born: 17 Jan. 1899; single; parents: Jacob C. CARTER and Dora BRUBAKER; death cause: "lagrippe, broncho pneumonia"; informant: father (Moshiem); died: 15 Jan. 1918; buried: Mountain Valley; record (1918) # 16.

JENNINGS, Blanch; age: 28 years; married; parents: G.B. ROLLINGS and Mollie __ (illegible); death cause: "typhoid fever"; informant: James COLLINS (Greeneville); died: 16 Dec. 1917; buried: Rheobeth; record (1918) # 17.

DAVIS, Mary Ann; born: 29 Jan. 1851; widow; parents: John B. HAWKINS and Esther BROWN; death cause: "heart failure"; informant: J. HAWKINS (Baileyton); died: 17 Jan. 1918; buried: Gass Shed; record (1918) # 18.

CUPP, John F.; born: 18 Jan. 1844 in Hawkins County; married; parents: Jacob CUPP (Hawkins County) and S_ (illegible) HECK (Hawkins County); death cause: "tuberculosis"; informant: G.F. LYNCH (Bulls Gap); died: 17 Jan. 1918; record (1918) # 19.

HENDRY, Mary Ann; born: 27 Apr. 1846; widow; parents: Ben CARTER and Honor HARDIN; death cause: "broncho pneumonia"; informant: W.E. HENDRY (Moshiem); died: 18 Jan. 1918; buried: Mt. Sinai; record (1918) # 20.

RIPLEY, Lucy; born: 29 Oct. 1872; married; parents: William MCCORKLE and Kate WEBB; death cause: "strangulated hernia"; informant: L.M. RIPLEY (Greeneville); died: 18 Jan. 1918; buried: Stone Dam; record (1918) # 21.

ROSS, J. Cad; born: 28 Aug. 1864; married; parents: John A. ROSS and Harriett __ (illegible); death cause: "lobar pneumonia"; informant: James ROSS (Afton); died: 18 Jan. 1918; record (1918) # 22.

GASS, J. Robert; born: 11 Feb. 1917; parents: Roy D. GASS and Jennie MORRIS; death cause: "spinal meningitis and pneumonia"; died in the 21st District, 20 Jan. 1918; buried: Gass Shed; record (1918(# 23.

FERGUSON, Noah Oliver; age: 1 year and 3 months; parents: Thomas FERGUSON (North Carolina) and Ada FOX (North Carolina); death cause: "acute indigestion"; informant: J.M. FOX (Greeneville); died: 22 Jan. 1918; buried: Red Hill; record (1918) # 24.

RANKIN, Jul_ (illegible) Howell; age: 14 years; parents: T.S RANKIN and Mary E. COILE; death cause: "appendicitis"; informant: father (Greeneville); died: 24 Jan. 1918; buried: Oak Grove; record # 25.

COOTER, Florence Emily; age: 59 years; married; parents: Charlie JONES (North Carolina) and Sallie SWINDELL (North Carolina); death cause: "pulmonary tuberculosis"; died in the 2nd District, 24 Jan. 1918; buried: Pisgah; record (1918) # 26.

BURGER, John; born: 16 Mar 1847; married; parents: Isaac BURGER and Rachel SMALL; death cause: "mitral insufficiency"; informant: J.A. BURGER (Moshiem); died: 25 Jan. 1918; buried: Albany; record # 27.

JONES, Ralf James; born: 13 Jan. 1918; parents: Robert JONES (Loudon County) and Lucy CUPP; death cause: "mal-formation, jaundice"; informant: N.A. CUPP (Bulls Gap); died: 27 Jan. 1918; buried: Phillippi; record (1918) # 28.

GIBSON, John Thomas; age: 50 years; married; parents: Calvin GIBSON (Kentucky) and Angeline RUSSELL; death cause: "pulmonary tuberculosis"; informant: Dudley GIBSON (Greeneville); died: 24 Jan. 1918; buried: Cedar Hill; record (1918) # 29.

LOLAR, Felix; black; age: 82 years; born: South Carolina; widower; parents: "unknown"; death cause: "senility"; informant: Ben PERKINS (Greeneville); died: 27 Jan. 1918; buried: Gass Cemetery; record # 30.

BIBLE, Cathleen; born: 24 Sep. 1917; parents: _ R. BIBLE and Winnie TAYLOR (Hawkins County); death cause: "rickets"; informant: George RADAR (Midway); died: 31 Jan. 1918; buried: Bible Chapel, 19th District; record (1918) # 31.

LOGAN, Infant; female; parents: Charles F. LOGAN and Willie E. BROWN; death cause: "hydrocephalus"; informant: father (Moshiem); died: 9 Jan. 1918; buried: Brown Cemetery; record (1918) # 32.

TARLTON, Infant; female; parents: father "unknown" and Nellie TARLTON; death cause: "stillborn"; born/died: 11 Jan. 1918; record (1918) # 33.

KIMERY, Edith; parents: Arbra C. KIMERY and Jessie KIMERY; death cause: "premature birth"; informant: Crete KIMERY (Afton); born/died: 17 Jan. 1918; buried: Herman; record (1918) # 34.

RENNER, Infant; male; parents: father "unknown" and Daisy RENNER; death cause: "stillborn"; born/died: 31 Jan. 1918; buried: St. James; record (1918) # 35.

DICKSON, Infant; male; parents: Harvy DICKSON and Elsey STILLS; death cause: "born dead"; informant: father (Greeneville); born/died: 7 Jan. 1918; record (1918) # 36.

KELLEY, Mary Reed; born: 26 Sep. 1911; parents: Robert J. KELLEY (Hawkins County) and Mary L. BAILEY; death cause: "entero colitis"; informant: R.T. KELLEY (Baileyton); died: 3 Feb. 1918; buried: Zion; record (1918) # 37.

LAWS, Franklin; born: _ 1846; age: 71 years; married; parents: Alford LAWS (North Carolina) and mother "unknown"; death cause: "unknown"; informant: Jacob LAWS (Baileyton); died: 4 Feb. 1918; buried: County Line; record (1918) # 39.

ERVIN, Thomas; born: 8 May 1884; single; parents: S.J. ERVIN and Josie KEKER; death cause: "pulmonary tuberculosis"; informant: father (Greeneville); died: 4 Feb. 1918; buried: Pine Grove; record # 38.

WOOLSEY, Laura; born: 18 Feb. 1860; married; parents: Samuel H. BAXTER and Elizabeth SHAULS; death cause: "cerebral hemorrhage"; died: 4 Feb. 1918; buried: Cedar Lane; record (1918) # 40.

WINKLE, George W.; age: 62 years; born: Washington County; married; parents: Jacob WINKLE (Washington County) and Caroline STRAIN (Washington County); death cause: "cancer of kidney"; informant: Don ALEXANDER (Greeneville); died: 5 Feb. 1918; buried: Philadelphia; record (1918) # 41.

EMERSON, Henry C.; born: 21 Feb. 1857 in Georgia; married; parents: C. EMERSON (Georgia) and _ AUSTIN; death cause: "invalid, with paralysis, clothing caught fire"; informant: Onie EMERSON (Greeneville); died in the 3rd District, 6 Feb. 1918; record (1918) # 42.

REAVES, Infant; male; born: 9 Dec. 1917; parents: Fain REAVES and Martha MCCOY; death cause: "bronchial pneumonia"; informant: F.C BRITTON (Greeneville); died: 7 Feb. 1918; record (1917) # 43.

DAY, James Franklin; born: 4 Feb. 1918; parents: James Franklin DAY and Maud Ethel LUTTRELL; death cause: "unknown, found dead in bed"; informant: father (Mohawk); died: 8 Feb. 1918; buried: Fairview; record (1918) # 44.

HERSCH, Sampson; age: 98 years; born: Germany; widower; parents: "unknown"; death cause: "senility"; died: 9 Feb. 1918; buried: Knoxville; record (1918) # 45.

COX, Mattie; born: 29 Dec. 1876; married; parents: W.G. DRAKE and Marga SAILOR; death cause: "hepatic abscess"; informant: W. Logan COX (Moshiem); died: 19 Feb. 1918; buried: Mt. Sinai; record # 46.

CANNON, Annie Mae; black; age: 6 years; parents: Malcom CANNON and Lizzie BROWN; death cause: "broncho pneumonia"; informant: Nan COOPER (Greeneville); died: 11 Feb. 1918; buried: Wesley; record (1918) # 47.

WELLS, Stephen George; born: 7 Apr. 1856; married; parents: Jacob P. WELLS and Synthia HARRISON; death cause: "apoplexy"; informant: T.C. WELLS (Greeneville); died: 13 Feb. 1918; buried: Price Cemetery; record (1918) # 48.

BOUGHER, James; born: 24 Jul. 1833 in Winchester, Virginia; widower; retired policeman; parents: Jacob BOUGHER (Maryland) and Mabeline H__ (illegible)(Virginia); death cause: "apoplexy (paralysis)"; informant: O.H. DOYLE (Chucky); died: 15 Feb. 1918; record # 49.

BURGNER, Margaret; born: 10 Oct. 1848; single; parents: C.C. BURGNER and Malinda FULLIN; death cause: "rheumatism"; informant: Mrs. S.M. BURGNER (Chucky); died: 15 Feb. 1918; buried: Pleasant Hill; record (1918) # 50.

DUGGER, James Newton; born: 26 Apr. 1900; parents: H.N. DUGGER and Alice SMITH; death cause: "spinal meningitis"; informant: father (Baileyton); died: 17 Feb. 1918; buried: Oakdale; record (1918) # 51.

ROWLAND, Michael; born: 29 Jul. 1836 in North Carolina; widower; minister; parents: Charley ROWLAND (North Carolina) and Mary SMITH; death cause: "bronchitis"; informant: Hester BOLDING (North Carolina); died: 18 Feb. 1918; buried: North Carolina; record # 52.

EVANS, Martha; born: 12 Apr. 1847; widow; parents: Michael MYERS and Sophia CARTER; death cause: "tuberculosis"; informant: J.M. MYERS (Moshiem); died: 18 Feb. 1918; record (1918) # 53.

BROOKINS, Mary; black; born: 19 Jan. 1888; married; parents: W.M. CROUDER and Mary CROUDER; death cause: "tuberculosis"; informant: Charles BROOKINS (Greeneville); died: 19 Feb. 1918; record (1918) # 54.

SEXTON, Mrs. Lucinda; born: 14 Nov. 1854; married; parents: Peter SIMPSON and Elizabeth H__ (illegible); death cause: "lagrippe"; informant: George W. SEXTON (Moshiem); died: 19 Feb. 1918; buried: Albany; record (1918) # 55.

LOWE, Wallace Henry; born: 17 Jan. 1918; parents: Andrew LOWE and Bonnie MORGAN; death cause: "croup"; informant: father (Moshiem); died: 19 Feb. 1918; record (1918) # 56.

GRAHAM, James; age: 82 years; widower; parents: George GRAHAM and mother "unknown"; death cause: "unknown"; informant: Will BALES (Greeneville); died: 20 Feb. 1918; buried: Harmon; record # 57.

RADER, James H.; born: 2 Feb. 1857; widower; parents: Ruben RADER and Cynthy HUNTER; death cause: "paralysis"; informant: Hubert SMITH (Surgeonsville, TN.); died: 21 Feb. 1918; buried: Mt. Hope; record (1918) # 58.

NEAS, Malissa; born: 9 Feb. 1848; married; parents: R.B. DARLING and mother "unknown"; death cause: "cirrhosis of liver"; informant: J.C. WINTER (Greeneville); died: 22 Feb. 1918; buried: St. James; record (1918) # 59.

HIGHSINGER, George; born: 29 Feb. 1890; married; parents: W.L. HIGHSINGER and Hannah LIGHT; death cause: "pulmonary tuberculosis"; informant: father (Greeneville); died: 23 Feb. 1918; buried: Mt. Bethel; record (1918) # 60.

GASTON, Myrtle Fern; born: 28 Nov. 1915; parents: John W. GASTON and Adda M. WALLER; death cause: "tubercular meningitis"; died in the 15th District, 24 Feb. 1918; buried: Providence; record (1918) # 61.

SHAW, N__ (illegible), Jr.; born: 24 Feb. 1918; parents: N__ (illegible) SHAW and Bonnie A__ (illegible); death cause: "premature"; died: 25 Feb. 1918; record (1918) # 62.

BRYAN, Ruth Dean; born: 20 Mar 1917; parents: Tom H. BRYAN and Sara E. IDELL; death cause: "bronchitis"; informant: S.N. BRYAN (Moshiem); died: 27 Feb. 1918; buried: Mt. Pleasant; record # 63.

WAINE, Minnie; age: 24 years, 2 months and 27 days; married; parents: Samuel Jackson MCCAMEY and __ BLAZER (Cocke County); death cause: "pulmonary tuberculosis"; informant: J.H. DUGGER (Baileyton); died: 28 Feb. 1918; buried: Bethany; record (1918) # 64.

HENSLEY, James Harrison; born: 1 Jan. 1918; parents: J.A. HENSLEY and Jane ARNOLD; death cause: "bronchial pneumonia"; informant: father (Baileyton); died: 28 Feb. 1918; record (1918) # 65.

BABB, Infant; male; parents: James BABB and Beckie BABB; death cause: "stillborn"; informant: father (Greeneville); died: 23 Feb. 1918; buried: Gass Shed; record (1918) # 66.

JONES, Thomas J.; age: 56 years; widower; parents: "unknown"; death cause: "pneumonia"; informant: J.H. WALKER (Afton); died: 1 Mar 1918; buried: Stone Dam; record (1918) # 67.

WOOD, Mancile Smith; age: 24 years; born: Washington County; single; parents: C.C. WOODS (Washington County, VA.) and Josephine BOOHER (Virginia); death cause: "pellagra"; informant: father (Greeneville) died: 1 Mar 1918; buried: Oak Grove; record (1918) # 68.

BURNS, John C.; born: 23 Nov. 1843; widower; parents: William BURNS and Westie SMITH; death cause: illegible; informant: S.E. BURNS (Moshiem); died: 8 Mar 1918; buried: Price Cemetery; record (1918) # 69.

BIBLE, Delay Alexander; born: 14 Jan. 1910; parents: Joe BIBLE and Ethel COX; death cause: "pneumonia"; informant: W.H. HARTMAN (Myers); died: 2 Mar 1918; buried: Mt. Pleasant; record (1918) # 70.

SMITH, Birtha; born: __ May 1909; parents: George SMITH and Sindy COMPTON; death cause: "broncho pneumonia"; died: 4 Mar 1918; buried: Chimney Top; record (1918) # 71.

DAVIS, James Canon; age: 68 years; married; school teacher; parents: William DAVIS and Jane ENGLMAN; death cause: "pneumonia"; informant: Mrs. E.J. DAVIS (Mohawk); died: 5 Mar. 1918; buried: Bible Cemetery; record (1918) # 72.

JUSTIS, Alfred; born: 25 Sep. 1832 in Tennessee; married; parents: John JUSTIS (Virginia) and Thurseve BROWN; death cause: "apoplexy"; informant: Nannie JUSTIS (Chucky); died: 5 Mar. 1918; buried: Pleasant Vale; record (1918) # 73.

FOWLER, Annah E.; born: 3 Jun. 1847; widow; parents: Samuel E. SNAPP and mother "unknown"; death cause: "angina pectoris"; died in the 10th District, 6 Mar. 1918; buried: Oak Grove; record (1918) # 74.

REED, Infant; male; born: 2 Mar. 1918; parents: Charley REED and Elizabeth WELLS; death cause: illegible; informant; father (Moshiem); died: 7 Mar. 1918; buried: Antioc Church; record (1918) # 75.

H_ (illegible), Jane; born; 14 Oct. 1857; married; parents: John RUTHERFORD and Sarah RUTHERFORD; death cause: "gallstone disease"; informant: Joe WARD (Afton); died: 7 Mar. 1918; buried: Fairview; record (1918) # 76.

HAROLD, Dodd; age: 17 years; parents: J.M. HAROLD and Ida DODD; death cause: "cretinism"; informant: father (Greeneville); died: 8 Mar. 1918; buried: Hebron; record (1918) # 77.

GASS, Isabel; born: 26 May 1847; married; parents: Jacob WHITE and Rebecca THOMPSON; death cause: "apoplexy"; informant: Henry CARTER (Baileyton); died: 9 Mar. 1918; buried: Gass Shed; record (1918) # 78.

ROSE, John W.; born: 22 Jul. 1859; married; parents: James H. ROSE and Elizabeth BULLEN; death cause: "suppose apoplexy"; informant: John W. PIERCE (Afton); died: 10 Mar. 1918; buried: Mt. Zion; record (1918) # 79.

HOLDERBY, Archie; black; age: "about 55 years"; born: North Carolina; single; parents: "unknown"; death cause: "apoplexy"; informant: J.C. KING (Greeneville); died: 10 Mar. 1918; buried: Winston Salem, North Carolina; record (1918) # 80.

DEAN, Joseph Ray; born: 17 Nov. 1916; parents: Joe DEAN and Orua HAMET; death cause: "bronchial pneumonia"; informant: David MELTON (Bulls Gap); died: 11 Mar. 1918; buried: Willoughbys; record (1918) # 81.

ELLISON, Jennie; age: 38 years; married; parents: J.P. EASTERLY and Louise DEVAULT; death cause: "operation for __ (illegible)"; informant: J.B. BELL (Greeneville); died: 11 Mar. 1918; buried: Whittenburg; record (1918) # 82.

MAU_ (illegible), Amanda Broyles; born: 28 Jan. 1836; widow; parents: Philip BROYLES and Ellen BROYLES; death cause: "general paralysis"; informant: H.M. WILHOIT (Chucky); died: 18 Mar. 1918; record (1918) # 83.

MALTSBERGER, Nancy; born: 12 May 1850; married; parents: James SHANKS and Malinda MAYS; death cause: "tuberculosis"; informant:

G.W.M. MALTSBERGER (Chucky); died: 17 Mar. 1918; buried: Union Temple; record (1918) # 84.

DAVIS, Florence; black; age: 60 years; married; parents: "unknown"; death cause: "unknown"; informant: Tom HAMILTON (Greeneville); died; 19 Mar. 1918; buried: Pruets Hill; record (1918) # 85.

GUIRE, Kelly; born: 22 Dec. 1851; married; parents: Hiram GUIRE and Louisa SHANKS; death cause: "gall stones"; informant: Melvina A. ARGENBRIGHT (Chucky); died: 20 Mar. 1918; buried: Milburton; record (1918) # 86.

PETERS, Elen Geneva; age: "about 2 years"; parents; Luther PETERS and Ethel GILLAN; death cause: "pneumonia"; died: 23 Mar. 1918; buried: St. James; record (1918) # 87.

NEUS, John T.; born: 8 Jul. 1837; married; parents: Philip NEUS and Elizabeth BOWERS; death cause: "mitral regurgitation"; informant: Clarence NEUS (Greeneville); died: 27 Mar. 1918; buried: St. James; record (1918) # 88.

BRABSON, Infant; male; parents: Thomas BRABSON and Josephine SUSONG; death cause: "craniotmy"; informant: W.H. DOUGHTY (Greeneville); born/died: 29 Mar. 1918; buried: Oak Grove; record # 89.

JOHNSON, Pearl; age: 23 years; married; parents: Ross GASS and __ WHITE; death cause: "pulmonary tuberculosis"; informant: Ben JOHNSON (Greeneville); died: 1 Apr. 1918; buried: Gass Shed; record (1918) # 90.

HUMBARD, Hazel; age: 17 years; single; parents: Ike HUMBARD and Mary MORRISON; death cause: "typhoid fever"; informant: father (Greeneville); died: 1 Apr. 1918; buried: Gass Shed; record (1918) # 91.

LINEBARGER, Nola; born: 9 Aug. __; age: 24 years and 7 months; single; parents: __ LINEBARGER and Martha LINEBARGER; death cause: "pulmonary tuberculosis"; informant: W.T. MASSEY (Greeneville); died: 1 Apr. 1918; buried: St. James; record (1918) # 92.

KENT, M.H.; born: 28 Sep. 1849 in North Carolina; married; parents: John KENT and Hariet BAULCH (North Carolina); death cause: "paralysis and rheumatism"; informant: William KENT (Moshiem); died: 3 Apr. 1918; buried: Brinirs Chapel; record (1918) # 93.

TELLACK, Annie; age: 35 years; married; parents: __ LANE and mother "unknown"; death cause: "pneumonia"; informant: James HOLBROOK (Greeneville); died: 3 Apr. 1918; buried: Oak Grove; record # 94.

HOLT, Infant; age: 8 days; parents: Scott HOLT and __ DEWITT; death cause: "hemorrhage"; died: 3 Apr. 1918; buried: Cedar Hill; record (1918) # 95.

HANNON, Infant; male; parents: Cecil HANNON and Mollie GRAHAM; death cause: "premature birth"; informant: James HANNON (Greeneville); died: 5 Apr. 1918; buried; Gass Shed; record (1918) # 96.

GRAY, Samuel A.; age: 2 years and 2 months; parents: W.H. GRAY and Ethel BRUMLEY; death cause: "pneumonia"; informant: S.T. BRUMLEY (Greeneville); died: 7 Apr. 1918; buried: Harmons; record (1918) # 97.

MALONE, Francis; age: 23 years, 2 months and 8 days; married; parents: John SMITH and Alice BROOK; death cause: "tuberculosis"; died: 8 Apr. 1918; buried: Gass Shed; record (1918) # 98.

BROWN, Infant; male; parents: Hilton BROWN and Nola BAILEY; death cause: "premature birth"; informant: Hitt BROWN (Chucky); died: 9 Apr. 1918; record (1918) # 99.

RICHARDS, Nadine; born: 7 Jul. 1907; parents: "unknown"; death cause: "obstructed bowel"; informant: W.T. WEYSOR (Greeneville); died: 10 Apr. 1918; buried: Watauga Valley; record (1918) # 100.

BEARD, Martha Pain; black; age: 89 years; born: North Carolina; widow; parents: "unknown"; death cause: "diarrhea"; informant: Will BEARD (Midway); died: 11 Apr. 1918; record (1918) # 101.

WADDLE, Francis; born: 5 Jan. 1850; parents: Rufus K. WADDLE and mother "unknown"; death cause: "lagrippe and brights disease"; informant: R.W WADDLE (Greeneville); died: 13 Apr. 1918; buried: Busheba; record (1918) # 102.

HAYS, Claud Lesley; born: 21 Dec. 1908; parents: Bowman HAYS and Ida BALES; death cause: "organic heart disease"; informant: Alex BALES (Jeroldstown); died: 13 Apr. 1918; buried: Cedar Lane; record (1918) # 103.

LIGHT, Martha; born: 3 Mar. 1884; single; parents: John LIGHT and Francis BARRETT; death cause: "nephritis"; died: 14 Apr. 1918; buried: Bethany; record (1918) # 104.

SMELCER, William Roy; born: 11 Mar. 1917; parents: A.C. SMELCER and Elsie B. BIBLE; death cause: "phlebitis"; informant: father (Midway); died: 14 Apr. 1918; buried: Warrensburg; record # 105.

JONES, Charles; age: 63 years; married; parents: Charles JONES and mother not stated; death cause: "brights disease"; informant: John RUSSELL (Greeneville); died: 14 Apr. 1918; buried; Susong Cemetery; record (1918) # 106.

HARMON, Henry; born: 14 Mar. 1826 in Tennessee; widower; parents: Jocob HARMON and Eliza STEALMAN; death cause: "rheumatism and senility"; informant: J.F. HARMON (Moshiem); died: 16 Apr. 1918; record (1918) # 107.

DEVATI, Elizabeth; age: 55 years; married; parents: Bernett WATTS and Elizabeth MIMMS (South Carolina); death cause: "neuralgia"; informant: W.A. DEVATI (Greeneville); died: 16 Apr. 1918; buried: Cedar Hill; record (1918) # 108.

WRIGHT, Mary Bell; born: 18 Apr. 1891; married; parents: Jessie OSTEN (North Carolina) and Jane GULLEY; death cause: "pellagra"; informant: James OSTEN (Mohawk); died: 18 Apr. 1918; buried: Mt. Hope; record (1918) # 109.

SPEARS, David Frank; born: 21 Sep. 1885; married; parents: R.S. SPEARS and Georgia WOODS; death cause: "lobar pneumonia"; informant: Mrs. D.F. SPEARS (Greeneville); died: 19 Apr. 1918; record (1918) # 110.

RAMSEY, Infant; female; parents: Ebb RAMSEY and Carrie HAWKINS; death cause: "suffocation"; informant: father (Moshiem); died: 20 Apr. 1918; buried: Mt. Carmel; record (1918) # 111.

HUNTER, Benjamin F.; born: 6 Jan. 1842; widower; parents: Harrison HUNTER and Annie __; death cause: "organic heart disease"; informant: James WARD (Chucky); died: 24 Apr. 1918; record # 112.

HAMMET, Bessie; born: 21 Apr. 1909; parents: Frank HAMMET and Mattie WAITS; death cause: "appendicitis"; informant: Fait WRIGHT (Mohawk); died: 20 Apr. 1918; buried: Mt. Hope; record (1918) # 113.

HALL, William A.; born: 8 Feb. 1846; widower; parents: William HALL and Elizabeth BIDDLE (Blount County); death cause: "nephritis"; informant: David HALL (Limestone); died: 21 Apr. 1918; buried: Oak Grove; record (1918) # 114.

HUFFMAN, Louvellie Belle; born: 22 Apr. 1876; married; parents: William G. GRANT (VA) and Ruth BROWN; death cause: "broncho pneumonia"; informant: Mrs. M.H. HUFFMAN (Limestone); died; 22 Apr. 1918; buried: Pleasant Vale; record (1918) # 115.

REESE, L.C.; born: 3 Jan. 1917; parents: Dave REESE and Lucy HAINER (VA); death cause: "pneumonia"; informant: father (Greeneville); died: 24 Apr. 1918; buried: Oak Grove; record (1918) # 116.

COBBLE, Elizabeth S.; born: 26 Dec. 1833 in Tennessee; widow; parents: James SMITH and Sarah SMITH; death cause: "hemorrhage of lungs"; informant: L.M. COBBLE (Midway); died; 25 Apr. 1918; buried: Pine Grove; record (1918) # 117.

GRAY, Becky; born: __ Jun. 1886 in Unicoi County; married; parents: Simon LOYD (Madison County, NC.) and Emie MCCURRY (Washington County); death cause: "child bed fever"; informant: Dr. LOVE (Greeneville); died: 25 Apr. 1918; buried; Shelton; record # 118.

FRASIER, Abner Julian; born: 21 Mar. 1840; married; parents: Abner J. FRASIER and Jane DINWIDDIE; death cause: "valvulor heart disease"; informant: Walter FRAZIER; died: 26 Apr. 1918; buried: Oak Grove; record (1918) # 119.

HAWKINS, George W.; born: 10 Apr. 1856; married; parents: Charles HAWKINS and Betsie JORDAN (North Carolina); death cause: "tuberculosis of lungs"; informant: B.A. HAWKINS (Baileyton); died: 26 Apr. 1918; buried: Zion; record (1918) # 120.

CHANDLER, Hurley; born: 17 Apr. 1898; single; parents: John Wesley CHANDLER (Washington County) and Martha JACKSON (Washington County); death cause: "lobar pneumonia"; informant: father (Chucky); died: 27 Apr. 1918; buried: Ebeneezer; record # 121.

MALONEY, Phoebe Ann; born: 13 Sep. 1848; widow; parents: William JONES (Virginia) and Martha JACKSON (Virginia); death cause: "lagrippe"; informant: B.A. JEFFERS (Moshiem); died: 28 Apr. 1918; buried: Carters Station; record (1918) # 122.

BIRD, W.N.; born: 4 Jun. 1849; widower; parents: Simeon BIRD and Elnor WADELL; death cause: "articular rheumatism"; informant: Henry A. BIRD (Greeneville); died: 30 Apr. 1918; buried: Harrison Church; record (1918) # 123.

CLOYD, James William; born: 12 Mar. 1846; married; physician; parents: William CLOYD and Julia WORTHINGTON; death cause: "_(illegible) and gastric carcinoma"; informant: Thomas D. CLOYD (Moshiem); died: 30 Apr. 1918; buried; New Bethel; record # 124.

BALL, Charles D.; born: 12 Sep. 1887; single; parents; David BALL and Matilda MALONE; death cause: "pulmonary tuberculosis"; informant: father (Moshiem); died: 30 Apr. 1918; buried: Albany; record # 125.

BROOKE, Infant; female; parents: William BROOKE and Francis ORWOOD; death cause: "born dead"; informant: father (Greeneville); born/died: 11 Apr. 1918; buried: Burnett Chapel; record (1918) # 126.

BAXTER, Infant; female; parents: Robert C. BAXTER and Mona ENGLISH; death cause: "stillborn"; died in the 17th District, 14 Apr. 1918; buried: Bethany; record (1918) # 127.

WILLIS, Thomas Jefferson; born: 18 Jul. 1851 in North Carolina; married; parents: Jetson WILLIS (North Carolina) and Caroline LASTER (North Carolina); death cause: "pellagra"; informant: Mrs. T.J. WILLIS (Greeneville); died: 4 Mar. 1918; buried: Romeo; record (1918) # 128.

HOUSTON, Howel; born: 25 Feb. 1845; married; parents: William HOUSTON and Malinda BRUMFIELD; death cause: "hemorrhage of brain"; died in the 18th District, 4 May 1918; buried: Bersheba; record (1918) # 129.

PENLEY, English; born: 1 Jan. 1859 in Virginia; married; parents: English PENLEY Sr. (Virginia) and Jane EST_ (illegible); death cause: "heart failure"; informant: James PENLEY (Jeroldstown); died: 5 May 1918; record (1918) # 130.

ARWOOD, Rachel; born: 5 Apr. 1846; widow; parents: "unknown"; death cause: illegible; died: 7 May 1918; buried: Poor Farm; record (1918) # 131.

SMITH, Minnie; born: 16 Nov. 1883; married; parents: Joe MASON and Harriett SCRUGGS; death cause: "cancer of uterus"; informant: J.L.

SMITH (Greeneville); died: 10 May 1918; buried: New Hope; record (1918) # 132.

MYERS, Nancy Matilda; born: 8 Oct. 1874; single; teacher; parents: J.A. MYERS and Talitha CARTER; death cause: "pellagra"; informant: D.E. MYERS (Moshiem); died: 13 May 1918; buried: Antioc; record (1918) # 133.

GANNAWAY, Samuel; black; born: 16 May 1848 in Virginia; widower; parents: "unknown"; death cause: "pneumonia"; died in the 10th District, 16 May 1918; buried: Colored Cemetery; record (1918) # 135.

FRYE, Vel_ (illegible) Victor; born: 9 Feb. 1900; parents: Ulysses S. FRYE and Dovie A. COX; death cause: "tuberculosis of lungs"; died at Moshiem, 18 May 1918; buried: Mt. Sinai; record (1918) # 136.

SPEER, Angie Magnolia; born: 14 Feb. 1865; widow; parents: Abraham COLLINS and Liza TELLER; death cause: "pulmonary tuberculosis"; died in the 10th District, 21 May 1918; record (1918) # 137.

CONKIN, Saul; born: 6 Aug. 1856 in Sullivan County; married; parents: Hagans CONKIN (Sullivan County) and Banaba CONKIN (Sullivan County); death cause: "cancer of liver"; died 22 May 1918; buried: Pleasant Hill; record (1918) # 138.

GASS, Mrs. D.A.; born: 4 Feb. 1845; widow; parents: Robert A. BROWN and Anna BROWN; death cause: "apoplexy"; informant: W.H. GASS (Greeneville); died: 24 May 1918; buried: Gass Shed; record (1918) # 139.

SENEKER, Daniel William; born: 15 Apr. 1867; married; parents: John A. SENEKER and Margaret N. CRAWFORD; death cause: "catarrhal jaundice"; informant: Sam SENEKER (Moshiem); died: 26 May 1918; record (1918) # 140.

DEATHRIDGE, James Houston; born: 11 Aug. 1893; single; parents: William DEATHRIDGE and Alice BAXTER; death cause: "tubercular meningitis"; died: 29 May 1918; buried: Bethany Cemetery; record (1918) # 141.

HARDIN, Tebitha; age: 86 years; widow; parents: __ CHARLES (Hawkins County) and mother not stated; death cause: "senility"; informant: Charles HARDIN (Greeneville); died: 29 May 1918; buried: Hardin Cemetery; record (1918) # 142.

CANNON, William; black; born: 21 Dec. 1917; parents: Malone CANNON and Lizzie DENTON; death cause: "flux"; informant: Lizzie CANNON (Greeneville); buried: Colored Cemetery; record # 143.

DAY, Willie; born: 20 May 1918; parents: John Richard DAY and Delie Ethel MCAMIS; death cause: "stillborn"; informant: Tuck STEPP (Mohawk); died: 20 May 1918; buried; Fairview; record (1918) # 144.

FILLERS, Infant; female; parents: J.D. FILLERS and Mary WILSON; death cause: "born dead"; informant: father (Greeneville); died: 5 May 1918; buried: Cove Creek; record (1918) # 145.

NOL__, Susan; born: 1 May 1831; married; parents: John RICKER and Delilah LYLES; death cause: "senility and fractured femur": informant: C.H. LAMB (Greeneville); died: 1 Jun. 1918; buried: Cove Creek; record (1918) # 146.

DINSMORE, Infant; male; lived 17 days; parents: S.G. DINSMORE and __ JONES; death cause: not stated; informant: W.G. GRAY (Greeneville; died: 1 Jun. 1918; buried: Pisgah; record (1918) # 147.

BURGNER, Talbert; age: 52 years; widower; parents: Crystal BURGNER and mother unknown; death cause: "cancer"; informant: Mack BURGNER (Afton); died: 8 Jun. 1918; buried: Philadelphia, TN.; record (1918) # 148.

ROBINSON, Maggie E.; age: 62 years; married; parents: Lonzo YARBROUGH and Mary NORTHINGTON, death cause: "malignancy of uterus"; informant: F.R. ROBINSON (Greeneville); died: 2 Jun. 1918; record (1918) # 149.

GILBERT, Kenneth Garfield; born: 16 Dec. 1916 in North Carolina; parents: George R. GILBERT and Alice RICKER; death cause: "ilio colitis"; informant: Jennie WILLIAMS (Greeneville); died: 2 Jun. 1918; buried: Pine Springs; record (1918) # 150.

HORTON, John Charles; born: 11 Nov. 1868; married; parents: James M. HORTON (North Carolina) and Rachel WEAVER; death cause: "unknown"; informant: J.R. HORTON (Limestone); died: 8 Jun. 1918; buried: Pleasant Vale; record (1918) # 151.

HILL, Ida; black; born: 8 Apr. 1897; single; parents: B.J. HILL (Virginia) and Ezbll A__ (illegible)(South Carolina); death cause: "tuberculosis of lungs"; informant: father (Greeneville); died: 8 Jun. 1918; record # 152.

CRUM, Wilbur D.; age: 23 years, 10 months and 1 day; single; parents: E. CRUM and Martha A. TAYLOR; death cause: "potts disease"; informant: father (Greeneville); died: 10 Jun. 1918; buried: Red Hill; record (1918) # 153.

ANDERSON, Louis K.; born: 7 May 1918; parents: J.J. ANDERSON and Nora OLER; death cause: "unknown"; informant: father (Chucky); died: 11 Jun. 1918; buried: Stone Dam; record (1918) # 154.

RICKER, Mary Ruth; age: 47 years; married; parents: George WRIGHT and mother not stated; death cause: "tuberculosis"; informant: V.E. RICKER (Greeneville); died: 19 Jun. 1918; buried: Cedar Hill; record (1918) # 155.

MILLER, Eldridge; born: 7 Feb. 1918; parents: Spencer MILLER and Roxie __ (illegible); death cause: "gastro enteritis"; died in the 4th District, 20 Jun. 1918; buried: Stone Dam; record (1918) # 156.

LEONARD, Maud; born: 2 Jun. 1896; married; parents: Thomas RICKER and Maggie __ (illegible); death cause: "pulmonary tuberculosis"; informant: father (Greeneville); died: 20 Jun. 1918; buried: Mt. Hebron; record (1918) # 157.

SMITH, Herman; born: 22 Mar 1916; parents: J.H. SMITH and Bessie B. MCNEESE; death cause: "typhoid fever"; informant: father (Baileyton); died: 23 Jun. 1918; buried: Lebanon; record (1918) # 158.

HENSLEY, Ursley; age: 66 years; born: Madison County, NC.; married; parents: Roderick SHELTON (Madison County, NC.) and Polly KING (Madison County, NC.); death cause: "organic heart disease"; informant: B.G. HENSLEY (Greeneville); died: 23 Jun. 1918; buried: Mt. Hebron; record (1918) # 159.

BROWN, Louise J.; born: 17 Oct. 1844; widow; parents: Joshua BERRY and Sarah WHITE; death cause: "gastritis"; informant: S.L. PENNINGTON (Bulls Gap); died: 24 Jun. 1918; buried: Pleasant Hill; record (1918) # 160.

DICK, Margaret Ann; born: 6 Jul. 1839; widow; parents: Jonathan MILBURN and Nancy SHANKS; death cause: "nephritis"; informant: J.A. SHANKS (Limestone); died: 25 Jun. 1918; buried: Stratford, Iowa; record (1918) # 164.

WILSON, Robert F.; born: 30 Nov. 1871 in Mountain City, TN.; married; merchant; parents: Madison T. WILSON and Sarah RANKIN;

death cause: "pulmonary tuberculosis"; died: 26 Jun. 1918; buried: Cross Anchor; record (1918) # 162.

CRUMLEY, Milton J.; born: 9 Mar 1861 in Sullivan County; married; merchant; parents: D.J. CRUMLEY (Sullivan County) and Dortha HARKLEROAD (Sullivan County); death cause: "pulmonary tuberculosis"; informant: Mrs. M.J. CRUMLEY; died: 26 Jun. 1918; buried: Timber Ridge; record (1918) # 163.

MARTIN, Sevier M.; born: 7 Mar 1867; single; parents: Frank R. MARTIN and Rachel Eveline KNUCKLES; death cause: "pernicious __ (illegible)"; informant: Grant MARTIN (Limestone); died: 22 Jun. 1918; buried: Providence; record (1918) # 164.

YEAKLEY, George; age: 19 years; single; parents: Johnson YEAKLEY and Lura BASKETT; death cause: "pulmonary tuberculosis"; died in the 20th District, 27 Jun. 1918; buried: Mt. Zion; record (1918) # 165.

CRABTREE, Betsy; born: 16 Mar 1823 in Tennessee; single; parents: William CRABTREE and Easter STONECIPHER; death cause: "apoplexy (stroke)"; died in the 15th District, 28 Jun. 1918; buried: Union Temple; record (1918) # 166.

NEWBERRY, Naoma; born: 24 Dec. 1861 in Hawkins County; widow; parents: P.K. NEWBERRY and Jane HANES; death cause: "paralysis"; informant: J.N. NEWBERRY (Bulls Gap); died: 28 Jun. 1918; buried: Rogersville; record (1918) # 167.

TWEED, Viola; born: 10 Apr. 1911; parents: James TWEED (North Carolina) and mother's name illegible; death cause: "dysentery"; informant: A.J. STEPHENS (Greeneville); died in the 9th District, 28 Jun. 1918; record (1918) # 168.

LANE, Nancy B.; born: 1 Aug. 1888 in Scott County, VA.; single; invalid; parents: William LANE (Scott County, VA.) and Martha LANE (Scott County, VA.); death cause: "pneumonia"; informant: James LANE (Baileyton); died: 29 Jun. 1918; buried: Caney Creek; record (1918) # 169.

PAINTER, Infant; female; parents: Y.K. PAINTER and mother's name illegible; death cause: "premature birth"; informant: father (Chucky); died: 9 Jun. 1918; buried: Stone Dam; record (1918) # 170.

PAINTER, Infant; female; parents: Y.K. PAINTER and mother's name illegible; death cause: "premature birth"; informant: father (Chucky); died: 9 Jun. 1918; buried: Stone Dam; record (1918) # 171.

MYERS, Infant; female; parents: Charles E. MYERS and Julia A. CARVER; death cause: "stillborn"; informant: father (Moshiem); born/died: 21 Jun. 1918; buried: Albany; record (1918) # 172.

LONG, Infant; male; parents: Lawson LONG and Alice AVINS; death cause: "stillborn"; informant: father (Moshiem); died: 21 Jun. 1918; buried: Albany; record (1918) # 173.

LAUDERDALE, Infant; male; parents: Carl LAUDERDALE and Ethel GREGG; death cause: "born dead"; died: 21 Jun. 1918; buried: Piney Grove; record (1918) # 174.

WADDLE, Mamie Dollie; born: 13 Jun. 1916; parents: Peter WADDLE and Tinie CANNON; death cause: "cholera infantum"; informant: father (Greeneville); died: 3 Jul. 1918; record (1918) # 175.

MORROW, John; born: 8 Jun. 1844; married; parents: Adam MORROW and mother not stated; death cause: "myocarditis and bornchitis"; informant: Mrs. MORROW (Afton); died: 8 Jul. 1918; buried: Shilo; record (1918) # 176.

CUPP, J.O.; born: 19 Mar 1844 in Hawkins County; married; parents: John W. CUPP (Virginia) and Levana HECK (Virginia); death cause: "paralysis"; informant: Charley KITE (Bulls Gap); died: 8 Jul. 1918; buried: Phillips; record (1918) # 177.

SHELTON, Ev__ (illegible); born: 13 Sep. 1878 in North Carolina; married; parents: N__ (illegible) SHELTON (North Carolina) and Ina SHELTON (North Carolina); death cause: "bit by a copperhead snake"; informant: James RANDOLPH (Greeneville); died: 9 Jul. 1918; buried: Shelton Cemetery; record (1918) # 178.

RADER, Malissie J.; born: 15 Jan. 1848; married; parents: Billey PHILLIPS and Malissie J. PHILLIPS; death cause: "heart disease"; informant: T.L. RADER (Mohawk); died: 10 Jul. 1918; buried: Willoughbys; record (1918) # 179.

BLACK, Buford Binum; born: 22 Mar 1905; parents: W.A. BLACK and Elizabeth DOTSON; death cause: "pulmonary tuberculosis"; informant: father (Chucky); died: 10 Jul. 1918; record (1918) # 180.

WILLIAMS, Eliza; born: 8 Oct. 1848; single; parents: Fanner WILLIAMS and Nancy RUTHERFORD; death cause: "acute indigestion"; informant: J. WILLIAMS (Bulls Gap); died; 10 Jul. 1918; buried: Pilot Knob; record (1918) # 181.

SOUTHERLAND, Infant; male; age: 2 months; parents: Sam SOUTHERLAND and Gertie PARK; death cause: "unknown"; informant: T.J. SOUTHERLAND; died: 11 Jul. 1918; buried: Mt. Carmel; record (1918) # 182.

JOHNSON, Glena R.; born: 29 Sep. 1916; parents: G.A. JOHNSON and Ella HARRISON; death cause: "diarrhea"; informant: father (Kingsport); died: 13 Jul. 1918; buried: family cemetery; record # 183.

TAYLOR, Joshua; age: 1 year and 11 days; born: Cocke County; parents: John TAYLOR and Sallie S__ (illegible)(North Carolina); death cause: "whooping cough"; informant: father (Moshiem); died: 14 Jul. 1918; record (1918) # 184.

CONLEY, William James; parents: Joseph CONLEY (Washington County) and Pearl NELSON (Washington County); death cause: "atelictosis"; born/died in Baileyton, 14 Jul. 1918; buried: Milburnton; record (1918) # 185.

MCMILLAN, Nancy; black; born: 1 Jan. 1882; married; parents: Jonas FRESH and Louisa BLUE; death cause: "cancer of cervix and surgery"; informant: John BLUE (Mohawk); died: 15 Jul. 1918; buried: Midway; record (1918) # 186.

HARTMAN, Emma Virginia; born: 9 Aug. 1882; widow; parents: John A. REED and Attamira BRITTON; death cause: "tuberculosis"; informant: W.H. HARTMAN (Myers); died: 15 Jul. 1918; buried: Mt. Pleasant; record (1918) # 187.

KERBOUGH, Elizabeth; born: 23 Dec. 1841; widow; parents: Robert LISTER and Fannie GARRISON (Virginia); death cause: "lagrippe"; informant: Robert MORGAN (Greeneville); died: 17 Jul. 1918; buried: Oak Grove; record (1918) # 188.

VESTAL, Ruth Jane; born: 7 Apr. 1918; parents: Doak VESTAL and Beulah E__ (illegible); death cause: "whooping cough"; informant: Mrs. VESTAL (Afton); died: 17 Jul. 1918; record (1918) # 189.

HUX, Julia; age: 41 years; born: Jefferson County; married; parents: __ LANE and mother not stated; death cause: not stated; informant: B.C. HUX (Greeneville); died: 18 Jul. 1918; buried: Susong; record # 190.

HYDER, William Hartman; born: 7 Sep. 1901; parents: James E. HYDER and Dillie I. BEALS; death cause: "tubercular meningitis"; died in the 14th District, 18 Jul. 1918; buried: Mt. Zion; record (1918) #191.

GREGORY, Bertrum B.; born: 2 May 1917; parents: Andrew N. GREGORY and Mary RAY (North Carolina); death cause: "cholera infantum"; died at Afton, 20 Jul. 1918; buried: Mt. Zion; record # 192.

A__ (illegible, Infant; female; parents: Fred A__ (illegible) and Ada BURGNER; death cause: "premature birth"; born/died: 21 Jul. 1918; record (1918) # 193.

DEVOTIE; Beulah Marie; born: 3 Apr. 1916; parents: John DEVOTIE and Addie GREAR; death cause: "__ (illegible) poison (accidental)"; died at Chucky, 21 Jul. 1918; buried: Cedar Hill; record (1918) # 194.

DARNELL, Rena Alice; born: 23 Aug. 1917; parents: Namon DARNELL and May JOHNSON; death cause: "whooping cough and bronchitis"; informant: father (Greeneville); died: 22 Jul. 1918; buried: Harrisons; record (1918) # 195.

LAFOLLETTE, Sadie; age: 47 years; married; parents: William C. SMELCER and Tilda ELLIS; death cause: "typhoid fever"; informant: Clark LAFOLLETTE (Greeneville); died: 22 Jul. 1918; buried; Hartman Chapel; record (1918) # 196.

HENSLEY, John; born: 11 Feb. 1849; single; parents: Abraham HENSLEY and Polly SELLERS (North Carolina); death cause: "pellagra"; informant: W.B. HENDRY (Baileyton); died: 22 Jul. 1918; buried: Locust Springs; record (1918) # 197.

LOWE, James E.; age: 63 years; born: Knox County; married; parents: Alfred LOWE and Sinda WEST; death cause: "nephritis"; informant: J.P. LOWE (Greeneville); died: 24 Jul. 1918; buried: Oak Grove; record (1918) # 198.

WALDREP, Wallace; born: 2 May 1863 in Madison County, NC.; married; parents: "unknown"; death cause: "tuberculosis of bowels"; informant: Robert R. JONES (Greeneville); died: 25 Jul. 1918; buried: Gethsemnia; record (1918) # 199.

BOLES, Flora; born: 14 Oct. 1875; married; parents: Ruben DOTSON and Lucinda MYERS; death cause: "pulmonary tuberculosis"; informant: B.J. BOLES (Chucky); died: 26 Jul. 1918; record # 200.

GREENE, Mary Catherine; born: 15 Mar 1851 in Virginia; married; parents: "unknown"; death cause: "dysentery and paralysis"; informant: Jacob GREENE (Limestone); died: 28 Jul. 1918; record (1918) # 201.

HENRY, Ida V.; born: 14 Nov. 1876; married; parents: John HOPE and Martha GOODIN; death cause: "struck by lightening, died instantly"; informant: James R. HENRY (Midway); died: 29 Jul. 1918; buried: Pine Grove; record (1918) # 202.

MOTTERN, James M.; born: 14 Sep. 1964; married; parents; William MOTTERN and Elizabeth SMITH; death cause: "neuralgia"; informant: Dan MOTTERN (Midway); died: 31 Jul. 1918; buried: St. Josephs; record (1918) # 203.

WALDROP, Infant; female; parents: L.D. WALDROP and Catherine E. __; death cause: "stillborn"; informant: father (Greeneville); died: 6 Jul. 1918; buried: Price Cemetery; record (1918) # 204.

RUDDER, Infant; male; born: 8 Jul. 1918; parents: Calvin RUDDER and Ruth E. LONG; death cause: "premature birth"; informant: C.A. RUDDER (Moshiem); died: 8 Jul. 1918; buried: Mt. Sinai; record (1918) # 205.

CARTER, Infant; male; parents: Daniel CARTER and Lula E. SMITH; death cause: "placenta previa"; informant: D.G. CARTER (Moshiem); born/died: 28 Jul. 1918; buried: Albany; record (1918) # 206.

DERRY, Sarah Ellen; born: 10 Oct. 1916; parents: Earnest DERRY and Lula Bell TAYLOR (North Carolina); death cause: "whooping cough"; informant: father (Mohawk); died: 2 Aug. 1918; buried: Warrensburg; record (1918) # 209.

COLYER, Margaret; age: 74 years; widow; parents: father "unknown" and Margarette BROTHERTON; death cause: "pulmonary tuberculosis"; informant: D.D. WILSON (Greeneville); died: 3 Aug. 1918; buried: Albany; record (1918) # 208.

KILLIAN, Mary Isabel; born: 1 Apr. 1918; parents: Tom KILLIAN and Effie WILBUR; death cause: "diarrhea and enteritis"; informant: Dellie WILBUR (Midway); died: 4 Aug. 1918; buried: Bible Chapel; record (1918) # 209.

FOCHEE, Ella; born: 15 Sep. 1853; married; parents: William K. JOHNSON and Mary EVERHART; death cause: "dropsy"; informant: C.S. FOSHEE (Johnson City); died: 4 Aug. 1918; record # 210.

WILSON, Gurlie B.; age: 1 year and 4 months; parents: H.R. WILSON and Maggie HANEY; death cause: "cholera infantum"; informant: father (Greeneville); died: 4 Aug. 1918; buried: Cedar Hill; record # 211.

CRUMLEY, Mary Catherine; born: 24 Jul. 1854; married; parents: John RUSH and Ethel B. BRIGHT; death cause: "cirrhosis of liver"; informant: G.R. CRUMLEY (Baileyton); died: 4 Aug. 1918; buried: Gass Shed; record (1918) # 212.

BLANTON, William E.; born: 21 Jul. 1851 in South Carolina; widower; parents: Clayton BLANTON (South Carolina) and mother not stated; death cause: "acute indigestion and lock bowels"; informant: M.A. BLANTON (Moshiem); died: 5 Aug. 1918; buried: Blanton Cemetery; record (1918) # 213.

COGBURN, J.V.; age: 2 years; father "unknown" and Clete COGBURN; death cause: "unknown"; informant: J.E. FRESHOUR (Greeneville); died: 6 Aug. 1918; buried: Cedar Creek; record (1918) # 214.

WAMPLER, James; born: 24 Apr. 1843; married; parents: Soloman WAMPLER (Virginia) and Polly SIPE; death cause: "traumatic peritonitis"; informant: James A. WAMPLER (Moshiem); died: 8 Aug. 1918; record (1918) # 215.

NEAS, Noah; age: "about 70 years"; widower; parents: Henry NEAS and Lydia __; death cause: "unknown"; informant: J.C. WINTER (Greeneville); died: 8 Aug. 1918; buried: St. James; record (1918) # 216.

LOVE, Eliza; age: 38 years; single; parents: W.A. LOVE and Mary FRESHOUR; death cause: "stomach and kidney __ (illegible)"; informant: W.A. LOVE (Greeneville); died: 9 Aug. 1918; record # 217.

STYKE, Annie; born: 1 May 1856 in Virginia; married; parents: Jackson ROWLAND (Virginia) and Sarah DEBOARD (Marion, Virginia); death cause: "dropsy and French measles"; informant: W.M. STYKE (Mohawk); died: 9 Aug. 1918; buried: Fairview; record (1918) # 218.

OWENS, Mary J.; age: 67 years; married; parents: J.M. OVERHOLSER and Kerie WOOLSEY; death cause: "pneumonia and tuberculosis"; informant: William OVERHOLSER (Greeneville); died: 10 Aug. 1918; buried: Oak Grove; record (1918) # 219.

BLACKBURN, Wesley; age: "about 81 years"; poor asylum inmate; parents: "unknown"; death cause: "paralysis"; died: 11 Aug. 1918; buried: Poor Farm; record (1918) # 220.

GLASCOCK; Edna; age: 15 years; parents: J.T. GLASCOCK and Minnie ERWIN; death cause: "appendicitis and peritonitis"; informant: father (Mohawk); died: 11 Aug. 1918; buried: Fairview; record # 221.

REAVES, James W.; born: 27 Apr. 1881; married; miller; parents: E.M. REAVES and mother's name illegible; death cause: "sarcoma of __ (illegible); informant: N.H. REAVES (Greeneville); died; 11 Aug. 1918; buried: Mt. Tabor; record (1918) # 222.

REEDER, Patsy; black; age: 71 years; widow; parents: "unknown"; death cause: "pulmonary tuberculosis"; informant: C.G. REEDER (Greeneville); died: 13 Aug. 1918; buried: Wesley Cemetery; record # 223.

MILBURN, John Lilburn; born: 28 Nov. 1916; parents: W.M. MILBURN and Bessie ARMENTROUT; death cause: "diphtheria"; informant: W.R. MILBURN (Limestone); died: 14 Aug. 1918; buried: Milburnton; record (1918) # 224.

PETERS, Margaret Ellen; born: 20 Apr. 1918; parents: J. Dan PETERS and Maude A. DOWNEY; death cause: "acute indigestion"; informant: __ MAUPIN (Chucky); died: 15 Aug. 1918; record (1918) # 225.

WILSON, Sallie Jessie; born: 3 Jun. 1853 in South Carolina; married; parents: A.M. C__ (illegible)(South Carolina) and Louisa HAIGOOD (South Carolina); death cause: "tuberculosis"; informant: R.R. WILSON (Greeneville); died: 16 Aug. 1918; buried: Oak Grove; record (1918) # 226.

BIBLE, James K.; born: 7 Sep. 1839; divorced; parents: Billie BIBLE and mother "unknown"; death cause: "brights disease"; died at Midway, 17 Aug. 1918; record (1918) # 227.

MOORE, Orval; born: 16 Aug. 1880 in Washington County; married; parents: Henderson MOORE (Washington County) and Eliza SHAFER (Washington County); death cause: "accident, large truck passed over lower part of his body"; died at Chucky, 17 Aug. 1918; buried: Union Temple; record (1918) # 228.

MCLAIN, M.; infant; female; parents: Thomas M. MCLAIN (Hawkins County) and Leathie SELLERS; death cause: "spinal meningitis";

informant: J.M. MCLAIN (Baileyton); died: 18 Aug. 1918; buried: Lebanon; record (1918) # 229.

GUINN, Infant; male; parents: F.C. GUINN and Pearl RUSSELL; death cause: "delayed delivery"; informant: J.O. REYNOLDS (Greeneville); died: 20 Aug. 1918; buried: Cedar Hill; record (1918) # 230.

INGLE, Bell; age: not stated; married; parents: Terry KENN (?) and Polly HALE; death cause: "mitral regurgitation"; informant: Dr. WHITE (Fall Branch); died: 21 Aug. 1918; record (1918) # 231.

JUSTIS, Florra; born: 7 Jun. 1886; single; parents: father not stated and Lucinda JUSTIS; death cause: "pulmonary tuberculosis"; died: 21 Aug. 1918; buried: Gass Shed; record (1918) # 232.

BASHOR, Levy Benjamin; born: 3 Oct. 1868 in Washington County; married; parents: John C. BASHOR (Virginia) and Julia MILLER (Virginia); death cause: "accidental, by saw in saw mill"; died in the 11th District, 22 Aug. 1918; buried: Washington County; record # 233.

LAMB, Julia; born: 28 Jun. 1904 in Raburn County, Georgia; parents: John R. LAMB and Orpha LAMB (Georgia); death cause: "typhoid fever"; informant: J.M. LAMB (Greeneville) died: 22 Aug. 1918; buried: Lamb Cemetery; record (1918) # 234.

THOMPSON, Salina; born: 23 Sep. 1850; married; parents: Jefferson BROYLES and Mary BITNER; death cause: "diarrhea"; informant: Burnie THOMPSON (Chucky); died: 22 Aug. 1918; buried: Union Chapel; record (1918) # 235.

HARMON, Emma Cassander; born: 15 __ 1837; age: 80 years, 9 months and 9 days; parents: Thomas PHILLIPS and Catherine RIGHTSEL; death cause: "senile dementia"; informant: R.P. HARMON (Mohawk); died: 24 Aug. 1918; buried: Harmon Cemetery; record (1918) # 236.

BURNETT, James; age: "about 75 to 80 years"; born: North Carolina; widower; parents: "unknown"; death cause: "pulmonary tuberculosis"; informant: Floris HARMON (Greeneville); died: 25 Aug. 1918; buried: Fairview; record (1918) # 237.

HARRISON, Martha Caroline; born: 28 Jun. 1851; married; parents: Simeon BIRD and Elenor WADDLE; death cause: "cerebral embolism"; informant: Nina F. HARRISON (Greeneville); died: 26 Aug. 1918; buried: Harrison Cemetery; record (1918) # 238.

ANDERSON, Gussie; age: 51 years; married; parents: J.C. KELLER and Nancy ROSS; death cause: "typhoid fever"; informant: C.A. ANDERSON (Greeneville); buried: Gass Shed; record (1918) # 239.

LOWRY, Bonnie May; age: 7 months; parents: James LOWRY and Lizzie FRESHOUR; death cause: "whooping cough"; died: 28 Aug. 1918; buried: Cove Creek; record (1918) # 240.

JOHNSON, John S.; born: 14 May 1838; married; parents: Stephen JOHNSON and Elizabeth KIKER; death cause: "colitis"; informant: S.L. JOHNSON (Greeneville); died: 30 Aug. 1918; buried: Zion; record (1918) # 241.

ROBINSON, Infant; male; parents: John ROBINSON (Cocke County) and Loura BLAZER (Cocke County); death cause: "stillborn"; informant: J.B. BELL (Greeneville); born/died: 4 Aug. 1918; record (1918) # 242.

DOTY, Infant; sex: not stated; parents: Auldon DOTY and Pearl WEEMS; death cause: "stillborn"; informant: father (Baileyton); born/died: 7 Aug. 1918; buried: New Lebanon; record (1918) # 243.

GREENE, Infant; female; parents: John GREENE and Mary SEADGHTON; death cause: "stillborn"; informant: father (Greeneville); died: 16 Aug. 1918; buried: Oak Dale; record (1918) # 244.

SMITH, Infant: female; parents: Will SMITH and Liza RAGSDALE; death cause: "stillborn"; informant: R.L. BROWN (Greeneville); died; 21 Aug. 1918; buried: Gass Shed; record (1918) # 245.

FORTNER, Infant; female; parents: John FORTNER and Ada COX; death cause: "stillborn"; informant: G.W. COX (Greeneville); died: 25 Aug. 1918; buried: Fairview; record (1918) # 246.

BRANCH, Infant; female; parents: Amos BRANCH (North Carolina) and Butha BRADLY; death cause: "stillborn"; informant: father (Greeneville); died: 30 Aug. 1918; buried: Jonesbro; record (1918) # 247.

MCAMIS, William Pleasant Anderson; born: 19 Feb. 1832 in Greene County; widower; parents: John MCAMIS and __ HILL (Jefferson County); death cause: "general paralysis"; informant: J.F. DOTY (Baileyton); died: 1 Sep. 1918; buried: New Lebanon; record # 248.

CURTIS, Flora F.; born: _ Sep. 1917; parents: Val CURTIS and Abi FRAZER; death cause: "diphtheria"; died: 2 Sep. 1918; buried: Lovelace; record (1918) # 249.

CHAPMAN, Infant; male; parents: J.W. CHAPMAN (Washington County, VA.) and Hannah HARMON; death cause: "premature birth"; informant: father (Greeneville); died: 1 Sep. 1918; buried: Harmon Chapel; record (1918) # 250.

WILLIAMS, Ada L.; born: 16 Sep. 1883; married; parents: J.K.P. KELLER and Alice CRUMLEY; death cause: "typhoid fever"; informant: Ronil WILLIAMS (Baileyton); died: 3 Sep. 1918; buried: Zion; record (1918) # 251.

MORELOCK, Rufer Burton; born: 27 Oct. 1898; single; parents: William MORELOCK (Hawkins County) and Adaline SMITH; death cause: "nephritis"; informant: Phronie MORELOCK (Baileyton); died: 3 Sep. 1918; buried: New Lebanon; record (1918) # 252.

RAGAN, Walter Carr; born: 13 Aug. 1917; parents: Henry C. RAGAN and Bessie BEACH; death cause: "tuberculosis"; informant: mother (Midway); died: 3 Sep. 1918; record (1918) # 253.

BALL, Fred Manson; age: 7 years and 17 days; parents: Charles BALL and Iva MCAMIS; death cause: "diarrhea"; died: 8 Sep. 1918; buried: Zion; record (1918) # 254.

PENLEY, Elsie Lee; born: 27 Apr. 1917; parents: James PENLEY (Virginia) and Vinie MORELOCK (Hawkins County); death cause: "pulmonary tuberculosis"; died in the 17th District, 12 Sep. 1918; record (1918) # 255.

MALONE, Elbert; born: 27 Jun. 1903; parents: Don MALONE and Hiley GASS; death cause: "tuberculosis"; informant: C.E. DAVIS (Greeneville); died: 12 Sep. 1918; buried: Mt. Pleasant; record # 256.

PITTS, Clyde Edward; born: 20 Mar 1917; parents: Thomas PITTS and Osie CARTER; death cause: not stated; informant: father (Midway); died: 14 Sep. 1918; record (1918) # 257.

REED, Louisa; born: 8 Oct. 1877; single; parents: Robert REED and Susan MCNEESE; death cause: "pulmonary tuberculosis"; informant: J.J. REED (Limestone); died: 15 Sep. 1918; buried: Dixon Chapel; record (1918) # 258.

FOX, J.M.; age: "about 20 years"; single; parents: Gussie FOX and mother "unknown"; death cause: "pulmonary tuberculosis"; died: 15 Sep. 1918; buried: Poor Farm; record (1918) # 259.

CARTER, Mary; born: 12 Sep. 1843; widow; parents: V.D. SMITH and Lucy CARTER; death cause: "carcinoma of bowels"; informant: W.H. ARCHER (Baileyton); died: 16 Sep. 1918; buried: County Line; record (1918) # 260.

KILLIAN, Effie; age: "about 27 years; married; parents: Ben WILBURN (Virginia) and Ella KINSER; death cause: "pulmonary tuberculosis"; informant: Tom KILLIAN (Midway); died: 18 Sep. 1918; buried: Bible Chapel; record (1918) # 261.

SUSONG, Elizabeth; age: 46 years; single; parents: A.E. SUSONG and Esther GREGG; death cause: "pulmonary tuberculosis"; informant: W.A. SUSONG (Greeneville); died: 21 Sep. 1918; buried: Susong Memorial; record (1918) # 262.

NEAS, Paul; born: 12 Sep. 1918; parents: Erscine NEAS and A. COOPER; death cause: "unknown"; informant: Jacob NEAS; died: 26 Sep. 1918; buried: St. James; record (1918) # 263.

CRUM, Katie Sue; age: 13 years; parents: E. CRUM and Martha A. TAYLOR; death cause: "pulmonary tuberculosis"; informant: father (Greeneville); died: 26 Sep. 1918; buried: Red Hill; record # 264.

ANDES, Emma; age: 28 years; single; parents: Wesley ANDES and mother not stated; death cause: "tuberculosis of lungs"; informant: M.D. BRIGHT (Afton); died: 27 Sep. 1918; buried: Quaker Knob; record (1918) # 265.

B_ (illegible), Ellie; age: 18 years; parents: Joseph B_ (illegible) and Mollie PALMER, death cause: "typhoid fever"; died in the 10th District, 27 Sep. 1918; record (1918) # 266.

SNAPP, Jessie May; age: 60 years; single; parents: S.E. SNAPP and Caroline M. BROYLES; death cause: "pneumonia and influenza"; informant: H.R. SNAPP (Greeneville); died: 27 Sep. 1918; buried: Oak Grove; record (1918) # 267.

RUDDER, William F.; born: 8 Apr. 1884; married; parents: A.J. RUDDER and Mary DAY; death cause: "typhoid fever"; informant: A.C. MCDONALD (Moshiem); died: 28 Sep. 1918; buried: Pilot Knob; record (1918) # 268.

BEEMER, Susann; born: 8 Sep. 1852; widow; parents: Enic RECTOR and Pelela PRESS (Washington County); death cause: "general

paralysis"; informant: Phronia MORELOCK (Baileyton); died: 30 Sep.
1918; buried: Lebanon; record (1918) # 269.
NEAS, Pauline; born: 12 Sep. 1918; parents: Erscine NEAS and A.
COOPER; death cause: "unknown"; informant: Jacob NEAS (Greeneville); died: 30 Sep. 1918; buried: St. James; record (1918) # 270.
MORRISON, Cara; born: 2 Feb. 1895; married; parents: Joe
MORRISON and Emma BRITTON; death cause: "typhoid fever";
informant: W.A. MORRIS (Baileyton); died: 3 Oct. 1918; buried:
Salem; record (1918) # 271.
TWITTERY, Andrew Farmer; black; born: 3 Oct. 1908; parents: Henry
TWITTERY (Rutherford County, NC.) and Fannie GILLESPIE; death
cause: "influenza"; informant: father (Bulls Gap); died: 3 Oct. 1918;
buried: Drake; record (1918) # 272.
ESTEPP, James William; born: 24 Aug. 1918; parents: Amos ESTEPP
(Yancey County, NC.) and Ela HENSLEY (Allegheny County, NC.);
death cause: "hives"; died in the 21st District, 4 Oct. 1918; record
(1918) # 273.
HAWK, Earl; born: 5 Oct. 1813 in Philadelphia, Pennsylvania; married:
theatrical manager; parents: not stated; death cause: "pneumonia
following influenza"; informant: Mrs. Earl HAWK (Ohio); died: 5 Oct.
1918; record (1918) # 274.
ANDERSON, Sam; born: 15 Jan. 1898; single; parents: Vick
ANDERSON and Daisy LAUGHTER; death cause: "influenza and
pneumonia"; informant: Mrs. Vick ANDERSON (Greeneville); died: 6
Oct. 1918; buried: Oak Grove; record (1918) # 275.
SEATON, Holloway; age: 3 years; parents: John SEATON and Nellie
TAYLOR; death cause: "whooping cough"; informant: J.L. LOWRY
(Greeneville); died: 7 Oct. 1918; buried: Cove Creek; record # 276.
OTEY, C.N., Jr.; age: 32 years; born: Wytheville, Virginia; married;
parents: C.N. OTEY (Bedford, VA.) and Ella M. SCOTT (Wytheville,
VA.); death cause: "influenza and pneumonia"; informant: father
(Wytheville, VA.); died: 8 Oct. 1918; buried: Wytheville, VA.; record
(1918) # 277.
GILLESPIE, Robert J.; black; age: 24 years; married; parents: Charles
GILLESPIE and mother's name illegible; death cause: "pneumonia";

informant: Eugene GILLESPIE (Bulls Gap); died: 9 Oct. 1918; buried: Greeneville; record (1918) # 278.

LOVEDAY, Curtis Monroe; born: 1 Mar. 1897 in Sevier County; single; parents: William LOVEDAY (Sevier County) and __ SHAW; death cause: "pulmonary tuberculosis"; informant: W.A. SHAW (Moshiem); died: 10 Oct. 1918; buried: Pine Grove; record (1918) # 279.

ELLENBURG, Nannie E.; born: 6 Dec. 1884; married; parents: Thomas DEBURK and Cal ERVIN; death cause: "Spanish influenza, child birth contributory"; informant: W.W. ELLENBURG (Moshiem); died: 10 Oct. 1018; buried: Mt. Pleasant; record (1918) # 280.

LAUDERDALE, Eliza; born: 14 Jul. 1829 (duplicate record shows birth 4 Jul. 1829); born: Greene County; widow; parents: Robert E. COCHRAN and Margaret EVANS (Virginia); death cause: not stated; informant: Robert LAUDERDALE (Greeneville); died: 11 Oct. 1918; buried: Timber Ridge; record (1918) # 281.

HOLLAND, Susan; born: 12 Jan. 1864; married; parents: Alfred REYNOLDS and Lucy Jane MOYER; death cause: "tuberculosis of lungs"; informant: C.N. HOLLAND (Afton); died: 12 Oct. 1918; buried: Doty Cemetery; record (1918) # 282.

CANNON, J.M.; age: 67 years; married; parents: A. CANNON and Sallie CORWELL; death cause: "angina pectoris"; informant: R.C. RENNER (Greeneville); died: 13 Oct. 1918; buried: Cove Creek; record (1918) # 283.

SHANKS, Cy Moore; born: 4 Jun. 1915; parents: S.L. SHANKS and Golden MOORE; death cause: "whooping cough and ileo colitis"; informant: father (Jeroldstown); died: 14 Oct. 1918; record # 284.

LANE, Thomas; black; age: 42 years; married; parents: William LANE and mother "unknown"; death cause: "typhoid"; informant: Tennie LANE (Greeneville); died: 14 Oct. 1918; buried: Wesley Cemetery; record (1918) # 285.

KELLER, Josephine; age: 13 months; parents: John KELLER and Myrtle LOWRY; death cause: "influenza and pneumonia"; informant: A. TAYLOR (Greeneville); died: 15 Oct. 1918; buried: Cove Creek; record (1918) # 286.

HARMON, Infant; male; parents: V.S. HARMON and mother's name illegible; death cause: "whooping cough"; informant: J.N. HOLBROOK

(Greeneville); died: 15 Oct. 1918; buried: Kidwell Cemetery; record (1918) # 287.

MIDDLETON, James; born: 16 Sep. 1842 in North Carolina; widower; parents: Lafayette MIDDLETON (North Carolina) and mother "unknown"; death cause: "uremia"; died: 16 Oct. 1918; buried: Pleasant Hill; record (1918) # 288.

BROWN, Lydia Anna; born: 29 Mar. 1872 in Hawkins County; married; parents: John LUSTER (Hawkins County) and Hannah MORRISON; death cause: "septicemia of mouth and throat"; died at Baileyton, 16 Oct. 1918; buried: family cemetery; record (1918) # 289.

KELLER, Chassic; age: 3 years; parents: John KELLER and Myrtle LOWRY; death cause: "pneumonia and Spanish influenza"; informant: A. TAYLOR (Greeneville); died: 17 Oct. 1918; buried; Cove Creek; record (1918) # 290.

BERRY, Carry; age: 30 years; married; parents: Grant G. ARNOTT and Margarete PETIT; death cause: "dropsy"; informant: A.J. STANBERRY (Mohawk); died: 17 Oct. 1918; buried: Mt. Hope; record (1918) # 291.

CONDUFF, Infant; male; age: 18 days; parents: A.L. CONDUFF and Martha Ann OWENS; death cause: illegible; informant: F.M. CONDUFF (Cedar Creek); died: 17 Oct. 1918; buried: Cedar Creek; record (1918) # 292.

ELLENBURG, George Franklin, Jr.; born: 6 Oct. 1918; parents: Walter ELLENBURG and Nannie DEBURK; death cause: "inanition"; informant: father (Moshiem); died: 18 Oct. 1918; buried: Mt. Pleasant; record (1918) # 293.

RECTOR, Ortha; born: 18 Oct. 1892; age: 26 years; married; parents; father "unknown" and Mattie COPLER; death cause: "pneumonia fever"; informant: James RECTOR (Greeneville); died: 18 Oct. 1918; buried: Mt. Pleasant; record (1918) # 294.

ILLEGIBLE, Child's death record; child lived 1 day; record (1918) # 295.

TWITTY, Beatrice; black; age: 21 years; single; parents: Henry TWITTY and Fannie GILLESPIE; death cause: "influenza and pneumonia"; died in the 6th District, 21 Oct. 1918; buried: Drake Cemetery; record (1918) # 296.

CANNON, James; age: "about 70 years"; married; parents: not stated; death cause: "organic heart disease"; died in the 3rd District, 22 Oct. 1918; buried: Cove Creek; record (1918) # 297.

LAMONS, George G.; age: 50 years; married; wagon maker; parents: W.A. LAMONS and mother not stated; death cause: "cerebral hemorrhage"; informant: Henry LAMONS (Greeneville); died: 22 Oct. 1918; buried: Oak Grove; record (1918) # 298.

AYERS, Von; born: 22 May 1917; parents: Bert AYERS (North Carolina) and __ HENSLEY (North Carolina); death cause: "Spanish influenza"; informant: R.C. HENSLEY (Greeneville); died: 22 Oct. 1918; buried: St. James; record (1918) # 299.

STARNES, Mary; born: 3 Sep. 1858; married; parents: John LINEBAUGH nad Jennie A. MALONE; death cause: "diarrhea and enteritis"; informant: J.S. BROWN (Baileyton); died: 23 Oct. 1918; buried: Zion; record (1918) # 300.

DAVIS, Inez; black; age: 2 years; parents: Charles DAVIS (North Carolina) and Inez ALUMS; death cause: "influenza and pneumonia"; informant: Carl ALUM (Greeneville); died: 25 Oct. 1918; buried: Wesley Cemetery; record (1918) # 301.

BOWMAN, Lura; born: 25 Aug. 1917; parents: James BOWMAN and Lizzie ARWOOD; death cause: "could not get doctor, flu"; informant; father (Greeneville); died: 25 Oct. 1918; record (1918) # 302.

THOMPSON, Cornelius; born: 17 Dec. 1841 in North Carolina; widower; parents: John THOMPSON (North Carolina) and Margaret RINEHART (North Carolina); death cause: "apoplexy"; informant: Burnis THOMPSON (Chucky); died; 26 Oct. 1918; buried: Union Chapel; record (1918) # 303.

HARMON, Emily G.; born: 5 Apr. 1825 in Tennessee; widow; parents: Robert MALONEY and Emily COOPER; death cause: "dropsy"; informant: Dana HARMON (Greeneville); died: 26 Oct. 1918; buried: Oak Grove; record (1918) # 304.

BISHOP, Walter E.; born: 7 Oct. 1911; parents: Thomas E. BISHOP (North Carolina) and Sarah E. FLETCHER; death cause: "influenza and pneumonia"; informant: T.E. BISHOP (Greeneville); died: 27 Oct. 1918; buried: Red Hill; record (1918) # 305.

VINEABLE, Caroline; born: 4 Nov. 1848; widow; parents: "unknown"; death cause: "pneumonia"; died in the 10th District, 27 Oct. 1918; buried: Salem; record (1918) # 306.

SELF, John Luke; born: 23 Jun. 1914; parents: J. Emmett SELF and Ethel J. RUSSELL; death cause: "convulsions, tubercular spine"; informant: father (Moshiem); died: 27 Oct. 1918; record (1918) # 307.

RADER, James Richard; born: 11 Oct. 1918; parents: Charley RADER and Martha GREGORY; death cause: not stated; informant: father (Greeneville); died: 28 Oct. 1918; buried: Salem Chapel; record # 308.

HALL, Eveline; born: 30 Apr. 1839 in Tennessee; married; parents: Pleasant JOHNSON (Hawkins County) and Francis GRAVES (Knox County); death cause: "unknown"; informant: J.A. HALL (Mohawk); died: 29 Oct. 1918; record (1918) # 309.

ELLIS, __ (illegible); female; born: 31 Oct. 1916; parents: Jack ELLIS and Jossie LAUGHLIN; death cause: "pneumonia fever"; informant: Mate ALEXANDER (Greeneville); died: 31 Oct. 1918; buried: Shilo; record (1918) # 310.

WHEELER, Infant; parents: James WHEELER and Pearl RIDDLEY; death cause: "suffocation"; informant: father (Bulls Gap); born/died: 19 Oct. 1918; record (1918) # 312.

RIPPETOE, Eliza Annie; born: 28 Jan. 1834; widow; parents: James COURTNEY and __ MCBROOM (North Carolina); death cause: "pneumonia"; died in the 6th District, 31 Oct. 1918; buried: Bent Creek; record (1918) # 311.

SHANKS, Billie; born: 3 Dec. 1917; parents: William R. SHANKS and Lillie BRANDON; death cause: "influenza and pneumonia"; died: 1 Nov. 1918; buried: Pleasant Hill; record (1918) # 313.

SWINEY, J.W.; age: 83 years; born: Carter County; widower; parents: James SWINEY and __ OLIVER; death cause: "nephritis"; informant: T.A. SWINEY (Greeneville); died: 2 Nov. 1918; buried: Fairview; record (1918) # 314.

ANDERSON, William George; born: 2 Sep. 1841; widower; parents: William ANDERSON and Eva HURLEY; death cause: "prostitis"; informant: J.C. ANDERSON (Mohawk); died: 2 Nov. 1918; buried: Bible Cemetery; record (1918) # 315.

FRYE, Hazel Pauline; born: 5 Mar. 1918; parents: John FRYE and Rebecca BARNES; death cause: "unknown"; informant: A.J. BARNES (Bulls Gap); died: 3 Nov. 1918; buried: Mt. Carmel; record # 316.

DAVIS, Catherine; born: 11 May 1912; parents: U.J. DAVIS and Jessie SMITH; death cause: "cardiac dropsy"; informant: father (Mohawk); died: 3 Nov. 1918; buried: Jernigan Cemetery; record (1918) # 317.

FRYE, Martha Pauline; born: 3 Mar. 1918; parents: John FRYE and Rebecca BARNES; death cause: not stated; informant: Jack BARNES (Moshiem); died: 4 Nov. 1918; buried: Mt. Carmel; record # 318.

IDELL, Maggie E.; born: 10 Nov. 1986; married; parents: "unknown"; death cause: "influenza and pneumonia"; informant: Henry IDELL (Midway); died: 4 Nov. 1918; buried: Moshiem; record (1918) # 319.

MITCHELL, Eliza; born: 16 Aug. 1894; single; parents: William MITCHELL and Dora E. THOMPSON; death cause: "influenza"; informant: father (Chucky); died: 4 Nov. 1918; buried: Cedar Grove; record (1918) # 320.

MITCHELL, John B.; age: 57 years, 5 months and 19 days; married; parents: not stated; death cause: "cirrhosis of liver"; informant: James MITCHELL (Greeneville); died: 5 Nov. 1918; buried: Oak Grove; record (1918) # 321.

DEATHRIDGE, Melvina; born: 19 Oct. 1841; widow; parents: William LOYD and Jane TADLOCK; death cause: "general breakdown"; informant: M.M. PULLIAM (Jeroldstown); died: 6 Nov. 1918; buried: Bethany Church; record (1918) # 322.

WILLIAMS, John Thomas; born: 1 Jul. 1836; widower; parents: "unknown"; death cause: "arterio sclerosis"; informant: Joe F. WILLIAMS (Limestone); died: 6 Nov. 1918; record (1918) # 323.

DUGGER, Infant; male; parents: S.A. DUGGER and Elizabeth BABB; death cause: "unknown, found dead in bed"; informant: father (Greeneville); died: 6 Nov. 1918; buried: Gass Shed; record (1918) # 324.

MARTIN, Frank; born: 27 Jun. 1835 in Tennessee; married; parents: Lewis P. MARTIN and Deborah REGISTER; death cause: "influenza"; informant: Grant MARTIN (Limestone); died: 6 Nov. 1918; buried: Providence; record (1918) # 325.

MATHES, George; born: 4 Aug. __; age: 71 years; widower; parents: James MATHES and mother "unknown"; death cause: "nephritis";

informant: J.D. MATHES (Mohawk); died; 7 Nov. 1918; buried: Fairview; record (1918) # 326.

REESER, Jessie Roscoe; born: 31 Aug. 1889; married; parents: Joseph M. REESER and Anna DOTSON; death cause: "epileptic convulsions, apoplexy"; informant: father (Limestone); died: 8 Nov. 1918; buried: Pleasant Vale; record (1918) # 327.

BLAZER, Aneglilne; born: 22 Dec. 1849; widow; parents: Wes SWATZEL and mother "unknown"; death cause: "organic heart disease"; informant: Blane RENNER (Greeneville); died: 8 Nov. 1918; buried: Caney Branch; record (1918) # 328.

HARTSELL, George H.; born: 27 May 1862 in Bedford, Pennsylvania; married; teacher; parents: Sebastian HARTSELL (Pennsylvania) and __ DIBORD (Pennsylvania); death cause: "tuberculosis"; informant: Mary L. HARTSELL (Limestone); died: 9 Nov. 1918; buried: Pleasant Vale; record (1918) # 329.

PITT, Florence; age: "about 33 years"; married; parents: John ARMSTRONG and Bet HALL; death cause: "influenza and typhoid fever"; died in the 17th District, 10 Nov. 1918; buried: Lovelace; record # 330.

JONES, Ada; born: 9 Dec. 1896 (?); age shown as: 12 years, 6 months and 1 day; parents: William JONES and E. WHEELER; death cause: "influenza and pneumonia"; died in the 7th District, 10 Nov. 1918; buried; Pilot Knob; record (1918) # 331.

MORRISON, Cora Pearl; born: 2 Oct. 1918; parents: Samuel MORRISON and Cora MORRIS; death cause: "premature birth"; informant: father (Baileyton); died: 10 Nov. 1918; buried: Salem; record (1918) # 332.

BRUNER, Minnie; born: 28 Feb. 1903; parents: Abner BRUNER and Exilonia VAUGHN; death cause: "pneumonia and influenza"; informant: Charles Davis (Baileyton); died: 12 Nov. 1918; buried: Caney Creek; record (1918) # 333.

KIDWELL, Mariah; born: 8 Jun. 1855; single; parents: Josiah KIDWELL (Jefferson County) and Eliza COUCH; death cause: "organic heart disease"; informant: J.F. BROTHERTON (Moshiem); died: 12 Nov. 1918; buried: Couch Cemetery; record (1918) # 334.

WARDEN, Roy Jr.; born: 8 Mar. 1918; parents: Roy WARDEN and Jennie May BARHAM; death cause: "influenza and pneumonia";

informant: father (Greeneville); died: 12 Nov. 1918; buried: Oak Grove; record (1918) # 335.

WILBURN, C.C.; age: 73 years; born: Virginia; married; parents: Benjamin WILBURN (Virginia) and Nancy STALEY (Virginia); death cause: "cerebral __ (illegible) and gangrene"; informant: Ross KINGSLEY (Greeneville); died: 13 Nov. 1918; buried: Mohawk; record (1918) # 336.

WALKER (?), Cynthia Florence; born: 8 Aug. 1855 in Virginia; parents: John S__ (illegible) and mother's name illegible; death cause: "peri corditis"; died: 16 Nov. 1918; buried: Cedar Hill; record (1918) # 337.

REYNOLDS, Eula Blanch; born: 9 Oct. 1913; parents: George REYNOLDS and Vernie HYDER; death cause: "intestinal obstruction"; informant: father (Baileyton); died: 16 Nov. 1918; buried: Mt. Zion; record (1918) # 338.

WILLETT, W.G.; born: 2 Oct. __; age: 60 years, 1 month and 15 days; married; parents: __ WILLETT and __ JOHNSON; death cause: "influenza and pneumonia"; informant: A.F. WILLETT (Bristol, VA.); died in the 13th District, 17 Nov. 1918; record (1918) # 339.

WOOLSEY, Alice; born: 11 Jan. 1825 in Greene County; widow; parents: David BIRD and Mary BIRD; death cause: "angina pectoris"; informant: F.H. WOOLSEY (Greeneville); died: 17 Nov. 1918; buried: Harrison Cemetery; record (1918) # 340.

CATRON, Columbus C.; age: 59 years, 2 months and 2 days; married; parents: Andrew CATRON and mother not stated; death cause: "nephritis"; informant: M.L. COBBLE (Midway); died: 17 Nov. 1918; buried: Sinking Springs; record (1918) # 341.

SAUCEMAN, Assalia; born: 13 Mar. 1866; married; parents: __ WHITTENBURG and Catherine BOLES; death cause: "influenza"; informant: J.T. SHIELDS (Greeneville); died: 19 Nov. 1918; buried: Pine Grove; record (1918) # 342.

SMITH, Augusta; born: 28 Oct. __; age: 17 years; single; parents: Will SMITH and Mattie TADLOCK (Washington County); death cause: "carcinoma of thyroid"; informant: W.M. SMITH (Baileyton); died: 19 Nov. 1918; buried: Oak Dale; record (1918) # 343.

HUMPHRIES, P.G.; born: 2 Nov. 1836 in Carter County; married; parents: Jessie HUMPHRIES (Pennsylvania) and Eliza HUGHES; death cause: "old age"; informant: M.F. HUMPHRIES (Greeneville); died: 21 Nov. 1918; buried: Cove Creek; record (1918) # 344.

TWEED, Jules; born: 4 Oct. 1884 in North Carolina; married; parents: Anson TWEED (North Carolina) and Elsie GILLAND; death cause: "unknown"; died in the 10th District, 21 Nov. 1918; buried: Bersheba; record (1918) # 345.

LINEBAUGH, Jacob; born: 14 Sep 1840; married; parents: Daniel LINEBAUGH and Kate LINEBAUGH; death cause: "organic heart disease"; informant: John M. LINEBAUGH (Baileyton); died: 23 Nov. 1918; buried: Zion; record (1918) # 346.

COX, Hattie; age: 25 years; married; parents: Jack JONES and __ DICKSON; death cause: "typhoid fever"; informant: S.J. MALONE (Greeneville); died: 24 Nov. 1918; buried: Malone Cemetery; record (1918) # 348.

MIDDLETON, James N.; age: "about 78 years; married; minister; parents: not stated; death cause: "paralysis"; informant: R.O. HUFFAKER (Greeneville); died: 23 Nov. 1918; buried: Strawberry Plains; record (1918) # 347.

KIMBELL, John; born: 25 Dec. 1910 in Virginia; parents: "unknown"; death cause: "lagrippe"; informant: W.J. WISOR (Greeneville); died: 26 Nov. 1918; buried: Seven Mile Ford; record (1918) # 349.

HENDERSON, Susan; black; age: 41 years; married; parents: __ GIBBS and mother "unknown"; death cause: "influenza"; died in the 10th District, 28 Nov. 1918; buried: Wesley Cemetery; record (1918) # 350.

BIRD, Virginia; born: 8 Jul. 1918; parents: Scot BIRD and Dollie PARK; death cause: "unknown"; informant: John PARK (Greeneville); died: 28 Nov. 1918; buried: Cove Creek; record (1918) # 351.

PIERCE, Rebecca J.; age: 76 years; widow; parents: __ PRITCHARD and mother not stated; death cause: "cerebral hemorrhage"; informant: E.P. PIERCE (Greeneville); died: 29 Nov. 1918; buried: Oak Grove; record (1918) # 352.

MORRISON, William M.; age: 3 years; parents: W.E. MORRISON and Ethel HARMON; death cause: "influenza and pneumonia"; informant: father (Greeneville); died: 29 Nov. 1918; buried: Oak Grove; record (1918) # 353.

MOORE, James Dexter; born: 26 Aug. 1908; parents: James J. MOORE and Sallie JONES; death cause: "accidentally hit in the stomach by flying __ (illegible)"; died: 30 Nov. 1918; record (1918) # 354.

SWATSELL, Infant; male; parents: Edgar SWATSELL and Cordie P_ (illegible); death cause: "stillborn"; informant: father (Greeneville); died: 2 Nov. 1918; buried: Harmons; record (1918) # 355.

PRESSLEY, Infant; male; parents: Harrison PRESSLEY and Mollie CARTER; death cause: "unknown"; born/died at Moshiem on 17 Nov. 1918; record (1918) # 356.

HARMON, Rufus; age: 55 years; married; parents: John HARMON and mother "unknown"; death cause: "influenza and pneumonia"; died in the 10th District, 1 Dec. 1918; buried: Mt. Vernon; record (1918) # 357.

GREENWAY, John; age: not stated; married; parents: James GREENWAY and Catey CANNON (Washington County); death cause: "pulmonary tuberculosis"; died: 2 Dec. 1918; buried: Susong Cemetery; record (1918) # 358.

ARTENBERRY, Elizabeth; born: 29 Mar. 1855; widow; parents: John B. BROWN and Terthenia NEAL; death cause: "influenza and bronchitis"; informant: P.D. ARTENBERRY (Afton); died: 2 Dec. 1918; buried: Gass Shed; record (1918) # 357.

FILLERS, Connie; age: 4 years; parents: Maynard FILLERS and Lizzie GREENE; death cause: "diphtheria"; informant: Scott FILLERS (Greeneville); died: 2 Dec. 1918; buried: Mt. Tabor; record # 360.

BROYLES, C.F.; born: 18 Oct. 1899; single; parents: Lon BROYLES and __ WILHOIT; death cause: "influenza and pneumonia"; informant: N.T. CONSTABLE (Greeneville); died: 2 Dec. 1918; buried: Red Hill; record (1918) # 361.

HANKINS, Harold; age: 4 months; parents: T.R. HANKINS and Clodie HARMON; death cause: "influenza and pneumonia"; informant: Ross GASS; died: 4 Dec. 1918; buried: Kidwell; record (1918) # 362.

HANKINS, Ruth; age: 5 years; parents: T.R. HANKINS and Clodie HARMON; death cause: "influenza and pneumonia"; informant: Ross GASS; died: 4 Dec. 1918; buried: Kidwell; record (1918) # 363.

BRADFORD, Ebba M.; age: 51 years; born: Vienna, Austria; married; parents: Carl STRAUB (Munich, Germany) and Henrietta SCHIELFORTH (Germany); death cause: "dropsy and Brights disease";

informant: C.S. BRADFORD (Greeneville); died: 4 Dec. 1918; record (1918) # 364.

CHARLTON, Maney; age: 21 years; single; parents: Harvy CHARLTON and Sarah DYKES; death cause: "influenza and tuberculosis"; died in the 17th District, 5 Dec. 1918; record # 365.

HAYS, Calmer Jessie; born: 9 Sep. 1918; parents: Jessie P. HAYS and Ella SMITH; death cause: "gastritis"; died at Jeroldtown, 3 Dec. 1918; buried: Pleasant Hill; record (1918) # 366.

DAVIS, John T.; born: 15 May 1847; married; parents: Thomas DAVIS and Martha HARTMAN; death cause: "brights disease"; informant: W.F. DAVIS (Greeneville); died: 5 Dec. 1918; buried: Oak Grove; record (1918) # 367.

BROOKS, Henry Allen; born: 4 Aug. 1915; parents: W.C. BROWN and Bessie GRAY; death cause: "influenza and pneumonia"; died: 5 Dec. 1918; buried: Pisgah; record (1918) # 368.

BOYD, Nolen; age: 15 years, 1 month and 4 days; parents: John P. BOYD and Elvina _ (illegible); death cause: "rheumatism"; informant: S.P. SENEKER (Moshiem); died: 5 Dec. 1918; buried: Craft Cemetery; record (1918) # 369.

CRITSELOUS, Noah R.; born: 8 Oct. 1854; married; parents: John CRITSELOUS and Jennie OTTINGER; death cause: "cancer of kidney"; informant: Luther CRITSELOUS (Greeneville); died: 6 Dec. 1918; record (1918) # 370.

CANNON, Willie Bell; age: 35 years and 3 months; single; parents: Ike CANNON and mother "unknown"; death cause: "pulmonary tuberculosis"; informant: Will MONTGOMERY (Greeneville); died: 1 Dec. 1918; record (1918) # 371.

HANKINS, Harmon; age: 4 years; parents: T.R. HANKINS and Clodie HARMON; death cause: "influenza and pneumonia"; informant: Ross Gass (Greeneville); died: 6 Dec. 1918; buried: Kidwell; record # 372.

EVERHART, Nancy Ellen; born: 31 May 1877; married; parents: Jack EVANS and Lucinda MELTON; death cause: "influenza and tuberculosis"; informant: Charles R. EVERHART (Mohawk); died: 7 Dec. 1918; buried: Phillips; record (1918) # 373.

HUFF, Wilson; born: 14 Feb. 1866; married; parents: John HUFF and M. SMITH; death cause: "mitral insufficiency"; informant: E.B. HUFF (Greeneville); died: 7 Dec. 1918; buried: Pine Grove; record # 374.

VANCE, Troy C.; born: 8 Nov. 1869 in North Carolina; married; merchant; parents: James VANCE (North Carolina) and Mary BUTLER (North Carolina); death cause: "appendicitis"; died in the 10th District, 7 Dec. 1918; buried: Oak Grove; record (1918) # 375.

VAUGHN, Lucille; born: 21 Mar. 1918; parents: Wiley VAUGHN and Phoebe BROWN; death cause: "influenza and pneumonia"; died in the 11th District, 8 Dec. 1918; buried: Ottway; record (1918) # 376.

CARTWRIGHT, Carl Otho; born: 16 Oct. 1917; parents: A.O. CARTWRIGHT and Rutha SOLOMAN; death cause: "influenza and pneumonia"; informant: father (Greeneville); died: 8 Dec. 1918; buried: Ottway; record (1918) # 377.

STARNES, Lorence Vernon; born: 8 Oct. 1917; parents: Ott STARNES and Lula BROWN; death cause: "broncho pneumonia"; informant: father (Baileyton); died: 8 Dec. 1918; buried: Underhill Cemetery; record (1918) # 378.

MALONE, Dora C.; born: 30 Sep. 1883; married; parents: Samuel LINEBAUGH and Kate MALONE; death cause: "septicemia, child bed fever"; died at Afton on 8 Dec. 1918; buried: Fairview; record # 379.

DODD, Maxine; age: 1 year and 1 month; parents: Coon DODD and May PARKS; death cause: "influenza and pneumonia"; informant: father (Greeneville); died: 9 Dec. 1918; buried: Hebron; record (1918) # 380.

PHILLIPS, Nellie May; born: 14 Jun. 1918; parents: A.L. PHILLIPS and C_ (illegible) CONSTABLE; death cause: "pneumonia"; informant: mother (Greeneville); died: 9 Dec. 1918; buried: Oak Grove; record (1918) # 381.

MYSINGER, Augustus H.; born: 10 Apr. 1881; married; parents: John MYSINGER (North Carolina) and Mary E. BIBLE; death cause: "influenza and tubercular spasms"; died in the 8th District, 10 Dec. 1918; buried: Mt. Pleasant; record (1918) # 382.

HOLLEY, Lawrence W.; age: not stated; married; parents: J.P. HOLLEY and Allig JONES; death cause: "influenza and pneumonia"; informant: Mrs. Bruce HARRISON (Greeneville); died: 10 Dec. 1918; buried: Mt. Hebron; record (1918) # 383.

CONSTABLE, Sam; born: 18 Dec. 1892; married; parents: N.T. CONSTABLE and Eva KING; death cause: "Spanish flu and pneumonia"; informant: John CONSTABLE (Roanoke, VA.) died: 10 Dec. 1918; buried: Cedar Hill; record (1918) # 384.

BROYLES, Pearl; age: 16 years; parents: Lon BROYLES and __ WILHOIT; death cause: "influenza and pneumonia"; informant: father (Greeneville); died: 11 Dec. 1918; buried: Red Hill; record # 385.

MORELOCK, Nancy; born: 2 Apr. 1883; married; parents: Will W. JEFFERS and Finey MALONE; death cause: "pulmonary tuberculosis"; informant: T.L. MORELOCK (Baileyton); died: 11 Dec. 1918; buried: Mountain Valley; record (1918) # 386.

EALY, Robert; age: 43 years; single; parent: James EALY and Jane RECTOR; death cause: "influenza and pneumonia"; informant: Will ROBERTS (Greeneville); died: 12 Dec. 1918; buried: Cedar Hill; record (1918) # 387.

HEDDEN, Consel Lee; born: 10 Jul. 1918; parents: William HEDDEN (North Carolina) and Lavina KELLER (Washington County); death cause: "broncho pneumonia"; died in the 16th District, 12 Dec. 1918; buried: Liberty Hill; record (1918) # 388.

BABB, Fanny Bell; born: 30 Dec. 1914; parents: Rufus BABB and Minnie KELTON; death cause: "influenza and pneumonia"; informant: S.W. DOTY (Afton); died: 12 Dec. 1918; record (1918) # 389.

HENRY, Allen; black; age: 83 years; single; parents: "unknown"; death cause: "syphilis"; died in the 10th District, 13 Dec. 1918; buried: Poor Farm; record (1918) # 390.

BROOKS, William; born: 13 Nov. 1917; parents: W.C. BROOKS and Bessie GRAY; death cause: "influenza and pneumonia"; died: 13 Dec. 1918; buried: Pisgah; record (1918) # 391.

HUNTSMAN, Grafford E.; born: 23 dec. 1903; parents: James Butler HUNTSMAN and Nelie ROARK; death cause: "influenza"; informant: father (Bulls Gap); died: 13 Dec. 1918; buried: Phillipi; record # 392.

LONG, Mary Elizabeth; born: 9 Feb. 1916; parents: Ira LONG and Minnie BULLINGTON; death cause: "pneumonia"; died at Moshiem, 13 Dec. 1918; buried: Willoughby; record (1918) # 393.

KESTERSON, Jacob Elbert; born: 16 Jan. 1889; married; parents: John KESTERSON and Nan REDINOUR; death cause: "Spanish influenza"; died in the 6th District, 13 Dec. 1918; buried: Mt. Hope; record # 394.

HARRISON, Lora; born: 5 Oct. 1914; parents: John HARRISON and Una MORELOCK; death cause: "whooping cough"; informant: father (Baileyton); died: 14 Dec. 1918; buried: Bernards; record (1918) # 395.

BAILEY, Mrs. George; age: "about 65 years"; widow; parents: "unknown"; death cause: "broncho pneumonia"; informant: Isaac SMITH (Jeroldstown); died: 14 Dec. 1918; buried: Pleasant Hill; record (1918) # 396.

COX, Alice; born: 4 May 1854; widow; parents: Milton ARCHER and Lucinda ROGERS; death cause: "influenza"; informant: Hugh COX (Chucky); died: 15 Dec. 1918; buried: Sulfur Springs, Washington County; record (1918) # 397.

RAMSEY, Johnie; age: 5 months; parents: George RAMSEY and Mattie RAMSEY; death cause: "influenza"; informant: Samantha SNYDER (Greeneville); died: 15 Dec. 1918; buried: Oak Grove; record # 398.

GRAY, Rucy J.; age: 66 years; married; parents: S. RAMBO and Sallie HARRISON; death cause: "pulmonary tuberculosis"; informant: Peggy GRAY (Greeneville); died: 18 Dec. 1918; buried: Pisgah; record # 399.

DUCK, Rexter; born: 15 Dec. 1888; married; parents: Daniel DUCK and Rachel FELLER; death cause: "lagrippe and pneumonia"; informant: W.B. DUCK (Greeneville); Died: __ Dec. 1918; buried: Mt. Hebron; record (1918) # 400.

JOHNSON, Mrs. T.F.; born: 10 May 1877; married; parents: James MILLER and Vina E. BOWERS; death cause: "tuberculosis of bowels"; informant: J.A. BROYLES (Greeneville); died: 19 Dec. 1918; buried: Red Hill; record (1918) # 401.

TAYLOR, Marvin Paul; born: 5 Sep. 1917; parents: Joe TAYLOR and __ (illegible) SMITH; death cause: "influenza and pneumonia"; died: 19 Dec. 1918; buried: Oak Grove; record (1918) # 402.

SMELCER, John M.; born: 24 Dec. 1882; married; parents: Ike SMELCER and Jennie HOPE; death cause: "influenza"; died: 19 Dec. 1918; buried: Hamons; record (1918) # 403.

SHANKS, James R.; born: 15 Apr. 1862; married; parents: Robert SHANKS and Mary Ann GIBSON; death cause: "apoplexy"; informant:

Mrs. J.R. SHANKS (Afton); died: 20 Dec. 1918; buried: Stone Dam; record (1918) # 404.

HUNTSMAN, Minnie B.; born: 28 Nov. 1918; parents: James B. HUNTSMAN and Ethel HAUN; death cause: "premature, mother had influenza"; informant: father (Bulls Gap); died: 22 Dec. 1918; buried: Phillips; record (1918) # 405.

FOSHE, Georgia L.; age: 33 years; married; parents: William KELLER and Jennie ROSS; death cause: "pneumonia and influenza was 8 months pregnant"; informant: John FOSHE (Greeneville); died: 22 Dec. 1918; buried: Gass Shed; record (1918) # 406.

RAZAR, Mary Elizabeth Cobble; born: 7 Apr. 1886; married; parents: Marion COBBLE and __ (illegible) MOFFET; death cause: "influenza"; informant: S.E. RAZAR (Midway); died: 23 Dec. 1918; record # 407.

MYSINGER, Harrold; born: 27 Dec. 1917; parents: Will MYSINGER and Fay CONSTABLE; death cause: "unknown, found dead in bed"; informant: father (Greeneville); died: 23 Dec. 1918; buried: Mt. Bethel; record (1918) # 408.

WISECAREN (?) __(?); female; born: 25 Oct. 1881 in Texas; married; parents: Joseph DAY and Martha LANE; death cause: "abortion followed by __ (illegible) fever"; died: 24 Dec. 1918; buried: Fairview; record (1918) # 409.

COFFEE, Mrs. Melvina; age: 83 years; born: Hawkins County; widow; parents: "unknown"; death cause: "organic heart disease"; died at Baileyton, 25 Dec. 1918; buried: family cemetery; record (1918) # 410.

MCKEE, Robert M.; born: 20 Dec. 1834; widower; retired lawyer; parents: John MCKEE (Ireland) and E. ANDERSON; death cause: "senility"; informant: John MCKEE (Greeneville); died: 25 Dec. 1918; record (1918) # 412.

HORTON, Bula Jane; born: 25 Dec. 1914; parents: father not stated and Emily HORTON; death cause: "diphtheria"; informant: Andy RADER (Chucky); died: 25 Dec. 1918; buried: Pleasant Vale; record # 411.

PINKSTON, G.T.; born: 15 Mar. 1854; widower; parents: not stated; death cause: "stroke or paralysis"; informant: G.J. PINKSTON; died: 26 Dec. 1918; buried: Bulls Gap; record (1918) # 413.

COUCH, Mrs. Venie; born: __ Oct. 1866; married; parents: George BUCHANAN (North Carolina) and Lina BUCHANAN (North

Carolina); death cause: "valvulor heart disease"; informant: Martin GABY (Baileyton); died: 27 Dec. 1918; buried: Price Cemetery; record (1918) # 414.

PARKER (?), Richard T.; born: 27 Dec. 1844; widower; parents: W.T. PARKER (?) and Anna STONE; death cause: "mitral heart disease"; died in the 18th District, 27 Dec. 1918; buried: Shilo; record # 415.

EMERT, Penelope; born: 24 Jan. 1858; married; parents: George W. CANNON and Maggie CORNWELL; death cause: "carcinoma of liver"; informant: John EMERT (Greeneville); died: 28 Dec. 1918; record (1918) # 416.

FRYE, James S.; born: __ Jun. 1887; married; parents: P.A. FRYE and Martha J. PIERCE; death cause: "septicemia originating from finger"; informant: John PIERCE (Moshiem); died: 29 Dec. 1918; buried: Mt. Carmel; record (1918) # 417.

BOWMAN, May; born: 30 Dec. __; age: 30 years; single; parents: W.F. BOWMAN and mother's name illegible; death cause: "influenza"; informant: T.J. BOWMAN (Greeneville); died: 30 Dec. 1918; buried: Gethseminie; record (1918) # 418.

BRANDON, Mary Jane; age: "about 76 years"; born: North Carolina; widow; parents: John RINEHART and Elizabeth BOGER; death cause: "articular rheumatism"; informant: Lillie SHANKS (Jeroldstown); died: 31 Dec. 1918; buried: Lovelace; record (1918) # 419.

SHELTON, Infant; male; parents: Robert SHELTON and Mary HIPS; death cause: "stillborn"; informant: J.V. ANDERSON (Greeneville); died: 5 Dec. 1918; record (1918) # 420.

BRASON (?), Infant; male; parents: C.G. BRASON and Pearl BROYLES; death cause: "stillborn"; informant: father (Greeneville); born/died: 14 Dec. 1918; buried: Oak Grove; record (1918) # 421.

CASH, Infant; female; parents: William M. CASH and Idie I. MCCURY; death cause: "stillborn"; informant: father (Moshiem); died: 16 Dec. 1918; buried: Browns Springs; record (1918) # 422.

Name Index

A__, Bonnie 257 Exbll 266 Fred 271 Infant 271
ADAMS, __ 113 Effie J 20 Exekiel 162 Melvina 20 Viola 113 WB 223
AIKEN, Sarah 229
AILSHIE, Nora 148
AISHIE, Infant 81 William 81
ALDRED, George Haskel 119 W M 119
ALDRICH, Alma Lee 203 Henry Martin 203
ALDRIDGE, Alice 130
ALEXANDER, Andy 182 AJ 164 AT 192 Bob 100 Bonnie 164 Bonnie Lee 129 Charles S 133 CW 87 Don 255 DD 213 Ed 182 Frank 164 182 HD 219 James 106 Jane S 221 Jess 108 John R 87 King 138 Margaret Elizabeth 133 Mate 283 William 87
ALL__, Alexander 113 Carl 113
ALLDIED, Dewy 75
ALLEN, Cela 155 Daniel 223 Daniel C 135 Danil 145 Henry Clay 208 Laura 74 Mariha 152 Nancy 29 Nannie 227 Phillip 208 Robert 135 Sam 145
ALLISON, Jammie 41
ALLRED, Ira Legetty 38
ALMAN, Mary A. 98
ALUMS, Carl 282 Inez 282
AMBERS, Vina 90
AMOS, Harry 62 Martha E 62

ANDERSON, Ada 237 Annie 99 144 Ben 196 CA 276 Dick 166 251 E 293 Gussie 276 Hull B 221 Infant 149 194 James 144 197 JB 194 JC 283 JJ 267 JV 294 Louis K 267 Mary E 230 Melinda 109 Memory 72 Mildred 28 ML 18 Robert 75 Sam 279 Vick 279, Mrs Vick 279 William 149 196 283 Mrs William 136 William George 283
ANDES, Emma 278 Wesley 278
ANDIES, Andrew 176
ARCHER, Milton 292 WH 278
ARGENBRIGHT, Melvina A. 260
ARMANTROUT, Fred 95 Bessie 274 Jessie 95 JG 95
ARMITAGE, Dollie 72 Isabel 232 James 170 L 197 Mary 7
ARMSTRONG, Elizabeth 112 Mrs JL 206 MB 6
ARNETT, James 249 Nannie 46
ARNIE, Mary 75
ARNOLD, Ida Vena 87 Jane 258 John 222 Major Henry 122 Manie 89 Mary 86 Mary C 132 Mary Jane 163 Mary J 118 Newt 182 Richard 182 Robert 87 122 222 225 Selena 32 Susie Ollie 122 William 225
ARNOTT, Grant G. 281
ARNOUL, Newton 36
ARTENBERRY, Elizabeth 288
ARTER, Gavenor 137 James 56 137
ARTERBERRY, PD 288
ARWOOD, Ed 33 Flora 99 Francis 200 Lizzie 282 Rachel 264
ASHLEY, __ 232 Joe 232
ASTES, Thomas 108

AURINS, Lee 13
AUSHIE, Brad M 65
AUSTIN, Armentie 112 Mary 197
AVINS, Alice 269
AYERS, Bert 282 Crofford 116
David Jones 116 JC 11 Lucind 12
LCH 119 Sallie 119 Samuel D 12
Samuel O 119 Von 282
B__, James 99 Joseph 278
BABB, Annie 190 236 AB 71
Beckie 258 Clarence 243 Cora
207 Daisey 140 Ed 140 Edd 236
Elbert S 147 Elizabeth 284
Ernest 185 Etta V 227 Fanny
Bell 291 George 40 Infant 236
258 James 128 258 Joe 104 Katie
137 Kittie Deborah 147 Lavada
199, Lizzie 116 Margaret 140
Mary 71 Mollie 9 Rufus 291
Sallie 236 Shadrack 183 SH 227
Trixie Maud 104 William 199
Willie Paul 243
BACHAM, William 93
BACON, Elizabeth 135 Susan 218
BAILES, Charlie 169 Lizzie 144
169 Maley 28 Mary E 1 Wice
169
BAILEY, Andrew 243 Andrew
Jackson 243 George A 5 Mrs
George 292 Infant 121 JH 57
Lousian 216 Lydia 192 Mary L
255 Nola 261 Osa Fern 121
Oscar 57 Pearl 215 Polly A 141
BAILS, Rebecca Jane 210 Soloman
160
BAIR, Barbara E 154
BAKER, Fannie 113 Mrs Jess 162
Johnathan Noah 113 Mary 223
Nannie E 107 Oscar Wilds 126
RR 126 Wilburn 126

BALDEN, Anderson 159 Ramen
159
BALES, Alex 261 Buford 96 CE
96 97 EO 141 Francis A 188 HH
210 Ida 261 Jessie 187 Joe 141
JW 96 141 249 Luther 188
Martha 33 Mary 239 Mary
Adeline 135 Nola 242 Rebecca
Jane 210 RR 218 Will 257 Zella
May 218
BALL, Charles 180 277 Charles D
264 David 264 Elizze 170 Fred
Manson 277 Infant 180 John
Franklin Charlie 175 Leroy 64
Mary 95 Nancy 243 Rufus 175
Sallie 216 SH 122 Thomas 124
BALLARD, George 238
BALLES, Marie E 80
BALLEU, JW 136 Ernest 225
Peter 225
BALLUE, Dollie 160 Peter 160
BALNS, Hunter 22
BANKS, Kizzie Lee 209 Sam 209
BANLEY, HV 50
BANSREL, Infant 28
BARB, Clifford 2
BARDING, SP 81
BARHAM, Ida 145 Jennie May
285 Mary A 33
BARKELY, ML 158 Edith
Josephine 180 George 180
BARKLY, George 107 Infant 107
BARLOW, Della 27 James Rose
46 Lura 244 Nancy 234 WH 156
Zona 168
BARM, Willy May 82
BARNES, AJ 284 Elmer W 111
Jack 284 John 129 Joseph 111
Lucy 129 Mashey 111 Rebecca
284 Robert S 75 Susan 170

BARNET, AJ 28 Lace 106 Lottie 105
BARNETT, Ike 108 Mabry M 141 WT 141
BARRETT, Francis 262
BARRIER, Robbert 79
BARRMON, SJ 87
BARRON, Ann 250
BARRY, George 10
BARTLEY, Annie Kate 156 Eliza Jane 135 JE 136 156
BARYHERD, John A 77
BASHAM, Dave 86 Lucretia 86
BASHOR, Ben 166 John C 275 Levy Benjamin 275 Peter 166
BASKET, Dessie 45 Estelle 166 Infant 2 18 John 9 Kermit 45 Louise F 141
BASKETT, Lura 268 Matilda 222 250 Richard 178
BASS, Anna Elizabeth 18 Daisy 236 Mariane 65
BASWELL, James 241 Leona 241
BATES, Adbra 218 Elizabeth 201 Rece 80
BATTAN, Emma 173
BAULCH, Hariet 260
BAXLEY, William 241
BAXTER, Alice 265 Barnet 163 Charles 121 Elizabeth 124 Infant 264 James 185 James M 89 John 89 Robert C 264 Samuel H 255 SP 124
BAYLES, Gurtie R 63
BAYLESS, ER 226 John Alexander 141 John H 226 Mrs JA 141 Luke B 141 Robert R 226 SE 158 Mrs WF 228
BAYSINGER, Polly 189
BEACH, Bessie 277 Nora 133

BEALS, Asbery 132 Dillie I 271 HH 132 Lydia Emily 132
BEAMER, Florence 62
BEARD, Harriet 145 Martha 261 Will 261
BEASON, H__ 109
BEBBER, Georgia 162 James 212 Manuel 238
BECHAM, Clarence 117 Hassie 117
BECK, Georgia Lee 216 Henry C 215 215 HC 215 Sarah Elizabeth 215
BEECH, Infant 247 John 247
BEEMER, Susann 278
BELCHER, Bertha Lucille 87 Rufus 87 Thomas 87
BELL, Bonnie 237 Henry 62 Jennie 82 JB 133 219 259 276 Sam 188 Samuel 82 Samuel Allen 82
BELT, Belle 38
BENCH, Infant 88 James S 88
BENNET, Zack 3
BENNETT, Bessie Naome 197 David 215 David A 197 HME 215
BENTON, Katie 227
BERGER, Margaret Jane 156
BERL, Martha 132
BERNARD, FM 122 Laura Cornelia 122
BERRY, Carry 281 Joshua 267 RA 163 TJ 129
BIBBES, __ 98
BIBBS, Frank 98
BIBLE, Alvin 162 Andra 174 Bertha U 230 Bertie Mae 209 Bessie 208 Billie 274 Capt John 168 Cart 209 Cathleen 254

Charles 98 Christian 61
Christopher 176 Clide 79 Cordie
234 CG 177 David 44 Delay
Alexander 258 Dessie 17 DD 171
Effie 173, Eliza 146 Elsie B 262
Emaline 156 Emma 61 Enoch M
240 Ezra 151 EM 240 Francis
Elizabeth 203 Mrs F 152 Grace
224 Hobert 206 Infant 171 Jacob
162 168 James Charles 206
James K 274 Jane 207 Joe 258
John 91 200 John (Capt) 168
John T 11, Josephine 140 JC 240
Lula 130 Mabel 203 Maggie 98
Mahalla 44 Marllia 162 Mary 63
219 Mary E 290 R 254 RJ 35
Seth 185 Thomas 69 158 Thomas
Stokley 151 Tommie 79 Truman
140 TA 206 Vista 147 William
209 William S 174
BICKERSTAFF, Mary Magdalene
248 ML 248
BIDDLE, Dorothy 214 Elizabeth
263 John M 41 120 JE 182 214
William 120 218 William J 218
BIERD, Bessie 187
BILLINGSLY, Alfie 143
BIRD, __ 82 Clyde 70 David 36
286 Hannah Jane 22 Henry A
264 Hugh 75 John 169 Mary 286
Robert 154 Scot 287 Simeon 264
275 Simon 208 Virginia 287 WN
264
BIREL, David 36
BISHOP, Thomas E 282 TE 282
Walter E 282
BITNER, Ben 206 Dosser 206
Mary 275 WR 151
BLACER, __ 257

BLACK, Allis 88 Barbara 192
Billie 102 127 Buford Binum 269
Ellen 9 114 Ida Bell 185 Infant
88 James 226 Jessie 127 Joseph
114 Josie 88 Mary 120 May 192
Pearl Lucile 150 Pery 226 Polly
Ann 35 127 Robert S 102
Thomas 29 127 Tom 150 WA
269, WC 154
BLACKBURN, Lucinda Alice
Kelley 151 Nancie 213 Wesley
274
BLAIN, Hugh 237 Josephine 237
BLAKE, Leda 140 Lou 208 Robert
38 Sylvester 177
BLANTON, Clayton 273 Julia
Ann 150 JB 233 MA 273
William E 273 WE 273
BLAZER, Andrew 92 Angeline
285 Eliza Ruth 127 Franklin 221
Joe 127 John 100 Lawe Ellen 185
Loura 276
BLEDSOE, Infant 153 Will 153
BLESS, Marth 158
BLEVIN, Joe 139
BLEVINS, __ 187 Infant 139 JS
183 Mary M 183
BLUE, Dollie 160 John 270 Louisa
270 Malinda 207 Peter 160
BOBSON, John 213
BODWELL, B __ 181
BOGER, Elizabeth 294
BOHANAN, John 150 Simon 150
William Thomas 150
BOHANNAN, John 165 Katherine
215 Neal 215
BOHANNON, C __ 165 Martha J
180 Neal 165 SJP 180
BOLDING, Hester 256 Howard
245 JA 239 Mark 245

BOLES, BJ 272 Catherine 286
David J 83 Flora 272 Jacob 83
Mary 183 Robert 72 Virginia 25
71
BOLINGER, Henrietta Catherine
166
BOLLEW, Sarah J Bertha 136
BOLLINGER, Louise 213
BOLON, Hazel 150 John 150
BOLTON, DF 52 Malinda 229
BONSALL, Sarah A 184
BOOHER, Josephine 258
BOOKER, Larie 177 William 177
BORDEN, Elija 223 Henry 195
Henry S 223 Minnie 126
Virginia 195 WM 223
BOSWELL, Charles Earl 117
Elliott 117 Luther 74 Polly Ann
93 Susan A 246
BOUGHARD, Cora Bell 236
Infant 234 JA 236 Mary Jane 128
Robert 234 WJ 128
BOUGHER, Jacob 256 James 256
BOULS, Infant 80
BOWEN, Marion 35
BOWER, Aden 81 Frank 221
Infant 81 221 Mira 14 Sallie 78
BOWERS, Charles 111 Elizabeth
260 Eva Nell 111 Infant 247
Jacob 166 James H 77 Lidie 184
Lula 207 Mary 170 175 Sarie
162 Vina E 292 Wesley 247
BOWHIE, Cart 65
BOWLAND, Stella 80
BOWLES, Ira A 14
BOWLIN, Bell 113 Nancy 113
Peter Filmore 113
BOWMAN, __ 194 Alonzo 94 AJ
104 Cecil 60 Charles M 201
Cora Patten 134 Dora 8 Dora B
133 171 DS 169 Ebb 186 Edna
61 252 Elender 104 Elizabeth
244 Ethel 97 Frank M 94 Guy
109 Hattie 23 James 282 John 94
171 230 Lukinsie 104 Lura 282,
Marion F 91 Mary 60 Mary
Elizabeth 82 Maud 53 May 294
Myrtle 61 Nela May 8 Nellie 60
Pearl 91 Polly 23 Rachel 37
Sallie 37 Smith 18 Susan 140 SA
104 TJ 82 294 William 104
Wilson 53 WF 94 97 109 294 WJ
94
BOWSER, Bertha 177 Charles 177
210 Charlie 118 CR 52 John 210
BOYD, Edgar 199 E_ 199 Jerre
223 John 199 John P 289 Lulo O
172 LC 179 223 Nolen 289 WB
131
BRABSON, Alexander 212 ED
212 Infant 260 Lucinda 228 LE
212 Thomas 260
BRADFORD, Andrew 228 CS 289
Ebba M 288
BRADLEY, Alison 83 Infant 83
James 296 Jasper 85 William
Lawrence 206 Wona 83 WL 207
BRADLY, Butha 276
BRAKEBILL, Elizabeth 203
BRANCH, Amos 276 Harvey 150
Infant 276
BRANDON, Edgar Mason 185
Etta 3 James 64 Lillie 283
Lucille 229 Martha Christina 190
Mary Jane 294 Roam 124 SD
185 Thomas G 191
BRANNON, Cora Mae 41
BRANON, Ellen 204
BRASON, CG 294 Infant 294
BRIANT, __ 118

BRICE, Infant 134
BRIGHT, __ 89 Bertie 164 Bill
230 Eliza 103 Elizabeth 178
Ethel B 273 Infant 33 MD 278
Rosa 74 Sarah Etta 158 WM 103
BRIGMAN, James Orval Lee 229
Laura 234 Nathaniel K 229 NK
92 Sarah 92 Stella 109 222 Stella
May 244
BRINSON, Jennie C 85
BRISCOE, Will 146
BRISENDINE, Carlos 11 Dewey
11
BRIT, John 67
BRITON, Mary A 229
BRITT, Louis 17
BRITTAN, George 200
BRITTON, Alice 241 Attamira
270 Catherine 6 Dora 200 Emma
159 279 FC 138 232 255 GD 97
Hannah 97 HC 116 James 97 241
JC 159 Kenney 159 Margaret 6
Mary Ann 159 ME 67 Wallas
185
BROBECK, Cecil 33 Dessie 42 JC
204 JG 204
BROBSON, JM 40
BROCKELL, Crawford 49
BROCKWELL, John R 91
Tennessee 91
BRODERICK, Polly 95
BROMLEY, Sarah Elizabeth 167
BROOK, Alice 261
BROOKE, Infant 264 William 264
BROOKINS, Charles 256 Ike 161
232 240 Isaac 216 Levenia 161
Mary 256 Pauline 216 Riley 224
240 Thidore 232 Willis 240
BROOKS, __ 64 Alfred 116 Burge
150 BB 171 FC 85 FS 31
Harrison 200 Henry Allen 93 289
Jake 64 John 249 Joseph 116 JA
249 Leo 245 Lizzie 89 Nellie
Clyde 32 Pearl 249 Pearl B 249
TW 116 William 93 200 291 WC
291
BROTHERTON, Elizabeth 168
Empress 183 Jennie 202 Joseph
Homer 189 JF 285 Margarette
272 Odie Elizabeth 225 Tilman
A 189
BROUGHS, Hattie 186
BROWCH, Chassie 161
BROWLES, WW 24
BROWN, __ 97 Anna 265 Arrie
108 Calvin F 131 Charlie Roscoe
10 Clara Ruby 115 CF 178 220
CS 200 Delia 131 Elizabeth A
134 Elmer C 131 Elsie 229
Emily Elizabeth 126 Esther 253
Flora C 198 George Peter 126 GP
230 GW 96 Harry 109 Hila 142,
Hila J 151 Hilton 261 Hitt 261
Infant 110 200 230 261 IB 123
212 J 128 Jack 244 James C 216
Jennie 48 79 John 217 236 John
B 7 288 John D 191 J Bradley
216 JA 96 138 218 JD 243 JM
104 JS 282 Kyle 109 Lila 178
Liza 30 Lizzie 256, Lolia May 96
Louise J 267 Lula 290 Lydia
Anna 281 Margaret 72 148
Marian 23 Mark 99 Martha A
195 Mary 186 Mary A 172 Mary
Nan Effie 138 Monroe 110
Nancy 175 Nancy G 172 Oliver
211 Oscar 99 Peter 187 220
Phoebe 290 Rebecca Jane 190,
Rhoda A 244 Robert 116 190 236
Robert A 265 Ross 4 Roy Doanl

191 Ruth 263 RA 179 190 RL
212 258 Sarah Elizabeth 157
Sarah J 236 Serenie 163 Suda
235 Sudie 116 Thurseve 258 Will
99 William 97 William
Alexander 217 William A 220,
William Bruce 243 Willie E 254
Willie Y 49 Wilson B 187 WC
289 WD 116 236
BROYLES, __ 189 Adam 101
Annie Lee 142 Arthur G 165 AN
181 Callie 58 Caroline M 278
Claud 101 CF 288 Dezzie 217
Elendar 118 Ellen 259 Emory B
118 EH 23 Florence J 101
Hannah 105 Horace 165 Infant
202 225 Jack 179 Jacob 216
Jefferson 275, John 89 131 142
197 John S 202 JA 292 JF 88
King 100 Lara 241 Lee Roy 38
Lon 288 291 LJ 38 LM 225 Mag
100 Martha 38 88 Mary 219
Mary Edna 206 Mary J 204 Max
F 206 Micher 210 M 197 Nat H
142 Nathaniel 118 Newton A 58
Oliver M. 217, Pearl 291 294
Phillip 259 Russell 225 Salina
131 146 Sam 179 SH 133 Venie
87 Virgie 244 Watsell 54 Will F
54 William A 210 WO 39
BRUBAKER, Dora 253 Margaret
154
BRUEBAKER, DA 154
BRUMFIELD, Malinda 264
BRUMLEY, Birthy 194 Cathrn 28
Ed 155 Ethel 87 261 Jud 155
Kenneth Ray 194 Laura 96 Olive
237 ST 261 WP 40
BRUMLY, Infant 182 S 182
BRUNER, Abner 285 Minnie 285

BRYAN, JM 245 Mary G 245
Ruth Dean 257 SN 257 Tom H
257
BRYANT, __ 249 AM 179 Calvin
58 Infant 239 Lula 158 Martha C
179 S 249
BUCHANAN, Ada 203 204
George 293 Lina 293
BUCKNER, Lorenza 121
BULLEN, Elizabeth 259 Mary 72
BULLINGTON, Edgar 45 Edna
232 Flora 139 Jessie 232 Minnie
178 291 Nancy 208
BUNCH, Nancy 211
BUPP, Bert 214
BURELL, Harriett 209
BURGER, Isaac 254 John 156 254
JA 254 Sarah Jane 130
BURGNER, Ada 271 Christian
140 204 242 Crystal 266 CC 256
DW 239 Florence 134 242 Infant
54 69 Isaac Mitchell 140 James
75 JH 140 Mack 266 Margaret
256 Peter 169 204 Mrs Peter 204
Ralph 239 Mrs SM 256 Talbert
266 William Gipson 242
BURGNON, Sallie 99
BURGON, Joe 20
BURKETT, Callie 111
BURKEY, __ 119 Hubert 42
BURKHART, Infant 38
BURNETT, George 103 James 275
Sarah 207
BURNS, John C 223 258 John E
223 SE 258, William 258,
William Carter 223
BURRELL, Martha 178
BURRIS, Anna 2
BUSHONG, Mary Elizabeth 93
BUTLER, Mary 290

BUTTER, FS 160
BYERLY, Agnes 158, WR 158
BYERS, Susan 163
BYRD, Callie 211 CR 210 211
   John 210
C__, Abraham 176 AM 274 Dollie
   221 Mattie 110 Sue 169
CAIN, Sarah 149
CALHOUN, Effa 53
CALHUT, Ellen 25
CALLETT, Margaret 80
CAMBEL, Bersheba 192
CAMON, Infant 244 Olivia 244
CAMPBELL, __ 87 Amanda 132
   Bessie 47 Bettie 18 Clyde 148
   Harlow 47 Hugh 87 Jacob 87
   John 13 81 JA 11 JD 189 Lisa 81
   Louise 138 Lula Elizabeth 215
   LP 83 123 148 Mae 83 Margaret
   123 Marion 241 Minnie 241 RE
   2 SAm 94 Winfred 56
CAMRON, Catherine 193 194
CANNON, A 280 Annie 224
   Annie Mae 256 Catey 288
   George W 294 Grant 221 Ike 289
   Infant 221 James 282 Jessie 44
   JM 280 Lafayette 209 Lizzie 266
   Malcom 256 Mallome 209
   Malone 266 Nellie 108 Samuel
   62 Tenie 269 William 22
   William FM 22 Willie Bell 289
CANON, Jane 176
CANTER, Mary 181 Samuel 67
CANTRELL, J 143 Mary Bell 103
CAPP, JO 101
CARDON, Dennis 215
CARICO, Lena 100 Lucy Alice
   100
CARLISLE, Joseph 68

CARMAC, Infant 199 Jessie 157
   Jessie J 199
CARMICLE, Sallie 96
CARMON, Darnell 31 Dollie 251
CARPER, Moses 113 Walter 113
CARR, Bazzle Clide 117 Charley
   Edward 117 Ola 217 Sherman 52
CARRISON, Howard 55
CARSON, Bob 186 236 Garland
   W 57 George 236 John R 196
   Lizzie 164 Roy 196 Samuel L
   196 Tenia 105 Thomas 248
CARTELL, Lizzie 90
CARTER, __ 128 Alfred 172
   Anderson 154 Anna 223 Annie
   155 Ben 253 Berry 63 Berton
   113 Betsy 185 Brolson 105 BF
   237 Carrie 163 Christina 77
   Daniel 172 272 Dot 236 DG 272
   Effie 149 Eliz Alice 143 Eliza J
   131 178 Ezekiel 206 FT 87
   Georgia 52 GR 114 Hassie 181
   Henry 78 259 Hyla 16 Ida 123
   Infant 15 66 105 165 237 272
   Irene 148 IP 187 Jacob C 253
   James 132 178 John 16 30 148
   John Biddle 78 John P 19 Joseph
   E 143 J Mc 162 JC 123 JD 201
   206 JP 136 Kate 197 238 Katie
   180 Kermit 20 Lee 77 Leona 56
   Liea Anna Ellen 113 Lucinda
   232 Lucy 278 Margaret 123
   Martha 16 Mary 278 Massie 198
   Mollie 288 MD 97 Nat M 237
   Osie 277 Patience 192 Patsie 164
   Robert 16 Robert Taylor 97 RB
   165 Sadie 66 Sis 221 Sophia 25
   Stringfield 221 Susan 8 Tilitha
   265 Verdie 253 William 206
   William M Brown 172 Willie

Ross 162 WA 101 WB 134 Zack 237
CARTRIGHT, Hazel 30
CARTWRIGHT, AO 290 Carl Otho 290
CARVER, Julia A 269
CASH, Infant 70 118 294 William M 294 Willie 118
CASSADY, George 2
CASTEEL, Bonie 51 Chassis 191 Hanah 7 Ida 51 218 Jerimiah 161 John 220 JM 92 161 Lena 251 Licy 189 Nettie C 191 Rachel 212 RT 220 T Henderson 35 William 161 220 William Marton 8 WW 191
CASTIEL, William 161
CATRON, Andrew 286 Columbus C 286 JB 144 Zenas 144
CAVENDER, Nancy 216
CAVERN, Nancy 138
CHAMBERLAIN, Gene 174 Infant 174
CHANDLER, Daniel 242 Elbert 68 Hurley 263 Jess 179 John Wesley 263 JW 216 Laura 179 Mary 242 Mary Ann 242 Mattie 186 Susie 159
CHANDLEY, __ 48 Horace 249 Margaret 249 William 25
CHANEY, Wyley 239 Eulret 39
CHAPMAN, Amanda 85 Archibald 201 Bettie 238 David 61 Ed 101 144 Ellen 120 Estella 214 EC 201 FC 85 GW 90 Infant 277 John Wesley Emmett 90 JW 277 Laura 144 Mary 101 Sallie 101 Sherman 85
CHARLES, __ 265
CHARLTON, Elizabeth 202 Harvy 289 John 217 LB 202 Maney 289
CHASE, John 117 Mary A 147 Pauline 166 Sam 166
CHATMAN, Infant 76 Lora 49 Sarah 50
CHEDESER, Mattie 159
CHENY, Louise 129
CHESNUT, Mollie 88
CHRISTIAN, Flora 83 JHM 35
CHRUCH, Ida Victoria 157 Edny 33 Nat 43
CINDUFF, J 142
CLARK, Al__ 227 Ellen 104 WC 227
CLAUD, Sarah 76
CLAYTON, Adeline 22 Elsie 189 Haney 189 Harold 63
CLEM, George Washington 149 Sindy 165
CLEMANS, Anna 237
CLEMMON, Essie 8 JL 8
CLICK, Gussie 238 GW 170 John M 245 John S 242 Patton 238 Rachel 59 Susana 210
CLIMER, __ 103 Celia 229 Ellen 42
CLINE, Mae 224
CLIPHAUT, Hannah 210 James 210
CLOUD, __ 251
CLOWERS, Edward 47
CLOYD, James William 264 John P 31 Larua 140 Mary 244 Thomas D 195 264 William 264
CLOYER, __ 128
COAL, Naunah R 55
COALMAN, WT 58
COATER, James H 15

COATES, Charles 84 Cloe 30
  Rufus Clide 84
COATNEY, Dana 214 Maggie 191
  Robert 191 Yank 214
COATS, CD 84
COB, Sinthey 95
COBBLE, __ 205 Allis A 127 AA
  127 Barbara 144 Bertha 229
  Elizabeth S 263 Ida 11 44 Infant
  127 James 42 177 John A 29 JL
  183 195 Kelly Love 46 LM 240
  263 Marion 293 Mary Effy 9 ML
  286 Nathaniel 195 Nela May 8 N
  9 Philip 183 Ricky 35 Sallie 125
  205 Tom 88 Washington 9
COCHRAN, John 183 Lilie Belle
  183 Robert E 280 William 219
COCKERHAM, James F 157 JC
  157
COFFEE, __ 173 Alice 235 Ed
  173 Infant 235 Melvina 293
  Mirna Jane 90 Richard A 173
  Willard 235
COGBURN, Clete 273 Elizabeth
  231 JV 273
COGDAL, Infant 47
COGDALE, Tildy 162
COILE, Mary E 254
COIN, May 184
COLDWELL, __ 97 Lee 68
COLE, Andrew 114 Robert 114
COLEMAN, Leneta I 238 OL 238
COLIER, Dula 171
COLINS, Charles 145 Robert
  Claud 145
COLLENS, Johnie 52 Nancy 52
  Ora 140
COLLET, __ 65 Infant 10 John
  178 Mary Emma 178 Melvina 2

COLLETT, Frank 17 Jane 178
  Marguarate 187 Mary 220 Ottie
  Berthold 238 Samuel 238
  William 19 WS 238
COLLIER, Alma Thelma 191
  Anderson 130 Henry 191 Meonie
  63
COLLINS, A 31 Abraham 265
  Carson 86 Chassie Viola 13
  Daniel C 13 Edith 152 Eliza Jane
  108 Elizabeth 182 English 100
  Jacob 100 James 112 150 253 Joe
  86 John 100 Johnie 65 Joseph
  112 JE 152 JK 51 Lizzie 30
  Lucinda Francis 174 LR 1 Madge
  M 13 Martha 13 86 Nancy 65
  Vinia 150
COLLIT, Laura 145
COLSON, Elija 233 EA 157 Oscar
  157
COLWERS, Elizabeth 72
COLYER, Andrew Jackson 125
  Charles 161 Ed 125 Etta 161 EF
  125 John 161 Margaret 272 Pearl
  146
COMBS, Robert 31
COMES, Elmer 215
COMPTON, Andrew 18 HC 223
  Nellie 18 Nola 10 Sindy 258
CONDUFF, Alvin 79 AL 281
  Ethel 174 225 FM 281 Ida Bell
  13 Infant 281 John 235 Matt 235
  Samuel 29 Susan Ann 13 Vici
  221 William A 79
CONK, Ronie 52
CONKIN, Banaba 265 Hagans 265
  Harry 147 M Eveate 220 Saul
  265 SB 220
CONKLIN, Mattie 64

CONLEY, Joseph 270 Nancy 11
William James 270
CONN, James 126 John 126
Robert 126
CONNER, Viola 14 Sarah 14
CONSTABLE, C 290 Clarissa 70
Fay 293 John 291 NT 288 291
Sam 291
CONWAY, Laura 101
COOK, __ 231 Anson King 131
EG 131 Oliver 122
COOLER, Charles 139
COOLEY, Hannah 62 WM 104
COOPER, A 278 279 Bonnie 231
Emily 282 James M 231 Landon
233 Nan 256 Nathaniel 233
Rachel 109 Robert 231 233 RN
109
COOTER, Barney 90 211 226
Carrio 133 Charles F 133
Charles R 187 CC 226 CR 187
Edith 93 Florence Emily 254
Gladys Aline 187 Harley 211
Henry 168 James E 114 James R
175 Jasper C 201 John 134 168
John Alexander 175 John M 90
235 Jones 135 JW 168 Maggie
Mae Ellen 114 Mary A 130
Mattie 186 Nora Alice 201 Pearl
169 Phillip 226 Roy K 175
COPLER, Mattie 281
COPLEY, Caroline 244 Gertrude
74
CORBY, James 23
CORNWELL, Florence 247
Maggie 294
CORWELL, Sallie 280
COSTLEY, Charles 59
COUCH, Arch 247 Eliza 285 Jode
221 Mary 163 Mary Ann 67 Opal
221 Polly Ann 146 Poluntine 67
Sallie 247 Valentine 170 Venie
293
COUGDAL, John 47
COURTNEY, Floyd Raymond 195
James 195 283 JL 195 Sophroina
195 Susan Victoria 110
COWARD, Amanda Melvina 249
JE 249
COX, Ada 276 Aleno 43 Alice 292
Annie 224 Bessie 129 Charles A
231 Charles N 237 Charles R
230 Daisy 206 Dallas Paul 231
Dovie A 265 Ethel 258 Frank
125 George 206 GW 242 276
Hareld 53 Hattie 287 Hugh 292
Infant 230 James Franklin 237
JM 121 Lela 199 Lemuel K 125
Lewis 207 Margaret 92 Mary 66
Mattie 256 Maxie 237 Silas 207
Susan 236 Susan C 242 UA 130
Walter 39 William 121 125 207
William C 121 W Logan 256
COYLES, Major 62
CRABTREE, AB 65 188 Betsy 268
Henry 170 John 170 Mamie Ruth
190 Sarah Florence 246 SP 246
Thomas E 190 William 268
CRADDOCK, John Carl 50 John
C 44
CRADIC, Herman E 235 Kyle 235
CRADLOCK, Abbical 213
CRAFT, Myrtle 167 William
Jackson 2
CRAMER, Louisa 52
CRASEMAN, Infant 196
CRASY, Infant 226 RA 226
CRAWFORD, Catherine 112
Charles F 147 Etta 3 Frank 113
Fred Hale 130 George 95 Jessie L

3 Margaret N 265 Ollie 185 RE
130 Sarah Margaret 96 Will 95
Zella 3
CREASMAN, Ben 196
CRISLEY, Emily 99
CRITSELOUS, John 289 Luther
  289 Noah R 289
CRITTENDON, Celia 82
  Washington 203
CROAKER, Mirann 167
CROFT, Joe 188 William 188
  William P 188
CROSBY, Andrew Jackson 135
  Infant 135 Mary Elizabeth 125
  RJ 242 William H 125
CROUDER, WM 256
CROWN, Ora Bell 138
CROXWELL, Margaret 66
CRUCY, Bertie 208
CRUM, Bell 157 237 Beulah 59
  Donna Elizabeth 157 Edna 119
  222 Eliza 120 Elmer 159 E 267
  278 Floy 60 Geneva 68 Infant 37
  John 118 John F 139 JF 157
  Katie Sue 278 Margaret J 216
  Mary 159 MA 23 Pearl 195
  Sparkling Janes 68 Tom 171 Wes
  139 Wilbur D 267 William 118
  William J 237
CRUMLEY, Abraham 102 Abram
  30 Alice 277 Benjamin Douglas
  102 Catherine 217 DJ 268 GR
  273 James 68 Jerome 220 John
  78 Lavie Pauline 220 Mary 138
  Mary Catherine 273 Milton J 268
  Mrs MJ 268 Perry 185
CRUMLY, John 78
CRUMM, Mary Ella 171
CRUSY, Infant 244 Sol 244

CULBERTSON, Caswell 88
  William 88
CULVER, William 61
CUNNINGHAM, Annie 29
CUPP, Alfred Allen 195 BA 232
  BS 156 Infant 214 Jacob 253
  John F 253 John W 269 Joseph
  Campbell 214 JB 156 JO 269
  Laurie May 195 Leroy 214 Lucy
  254 Myrtle 131 NA 254 Will 214
CURD, Abraham 245
CURTIS, Flora F 276 Gladys
  Geneve 185 Val 185 276
CUTSHALL, Ana Ruth 251
  Andrew 130 Andrew J 103 Asa
  91 BR 119 Darous 209 Elbert
  Anderson 103 Ellen 8 Ellen Faye
  138 Elmer Hubert F_ 54 Flora
  203 Frederick 79 Infant 21 James
  247 James Perry 39 Jennie
  Elizabeth 208 John 248 250 JH
  141 Lowell Edward 119 LC 69
  Martin 92 Mary 21 Mary Jane 55
  Maudie Pauline 103 Mirlin 54
  Nanie 170 Newton J 251 NJ 130
  136 Orpha 136 Paulen 103 Sam
  128 170 Sarah Ann 200 Stanley
  Hugh 208 TM 130 Virgil 68
  Virginia 141 William 247
  William M 208 WM 136
CUTSHAWL, Evie 234 Jake 125
DAIRS, Mollie 211
DALLINGER, James Authur 129
  Spencer 129
DALTON, Millie 172 Sallie 147
DANIELS, John B 14
DARLING, RB 257
DARNELL, John 22 Namon 271
  Rena Alice 271
DAUD, Manda 177

DAUGHERTY, Ethel 191
DAUKINS, __ 146
DAULTON, Ruby 149
DAVENFORT, Hannah 72
DAVENPORT, Charlie 177 Ellen 22 Mary 202 MH 106
DAVIS, Belle 232 235 Catherine 284 Charles 282 Charles M 169 CE 84 211 220 236 277 Decatur 94 Eliza 157 Elizabeth 151 Ella 245 Elmer 178 Mrs EJ 258 Florence 260 Gena 219 Glennie 193 Guy 35 Henry 24 Inez 282 Infant 19 159 169 Isaac 38 James 101 James Canon 258 Jesse 155 198 Jesse Emerson 198 J 155 John 94 116 235 289 John T 289 Joseph A 80 Lana 19 Lizzie 94 M_ 241 Mark 232 235 Mary 76 Mary Alice 219 Mary Ann 253 Nancy C 126 Nomie 183 Odessa 122 Orrin 36 Peter 164 Powell 239 Rushia 58 Sam 55 Steller E 80 Susa 103 Susan 104 Susan T 219 SW 219 Thomas 289 Thomas A 155 Tom 159 TER 239 UJ 284 Vinie 145 William 245 258 William Abner Center 167 Willie 116 Willie James 167 WF 289 WS 198
DAY, ET 146 James Franklin 255 James R 167 John 167 John Richard 266 Joseph 293 JF 167 Mary 278 Mollie 187 William 70 Willie 266
DEAN, Alonzo 235 Andy 191 225 235 Anna 191 Davey Andrew 47 Emma Lee 191 Henry 225 Joe 259 Joseph Ray 259 Sallie 225 Thomas 225

DEARSTONE, Bartia 205 Bob 239 George 126 Grant 239 Henry 126 Jacob 239 James Kennith 242 JA 242 William M 126
DEATHRDIGE, Andy 158 James Houston 265 Melvina 284 William 265 William M 168
DEBOARD, Sarah 273
DEBURK, Florence 240 Martha 176 Nannie 281 Thomas 280
DECK, LV 207 Rome 207
DEEN, Alice 153
DEERSTONE, Minnie 204
DENNY, Lucy A 224
DENSMORE, Vinia 99
DENTON, Daisy 209 George R 224 Jennie 224 Pauline 224
DENWIDDIE, JM 241 Vera 241
DEPEW, Eliza 17
DERRIL, Irene 126
DERRY, Earnest 272 Sarah Ellen 272
DETHERAGE, Birt 54
DETHRGE, Mable 18
DEVATI, Clark 165 Elizabeth 262 Pearl Ruth 165 William 165 WA 262
DEVAULT, David 237 John A 237 Louise 259 Mary E 73
DEVOTIE, Beulah Marie 271 John 271
DEWITT, __ 261 Fred 248 Willie 156
DEZARN, Fannie 199
DEZORN, Effie 239 Fannie 235 James 239
DEZZARN, Nancy Ellen 86
DIBORD, __ 285
DICK, Margaret 267
DICKERSON, Mary M 88

DICKSON, __ 287 Gladis 3 Harvy 255 Irene 245 James 213 Julia 154 Logan 213 Lola Vernel 200 Mary 245 William Blaine 200
DILAN, James 120
DILLON, Mary 44
DINKINS, Danil 190 William 190 William J 190
DINSMORE, Infant 189 266 SG 189 266
DINWIDDIE, Jane 263
DIXON, __ 64 Alex 112 Bertie 73 Charles 233 Clyde 65 Eller 39 Etta Mae 244 G_ 100 George 39 Hermon 63 HG 224 Infant 75 King 138 Mary 86 Minnie 101 Sue 31 Thelma 100 William Tell 75
DIZAM, Effie L 100
DLON, NJ 114
DOAIN, Nancy 154
DOAK, Dr Hubert 61 Margaret 53 Mathew 53
DOBBINS, Andy 123 Berthire 134 Nancy 11
DOBSEN, Louise 120
DOBSON, __ 109 Calvin 213 Caroline H 32 EB 101 224 HE 117 Infant 224 Thomas 32
DOCKERY, George 59
DODD, __ 228 Coon 290 Florence 161 Ida 259 JR 194 Margaret 210 Maxine 290
DOKE, Alexander M 188 Sue V 188
DOLTON, James 107
DOTSON, Anna 285 Blanch 20 Elizabeth 269 Frank 244 James 197 Loretta Estelle 197 Ruben 272 Samuel Rhuben 197 UT 197

DOTY, Allen 241 Alphius 19 Auldon 276 Ely May 52 Infant 241 276 JF 276 Roy 52 SW 184 291
DOUD, E 169 James 168 Patrick 168
DOUGHTY, John H 35 WH 260
DOUGLAS, WR 145
DOUTHAT, Chassie 96 Jessie 212 OE 96 Robert Powell 102 RP 212 Vincin Aster 102
DOWNEY, Martha Jane 200 Mauda A 274
DOWNIE, Feletie A 74
DOWNY, Mack 178
DOYLE, OH 256
DRAIN, James 77
DRAKE, James Edgar 131 William T 131 WG 256
DUCK, Daniel 292 Rexter 292 WB 292
DUDLEY, Eliza Jane 180
DUGGER, Edd 220 Elizabeth 243 HN 256 Infant 284 James Newton 256 J 110 JH 257 Lucinda 220 Margaret E 211 Mattie Jane 100 ME 220 Newt 110 OM 126 RR 110 SA 284 William 228
DULANEY, Infant 37
DUMERON, Infant 138 Moses S 138
DUNBAR, Ben 142 John A 142 Louise 24 Virgie 104 WC 142
DUNCAN, Aaron 212 Alfred 246 Anna 77 Annie 176 Belle 182 Brooks 250 Ethel 77 George 152 179 Goober 41 John 212 Louisa 212 Thomas 249 Will 113

DUNN, Bert C 216 Georgia 112
  Glenna 193 John 150 216 Nina J
  216 Sam 102 Samuel M 150
  Sarah 150 Susan 102 SM 193 SN
  112
DUNWOODY, Amanda 65 John 6
DURHAM, Elizabeth 249 William
  252 William Francis 252
DYAL, Infant 221 John 221
DYER, Bertha 152 Bertha Jane
  115 Charlie 82 Elizabeth 143
  Fred 155 Infant 82 James 229
  James Luther 229 JT 152 JW 102
  Madlin 155 WS 143
DYKE, Chassie Carter 221 Infant
  66
DYKER, Gus 129 Lucinda 124
  Charley 239 Clarence 3 Essie 18
  Idahm 223 James 20 223 Jasper
  64 John 129 JA 129 Lillie
  Victory 100 Mary Walsey 10
  Ruth 124 Sarah 289 Thomas 100
  239 William 117
E__, Andrew 230
EADS, Mrs Annie 74 Julia 192 LH
  192 SH 59
EAKIN, Kathrin 236 Mrs Roy 249
EALEY, Joe 205 Rebeca 205
EALY, James 291 Robert 291
EARLY, Elsa 150 George W 200
  William 150
EARNEST, Kate
EARNEST, Mariah 99 Rhoda 107
EAST, George T 251 Thomas 251
EASTEP, Rebecca Liza 100
EASTERLY, Carl 12 Catherine
  127 Elbert 73 Frank 46 FP 82 HT
  252 JP 259 Kate 47 Matilda Ann
  81 Reuben 245 Virginia 167
  William A Clark 245 W Carl 25

EDINGTON, Eric 202 Infant 202
EDMONS, Bessie 223 Martha 236
  Mirah 229
EDWARDS, Callie 193 Dicie 139
  140 James H 55
EISENHOUR, Eva 243 Peter 218
ELENBURG, Adam 203 John 203
  Sarrah 227
ELKHART, Belle 189
ELKINS, Basil 213 Rice 217 Sarah
  E 217 Thomas 226
ELLENBURG, Adam 180 204
  George Franklin Jr 281 Harriett
  134 Henry 106 John 106 180 204
  Julia 134 LD 106 Mary 180
  Nannie E 280 Walter 281 Willie
  40 WW 280
ELLER, Manila 167
ELLIOT, Augusta 31
ELLIS, __ 283 Bill 190 EB 83
  Infant 190 Jack 283 Joseph 180 L
  107 Mary 132 MD 163 Nancy
  163 Susanna 49 Tilda 271
ELLISON, Jennie 259
ELRNESS, Mary 162
ELROD, Essie M 238
ELWELL, Joseph W 136
EMERSON, C 255 Henry C 255
  Onie 255
EMERT, John 294 Penelope 294
EMMERT, J 251 Andy 251
  Charles 251
ENGLE, __ 217 Sallie 89
ENGLISH, A_ 214 AJ 214 HE 128
  Mary 214 Milton 214 Mona 264
  Sarah 174
ENGLMAN, Jane 258
EPPERSON, Mary 213

ERVIN, Cal 280 Elbert E 206
James 206 Nellie 247 SJ 255
Thomas 255
ERWIN, Minnie 274 Onie 71
ESTEP, John 128 Mary 248
ESTEPP, Amos 279 James
  William 279
EST_, Jane 264
ETTER, George Alexander 147
  Peter 170
EVANS, Calvin 209 Caroline 153
  Charles L 118 Child 161 Dave
  90 105 Effa 148 Hamilton 203
  Hillie 105 Jack 232 289 James 90
  Katie 147 Margaret 153 280
  Martha 256 Perry 69 Robert 209
  Robert M 160 Samuel 160 161
  WR 153
EVERETT, Manda 47
EVERHART, Bessey 6 Charles R
  289 Clayton 46 James 225
  Kathleen 78 Mary 273 Mary A
  143 Nancy Ellen 289 Stella 6 46
FAIR, Bud 183 Eli 84 George
  Washington 183 Mandy 205 TM
  84
FAN, Edgar 76
FANN, Fred 181 Gennie E 181
FANNING, Annie 60 Oma 23
  Sarah 37
FANNON, Charles 179 Henry 91
  Infant 23 John 174 Julia 97 109
  Lillie 179 Peggy 62
FARBY, Green 201
FARLEY, Francis H 122
FARNSWORTH, Catherine 69
  Ganett 135 George 161 Harriett
  227 Jane 129 Joe 246 John 246
  Lillie 130 Loyd 106 Thomas 227
  Thomas J 246 Tom 163

FARRIS, E Campbell 225 Robert
  15 Samuel 15 225
FASCHIR, Bird 79
FASHIE, Mrs William 148
FEAGINS, FJ 124
FELLER, Rachel 292
FELLERS, Lucy 179 WA 23
FERGUSON, Frank 53 Mary 219
  Noah 253 Thomas 253
FERIRIL, Martha 40
FERRELL, Charles 152
FIELDS, __ 142 Ralph 16
FILEPS, Gabril 63
FILLER, Bird 60
FILLERS, __ 131 Clarence 14
  Connie 288 DH 195 DW 105
  Emily 136 Fanny 60 68 Hazel
  Rovina 195 Infant 23 266 Isaac
  151 John 142 Joseph 197 Josie
  171 Junior 195 JD 266 Maggie
  77 Martha Jane 120 May 37
  Maynard 288 Sarah 24 123 Tom
  171 Wilber Cleveland 171
FINCH, Anna Catherine 92
  Larance 92
FINCHER, David B 147 John E
  194 Joseph 147 RB 147
FINCHUM, Cora B 220
FINK, George W 229 Mary 221
  William P 229
FISHER, LH 123 Mary Elizabeth
  123
FITZGERALD, George 182
  William 182 William A 182
FITZSIMMONS, Mary 223
FLETCHER, John 60 Sarah E 282
FLOWERS, George 121
FLUKS, Margaret 27
FOCHEE, Ella 273
FOLKS, FO 213 Leonard 213

FORD, Dolly 177 JB 169 197
Rhoda 111
FOREMAN, John 250 Nancy 250
FORHIE, Martha 39
FORT, Rev 92
FORTNER, George 93 George Sr 93 GF 251 Infant 276 John 62 276 Lucy 179 Mary 27 Oma May 251 Ruby 31 44 WE 93
FOSHE, Georgia L 293 John 293
FOSHEE, CS 273 Margaret 203 John 91 105 Kisa 211 Prescilla 91 William 91
FOSTER, __ 165 Ann 91 Clodie 158 JS 158 Nora 223 Robert 165
FOULKS, JF 230 Mildred Vivian 230
FOWLER, Annah E 258 Buna 81 Francis 126 Manerva 179 William Francis 126
FOX, Ada 253 Ben 233 Benjamin Marion 233 Clifford 134 Etta 152 Eva Kate 134 Frank 226 Gussie 277 Infant 94 James 219 JD 217 JM 253 277 Liew 64 Pink 226 Robert L 233 Rubie 226 Samuel 134 Serence 76 Synthia 251 Worley 94 WJ 86
FRACKER, Sarah 106
FRAICAR __ 177
FRAKAR, HH 50 Sarah 49 Rethia Jane 211 TTM 211 William M 149
FRANKLIN, Emmaline 79 Henry 86 James 224 Layruth 224 Polly 85
FRANSWORTH, __ 234
FRASIER, Abner Julian 263 Abner J 263 JJ 197

FRAZIER, Abi 185 276 Margarette 216 Moe 199 Walter 263
FREEBORN, Margaret 157
FREEMAN, Catherine 110 Charles 174 David 135 Jennie 211 Jim 110 John 174 Nathan 174 Scot 50 Will 135
FREMAN, Kittie 94
FRENCH, Dus_ 230 Elizabeth 210
FRESH, Jonas 270
FRESHENS, Annie May 80
FRESHONS, Rebecca 14
FRESHOUR, Andrew 180 Charles 143 CW 235 Elizabeth 142 Infant 142 JE 273 Lavona 109 Lizzie 276 Mary 273 Michael 209 Scott 177 Vennie 235
FRIDDLE, Infant 32
FROST, Nancie 126
FRY, Dovie 2 Mrs EF 192 Henry 2 Infant 2 James Soloman 192 Martha 93 Mary J 222 Susan 203 Tom 90
FRYE, Hazel Pauline 284 James S 294 John 284 Martha Pauline 284 PA 294 Ulysses S 265 Vel_ Victor 265
FUKLERSON, Crocket 105 JM 199 Poff 51
FULKS, Alex 155 Sallie 162
FULLER, Malinda 140 204 242
FULLIN, Malinda 256
FULLINS, Eliza Jane 123
FULWILER, Sallie 124
FYAN, Mattie Jeniva 199
G __, Nellie 111 Susan 233
GABY, Artie Minte Couch 170 Dorthia Ann 16 Homer Wane 15 Inlia 16 Martin 294 William 170

GADDIS, Jessie 94 127 John 94 127 Lillie 7 Mack 112 Rean 94 Redmon 127
GAGELY, Mrs. Anna 45
GALASPIE, Loreta 56
GALLIEN, Houston 62
GALSCOCK, James 128
GAMMON, Doss 151 Eliza Ellen 100 LA 101 RJ 81 96 William 246 WR 151
GAMMONS, George W 228 Lou 238 Lulu B 198
GANNAWAY, Samuel 265
GARBER, Charlie 236 Christie A 27 Jacob N 153 Josie Carter 236 WM 249
GARDNER, Alfred 163 AD 125 Henry Lorenza 163 Infant 19 68 88 James 83 Joseph 88 Mary Jane 22 Olive 56 Sarah 19
GARGER, Jacob 153 William 153
GARLAND, Elijah 242
GARRETT, __ 222
GARRISON, Fannie 270
GASS, Cate 64 Conrad 4 David A 244 Mrs DA 265 Elizabeth 130 185 236 Elzie 190 Flora 182 GG 236 GH 228 GR 93 Henderson 148 Hiley 277 Hilie 30 Howard Clayton 148 Infant 30 187 Isabel 259 James Edwin 234 Joe 4 246 John 93 Joseph 184 J Robert 253 JB 234 Loura 201 Mattie 243 Minerva 149 MW 28 Ross 260 288 289 Roy D 253 Sarah 228 Srigfield 120 SM 201 Thomas 120 Willard 234 William 187 WH 265 Zola 184
GASSETT, Elizabeth 227 Estel 227 Mattie 227

GASTON, John W 257 Myrtle 257
GENTRY, Bobie 54 Carl 60 Cloyd R 174 Emeline 86 Ernest Edward 43 Ervin 57 Frankie 107 George 36 Gracie 225 James 23 Thomas 174 225
GEORGE, Luvena 151
GERDNER, John 109
GERNUER, Winnie 105
GIBBS, __ 287 Daniel Fox 198 Dave 107 Florence 107 Joe 169 198 William R 198
GIBSON, Andrew J 248 Calvin 254 David L 157 Dudley 254 Eva 248 John 248 John Thomas 254 JE 157 Mary Ann 292 WC 209
GILBERT, George R 266 Jane 146 Kenneth Garfield 266 Sarah 53
GILBRATH, Edith 226 JW 226
GILDON, John 101
GILGON, Virgie 234
GILLAN, Ethel 260
GILLAND, Elsie 287 Gwen 186
GILLESPIE, Charles 279 Eugene 280 Fannie 279 281 Robert J 279
GILLIAM, Mary 226
GIRDNER, Catherine 109 Sarah A 115
GLASCOCK, Edna 274 JT 274 Matilda 128
GLASPIE, Allice 5
GLASS, Daniel Sherman 242 Smith 242
GLASSCOCK, Granville Jackson 203 James 203 James F 203
GLEUDMON, Infant 57
GLOVER, Infant 125 Ollie 125
GODSEY, Charles 143 Joe 143
GOGDILL, Joe 116
GONAS, John 137 Sarah 137

GOOD, Elizabeth 32 Florence 72 Jacob 121 James K Polk 250 John 165 250 Joseph 111 JW 227 Maggie 250 Mary Hellen 51 Mattie 165 Michell W 111 ME 127 Nancy 164 Russell 72 William W 121
GOODE, John 227
GOODIN, Charles H 201 Martha 272 Ruth Inell 201
GOODMAN, Columbus 84 Minerva 252 TE 252
GORBER, Will 127
GORDD, Josie I 67
GOSNELL, BF 208 Katie 122 Major 122 Melenia B 78
GOSSETT, __ 165 Infant 165
GOSWELL, Millie 135
GOURLEY, Julia 240
GRACEY, WG 189
GRAGG, Elbert 124 Hannah May 124
GRAGLEY, Chassie E 132
GRAHAM, AT 28 Bessie 49 63 Eliza Ann 27 George 193 257 Infant 1 James 232 257 Mattie 249 Mollie 261 Roy 232 RG 218 Synthia 249 William A 193
GRANT, William G 263
GRAVES, Francis 283
GRAY, Amanda 102 107 Andrew P 1 Andy C 102 AW 41 Becky 263 Bessie 289 291 Bunion 77 Caroline 221 Cecil 102 Crawford 24 Cy 97 DJ 123 Earl 240 Ema Elizabeth 87 Eva 88 102 Flora 208 Fred 116 240 GS 24 Ida 38 James 26 John 21 130 John Trig 97 Lavada 24 Mandy 108 Mary 45 108 188 Moice 38 Peggy 292 Roxe 88 Rucy J 292 Samuel A 261 Ted 115 Troy 37 VS 188 Walter 88 102 William 87 WA 24 WG 208 266 WH 261

GRAYHAM, __ 185 Abraham 45 Mary 9 Jane 25
GREAR, Addie 271
GREEN, Georgie 142 Kate 25 Myrtle 24 Sallie 159
GREENE, Anna S 59 Clyde 247 Enos 176 George W 176 Infant 276 Jacob 272 James Walter 246 John 276 Lizzie 288 Martha G 176 Mary Catherine 272 Mathes 248 Stewart 248 WH 246
GREENLEE, Charles 165 James 288 Jesse J 48 John 288
GREER, __ 150 Alice 127 Carry 25 Cas 71 Elmer Ayers 12 Emory 25 Esther 196 278 John 156 Joseph 39 Julia 158 Jusie 25 Kate 158 Marshall 156 Melvina 49 Minnis 137 Robert 47 Sarah 201
GREGLEY, EF 132 Andrew B 271 Bertrum B 271 Jim 62 Martha 283 Mary 175 Sarah A 125
GRIERS, Hiram 227 Robert Gray 227
GRIFFEY, Steve 90
GRIFFIN, Dixie Mae 231 Robert W 231
GRIGSBY, Annie 105 Cordie 221 SJ 232
GRUBB, Alexander 172 John William 172
GRUBBS, __ 246 Frank 111 Willie 111
GRUEY, Laura 92

GUDGEN, __ 178 Infant 178 Anis
  63 George Walter 149 Steve 149
  Walter 148
GUFFIE, __ 134 Lee 134
GUINN, FC 275 Infant 275 PM 41
GUIRE, Hiram 260 Kelly 260
GULLEY, Jane 262
GUNTER, Caney H 115 GW 171
  Marietta 226 Oliver Moses 171
  Rubie 115
GURGER, Infant 1
GUSNELL, Dock 246 Hester 246
GUTHRIE, __ 136 Anderson A
  153 Andrew 188 AA 131 Hascal
  131 Joseph K 189 Lindell 153
  Mollie 163 William 148 167
  William Thomas 148 WT 148
  H__ Anis 125 Clara 179 Daisy 172
  David R 63 Elizabeth 257 Jane
  259 Mabeline 256
HAGOOD, Elizabeth 97 WM 97
HAIGOOD, Louisa 274
HAINER, Lucy 363
HAINNER, RA 159
HAINS, Ray 171
HAIR, George 80
HAIRE, Henry 207
HALE, Conway 11 Elizabeth 170
  Gladys Robal 248 HH 184 Infant
  184 Polly 275 SP 11
HALL, AW 127 Bet 285 David
  222 263 David E 112 250 Donna
  235 Effie 117 Eliga 127 Eveline
  283 Francis 247 John 112 JA 283
  Mary 121 Mary Cecil 222
  Mchoge 127 Martha J 74 Peggy
  121 Stanley M 64 Tennessee
  Payne 93 William 263 William A
  263 WA 195 WM 222 250
HAMET, Marah 53 Orua 259

HAMILTON, Mary 39 Tom 260
  Emeline 178
HAMLIN, Per__ 171
HAMMER, Lena 204
HAMMET, Bessie 262 Frank 262
HAMMOND, PL 143 Ruth Evelyn
  143
HAMPTON, B__ 54 Margaret 104
  Nancy 123
HANARD, Drelvie 49
HANEY, Calvin 130 Maggie 273
  Troy 57
HANIE, Ethel 127
HANKINS, E 251 Elizah K 49
  Harmon 289 Harold 288 John E
  27 John E Sr 130 Kidwell 98
  Laura 104 Nancy 98 Robert 190
  Ruth 288 TR 288 289
HANKS, Martha Jane 92
HANNAH, George 105 John W
  105 Cecil 261 Infant 261 James
  261
HANSEL, WJ 46
HARBARGER, IA 111
HARDEN, Robert R 27
HARDIE, Margaret 104
HARDIN, Charles 224 265 Cora
  200 Honor 253 John 253 Neal
  224 Rebecca 188 Tebitha 265
HARE, Abraham 144 John S 144
  Lane J 144
HARISON, Lucy 48
HARKLEROAD, Dortha 268
  Infant 83 142 Myrtle J 83 MJ
  142
HARMAN, Cleo 192
HARMON, Alice 135 Bessie 63
  Catherine 165 Catherine M 181
  Charles Elbert 176 Clodie 288
  289 Cloyd Vernon 148 Dana 282

Delia 40 196 DM 17 DW 177
Eliza 206 Elizabeth Beatrice 110
Emily G 282 Emma Cassander
275 Ethel 287 Floris 275 George
F 29 Hannah 277 Harrison C 205
Henry 262 Inez 196 Infant 280
Isaac D 196 Jacob 228 262 Jacob
Luther 205 James Edward 45
James F 138 Joe 7 173 205 Joe M
98 John 125 138 200 205 215
216 288 JB 125 JF 110 262 JL
136 JM 98 Mrs JS 205 JW 228
Keneda 209 Larinda C 115 Lillie
138 Lydia 176 LV 209 Margaret
209 Martin 78 Mary 98 236
Mordica 176 Moses Piny 125
Nannie 114 Onie F 63 Pearl 31
Pete 135 Peter 135 Robert 200
Robert L 136 Rufus 288 RP 205
221 275 Sarah 98 Simon B 136
Sparkling B 180 Susanna 108 SB
238 Taylor 228 VS 280 William
C 148 William Z 209 WT 134
HAROLD, Dodd 259 Elizabeth 74
Ella 129 JM 259 Laura 212
HARPER, Nancy 12
HARRIS, __ 206 Alfred 106 Elen
71 Francis Morrison 106 GD 66
Katie 150 Margarette 12 RD 241
William 47 116 Willie Kate 241
HARRISON, Alex 179 AL 106
Benjamin W 191 Bonnie 177
Mrs Bruce 290 Caleb A 118
Catherine E 70 DP 191 Ed 92
128 Elizabeth 57 Ella 270 Emma
129 Eulalia Margiria 118 Francis
130 George 190 Gertrude E 118
Grover 61 Ida 105 Infant 138
James 73 Jeremiah 191 Jessie
128 Joe 194 John 95 292 Lora

292 Margaret 198 Martha
Caroline 275 Melvin 194 N 230
Nina F 275 Rhea Aelene 21
Sallie 176 292 Synthia 256 SB
59 Wade Gahagan 130 Will 137
William B 138
HARROLD, Ann__ 128 EL 120
238 Lewis 120 Mary A 238
Nancy E 120
HARSHBARGER, Eugenia 149
HART, Bell 215 CM 140 215 Pearl
140 Tilman 215
HARTMAN, Charles Morris 155
Elsie Jane 28 Emma Virginia
270 Enoch 77 Fannie L 189 JP
171 JT 198 Lois 19 Lora 138
Marshall 171 Martha 289 Mary
81 166 Myrtle M 58 Myrtle M 58
Ollie Belle 151 Sarah A 139
Susana 149 TC 189 Vern 198
William 171 William H 155 WH
258 270
HARTSELL, Abraham 209
Charles C 209 George H 285 JS
209 Mary 17 Mary L 285
Sebastian 285
HASH, Callie 230 William 230
HASHBURGER, William
Alexander 240 ZS 240
HASKER, Mechitable 107
HASS, Margaret 190
HATLEY, Hobert 220
HAULSLEY, Serrih 40 WH 40
HAULTY, Ada 85
HAUN, Andrew 143 Charlie H 131
Elax 143 Eli 207 Elizabeth 143
Ethel 178 293 Florence Elizabeth
88 Hannah E 238 Hazel 5 Jacob
Daniel 143 James 131 176 Jim
176 John 88 John R 181 JH 181

Leona G 214 Lewis Cosmo 181
Martha Isabell Johnson 143
Orbie Mable 131 William 102
HAWK, Earl 279 Mrs Earl 279 FA
139 John 240 Lavina 139
Penelope J 240 William 240
HAWKINS, BA 263 Carrie 262
Charles 263 Ema Virginia 7
George 151 George W 263 GS
236 J 253 James Willis 151 John
236 John B 253 Mary A 82 Nora
115 SS 150
HAWS, Beryl 29 Orville H 122
HAYNES, Mary Elizabeth 97
Rachel 239
HAYS, Aaron 174 Amon 108
Annie 61 Bowman 261 Calmer
Jessie 289 Claud Lesley 261
Debora 237 Eliza 192 Elizabeth J
149 Essie Caldonia 250 Evret
195 George 172 Harriett 108
Harriett C 32 Infant 3 Jessie P
289 John H 153 John S 174 John
W 195 Joseph 153 Joseph H 3
Lexie Glenda 3 Malisa 153
Marion 172 235 Moliss 163 RA
198 Tilda 235 William
Alexander 3
HAYSE, Fannie Jerrels 213 GS
213 Paggie 108
HEADWICK, Malinda Jane 134
William M 134
HECK, Carl 142 Charles 111 Mrs
Charles 112 Levana 269 Maggie
67 Stewart 111 S_ 253
HEDDEN, Consel Lee 291
William 291
HELTON, Dugger 53 John 20
Marry 215 Robert 181
HEN__, Matilda 249

HENARD, Louis C 85 Madison 85
Naoma Jane 237 RC 237
HENDERSON, John 179 Malisa
43 Susan 287
HENDRIX, __ 108 Otis 114 Sarah
194
HENDRY, Alma Modene 161 Bill
198 Clara 174 Jo 198 Joseph 198
228 Lilior 80 Mary Ann 253 SA
161 WB 161 271 WE 253
HENRY, Allen 291 Ben A 240 BF
44 240 Ida V 272 James A 58
James R 272 John 117 235 Linda
117 Thomas A 26
HENSEL, Georgia 51
HENSHAW, Louisa 230 Nancy
27 William 230 Willison 162
HENSLEY, __ 282 Abraham 271
Amos 133 Andrew 243 Benjamin
247 Birtha 81 Blanch Gladen
217 Bonnie 248 BG 267 Cathern
130 Cora Belle 56 Ela 279 Eliza
248 Enoch H 133 Eula 200 202
Eva 250 Evert 59 Frank Winston
105 Garfield 220 GH 243 248
GW 250 Infant 60 James
Harrison 258 Jennie 147 Jesie
243 John 271 John Sr 247 Joseph
69 Josephine 243 Julia Mae 69
JA 258 Mary 179 Mary Edith
220 Michael 86 Minnie 60 169
MH 147 RC 282 Thomas H 105
Ursley 267 Vena 54 Walter 90
WM 81
HERMIN, Mamie 149
HERSCH, Sampson 256
HERTEN, WJ 27
HETTIE, PJ 12
HEUX, Alice 32
HICK, Mandy 184

HICKS, Betsie 177 181
HICKSON, JR 63
HIGGINS, Albert 243 Irvin 243
HIGHSINGER, George 257 WL 257
HIGHT, Ruth Maude 143
HILL, __ 276 Bertham B 138 BJ 266 Carl King 85 Hugh Jasper 85 HJ 85 Ida 266 Jasper 85 Jimmie G 240 William 36
HILTON, Elizabeth 102 Kizzie 209 Robert 102
HIPS, Mary 294
HITE, Martha 105
HIXON, Andy 214 Arthur 214 Ina Ruth 214
HIXSON, Grover C 195 William H 195
HOGAN, Adolphus 47 Frank Bell 119 Hunley 119 Lola Lee 77 Nancy 139 Sarah Cobble 195
HOISTONON, JR 114
HOLBROOK, James 261 JN 280
HOLDER, Mollie 12
HOLDERBY, Archie 259
HOLLAND, __ 190 Bruch 198 Claud 238 CN 280 Kittie 92 Luley Bell 228 Mary 112 Montie Maud 198 Omer 198 Susan 280 William Howard 238 William H 145 W Bruce 238 WH 228
HOLLEN, Card 151 Osker 76
HOLLEY, Helen 99 JP 290 Laura 219 Lawrence W 290 WM 99
HOLLOWAY, Mamie 116
HOLT, __ 108 Albert 43 Catherine 112 137 Ed 105 109 Evaline 163 Infant 261 Jacob 109 James 15 John 109 Lotta 113 Luther 161 Marion 105 Melvin 192 Sarah 43
Scot 105 Scott 161 163 261 Sparl 108
HOLTSCLAW, Joseph 112
HOLTSWANGER, Francis 222
HOMER, John 210
HONEYCUT, Infant 172 Robert 116 W Bruce 172
HONYCUT, Henry 80
HOOD, Alex 133 JA 202 Leona 133 Liney 48 Sallie A 187
HOOK, Lawrence Norman 222 SL 222
HOPE, __ 146 Caroline Matilda 19 Helen Leona 99 John 99 Lon 99 Pash 56
HORTON, Annie 120 Bula Jane 293 Emily 293 James M 266 John Charles 266 JR 266 Mart 152 Rachel 91
HOSEBERGER, Blanche 175
HOUSE, Ethel 231
HOUSLEY, Benjamin Franklin 90 Howell 90
HOUSTON, Birtie 109 Emily 202 Howel 264 Isaac 122 James 122 JG 93 Martha 118 Meneva 93 Penelope 39 Rankin 122 Wayland Lee 130 William 130 264 WA 249
HOWARD, Hamilton Baldwin 104 Joseph S 104 Mary 135 Samuel 104
HOWELL, GM 251
HOWS, Deborah 104
HUBBARD, Charlie 159
HUDDLESTON, Prescilla 109
HUFF, Ella 128 EB 290 John 290 Julia K 228 Levina 76 Mrs Noah 71 Wilson 290

HUFFAKER, Robert D 138 RO
287 Wanda Deforest 138
HUFFMAN, Fannie Maxine 152
Louvellie Belle 263 Mrs MH 263
Robert 152
HUGHES, Archibald 104
Benjamin H 148 Eliza 286 Grant
104 Hiram B 218 James 109
James H 148 J Lafayette 218
Laura 109 Thomas 104 WP 148
HULL, Alfred 70 DM 63 Eula Bell
131 Isaac Bonham 231 John 123
John M 131 134 231 JM 231
Mary Ruth 36 Milton 172 TS 93
HULSE, Mary 7 Sarah 51
HULSEY, Infant 12
HUMBARD, Bob 200 Hazel 260
Ike 260 Meldrid 200 Susanne 45
Hazel 241 IW 241 Rachel 179
HUMPHREY, Maude 115
HUMPHREYS, Clarence 78 Eliza
20 Annie Lucy 194 Cora 140
Elizabeth 250 Jessie 286 Mrs JT
194 Mande 219 Maud 175 MF
287 PG 286 SH 194
HUNEYCUT, Henry 20 Lizzie 164
Robert 164
HUNT, Catherine 243 Elen 66
Flora Bertha 26 GB 77 Rebecca
82 Sarah Jane 82 Susan 211
Susiana 3 William 233
HUNTER, Benjamin F 262 Cynthy
257 Georgia 126 Harrison 262
Katherine 95
HUNTSMAN, Gay Nell 178
Grafford E 291 James Butler 291
James B 178 293 J Butler Jr 231
JA 120 JB 127 231 Minnie B 293
Mrs NJ 120 Ruth Butler 127

HURLEY, B_ 203 Caroline 162
Clearly 184 Eva 283 GF 176
Maria 158 Miss 168 Rachel 96
Susan Kate 114
HURST, Callie 198 WA 219
HUSTON, Fannie 156 WA 249
HUTCHINGS, Selestra 157
HUTCHINSON, __ 200
HUX, __ 81 BC 271 Charles 146
Cora 74 Dovy 74 Edd 233 Gladys
146 Infant 49 James 57 Julia 271
Rosa Mae 233 William 98
HYBARGER, Infant 111
HYDER, __ 132 Drucilla 205 Ella
83 Hariet 116 Harriett 164 James
E 271 James F 22 John T 181
Opal 181 Vernie 286 William 10
William Hartman 271
IDELL, Henry 191 250 284 Iny
Mae 250 John Clyde 191 Maggie
E 284 Sara E 257
ILSHIE, __ Mrs 81
INGLE, Bell 275 Cenith 217 Ellis
B 105 217 Maud Duncan 105
Thomas 217
INMAN, __ 107
INSCORE, Edgar 232 Edna 48 Joe
232 Mattie 163
INSEARE, JH 28
IRVIN, Minnie 128
IRVING, Lucy 213
ISAM, Arther 238 Jake 238 Kate
238
ISELY, Jane 95 JM 95
ISHAM, Gordon 157 Jacob 147
Marion Franklin 147
ISLEY, Alpha 172 Wilburn 27
ISOM, Gordon 88 John Henry 88
Mollie 88
IVINS, Alpha Carolina 106

JACK, Ira T 107 Melvin Leroy 107
ML Jr 107 Mrs ML 150
JACKSON, Bettie 64 Beulah V 14
BE 137 Charles 168 202 Emeline
218 HC 202 HN 172 Infant 202
James K Polk 172 James T 147
202 Jane 64 Jessie 210 John M
137 JKP 106 Martha 263 Mary
Alice 106 Otha Lee 173 Robert
157 RC 10 Sallie 124 Sarah 94
Steve 218 Taylor 172 Thomas
202
JAMES, Charles 19 Dona 183
Flora 139 Louise 36 Martha 166
JANES, Andrew Jackson 170
Berley 5 CJ 213 GA 38 Jack
Bernard 213 John 170
JARRELL, JM 211
JEFFERS, Briney 191 BA 263 DC
71 Emma 244 Essie 20 Infant 20
J 205 James 160 James H 214
Joseph Wheeler 132 John 214
Lucy Lee 71 Maggie 214 Robert
Taylor 26 Ruphus 3 Samuel E
132 SE 91 Will W 291
JEFFRIES, James 164
JENKINS, Elizabeth 139 Gabral
139 Infant 9 John 207 Joseph 95
JM 193 Mary 209 Sallie 86
JENNINGS, Billie 85 Blanch 253
DW 223 Effie 163 Elizabeth 151
Homer 49 JK 24 Kennedy H 37
Malinda 29 MR 136 Roy 189
Samuel 189
JERRELS, MF 213
JESTES, Serel 27
JOBE, Can 237 Joseph Russell 53
Lessie 237
JOHNSON, _ 286 Addie 2 Alex
32 59 Alice 41 Amy 119 Andrew
168 Annie 94 Azylda 226 AJ 100
AS 37 Barbara 28 Barbara
Elizabeth 94 Ben 260 Charles M
237 CA 124 CG 93 David 36
Della N 196 Dora 212 Dora Belle
92 Dora B 206 Elmer 198 Ervin
Emmett 119 E Ellen 167 Frank
45 Fred 199 G_ 198 Georgia 89
Glena R 270 GA 270 GW 198
Harrison 119 Henry 154 Hester
Virginia 154 Iley 87 Infant 21 68
142 199 237 Jadie 93 James 137
146 156 James Sr 146 Jim 188
226 John 89 156 John 204 John
S 276 Julia 171 JL 143 KM 119
222 Laura 119 138 Lawrence 24
Lee 196 Lillie 143 Lucile 60
Lura Anna Cutshall 103
Margaret 93 Marsha 222 Martha
47 Mary 179 Mary E 80 Matilda
21 May 271 Nancy 230 Nancy J
237 Other 188 Pauline Ruth 204
Pearl 260 Pleasant 283 Rachel
154 Retty 245 Robert 119 Rufus
222 Ruth 154 Sarah VAn D 58
Stephen 276 SL 276 Thomas 119
TA 142 Mrs TF 292 William 168
William H 200 William K 273
Willis 94 WE 93 WF 25
JONES, _ 226 266 Mrs _ 248
Ada 180 285 Alex 178 Allig 290
Anna May 107 Annie 37 Bertha
180 Betsey 191 Brabson 219
Caney 120 Cathern 195 Celia V
23 Charles 73 262 Charles P 180
Charlie 254 CE 123 Daniel 125
Dave 107 David 206 Ed 148
Edith 233 Elic 95 Eliza 103
Elizabeth 206 Elmer A 57 Febia
125 Florence 81 Fred 186 Garret

72 Gass 218 Glena 186 Hazaline
57 Henry 230 Horton 103 172
Mrs HO 223 Infant 4 43 57 96
172 218 Irene F 210 Isabelle 182
Jack 287 James 235 Jane 131
Jennie 43 233 Julia 60 J Marion
210 JH 109 JL 167 JM 210 216
Kin 115 Laura 55 Licindy 183
Lila 116 L Clark 235 Maggie
161 Margaret 183 Mrs Marion
216 Mary 160 223 Mollie 132
218 MC 233 N_ 205 Naoma 5
Nettie 82 Oscar 120 R 143
Rachel 98 Ralf James 254 Robert
254 Robert R 271 Ross 167 RE
98 Sallie 288 Samuel 212 Sarah
189 Sarah M 143 Sheridan 96
SD 212 Thomas J 258 Tildy 232
TM 140 William 206 263 285
William Maynerd 178 WC 132
WE 125 235 WM 98 YJ 248
JORDAN, Betsie 263 Charlie 40
Emily 252 JW 201
JUSTIC, Sarah J 211
JUSTICE, _ 91 Daniel K 214
Donald 78 Elizabeth 132 Ethel
51 Hannah J 26 Henry 4 Jacob 8
James 4 5 LR 94 Maggie 8
Margaret Ann 214 Mary E 83
Polly Ann 89 Mrs RC 94 Robert
94 Ruth 160 TT 27 William
Elbert 83 WA 83
JUSTIS, Alfred 258 Anderson 236
Florra 275 Jacob 185 201 James
Eugene French 201 John 258
Jonnie 185 Lucinda 275 Mamie
119 Margaret Ann 15 Margaret
Elizabeth 236 Margaret H 15
Martha 9 Nancy Ann 102 Nannie
258

K_, Rebecca 120
KAHL, Alice 249 John 32 Roy 57
KEE, Mary 92
KEEBLER, Mary S 92 Sana 170
KEELE, Matilda 157
KEELER, John R 89 Wash 89
KEENER, Roxie 248
KEICHER, Aaron 114 Minnie 114
KEIFER, Bersheba 192 James M
192
KEKER, Josie 255
KELEY, Nora Murtel 119
KELLER, _ 199 Bonnie 104 BF
84 Chassic 281 CD 106
Elizabeth 84 Ellen 167 Ena 102
HD 223 James KP 184 Mrs
James KP 15 Jane 30 John 280
281 Josephine 280 JB 104 JC 276
JKP 277 JM 38 Lavina 291
Major 19 Mary Jane 109 Phillip
184 Sarah 164 Sindia 19 William
144 293
KELLEY, _ 152 Ethyl S 127
Ettie 240 George 19 Hugh 19
Javis 109 John 240 JC 130 157 JJ
227 Luke 227 Martha J 130 Mary
Reed 255 Robert J 255 RT 240
255 Samuel 151 William 66
KELLIM, Milburn 203 Mona 203
Robert 203
KELLY, Dana Milburn 137 Jeff
137
KELTON, JC 187 Martha 227
Minnie 291
KENIERY, Elizabeth 186
KENN, Terry 275
KENNEDY, Fanney 22 Lanisa L
19 Rhoda 53 Samuel 206
KENNEY, Colman Campbell 110
Daniel 151 Eliza Jane 232 Elmer

208 Infant 199 208 James 110
John 227 JM 110 Laura V 114
LD 232 LK 199 Nancy 249
Nancy L 191 Sarah 151 Sarah
Madu 106 Willie Good 197 WA
151
KENT, Harriet 70 John 260
Martha Jane 179 MH 84 260
William 260
KERBAUGH, Mrs John 177
KERBOUGH, Dale 40 Elizabeth
270 Mrs James 181
KERGOUGE, Martah M 72
KERTZ, Eviline 226
KESLING, Cattie 96
KESTERLING, Fred 167 RN 167
KESTERSON, Florence 185 Jacob
Elbert 292 John 96 292 Riley 96
Sarah Adaline 167 Thomas 162
KESTON, JV 26
KETRON, AC 147 John Thomas
147
KEY, Albert 158 John 158 Nona
113
KEYES, Elizabeth 78
KEYS, Aaron 166 Aaron Jr 166
CH 128 Margaret 99 NA 167
KICK, Steward 184
KIDWELL, Alice 233 Cecil Paul
245 E 83 Elijah 146 Ettie 137
George W 245 John 146 Josiah
285 Mae 148 Mariah 285
KIFER, Infant 44
KIKER, Elizabeth 276 JS 161
KILDAY, Alexander H 106 Mary
20 Mattie 65 Mourie 18 Nettie
110 Willard Lee 106
KILGORE, __ 97 Ellen 127 SS
108 Willis 190

KILLIAN, Effie 178 Jacob 158
Joseph Huff 158 Martha Diana
207 Mary Isabel 272 Tom 272
278 WG 207
KIMBELL, John 387
KIMERY, Arbra C 254 Crete 254
Edith 254 Jessie 254
KINCHLOE, John 142 Birtha 89
Elizzie 89
KING, Charles J 115 Elisha S 154
Eva 291 ES 115 George 112
Infant 1 John 154 JC 259 Mary
44 Mollie 251 Perrie 55 Polly
267 Ruth 56 Sarah 217 Thomas
21 44
KINGSLEY, Ross 286
KINNURY, Jacob 94
KINPP, Guy 22
KINSER, Ella 278
KIRK, __ 96 Andrew 162 Buford
230 Clara L 43 Culman 32
Dorothy 230 Elbert 227 Ellen
227 Flora 155 219 John 120
Joseph 98 Joseph A 109 Joseph
Granville 227 JF 152 JW 101
Lemuel C 98 Levina 76 Luona 42
LV 98 Martha Florence 162
Mines Ralph 152 Mollie 42 Ona
88 Orville 96 Richard 155
Thomas Edward 47
KISER, AD Jr 129 CM 129 Infant
129
KISK, John Leonard 48
KISTERSON, Rettia 133
KITE, Alfred 140 210 Charley 269
Charley R 156 DL 168 GW 114
Infant 16 Joe 139 John 114
Lasarath 17 Mary 210 Matilda
17 Pauline 168 Robert 114 Sallie

175 Sallie Kate 156 Silvins Joe 139
KNICELY, Charley 201 Lanise 201
KNIGHT, Ambrose 156 Belle 143 Blaine 156 Dellie E 72 Edith 182 Emma 156 George 176 Greenville 21 GW 162 Homer Price 121 Infant 48 162 John 95 Joseph 76 Lizzie 233 Nancy M 176 RF 70 Will 95 WM 121
KNIPP, Elsie 22 Mary 35
KNITHT, Bertie 178
KNOTT, Lasey 29
KNOWLES, George 203 Henry Washington 203 William 204
KNUCKLES, Ed 174 Eveline 268 Moses Isaik 174
KOHL, James 234
KOONTZ, Grace 100
KORTZ, Eslaine 141
KRUNKELTON, Kate 186
KUKER, Rebecca 164
KYKENDALL, Avery 219 Avery A 155 Clarence 226 Flora 155 Infant 226 Milta 29 Neavele 219 Neple 155 Price 226
KYLE, Houston 114
KYLES, Jack S 131 Salina S 131
L_, Alex 164 Carrie 144 Nancy 168 Christie 92
LACEY, Isaac 166
LADY, Cora 153 220 Emery 153 Emory 220 Margaret 90 Oneal C 153 Orval D 220 Polly 168 231
LAFOLLETT, Benjamin 185 Scott 168
LAFOLLETTE, Clark 271 Joseph 1 Sadie 271

LAMB, Alice 29 Bertha Lois 97 CH 266 Earnest 97 John R 275 Julia 275 JM 275 Minnie 29 Orpha 275 William 30
LAMBERT, Corda 102 JA 81 Mary 81 Polly Ann 127
LAMBERTSON, Florence 40
LAMONS, E_ 200 George G 282 Henry 282 Sallie 89 WA 282
LANCASTER, Eustis A 116 John B 116
LAND, Manda 181
LANDRES, John 89
LANE, __ 107 261 271 Alf 116 Charles Lonzo 191 Crocket W 208 Eliza 12 Grayson 222 James 150 268 Joe 222 John 124 JD 12 JF 112 Katherine 112 Kizziah 220 Martha 268 293 Mary J 222 Milbord 19 Nancy B 268 Patsy 28 Patton 248 Pery 50 Sallie 116 Sam C 249 Sarha Jane 233 Sophia 49 SC 191 Tennie 280 Thomas 280 Viola 43 Virginia 248 William 233 249 268 280 WE 208
LASTER, Andrew J 172 Caroline 264 Ham 167 H Dave 167 Laura Annie 167 Martha Lelah 172 William Edward 167
LATHAM, Susan 240
LATHEM, Susan 97
LATMONS, Jay 13
LAUDERDALE, Angeline 232 Benjamin Franklin 231 Carl 269 Eliza 280 George 231 Infant 269 Nancy 88 Robert 280
LAUGHLIN, Ema 251 Josie 283 JH 141
LAUGHTER, Daisy 279

LAUGHTERS, Faun 5 Lawrence 5
LAUGHTNER, Eliza 98
LAURY, HV 250
LAUTHTLIN, William 140
LAWING, Elbert Ambros 97
  Grace 91 JF 97 WW 97
LAWLESS, Willie 47
LAWRY, Pearl L 250
LAWS, Alford 255 Charley 33
  Dave 163 Dora 53 Effie 37 Flora
  236 Franklin 255 GW 236 Infant
  37 53 104 Jack 163 Jacob 255
  Laura 226 Lillie 33 Margaret L
  33 Nola 230 Thomas 230 Tilda
  53 Tom 104
LAWSON, Etta 214 George 194
  John A 224 JM 218 Ruth 183
  Sherman 224
LAYUCK, Eugene 2
LAZENBERY, Eldridge Hausel
  199 George 199
LEE, Bonnie 105 Lula V 192
LEGARD, CW 165 Helen 165
LEGEND, CW 174
LEMANS, Lida 142
LEMING, James 155 Samuel 155
  Samuel W 32 Tempa 219
LEMONS, Mercia Elizabeth 200
  Samuel 184 Wesley 184
LENTZ, JM 225
LEONARD, B_ 141 Bettie J 141
  Callie 165 Jake 55 Maud 267
LESEN, Emma 28
LEWIS, James 21 Martha L 246
  Noel 246 Thomas 21
LIEBS, JH 176 Letha May 176
LIGHT, Catherine 97 E_ 141
  Gilbert 68 Hannah 257 John 262
  Martha 262
LILLIAN, Joseph Huff 158

LILLY, S Walter 166 Warren 166
LINEBARGER, __ 260 Ada B 202
  Alpha I 39 Fox 151 G Fox 151
  Hobart L 91 Infant 151 James A
  91 James H 46 Martha 260 Nola
  260
LINEBAUGH, Catherine 150
  Daniel 287 Elizabeth 7 84 Jacob
  287 John 31 163 282 John M 287
  Kate 287 Minnie 234 Pop 197
  Rebecca A 7 Samuel 290
LINK, Caroline 73
LINSER, Linie 205
LINTIAUM, Martha 218
LINTZ, Bell 192 Dewey 234
  Emma 191 Infant 234
LIPTRAP, Tomas 2
LISTER, Daisy 83 George 165 GW
  41 Hattie Virginia 165 Jaunita M
  33 John 105 Julia 197 Mary 209
  Robert 270 Sam 197
LITTLE, Nat 18
LIVINGSTON, Lena Belle 229
  Lonnie 229
LIVINGSTONE, Dona 178 John
  W 205
LLOY, Margarette 13
LOCK, Hattie 107
LOGAN, Andrew J 106 Charles F
  254 Hellen 123 Infant 254 MF
  123
LOLAR, Felix 254
LOLLER, Etta Eva 173 William
  173
LONES, AJ 190 Margaret 190
  Tom 190
LONG, AB 70 AW 27 Carrie Bell
  240 Carrie G 132 CW 114 Dock
  90 EL 240 Infant 269 Ira 178
  291 John 27 JR 70 JS 90 Lawson

269 Mae 111 Mary Elizabeth 291
Mima Jane 90 Otha 178 Ruth E
272
LONGMIRE, JA 138
LOONEY, Homer 122 Infant 171
Lilly 122 Mary Eveline 230
Michael E 171 Ruben Earl 122
WM 98
LOTH__, Susan 228
LOUDERBACK, Mahach 106
LOUDERMILK, Daisy 143
LOUGHLEY, Frank 224
LOVE, AB 102 BW 132 CS 124
Dr 131 263 Eliza 273 Elizabeth
22 Ethel 59 Hube 116 J 192
James L 192 Jay 116 JC 196 L_
132 Luven M 240 Mable 184
Mary 31 34 Odeca A 34 Oscar
196 Rote 57 Venie 224 Vice 179
Vinie 152 William E 196 WA
273_
LOVEDAY, Curtis Monroe 280
William 280
LOVELL, John 235 Sallie 235
LOWE, Alfred 271 Alonzo 105
Andrew 257 Delia Alice 182
Elizabeth 245 Emma 89 ER 205
Frank 163 George 105 Grover
Lafayette 205 Henry R 28 James
E 271 John Robinson 215 Joseph
163 JC 215 JP 271 Myrtle B 28
Tom 182 Wallace Henry 257
Will 55
LOWERY, Clarence 209 Dalie
May 209 Elbert 34 Infant 183
Mary 239 Mary Ann 90 William
183
LOWRY, Bonnie May 276
Catherine 176 Charlie 194 Dovie
226 HV 191 James 276 Jessie

193 194 JL 279 Mattie 196
Myrtle 280 281 Pearl Sus 191
Sallie 193
LOYD, Alice 205 Allis 180
Burlow 36 Charles 131 John 180
Julia 52 JM 86 Melvina 202
Nancy 19 Simon 263 Sinda 51
Thomas 180 William 284
LUCAS, Callie 78 Jane 240 Mary
122
LUITZ, John M 124
LUMBERTSON, Alice 8
LUSTER, Clinton 228 Henry 193
H Dave 167 Jack 241 James 115
Jennie 115 John 139 281
Lorenda 4 Peter 115 Robert Noah
147 William 228
LUTTRELL, Cat 160 Dolphes L
14 George 58 GW 72 JH 178
Katherine Lou 178 Laura 56
Martha 57 Maud Ethel 255 Ota
161 Robert 118 Robert J 47
Thebia 14 TJ 245 Mrs TJ 245
LYLE, Jane 123 Robert 249
William 249
LYLES, Delilah 266
LYNCH, Annie Lytisa 98 Cordie
200 George W 231 GF 253
Joseph 103 Josephine 197 Sarah
231 WK 5
LYONS, Lizzie 142
M_, Mary 175 Susan 196 Rettie
231
MACE, Adilia 177 Emmie Evalon
213 George Washington 139
Hannah 68 Mary 139 Sarah 103
MADISON, Gullum 224
MAGEE, Clara Lee 216
MAHONEY, Anna 17 Belle 173
John 173 Wesley 173 WF 173

MAINES, Nancy 110
MALINE, HB 164 John 164 John D 164
MALLONE, Roy 16
MALONE, __ 163 Andy 4 192 Annie Elizabeth 244 AB 192 Bewley 4 Charlie 166 CA 167 Della 173 Don 185 277 Dora C 290 Duncan D 211 Effie 96 Elbert 277 Elizabeth F 201 Finey 291 Francis 261 George 43 229 Gurtie 192 Humphrey 84 Ida 148 James H 211 Jennie A 282 John 89 229 236 Joseph 185 Kate 290 Lizzie 185 Lou 191 Mandy Beatrice 8 Margaret 246 Martha Jane Keller 167 Mary 30 166 181 Mary Ann 30 84 Matilda 264 Olive 79 Rebecca 112 Roy 67 Samuel E 244 SJ 287 Truly 51 Vida 220 William 84 138 236 WA 101 WH 230
MALONEY, George A 66 James 191 JJ 146 Lea 155 Martha J 126 Phoebe Ann 263 Robert 282
MALTSBARGER, Cathern 187
MALTSBERGER, Cahterine 185 GWM 260 Harvy 50 Nancy 259
MANAR, Nancy 141
MANESS, Alfred 120 Alfred Allen 120 Aflred A 218 AA 218 Charley 218
MANIS, Rebecca 243
MANUEL, Edith 57 Infant 43 44
MANUL, Fred 54
MARION, L_ 52 Lula Bell 113
MARISETT, Millie 35
MARKS, JW 182
MARKWOOD, Lelia 193
MAROK, Nancy Jane 222

MARROW, Maud 129
MARSHAL, AE 96 Guy 76 Lendin Vincen 96
MARSHALL, Ailent 22 Annie 162 AE 152 Clifford 41 Edith 152 Eva Elizabeth 75 Jack 135 John 109 JC 83 103 111 118 121 Lilly 122 Lou 151 LB 1 Martha M 90 Mary Caroline 190 Minnie 121 Robert 121 Veral L 12 Willie Kate 42
MARTIN, Birdie Kate 42 Bob 149 Frank 284 Frank R 268 Grant 268 284 Jennie 149 Lewis P 284 Margaret A 154 Robert 42 Sevier M 268
MASNEL, Ann 22
MASON, DC 166 Joe 264
MASSEY, Emma Carter 204 Emma C 203 GF 166 James 203 James B 204 Julia A 166 JB 203 WT 260
MASSIE, Rachel 69
MASSY, Edward Milburn 95 Guder 95 GF 96
MATHER, Fannie 197
MATHES, Chester Lee 222 Cordie 126 George 284 Henry 185 James 284 JB 197 JD 285
MATHEWS, Lewis 24 SF 96
MATHIS, Bob 185 Infant 109 244 Wilber 109 Wilbur 222 WH 244
MATIABURGER, Haley 170
MATTHEWS, EW 173 Jacob Lafayette 110 John Thomas 173 Tilda Ann 96
MAUK, AH 151 Jake 25 John 151
MAULDIN, John 120 Will 120
MAUPIN, __ 274 Jit 100
MAUSHLER, Margaret 140

MAU_, Amanda Broyles 259
MAXWELL, RC 41
MAY, Nancy J 38
MAYERS, Emoline 17
MAYEST, Lizzie 178
MAYS, Mabel E 165 Malinda 124 259
MCABEE, John 145 Susan 145 Thomas 66
MCAFEE, Eliza 95 Leonard King 95 Marion 95 Sallie 236
MCAFERS, __ 169
MCAMIS, __ 150 Alfred 202 Delie Ethel 266 Elbert 87 Eva 180 George D 202 Iva 277 John 6 276 Martha C 239 Mrs Jimmie 45 Nancy 44 Nancy Catherine 117 Robert 55 Thomas 135 Thomas Sr 135 William Pleasant Anderson 276 WA 135
MCANIS, Archibald 4
MCANNIS, Loyd 50
MCBROOM, __ 283
MCCALL, Elizabeth 121 John 101 Louise 101
MCCALLISTER, Lee 214
MCCAMEY, HP 167 HS 158 Joe 251 Kenneth 251 Lydia May Belle 29 Samuel Jackson 257
MCCAMPBELL, Edward 234 John 234
MCCAMY, Mary 217
MCCANISH, James 52
MCCARNEY, HP 147
MCCLAIN, Bessie 117 Dan 180 David 27 Louise 180 Mary 164
MCCLURE, Elizabeth 188 John 171 Lizzie 92
MCCONNELL, Orpha 9
MCCORD, Elizabeth 197

MCCORKLE, Catherine 206 Floy 125 William 253
MCCOWN, Bess 42 Mary 42
MCCOY, Ben 140 David 142 Dock 142 Elis 161 George W 161 Infant 8 James 61 JW 116 Martha 255 Mollie 209 Polly A 130 Robert 152 184 Shafter 161
MCCRACKEN, James 115 Robert 115
MCCRARY, Joseph 219
MCCRAVY, Benjamin 248
MCCRAY, Edith 2 Jennie 18
MCCROSKY, Roxie Leona 68
MCCULLUM, CW 103 Jasper 178 John 178
MCCURRY, __ 186 Belle 163 Emie 263 Ida 118 John 112 JH 250 Katherine 102 Letha M 238 Minnie 247 Samuel P 250
MCCURY, Idie I 294
MCCURY, Richard 121
MCC_, Florence 173
MCDADE, Addie 169
MCDANIEL, Fanny 224
MCDAVIS, Mary A 247
MCDONAL, Dessie 70
MCDONALD, AC 278 Davis L 247 Effie 157 Herman 31 Infant 247 James 66 Jane 231 John 134 June 198 Mary 117 Minnie 140
MCFALLS, Celia 213
MCFARLAND, __ 237 Florence 180
MCFERRIN, Mrs JG 105
MCGAMERY, Clarnce 159 Infant 159
MCGEE, Clide 252 Daniel 252 Ed 91 Edd 136 216 Infant 91 Lora

Anza 136 Maggie 91 Mary 121
RE 121
MCGHEE, Adriane 212 Walter
 212 William 212
MCGINLEY, Miss NI 57
MCGUFFIE, Adie 162 Lida F 150
MCGUIRE, Jonathan 97 Limon B
 97 Mrs LB 97 MF 66
MCINTURF, Infant 61
MCINTURFF, Sarah Ann 154
MCKAY, __ 66 Arrah W 157 BM
 70 FH 157 Robert 157
MCKEE, John 293 Robert M 293
 Sally P 41
MCKFFIE, Lillie 117
MCKINNEY, Eliza 120 Jennie
 211 Jerry 211 Marshall 76 Will
 211
MCLAIN, CJ 85 Hobert 33 JM 275
 Leonard Mitchell 83 M 264 Mrs
 SH 183 Thomas M 274
MCMACKEN, RF 10 John 141
 John L 246 RF 246
MCMACKINS, Elizabeth 117
MCMILLAN, Lidia 5 Lou 203
 Mary E 35 Nancy 270
MCMILLEN, Daner 152
MCMURTY, Pheba 118
MCMYSTIC, Bettie 132 Vol 132
MCNABB, Earle 208 Lula A 91
 Walter 91 203 William A 208
 William A 208 WA 203
MCNAMAR, Jennie V 31
MCNEAL, Mattie 190
MCNEESE, Bessie B 267 Francis
 Marion 157 Mrs FM 157
 Grovenor 239 Infant 7 45 IP 32
 Lacy 17 Rolina 1 Samuel 157
 Sarah 148 Susan 277 Wiley 168

MCNEW, Charles 202 219
 Charles D 135 Charles D 135
 Charley 115 Charley D 175 CW
 115 Garfield 175 Infant 115 175
 Irene 219 James 135 202
 Josephine 58 WR 135
MCPEARSON, Alex 71
MCPERAN, Laura 5
MCPERSON, Joe Jr 172
MCPHERSON, James Robert
 Alexander 156 L_ 172 LA 178
 Sarah 153 Tailor 156
MCQUEEN, Bert R 218 HO 218
MCSINGER, Mary E 40
MCWAMAR, Jennie V 31
MC_, Margaret 215
MEAL, James R 15
MEFFORD, Nancy 86
MEIRIEL, Frank 50
MELONE, MB 89
MELTON, Charlie 198 David 259
 Dollie 232 James E 78 John 120
 198 John Jr 120 Johnie Livi 46
 Lewis E 161 Lucinda 289 LE 161
 Martin Colombus 161 Rettie 13
 Sam 163 Silas 120 William 13
 Willie Ardell 163
MERCER, Charles 223 Hannah
 201 James R 86 JD 223 Martha
 Ann 206 Mikel 211 Sarah 85
MERCY, Fred L 134 211 Freda
 Lenore 134
MESINGER, John 69
METCALF, Absolom 147 Hiram
 147 SE 147
MIDDLETON, Abagill Hays 174
 David 117 James 281 James N
 287 Lafayette 281 Maggie 11
 Mariah Jane 1 Rosa 6 18 65
MIKLE, Pheba 170

MIL_, Rachel 125
MILBURN, John Lilburn 274
  Jonathan 267 Joseph F 184
  Joseph P 211 JJ 184 Mary 211
  May 184 WM 274 WR 274
MILIGAN, James 193
MILLER, Abraham 135 AM 166
  Barbe 118 Caroline 69 Cecil 64
  Della 73 Eldridge 267 Elizabeth
  123 Felix 54 Florence 22 Frank
  207 Gertrude 168 GM 102 Infant
  145 James 292 Jasper 153 Joe
  145 John N 6 Julia 275 Mary 89
  Mary A 152 Ruth 153 Sallie 207
  Sarah 69 248 Sarah Jane 130
  Spencer 267 Susan 166 Thomas
  242 Twoney 118 WA 152
MILLIGAN, Dewey 4 John 192
  WW 192
MILLS, Everhart 14 WB 125
MILTON, Elizabeth 26 Lula
  Albertie 45
MIMMS, Elizabeth 262
MITCHEL, Caty 55
MITCHELL, AJ 26 Bruce 156
  Edward 107 Eliza 284 EB 108
  Fannie 75 George W 156
  Hughley 132 James 140 229 284
  Jesse 37 John B 284 John J 229
  JJ 159 Katie 72 Lizzie 105
  Lucretia 24 Lucy 140 Minnie 159
  Mollie 194 Thomas 24 177 Will
  K 229 William 107 284 William
  R 108 111 Willie Kate 177 WT
  90 159 182 186 204 241
MOCUIER, Jennie 94
MOFFETT, __ 293
MONGER, Ann 200
MONK, Rolie 176 Whittny 176

MONTGOMERY, Cathrn 32 Ella
  91 103 154 184 Ransom 200
  Will 200 289
MONTUTH, S_ 185
MOODY, Elizabeth 193 J 193
  Mary 121
MOON, __ 103 Marilu 210
MOONEYHAM, James A 137
  Orpha 137 162 Samuel 162
  William 162
MOOR, Ricina 250
MOORE, Andy 173 Arch 20 AJ 66
  AN 56 Belle 93 Bonnie May 141
  Carrie 208 Dr 220 Edward 217
  Eliza 84 Enoch 242 Golden 280
  Henderaon 274 Hubert 70 Infant
  1 James Dexter 288 James J 288
  Jane 117 John 93 John R 217
  Mrs John R 217 J Carson 124
  138 141 163 168 Marlina
  Hartsell 146 Mary Elizabeth 107
  Milburn Ingle 141 Nellie 97
  Orval 274 Parley 173 Sarah 1
  SW 214 Taylor F 71 Toledo 52
  William Sherwood 146 WC 169
  WP 107 WS 219
MOORELOCK, Royan 171
MOPPIN, Lydia 1
MORELCOCK, Mary Elizabeth
  245
MORELOCK, Alex 44 Ana 3 BW
  14 Charlie A 225 Charlie B 83
  CA 92 Daisey E 137 DA 207
  Elbert Alexander 123 Elvira 125
  EA 123 134 245 Hannah 112 HL
  242 Ida Carter 134 Infant 225 J
  215 Jacob 58 James 126 171 Jane
  245 JM 125 JW 93 234 248
  Louise 206 Lucretia 77 Michael
  34 Mike 83 Montie 10 Nancy

291 Oletha 63 Phronia 277 279
Richard 125 Rufer Burton 277
SF 217 TL 291 Una 292 Vinie
277 Virginia Preston 217
William 277 Willie Lee 123
MORGAN, Bonnie 257 CB 92 155
Felix Elbert 84 Frank 232
Hannah 226 James Abel 199
Laura Myrtle 84 Nancy 199
Rebecca Malinda 233 Robert 199
270 Thomas 155 Till 55 White
199 Wiley 155 William 242
MORIS, Silvie 121
MORRIS, Adam 94 Burton Arnold
89 Cora 285 Fred 89 93 Harriet
246 Henry 78 Jennie 253 Joe 86
Landon 93 Mattie 234 Nancy 217
Raymond 86 Rhoda E 208 Sallie
113 Sarah 235 WA 279
MORRISON, Anna 112 Benson
239 Cara 279 Charles 33 Cora
Pearl 285 Dellie 17 Elmer 112
Francis 106 Gilbert M 201 GN
84 Hannah 281 Infant 67 106
Jacob 95 Joe 279 JB 111 JC 86
JR 173 Louise 189 Martha 67 173
Mary 106 208 241 260 Mary
Evaline 239 Orville 86 Robert
Earnest 7 Roy A 189 Rufus 208
228 239 Ruste 74 Sam 95
Samuel 285 Thomas 157 Tilda
Ann 95 William M 287 WE 287
YJ 19 __ Ray 111
MORROW, Adam 269 Emma 61
John 269 Nellie 159
MOSIER, Daniel 203
MOSUER, Hariet 87
MOTTERN, Dan 272 James M
272 William 272
MOUHEAD, JA 41

MOWE, Jacob 99 Mrs Jacob 99
MOYER, EJ 138 Lucy Jane 280
Mary 138
MULKIE, Anna 226
MULLENDORE, George 26
Newton 123
MULLINDON, David 127 Jacob
Newton 127
MURDOCK, Angeline 228
Crumley 251 Samuel Hobart 251
MURKY, Margaret A 141
MURR, Jimie 184
MURRAY, Cena 97 Lillie 147
MURRELL, James A 174 Sarah
Ann 174
MURRH, Bruce 26
MURS, Lucinda 119
MYERS, Anna 83 A Inell 150 Bell
20 Bill 205 Charles E 269 Clara
28 Clinton 233 Cora Carter 66 C
Festus 150 CF 119 Della J 135
DE 265 Eliza 119 Henry C 153
Hue Orland 153 Infant 66 269
Jacob 29 James 119 John 96 JA
265 JH 166 JM 91 123 256 JR 82
Lacy 189 Lucinda 272 Martha 20
163 Martha E 50 Michael 256
Rosa May 40 Nancy 172 231
Nancy Matilda 265 Newton 89
Rubie 237 Tommie 79 William
82 Wila F 80
MYSINGER, Augustus H 290 AH
205 Catherine 207 Gussie 205
Harrold 293 John 290 JM 105
113 Martha 54 Sarah 186 Will
293
NAFF, Martha 86
NAIL, Eugene 197 John 197
NAUGHTY, Nancy 208
NAVE, RL 234

NEAL, Elmer 112 Harell F 15
  Hazel 67 Howard F 55 James 16
  Nola 73 Terthenia 288 Virna G
  15 William 153
NEAR, Jacob E 78
NEAS, __ 202 Elma Ruth 122
  Erscine 278 279 Henry 273 Jacob
  279 JW 122 139 Malissa 257
  Margaret 34 Nettie 14 Noah 273
  Paul 278 Pauline 279 Susan 128
  139 Tabat C 122
NEASE, Mary Ann 39
NEILSON, James R 128 William
  Huff 128
NELSON, Bertha 10 Goolie 54
  Henry F 59 Jane 181 Joseph M
  38 JF 174 JW 174 Lee 87 Nancy
  128 Pearl 270 R 126 Will 193
  William 87
NERTON, Eliza 86
NESS, Albert H 202 Infant 202
NEURMAN, Samuel 162
NEUS, Clarence 260 John T 260
  Philip 260
NEWBARY, Leahr 15
NEWBERRY, JN 268 Naoma 268
  PK 268
NEWMAN, Joel Thomas 100
  Thomas 100
NEWSOME, AF 162 Infant 162
NICELY, CH 168
NICHOLS, Martha A 181
NOEL, JA 223 Margaret E 223
NOELL, Catherine 199
NOLLINGTON, Manervy 153
NOL_, Susan 266
NORTHINGTON, Mary 266
NORTON, __ 123 Artie 133 Bettie
  89 Flossie 22 George 211 George

Arnold 211 Infant 8 59 Jacob 164
  John 243 Nancy 85 Ollie 60
NUNLEY, Bennie Crede 229
  Corbet 240 Corlie Lea 229
  Taylor 240 Vernie 240
NUNNELLEY, Corbet 226 Ronnie
  C 226
OELER, Nannie 42
OLER, JM 85 Mary 85 Nora 267
OLINGER, Clive 140 Infant 140
  Mary 210
OLIVER, __ 283
OLLINGER, Belle 160
ORR, Fannie 125
ORWOOD, Francis 264
OSBORNE, Pearl 187 WS 25
OSTEN, Jessie 262
OTEY, CN 279 CN Jr 279
OTINGER, Massie 149
OTTINGER, __ 119 Christian 243
  Eliza Jane 118 Essie 101 229 FM
  243 GM 118 Harriet 132 Henry
  128 Jacob 101 128 Jennie 289
  Kathern 100 L_ 101 Mandy 46
  Martha Francis 118 Ollie 96 OE
  96 PC 243 WW 118
OVERHOLSER, Christopher 81
  James William 177 John
  Madison 81 JC 177 JM 273
  William 273
OVERTON, __ 183
OWEN, David Webster 233 Mrs
  DW 233 Mary 98 William 233
OWENS, Dora B 94 James 162
  199 Lucusa 199 Marion 209
  Martha Ann 281 Mary 241 Mary
  J 273 Melton Glover 98 Pahthe E
  247 Samuel Robert 162 Sewell V
  98 Thomas 171
P_, Cordie 288

PA_, Buster 42
PACK, Carl 193 Infant 114 Noah
  114 Noah L 201 Noah L Jr 228
  Noah L Sr 228 NL 201 Tom E
  193
PACKER, Alice 218
PACKSTON, Elzie 137
PAINTER, Alfred 59 Birtie 206
  Charles 234 Frana 169 Frank G
  215 George 215 Infant 234 268
  269 Mary 131 Mary Jane 164
  Osea 24 Rosa 5 Sarah Elizabeth
  124 SJ 222 WM 165 YK 268 269
PALMER, Gabe 210 Mary 81
  Mollie 278 William A 210
PARENAN, Sarah 141
PARENANS, Claud 141
PARHAM, Gertie 103 PC 103
PARK, Anson J 191 Dalphus
  Alexander 191 David F 191
  Dollie 287 Gertie 270 John 287
  Thomas 109
PARKER, Effie 231 Lizzie 41
  Mary F 83 Richard T 294 WT
  294
PARKS, May 290
PARMAN, Curtis Jay 136
  Elizabeth 246 Gipsie 39 Infant
  169 Jay 136 Lee 169 Lorence 136
  LF 136 Mary 198 PC 100 169
  Sarah 139 William 169
PARRIS, Susan S 121 Troy 121
PARRY, Jennie 83
PARSON, Roda 162
PATE, Fannie 201
PATRICK, Alfred 155 Ida 155
  Nancy 245 William 245
PATTEN, Roy R 188
PATTERSON, Bruce 213 Cleta
  213 David B 137 Nola 83
  Thomas 137 Will 137 YM 3
PATTISON, David B 146 James
  W 146
PATTON, Infant 220 James A 192
  John Earnest 215 JD 192 JN 215
  Melvin D 242 Roy R 220 Sallie
  Seneker 216 Thomas 188
  William P 188 Willie J 242
PATY, Allen 244 Infant 244
PAXTON, Alfred 96 Ellen 96 137
  Harman 137 Mit 96 Tiny Vetrice
  35
PAYNE, Bessie 116 Bevin
  Wheeler 93 Charlie 116 George
  Valentine 93 GC 228 HC 116
  HM 116 Lillie 104 Mary 118
  Will 211
PEARCE, Addie A 121 HM 249
  Joel N 249 Virginia 199
PEARSON, Elizabeth 177
  Loucinda 223 Mable E 211 SD
  211
PEIRCE, Belle D 26
PENCE, Edward 108
PENLEY, Elsie Lee 277 English
  264 English Sr 264 James 264
  277
PENNINGTON, Dr 186 SL 198
  267 Zoed 168
PERKINS, Ben 254
PERSON, Mose 195
PETERS, BF 200 202 Cecil 200
  Cecil Cloid 202 Earnest G 34
  Elen Geneva 260 Fannie 176
  George 21 Infant 39 Jacob 34 J
  Dan 274 Katie 183 Katy 169
  Luther 260 Margaret Ellen 274

Nancy Emmaline 185 Paul 207
Wesley 207 Yank 9
PETIE, Margaret 281 Rebecca 184
PHILLIPS, __ 160 Annie 238 AL
  290 Biley 269 Birtha 101 Carl 21
  Dave 238 David 144 Doak 144
  145 Fred 21 Harvey 117 Jim 144
  John 117 Katherine 45 Malissie J
  269 Marg 83 Mattie 220
  Minuard Hampton 157 Nathan
  144 145 Nellie May 290 Riley
  144 145 Thomas 275 WR 157
PICKENS, Elizabeth 132
PICKERING, Alfred D 173
  Clarence Weaver 173 Honey 123
  Infant 30 Mary 136 213 Puris 2
  TB 213 __ Lillie 159
PICKLE, Elizabeth 143 John 143
PIERCE, Alfred 113 Cathern 135
  Edward 75 Elizabeth 43 EP 287
  Florence 110 Floyd 113 Mrs
  Floyd 113 GB 71 John 230 294
  John W 259 Martha 95 Martha J
  294 Mary 233 Rebecca J 287
  Sarah F 110 William 135 Winnie
  127
PIGMON, Vida V 131
PINKERTON, Cinter C 45 Mollie
  103 Robert 103
PINKNEY, TB 236
PINKSTON, GJ 293 GT 293
  Jackson 86 JM 238 Sousan 207
PIPER, Albert M 129 152 Charles
  Wesley 129 Grace 129 James A
  152 Joe Keebler 92 John 152 WF
  92
PITT, Dawson 236 Florence 285
  Haysel 51 John 160 Lydia May
  124 Mary 55 Nettie 160 Paul 51
  Wharton Bisson 160

PITTS, Alpha 88 Andrew 221
  Asabelle 35 Bettie 9- Clyde
  Edward 277 Fern 229 Infant 221
  229 Katie 92 Lucy 221 Thomas
  277
PLEASANT, WF 223
POE, __ 125 GW 153 Henry 201
  208 Infant 70 170 173 John 170
  192 JH 208 JW 173 Lizzie Kate
  208 Mary 53 Pauline 208 Pery
  201 Robert 208 Rosa B 192
  Thassa 222
POPE, Dora 134 Taylor 163
POTTER, JT 126 Mary 115
POWELL, Cane 192 Maggie 192
  Sarah Rhine 110 William 110
PRATHER, Emmett 54 Eunice 245
  Onetta 77
PRESLEY, Rachel C 155 Ralph 15
  RB 80
PRESNELL, Bertha 109 Dave 109
  John 216 Nellie 210
PRESS, Pelela 278
PRESSLEY, Harrison 288 Infant
  288 Sherman 225
PRICE, Bettie 236 Caroline 213
  Charles M 148 Denver 75 Edwin
  213 Mrs Glen 142 GB 101 Henry
  148 Infant 37 James Edwin 104
  Lem 142 Martin 148 Mollie 16
  Nettie 8
PRITCHARD, __ 287
PRUETT, __ 186 Dollie 173
PRUITT, JA 219 Mollie 91 Newt
  219 Samantha 12
PULLIAM, M_ 132 Madison 87
  Margaret J 132 Milton M 87 MM
  284
QUINN, Mabel Ruth 147 Walter
  147

QUINTON, Florence 180 Leroy 67
R_, Florence 130
RABY, Mamie 182
RADAR, George 254 Hugh Vallie 119
RADE, Peter 88
RADER, _ 177 A 170 Andrew J 214 Andrew J Sr 214 Andy 293 Bula Louisa 175 Charles 186 Charley 252 283 Clark 176 Cornelius 115 Daniel 170 202 Dave 321 Emaline 133 Ester 209 Eva 192 Florence Addie 103 Frank Lee 192 Gale 231 George 12 Henry 153 170 Infant 153 186 Isabel 188 James 119 252 James H 257 James Richard 283 John 202 JA 8 JH 122 JL 170 Lena Branch 231 Mrs LA 195 Malissie J 269 Mamie Lee 201 Martha 137 Martin 168 Mary Jane 136 Mary Tennessee 168 Nancy 115 138 145 Nannie 251 PE 175 Rinda 168 Roy Frank 175 Ruben 257 Sarah 171 175 252 Sarah Angeline 228 Susan 124 SR 186 TL 269 Uless G 103 William 115 145
RADNLES, Cary 190
RADNOUR, Tola 204
RAGAN, Arthur 9 Henry C 277 James 9 Walter Carr 277
RAGSDALE, Bessie 5 Elizabeth 4 184 George 160 Liza 276 Lyde 212 Nan 7 Nyoma Steller 160 Sarah 192
RAMBO, Sallie 60 S 292
RAMSEY, Ebb 262 George 292 Infant 262 James 92 Johnie 292 Mattie 292

RANDELL, John 149 Mary 149
RANDLES, Cary 188 EB 190 Infant 188
RANDOLPH, George 23 James 269
RANKIN, Eileen 45 EK 144 Infant 144 Jul_ Howell 254 Lewis 138 Margarite 61 Richard 138 Sarah 267 TS 254
RANKINS, James 215
RATHDGE, Edith Johnson 95
RATLIFF, M 83
RAWLINS, Hannah 139
RAY, Infant 24 Lottie 8 Mary 271 Nely 129
RAZAR, Mary Elizabeth Cobble 293 SE 293
RAZER, Dora 140
REAMINE, JE 2
REATHERFORD, Mary 71
REAVES, Betsey 60 Ed 76 248 EM 274 ES 179 Fain 255 Flora 250 Hurse 60 Infant 23 179 255 James W 274 Jennie I 202 JE 163 JG 227 Major James 55 NH 274 OM 250 Polly 76
RECTOR, Carl 193 E_ 205 Enic 278 Eugene 193 James 281 Jane 291 John 205 Ortha 281
REDINOUR, Nan 291
REDMON, Nancy 218
REDNOUR, JW 96 Mary 195 Nannie 244
REED, Alta Mira 139 AB 141 Caroline 209 Carrie Bell 240 Challey 259 Chassie 58 Daniel B 139 Eliza 219 Infant 1 9 10 259 James 17 John 132 240 John A 270 JF 239 JJ 277 JM 139 Katy 10 Louisa 277 Lula 205 Martha

Alice 65 Mary 106 Nellie M 132
Robert 106 277 Sam 6 Sarah 10
Soloman 90 Susan 239
REEDER, __ 132 CG 274 Patsy 274
REEL, Infant 199 WE 199
REESE, Dave 263 LC 263
REESER, Jessie Roscoe 285 Joseph M 285
REEVE, Fred A 58 Fred Smith 137 Horace 245 Pauline 245 Roy 137 T Smith 137 TS 239
REEVES, FA 230 Josephine 230 JC 190 Vesta Anna 190
REGISTER, Deborah 284
REINER, Blaine 221
REMINE, Darvin Keith 142 HC 142
RENNELS, Samuel 246
RENNER, Andrew 174 Blaine 285 Daisy 255 David 139 Ida 222 225 Infant 130 255 Penelope 91 RC 280 Will 130 WA 224
REYNOLD, Margaret 188
REYNOLDS, __ 196 Alfred 1 280 Bert 243 Brazelton 243 Catherine 4 Cleo 51 Crawford 92 Crocket 200 Elizabeth 228 Emerson 148 Eula Blanch 286 George 286 Georgia 200 Hazel 94 Infant 115 175 Jack 246 James 4 243 Jane 103 John 115 160 175 JO 275 JR 46 Manerve 7 Martha 204 Nancie Jane 84 Nancy 230 Nora 153 Sarah 246 Susan 145
RHEA, Bob 196 EN 239 Hettie 239 Jim 107 Kizih 88 Mary 178
RHODES, Alberta 110 Clyde 94 James 110 Jeanett 94 Will 94

RICE, John 146 Thomas 146
RICHARDS, Adaline 167 Bettie 228 Nadine 261 Sarah 167 Sarah J 172
RICHARDSON, Elizabeth 113
RICKER, Ada Maud 230 Alice 266 Bettie 115 Christopher 136 Columbus 104 CC 104 Dora 23 Elizabeth 75 FK 29 Hassie 62 Infant 37 James Martin 130 James W 164 John 207 266 Lania 165 Mary E 118 Mary Ruth 267 Mattie May 243 Nancy 136 247 Nora 91 Richard 165 Roy Roscoe 130 RE 164 Silas 136 Taylor 158 Terry 158 Thomas 267 Velma 60 Virtie 104 VE 267 Walter 150 Warren 123
RICKLE, Theodore 75
RIDDLE, George 212 Laura 212
RIDDLEY, Pearl 283
RIDNOUR, Mary 187
RIGERS, Sarah 172
RIGGINS, Cordie 252
RIGGS, Elbert 184 Infant 184
RIGHTSEL, Catherine 275
RIKER, Infant 53 Sarah 29
RILES, Al 187 Etta 210 James 210
RILEY, Alice 12 Annie 46 Mary Virginia 201
RINEHART, John 294 Margaret 282
RIPLEY, David S 204 Infant 204 Lucy 253 LM 253
RIPLY, Blumfield 199
RIPPETOE, Eliza Annie 283
RITE, Glennss 28 Guy 63
RIVERS, Raymond 25
ROARK, Nellie 291

ROBERTS, __ 145 154 Annie 54
AA 251 Bruce 87 210 244 Cora
87 181 Curtis 86 Fitzhue F 124
GW 192 Hannah 173 Infant 54
87 244 Patsy 25 Sarah J 251
Sarah M 18 Thomas O 251
Vernie 3 Will 291 William H
124
ROBERTSON, Deborah 121 Lula
Eudra 126 WW 6
ROBESON, Lula 230
ROBINSON, Bettie 162 BT 115
FR 266 Infant 276 Infants 47 IV
158 Jess 158 John 276 Kate 245
Maggie E 266 Mary 193 Mrs 158
William Elmer 48
ROBISON, Alexander 81
ROCK, Alexander 226
RODDY, Elizabeth 122
RODGERS, Ellen 145 Frank 145
James 145 Nellie S 102 Paggie
131 Theodore Roosevelt 102
William 102
ROE, Flora 52 Florencd 52
ROGERS, Annie 88 Charles
Newton 100 Charlie R 38
Glennie 242 Hobart 24 HF 242
James P 100 Joseph 223 Lila 24
Lucinda 292 Manson 207 Mollie
207 SF 150
ROLLENS, GB 80 253
ROLLINGS, GB 80 253
ROLLINS, DH 130 140 Essie
Anna 130 Liza 110 Rovena Bell
140 Viannie Shelton 85
ROODA, Edna 32
ROSE, Bob 21 Mrs EM 52 James
H 259 John W 259 Ninnie 10
ROSS, Elizabeth 176 Fred 41
George E 161 James 81 167 253

Jamse Sr 81 Jennie 293 John A
253 Jonnie 144 J Cad 253 Nancy
276 Nancy A 44 Sue R 147
ROWLAND, Charley 256 Jackson
273 Michael 256
ROYAL, Ida 57
RUBBLE, __ 171
RUBLE, Hariett 85 Polly 84
RUDDER, Andy T 187 AJ 278
Calvin 272 CA 272 CH 244
Ernest H 244 Infant 244 272
James Alexander 231 Johnson
187 231 Mrs JA 231 Matilda
Bales 187 RG 187 William F 278
RUDE, Lillie 144
RUMBO, Annie 182
RUPE, Littie 1
RUPERT, David Dariua 34 Infant
241 Viola 14 William 241
RUSH, __ 157 Catherine 192
Infant 81 John 273 John K 81
Louis 210 Martha 64
RUSS, Anna 227 Margaret 196
RUSSEL, Mrs Louisa 26
RUSSELL, __ 126 209 Angeline
254 AD 48 AE 193 Bert 156 DE
252 E_ 236 Ethel J 283 Finley
227 Jennie 227 John 262 Mary
Jane 193 Pearl 275 Sallie 99
Samuel T 187 Sue 99 Thomas A
187 Walter 62 William 143 WM
42
RUSTON, Mary 113 223
RUTH, George 202
RUTHERFORD, Burnas Nasine 6
John 259 Nancy 270 Sarah 259
RUTLEDGE, Ed 252 Lee Andrew
King 252
RYAN, William P 199
RYLER, Alexander 66

S_, John 286 Nancy 225 Nancy Jane 46 Sallie 270
SAILOR, Marga 256
SALES, Lew 159 Mary 211
SALTERS, Emma 222
SALTS, Aleck 51 Allen 227 Andrew J 227
SALYER, Jacob 237
SAM, Sophia 48
SAMONS, William O 74
SAMS, Robert 166
SARTIN, John 183
SATTERFIELD, Maude 221
SAUCEMAN, Assalia 286 Infant 224 Wilbur 224
SAULS, Martha 253 O'dell 229
SAULSBURG, Louise 48 William 48
SAULTS, Alice 252
SAUSLBERY, Pearl 74
SAVILLE, Cora N 105 WT 105
SAYLER, Edith 16 John 16 221 JKP 221 Katie 154 Gussie 123
SAYS, Robert 51
SCHILEFORTH, Henrietta 288
SCOT, James 40
SCOTT, B_ 251 Hercelese 33 James 33 John 181 Lydia 131 Maggie 161 216 232 Mark L 246 Pain 131 Rachle 10 Rebecca 93 Roy 181 William C 131 William Thomas Lacey 247
SCRUGGS, Alma 11 Charles 151 Emma 46 EC 203 Harriett 119 264 Huse 173 Sallie 151 Sarrah 203 Susan 173
SCULLY, Rebacca 162
SEA, Amanda 227 James 227 WD 227
SEADGHTON, Mary 276

SEATON, BT 23 Clarence 252 Cora May 194 Edna Helen 188 Florence 107 Henry 188 Holloway 279 Ira 124 Joe 176 194 John 194 279 Lydia Kate 188 Martha J 251 Monroe 252 Sallie 58 Sidney 107
SEAVERS, Ida Fox 219
SEAY, HC 88 Rubin F 28 Sarah 219
SEDGMYTON, AJ 196 Infant 196 May 196
SEETLES, HI 26
SELF, __ 134 Clayton 216 Dorthy Maxine 151 Ethel Irene 187 Infant 115 152 John Luke 283 Josiah F 197 J Emmett 283 JB 232 Malinda 228 ML 232 Robert 152 Robert M 115 Sarah Eveline 205 S Harriett 68 SH 126 William K 151 Willie G 199 WR 1
SELLERS, John 231 Leathie 274 Polly 271
SENEKER, Daniel Silliam 265 John A 265 LP 241 Sam 265 SP 207 216 289
SETZER, Infant 169 LB 169
SEWELL, Will 186
SEWLCER, Charles 169 Martha 169
SEXTON, Arthur 69 Bart 123 Cordie Elnora 142 Ed 142 Emaline 69 George 89 Infant 123 John 146 JR 69 Lena 86 Lucinda 257 Miller 156 Minnie 101 Sarah 184 William 69 William Henry 142

SHACKLEFORD, Enoch 77 Infant 112 John 145 John H 112 Mary S 145
SHAFER, Eliza 274 Ola 10 William 18
SHANKS, Ambrose 106 Billie 283 Cy Moore 280 Elizabeth 198 GMD 106 Infant 175 James 124 132 175 259 James R 220 292 JA 267 JM 193 Mrs JR 293 Lillie 294 Lizzie 142 Louisa 227 260 Lucille 229 Mary A 219 Nancy 267 Rebecca 96 Rhoda 87 Robert 292 SL 280 William R 283 WR 229
SHARP, Savana 194
SHAULS, Elizabeth 255
SHAW, _ 280 Clyde 170 Dave 208 James 95 Lou 8 L 108 Nick 104 N_ 257 Pinkney Monroe 95 Rick A 170 Thomas 108 Thomas Greene 108 TM 95 WA 280
SHEFFEY, Alfred K 126 Annie Vistie 173 175 John R 35 Leonie 71 Marion 126 Neriva 219 Robert 187 RF 221 Texas 76 TK 175
SHELTON, Ales 49 Baxter 164 Brown 164 Daphne 23 Elizabeth 181 Ev_ 269 Genettie 36 Ina 269 Infant 36 294 Mande 225 Margaret A 164 Martin 85 N_ 269 Peter 31 Robert 294 Roderick 160 267 Sallie 243 Sarah 155 249
SHENAULT, Harry 61
SHEPARD, William 62
SHEPPARD, John 297
SHEROTT, Mary 45

SHIELDS, Alpha 156 Infant 25 Ivin 47 John 132 JT 286 Polly 223
SHIPLEY, Birdie 225 Ettie 161 George E 193 John 193 JC 193
SHORES, Charles 144 John 144 Joseph 144
SHORT, Martha 86
SHOUN, AN 159 Gladys 195
SHOWMAN, Sallie 218
SHOWMOR, Mrs Scott 111
SHULDS, JKP 25
SHUW, James 129 Nic A 129
SIMONS, Ida 51
SIMPSON, _ 98 Henry 155 HA 155 Lizzie 133 Peter 155 257 RW 152
SIPE, Corbett 205 James 205 Polly 273
SISK, Nattie 120 Toliver 120 William 120
SITZER, Gertrude 156 Jerrie 156
SIZEMORE, Katherine Josephine 111
SKEEN, James B 168 Penington 168
SKELTON, George Washington 91 Mrs ME 91
SKYLES, John H 146 John W 146 Mollie 192
SLAGLE, Addie 106
SLEDAM, Mae 108
SLIGER, Gertrude 153
SLUDER, Infant 128 James 79 William 128
SMALL, Rachel 254
SMELCER, Alice 111 AC 262 ES 176 Henry 103 Ike 292 Infant 114 James Claude 114 John M 292 Kironie N 103 Maggie 136

Maggie D 216 Martha Jane 98
William C 271 William Roy 262
SMELLER, Eula M 234 James 44
SMILEY, Samiel 128
SMITH, __ 111 292 Adaline 277
Agnes 225 Alden 160 Alice 150
256 Alice Belle 220 Amanda 59
Amos 158 Augusta 286 AL 175
Barbary 214 Birtha 258 Bula 10
Charles 112 Claude E 149
Cornelius 184 Crofford 185
Dorthy Estell 16 Edgar 146
Elizabeth 180 195 244 272 Ella
289 Ellen 100 Elliott Benjamin
159 Esther 30 Evey 52 Florence
Lela 96 Frank 21 George 173
258 Gilbert 78 Grace B 112 GH
159 Hailey 106 Harry 244 Hassie
59 Hattie T 241 Herman 267
Hubert 257 Ida A 145 Infant 11
160 179 185 212 276 Irene 51
Isaac 218 292 James 263 James
Alexander 218 James C 145
James N 184 Jessie 160 284 John
261 Jordan 159 Joseph 62 Josiah
96 JF 146 JH 267 JL 40 265 JS
106 Katherine E 134 Kyle
Vincent 146 Lula E 272 LE 244
Mabel 149 Mandy 99 Margaret
31 46 Margaret A 96 Margaret L
73 Margarette E 223 Martha 173
183 196 Mary 56 93 256 Mary A
147 252 Mary Catherine 16
Melissie 203 Minnie 264 M 290
Pansler 141 Polly Ann 114
Rachel 217 Rebecca J 185 Ross
179 Sallie 116 Sallie M 72 Sam
243 Sarah 263 Sarah Alice 50
Sarah Francis 99 Soloman 117
Stella 182 Valentine D 232

Vertie 123 VD 278 Westie 258
Will 179 212 276 286 William
158 182 William Alexander 182
William Talmage 16 WA 56 WH
67 WM 286
SMITHSON, George 172 James
171 172 JF 155 LW 172
SMITHTON, Infant 252 TH 252
SMOKER, Bell 227 John 227
SMOTHERS, __ 250
SNAPP, Edilene 107 HR 278
Jessie May 278 Kate 165 Robert J
107 Sam 204 Samuel E 258 SE
278 Thomas 204 WM 107
SNIDER, Nancy 166
SNODDY, Miles 42
SNODDY, Tulmon 119
SNOWDEN, Dewey 186 Newton
186 Tom 186
SNYDER, Darius 178 Samantha
292 Truman 178
SOLOMAN, Bessie 240 Fannie 86
George W 86 Huston 107 Infant
107 Jack 86 JM 81 Lena E 58
Loeta 81 Rutha 290 Selma 25
SOUTHERLAND, Infant 270 Jake
180 James 218 Jeroy 82 Martha J
34 Mattie E 215 216 Paul 82
Phillip 133 Rossie Pearl 241 Sam
270 TL 270
SOUTHERN, Francis Mae 135
SOWERS, Ida 213 Jacob 213
James B 213
SPEAR, Elizabeth 17
SPEARS, David Frank 262 Mrs
DF 262 Eliza Jane 170 Jerome
170 Kenric 177 181 Marion 154
Mattie 197 Ruth L 36 RS 262
Thelma 154 Will 154 William
170

SPEER, Angie Magnolia 265 AM
 183 John R 122 Ottie 122
 William King 122
SPEERS, Martha Louisa 53
SPEN__, Lettie 84
SPRINKLES, __ 121
SQUIBB, AJ 197 Bell 239 Clifford
 197 CP 6 Hugh Paul 197
ST HILAS, Joseph 2
ST JOHN, JF 244
STACY, David L 248 GC 248
STAFFORD, __ 81 Ermel Mary 9
 Thomas 42
STALEY, Nancy 286
STALL, MM 247
STAMER, Lilly Maud 182
STANBERRY, AJ 281
STANTON, Bessie 85 John 249
 Sarah 160 Sol 85
STARNES, Allis 102 Anay 4
 Charity Victoria 205 Hiram 184
 Infant 200 Jennie E 56 Landon C
 183 Lorence Vernon 290 Luna
 200 Marion 183 Mary 282
 Melvina 56 Mrs Jimie 15 Ott 290
 Rutha Lucinda 7 Sarah 231 Vern
 102 WA 231
STARNS, Wyan 33 Lucy Mataline
 111 Oka R 18 Sam 111
STATON, Elizabeth D 226 Hugh
 226 John 141 Robert 141
STEALMAN, Eliza 262
STEEL, Katherine 139 MH 139
STEELE, MH 11 Sallie 13
STEP, Elizabeth 111
STEPHENS, Alice 129 AJ 268 AJ
 Sr Hassie 206 Samuel 129 SJR
 129 William 115
STEPP, Tuck 266

STEVENS, __ 212 Jack 223 JN
 223
STILL, Ella Bell 103
STILLS, Birdie Josephine 14 Elsey
 255 Sista 29 Sue 179
STINES, JE 98 RM 98
STINKER, Lydia 220
STOKES, Claude 99 Maynard C
 73
STONE, John 186 Sam 186
STONECIPHER, Easter 268 Susan
 147
STONES, Margaret 124
STONESBURY, IH 124 Mrs __
 124
STORY, Carrie 27
STOVER, Elizabeth 105
STRAIN, Caroline 255
STRAND, Lydia 131 Oline 144
STRAUB, Carl 288
STRAUD, James Jr 168 James
 Sentre 168 Thomas 168
STREET, Aught 54
STROND, Fred 201 Lula 201
 Nancy 13 Nora 102 212
STRONDS, Lyda 153
STRONG, __ 117 Callie 206 John
 117 Kate 184
STROUD, Martha S 173 Rosco 46
 Sarah Elizabeth 98
STUART, Anna 133 Bud 133
 David 112 Henry 133
STULTZ, Sally 183
STURM, Alphonso 183 John W
 183
STURM, Stella 93
STURNS, Iretta 42
STYKE, Annie 273 WM 273
SULLIVAN, Alfred 14
SUMMERS, John 105

SUNCEMAN, Infant 133 Roy 133
SUSONG, AE 73 196 278 Carl 154 Dean Fox 26 DS 196 Elax 195 Elizabeth 278 Gabriel L 154 Hallie 248 John 92 154 John Elmer 77 Josephine 260 Mary 206 Nellie 110 Nicholas A 196 Sallie 195 Sara 92 WA 92 278
SUTHERLAND, Charlie 62 Mary 62 SD 133
SUTTLES, Berthy 82 115 Charlie 82 Infant 82
SWANGER, Annie 251 Robert 251
SWANSON, Aurbrey 22
SWARTZ, JL 149
SWATSEL, Bruce 90 Caroline 207 Ester Mae 69 Infant 90 Jennie 193 Nellie Bell 75
SWATSELL, Alice 131 Amanda 189 Brad 189 Edgar 288 Infant 288 Lucy F 182 Ray 189 Rhote 189 Robert 182 RA 89
SWATZEL, S Jane 216 Wes 285
SWATZELL, Charles 232 Clara Elizabeth 232 Emma 218
SWEENEY, Nancy 160
SWEENY, Martha 245 Clarence Alden 230 Lowel Edgar 230
SWIFT, Willie Clyde 49
SWINDELL, George C 67 Sallie 254
SWINEY, James 283 JI 166 JW 283 Rebecca 166 TA 283
T_, Sada 177
TADLOCK, Jane 284 Lewis 61 Mattie 286 Infant 250 254 Nellie 254 Worley 250
TATES, Blanch 26

TAYLOR, __ 143 A 209 280 281 Alvira Williams 135 Bula Clide 163 Cart 177 Dave 251 David 83 Frank Garfield 124 Henry N 97 Infant 251 James 178 James N 118 163 Joe 192 John 270 Joshua 270 JM 84 Lula Bell 272 Martha A 267 278 Marvin Paul 292 Mary 248 Mary Kate 88 Matilda 203 204 Mattie 12 Nellie 194 279 Price Hiram 84 Robert Carson 124 Sadie Christiana 226 Tildy 180 William 83 190 Winie 178 254 Winnie Ruth 118
TEAGUE, Florence 161 Pauline 55
TELLACK, Annie 261
TELLER, Liza 265 Margaret 240
TELOEAT, Maty E 27
TEMPLE, Julia 215 MJ 215
TERFINE, Armenta 112
THACKER, Cordie 175 Infant 247 Jane 150 SD 247
THOMAS, Addie 43 Barnie 82 Clementine 148 167 Jerry 40 Rhena 238 William 237
THOMASON, George 21 James 183 John P 204 Joseph M 204 William S 183
THOMPSON, Alex 220 Becky 228 Burnie 275 Cornelius 282 Dora E 284 Edward 140 Hauer 11 Henry 140 189 Infant 5 James 72 220 John 282 Mary 150 Mary E 117 Mattie 32 Mollie 8 Ollie 60 Rebecca 259 Salina 275 Seo 59 WH 140 190
THORNBURG, Alies 64 Callie 246 Leonard 128 Noah E 128
THORNBURY, Blanch 20
THURNBURG, Blanch 3 Earnest 3

TILSON, Bruce 125 Joseph 201
Ralph 159 Sam Flemings 125
TINE, Lizzie 199
TINSLEY, Charles 229 James 222
238 Major 238
TIPTON, Frankie 239 Lee 159
Sarah 159
TISLEY, Velma Ruth 229
TITTLE, Lou C 171
TOLIVER, Bertha 65
TOLLIVER, John Idris 134 Nancy
Jane 210 WD 134
TOME, Clarissa 212 Oma 212
TOMPSON, EP 112 Marthie 112
TOOMEY, AE 101 Rachel 102
TORBETT, Hugh C 43 Mattie 43
Walter R 43
TRAVIS, Atta 134 Sidney 211
TREADWAY, Sarah 116
TRELLORS, Byrd 113 JS 113
Woodrow Wilson 113
TRENT, Mattie 44
TRIVET, Kiciah 157
TROBAUGH, __ 245 George 136
TUCKER, A 220 Alexander 216
GB 97 Mrs JN 237 Nathan B 216
Polly 85
TULLACK, Will 164
TULLOCK, Davie 177 JW 177
Smith Reave 177
TURNELL, Lee 175
TURNER, Maltrie 207 William
207
TWEED, Abner 200 Anson 287
Hester 85 James 268 John 181
Jules 287 M_ 246 Mary Jane 213
Viola 268
TWITTERY, Andrew Farmer 279
Henry 279
TWITTY, Beatrice 281 Henry 281

UANR, Carl 33
UDELL, __ 152
UNDERHILL, Nettie 211
VAILES, James 184
VANCE, Bert 137 Fannie 224
James 290 John C 137 Martin B
137 Rufus 105 Troy C 290
William 224
VAUGHN, Elizabeth 140 Exilonia
285 Louise 150 Lucille 290 Ray
150 TW 79 Wiley 290
VEST, Lawrence 17
VESTAL, Doak 270 Infant 121
186 Lena 238 Paris 121 Ruth
Jane 270 WP 186
VIENABLE, Caroline 283
VOILES, James 184
W_, Amanda 187 Greene 6 Sarah
6
WADDEL, Tom 142
WADDELL, Mrs James 99
WADDLE, Arch 29 AW Justina
133 Bessie 235 Blevins 206 Dana
Lyle 217 Elenor 275 EC 89 Felix
89 Francis 261 Green 212 James
204 236 JB 217 241 JH 212
Laura E 133 Lura S 137 Mamie
Dollie 269 Mart 221 Mat 37
Peter 269 Fufus K 236 261 RW
261 Sam 246 Sana 170 Sue 194
William 221 246
WADELL, Elnor 264
WAGNER, Buford 83 John 83
Paul 47
WAGONER, Amy 190
WAIN, Cordie 234 Elizabeth 103
George W 234 William 239
WAINE, George 252 Minnie 257
William 252

WAITS, Bell 133 Belle 187
  Georgia 68 Mahala J 17 Mattie
  262
WAKLER, Gabral 139 Mary Lou
  147
WALDREP, Wallace 271
WALDROP, Francis Marion 243
  Infant 272 LD 272
WALKER, Anderson 117 Cynthia
  Florence 286 Elizabeth Jane 114
  John 154 164 John B 99 JH 258
  Mary 246 Neyotte 155 Samuel
  108 Sarah 139 246 William 114
WALL, Candice 90
WALLACE, Nona 53
WALLER, Adda M. 257 William
  88 William E 88
WALLIN, Anietta 103 Ben 103
  Benjamin Fox 228 Bessie F 85
  Infant 85 JM 85 Rachel C 228
  Thomas J 228 TJ 68
WALLY, Maglin 185
WALTER, RL 113
WALTERS, Alpha Isabel 91
  Fowler 191 GA 191 GR 216
WAMPLER, Barbara 192 Dempsy
  148 Flora 81 Isaac 123 James
  273 James A 273 Soloman 123
  273 William Webb 148
WARD, __ 114 Elizabeth 79
  James 262 Joe 259 Manda 198
  Mollie 92 Oma 208 RA 163
WARDEN, Clyde 208 Jess 89 John
  208 Nancy 90 Roy 285 Roy Jr
  285
WARDON, Flora 89 Jess 99 Mary
  Ema 99
WARE, SC 110
WARN, Robert 30

WARNER, Mrs MA 195 Nellie
  Margarette 195 Susan 234
WATKINS, Ella 242
WATSON, Elbert 188
WATTENBERGER, Enoch Baker
  186 Nirva Francis 146 Sarah 229
WATTS, Bernett 262
WEBB, James 206 Kate 253
WEBBER, George 250
WEBSTER, Eliza 67 Rebecca
  Sayler 221
WEEMS, Bernet 188 Callie 210
  CP 89 Earley 38 Elizabeth 110
  George 157 George Jones 157
  Infant 119 John 95 JE 206 Mrs
  JG 158 Marion 4 Mary 48 Mattie
  36 Mollie 218 Mrs JC 95 Nancy
  Ann 17 Pearl 241 244 276 Sallie
  81 SJ 119 Temple 89 Ula F 206
  WR 151
WELLER, Nancy 89
WELLES, Mary 84
WELLS, Elizabeth 259 FW 250
  Humphries 99 Ida 116 Jacob P 39
  256 Malinda 242 Mary 184
  Moses 237 MH 250 Sid 184
  Sidney 48 Stephen George 256
  TC 256 WH 250
WERNER, NL 39
WEST, Carrie 78 James 213 James
  Hesekiah 213 John WF 56 Lulia
  Lee 67 Sinda 271 WH 101
WESTMORELAND, Infant 101
WEYSOR, WT 261
WHALOCK, Martha 81
WHEELER, E 285 Henry 160
  Infant 160 James 195 283 Nora
  172 Will 160
WHITAKER, Infant 127 Jessie 252
  John 127 JT 126 Sarah 217 252

WHITE, __ 260 Archibald 50
Burthie 7 Carl V 5 Carrie Rita
206 Dr 275 Elbert Carl 127 Elisa
175 Eliza 118 Elizabeth 172
Emaline 242 Floyd 181 Floyd H
99 Francis 13 Francis M 73
George W 187 Infant 65 161
Jacob 34 118 239 259 Jake 230
James 228 Jerold 224 John 74
175 184 187 Joseph 175 Julie
188 JH 233 JR 127 181 JS 102
Lake 154 Laura 7 Lissie 103
Loura E 239 Margaret A 145
Martha 191 Mary 181 233 Mary
Suda 7 Matilda 4 Minnie 226
Minnie Kate 110 M Elizabeth 7
Nancy 156 Nannie 198 Pauline
230 Ross 100 Rubie Osibell 100
Sarah 175 267 Sarah Ann 154
Sylvia Edna 99 Vernie A 99
Viviane 224 William E 161
Willie 229 240
WHITESIDES Virgia 170
WHITSON, Infant 143 182 Lidie
182 Will 143 William 182
WHITTAKER, Mary Ellen 126
WHITTENBURG, __ 286 Effie
129 WS 129
WICKER, Sallie 185
WILBUR, Dellie 272 Effie 272
WILBURN, Ben 98 278 Benjamin
98 286 CC 286 JJ 246 Mack 138
Margaret 98
WILEY, John 211
WILHOIT, __ 288 291 Ania 225
Charles 130 Dailey 104 David
225 Dorthe E 235 DC 235 Ella
100 EM 25 George 225 George
Click 37 Harry 241 Henry 249
HM 259 Jacob 189 Janette Ricker
123 John 42 186 John P 70 John
W 219 JA 93 JC 139 JSJ 219
WILHOIT, Manuel 142 Mary Blair
219 Nancy 110 Nina 241 Samuel
S 186 Sarah 197 Simeon 139
William 38 WC 224
WILKERSON, Ana 127 JH 133
KT 133 Lizzie 89 Richard
Thomas 133 RS 241 RT 241 RW
98
WILKINS, Hattie 90
WILKISON, Charles C 204 Infant
204
WILLARD, Eliza 164
WILLBORN, Corra 9
WILLET, Joe 126 Lillie 126
Margaret 40 Martha 87
WILLETT, __ 286 AF 286 Lillie
105 Roy 189 WG 286
WILLHOIT, Dulice 58 Ella 55
Emanuel 139 Nancy E 39
WILLIAMS, Ada L 277 Allen 197
Bruce 117 145 Carl 74 Catherine
174 Chassie 101 Cynthia 72
Dowell 82 Eliza 270 Etta 120
Fanner 270 Florence 117 Francis
126 Frank 152 Hannah 189
Harriett 82 Infant 76 J 270 James
W 197 229 Jennie 111 166 266
Joe 181 Joe F 284 John 135 145
John Thomas 284 JF 135 JW
197 Laurce 9 Lena 41 Lillie M
232 Mamie 109 Mary Alice 86
Mary E 181 Mary S 152 Minnie
247 Nat 126 Nevil 174 Ronil 277
Sinie 167 Thomas R 15 Warn 74
Will D 86
WILLIAMSON, Elizabeth C 58
JW 23 Sallie 124 WT 78

WILLIS, __ 112 CD 182 Dode 188 Jetson 264 John 197 JW 197 Lyle 197 Mary 244 Thomas Jefferson 264 TJ 264 Worley 244 WW 182
WILLISON, Dora 239
WILLOUGHBY, Eliza 207 Elizabeth 119
WILLS, Bertha 79 Gussie 174 Nancy Emeline 84 Thomas Coke 84
WILLSON, Elizabeth 168 Ida 122 Margaret Ann 75 Oliver P 56
WILSON, AG 82 251 Ben 239 Bess 246 Charley 115 DC 189 DD 272 Ed 150 Edie 249 Elmira 101 Elsener 90 Florence 81 Gurlie B 273 Gussie 150 HR 273 Infant 82 251 Jennie 6 Joel 187 John 117 144 234 JB 189 245 JH 80 Madison T 267 Margaret 22 144 Mary 266 Mayanrd B 239 MT 187 Narsessis 41 Nat 87 Ollie 115 Robert F 267 RF 187 RR 274 Sallie 42 Sallie Jessie 274 William 92 101
WILTIE, Susan 161
WINKLE, George W 255 Jacob 255
WINREY, BF 1
WINSLOW, Walter S 18
WINTER, JC 257 273
WISECAREN, __ 293
WISECARVE, Harmon 158 HM 158 James 158
WISOR, M.J. 171 179 287
WITT, Alma 41
WLADROP, Willie 243
WOLF, Pearl 193
WOLFE, Hettie Maranda 83

WOOD, __ 169 Annie 171 David L 246 Mancile Smith 258 William 169
WOODFIN, Chassie 108 Matilda 32
WOODS, __ 93 CC 258 Ernest 153 156 Essie 235 Georgia 262 Infant 48 John 90 212 Lucinda 129 Mary 214 Nancy 36 Polly 211 RF 235 Stella T 153 Steve 45 Vina 43 Willie 214
WOOLSEY, Alice 286 FH 286 Kerie 273 Laura 255
WORTHINGTON, Julia 264
WRIGHT, AL 205 Ellen 201 EM 182 Fait 262 Francis A 197 George 194 267 Harral 194 John 128 JT 129 Lewis 129 Mary 203 Mary Bell 262 Mary L 97 Sula 205
WYAN, Lavina Cathern 121 Peter 121
WYATT, Charles 247
WYKLE, Myrtle 179 WD 179
YARBROUGH, Lonzo 266
YEAKLEY, George 268 Johnson 268
YEARWOOD, Florence M 157
YOAKLEY, George 10 30
YOKLEY, Anderw J 185 Betty 31 Cars Milton 185 Evelina 134 GA 175 GW 68 Mollie 175 Percie 217 Rebecca 31
YONES, WR 171
YOST, James D 72 Will D 75
YOUNG, BA 243 Crockett 169 183 Eliza 109 Gertrude 66 Hester 88 James H 169 JO 167 191 Mary 107 Samuel 243 William K 183

www.ingramcontent.com/pod-product-compliance
Lightning Source LLC
Chambersburg PA
CBHW060940230426
43665CB00015B/2012